Defining Medievalism(s) II

Studies in Medievalism XVIII

2010

Studies in Medievalism

Founded by Leslie J. Workman

Previously published volumes are listed at the back of this book

Defining Medievalism(s) II

Edited by
Karl Fugelso

Studies in Medievalism XVIII 2010

Cambridge
D. S. Brewer

© Studies in Medievalism 2009

First published 2009
D. S. Brewer, Cambridge

ISBN 978–1–84384–210–1

ISSN 0738-7164

D. S. Brewer is an imprint of Boydell & Brewer Ltd
PO Box 9, Woodbridge, Suffolk IP12 3DF, UK
and of Boydell & Brewer Inc.
668 Mt Hope Avenue, Rochester, NY 14620, USA
website: www.boydellandbrewer.com

A CIP catalogue record for this book is available
from the British Library

The author and publishers are grateful to all the institutions and individuals
listed for permission to reproduce the materials in which they hold copyright.
Every effort has been made to trace the copyright holders;
apologies are offered for any omission, and the publishers will be pleased to
add any necessary acknowledgement in subsequent editions.

This publication is printed on acid-free paper

Typeset by Pru Harrison, Hacheston, Suffolk
Printed in Great Britain by
CPI Antony Rowe Ltd, Chippenham and Eastbourne

Studies in Medievalism

Studies in Medievalism provides an interdisciplinary medium of exchange for scholars in all fields, including the visual and other arts, concerned with any aspect of the post-medieval idea and study of the Middle Ages and the influence, both scholarly and popular, of this study on Western society after 1500.

Studies in Medievalism is published by Boydell & Brewer, Ltd., P.O. Box 9, Woodbridge, Suffolk IP12 3DF, UK; Boydell & Brewer, Inc., 668 Mt. Hope Avenue, Rochester, NY 14620, USA. Orders and inquiries about back issues should be addressed to Boydell & Brewer at the appropriate office.

For a copy of the style sheet and for inquiries about **Studies in Medievalism**, please contact the editor, Karl Fugelso, at the Dept. of Art and Art History, Towson University, 8000 York Rd, Towson, MD 21252–0001, USA, tel. 410–704–2805, fax 410–704–2810 ATTN: Fugelso, e-mail <kfugelso@towson.edu>. All submissions should be sent to him as e-mail attachments in Word.

Acknowledgments

The device on the title page comes from the title page of *Des Knaben Wunderhorn: Alte deutsche Lieder*, edited by L. Achim von Arnim and Clemens Brentano (Heidelberg and Frankfurt, 1806).

The epigraph is from an unpublished paper by Lord Acton, written about 1859 and printed in Herbert Butterfield, *Man on His Past* (Cambridge University Press, 1955), 212.

Studies in Medievalism

Two great principles divide the world, and contend for the mastery, antiquity and the middle ages. These are the two civilizations that have preceded us, the two elements of which ours is composed. All political as well as religious questions reduce themselves practically to this. This is the great dualism that runs through our society.

Lord Acton

Editorial Note

As noted by several essayists in this volume of *SiM*, medievalism has become a "growth industry." In the last decade or so, the number of conferences and publications related to our field has exploded, particularly in response to the *Beowulf, Lord of the Rings*, and Harry Potter movies. But as even that short list suggests, multiplicity has led to something of an identity crisis. Scholars have increasingly asked to what degree and in what form a work must refer to the Middle Ages if it is to qualify as medievalism. Must it respond directly? Or can it refer to the Middle Ages via one or more intermediaries, such as J. R. R. Tolkien? Does its perceived tone and/or integrity matter? And what about its faithfulness to the Middle Ages? Indeed, how do we define the Middle Ages?

In our last volume, eight scholars attempted to answer these questions while characterizing medievalism and its origins. But, as many readers have noted, there is much more to be said on these matters. So here, as a kind of sequel, in the first section of this volume, a further seven scholars define the field. Some overtly build their discussion on the essays in *SiM* 17, while others react more to external literature; some wrap their definition around examples, while others wrap their examples around a definition; and some stay well within the traditional boundaries of medievalism, while others venture far beyond them. Yet all seven provide highly insightful commentaries that help bring our field into focus. Veronica Ortenberg West-Harling underscores the escapist tendencies of medievalism, particularly as they have emerged in the Heritage industry. Nickolas Haydock frames medievalism in relationship to "excluded middles." Richard Utz calls for a demonstrated awareness of our and our subjects' correlations to temporality. E. L. Risden celebrates the breadth and pedagogical advantages of our field. Carol L. Robinson and Pamela Clements combine to define our field via neo-medievalism. And Jane Chance characterizes medievalism in relationship to researching and teaching New Medievalisms in film and literature.

The essayists thus lay a foundation for our second section, whose eight articles apply, rather than directly address, theories about our field. In "Is Medievalism Reactionary? From between the World Wars to the Twenty-First Century: On the Notion of Progress in our Perception of the Middle Ages," Alain Corbellari traces the supposed evolution of medievalism over the last eighty to ninety years. In "Gustave Doré's Illustrations for Dante's *Divine Comedy*: Innovation, Influence, and Reception,"

Aida Audeh examines manifestations of medievalism in perhaps the most famous illustrations of the nineteenth century. In "Soundscapes of Middle Earth: The Question of Medievalist Music in Peter Jackson's *Lord of the Rings* Films," Stephen Meyer excavates an often overlooked aspect of a major subject in recent medievalism. In "Now You Don't See It, Now You Do: Recognizing the Grail *as* the Grail," Roberta Davidson compares modern cinematographic attempts to portray an (almost) unrepresentable medieval icon. In "From the Middle Ages to the Internet Age: The Medieval Courtly Love Tradition in Jeanette Winterson's *The Passion* and *The.Powerbook*," Carla A. Arnell highlights a major medieval topos in works by an extraordinarily well-informed novelist. In "New Golden Legends: Golden Saints of the Nineteenth Century," Clare A. Simmons examines Victorian spins on Jacques de Voragine's thirteenth-century *Golden Legend*. In "A Remarkable Woman? Popular Historians and the Image of Eleanor of Aquitaine," Michael Evans discusses the many liberties taken with a twelfth-century queen in twentieth-century historical fiction and fictional history. And in "The New Seven Deadly Sins," Carol Jamison reports on recent incarnations of a medieval preoccupation.

Our authors thus test the observations and conclusions of our essayists, as the latter propose broad contexts in which to locate studies of medievalism. And in this exchange across theory and practice, we have attempted to ground our field a little more, even as we have opened it up to new horizons, even as we have affirmed its tremendous potential for sustained growth.

Medievalism as Fun and Games[1]

Veronica Ortenberg West-Harling

Medievalism hides in many guises in contemporary culture, of which four will be examined here.[2] One is the popular literature of fantasy fiction and crime novels. Another two are the world of Heritage – covering medieval sites, theme parks, and a vast retail industry of artifacts – and, partly associated with it, the historical re-enactment scene. Last but not least is the development of war and strategy Internet games.

The origins of the fantasy fiction genre may go back to William Morris,[3] but its real modern roots are in Tolkien's *Lord of the Rings*. Fantasy fiction invents myths, legends, and characters situated in a world before time, doing heroic deeds and achieving impossible tasks with the help of magical creatures (beasts, demons, magicians). These illustrate the importance of man's understanding of, and working with, the natural world, which ultimately brings about wholeness and happiness.[4] At its best, the genre produced J. R. R. Tolkien and Philip Pullman; at worst, a plethora of run-of-the-mill fantasies meant for rapid consumption. Fantasy fiction's main writers, such as Anne Rice, Ursula Le Guin, Stephen Lawhead, and Robert Jordan, use titles such as *The Dragon Reborn*, *Lord of Chaos*, *A Crown of Swords*, *The Belgariad*, *The Malloreon*, the *Prydain* series, the *Song of Albion*, all featuring heroes, places, or gods' names with a Celtic resonance, from Sauron and Galadriel to Nynaeve, Aviendha, Amyrlin, Caemlyn, and Belgarath. These suggest to the readers' minds a world before time, inhabited by supernatural creatures, powers and heroes, fabulous myths and legends, where good triumphs over evil, and love and heroic deeds are rewarded. This has been increasingly associated with the idea of the "Celtic" world, equated with some kind of primitive

Eden, appealing to the myth of the roots of western civilization, and hence to a feeling of return to a national and ethnic past.[5] Such roots can be variably chosen in the countries of the Celtic fringe in the UK, in England where they are felt to be a more ancient national past than the Saxons (almost in the manner of the "native" cultures of America), and in the US because it links immigrant groups to their European roots. Fantasy fiction appeals to an adult audience, giving it an escape from daily drudgery and a too-rational surrounding world, and an opening for thinking about major life issues not always addressed by mainstream fiction, enacted by colorful characters in exciting life-threatening situations. The genre is used for escapist purposes, perhaps especially in the English-speaking world, where the ethics of Puritanism and a strong work culture predominate, and is non-gender-specific, appealing to both men and women.

Medieval crime fiction shares some of these features.[6] In the 1980s a revolutionary novel, Umberto Eco's *Name of the Rose*, which brought worldwide success for its author, ensured respectability for the genre and opened it up to followers. A wide range of historical periods has been used since, from Ancient Greece and Egypt to the 1950s; none, however, as much, if with variable success, as the Middle Ages. The first really successful novels were Ellis Peters' Brother Cadfael stories.[7] They spawned a series of television films and a medieval theme park, the Shrewsbury Quest. Apart from the Cadfael books (set in Shrewsbury during the civil war between King Stephen and the Empress Matilda in the 1130s and 1140s), the number of series written between 1990 and this year has now gone into double figures. They are set, chronologically, from sixth-century Byzantium and seventh-century Ireland onwards, until they start clustering in every century of the later Middle Ages from the twelfth century onwards. First set in London, Oxford, and York, they moved on to, for example, Kent and the West Country in England, then further away geographically to France, Spain during the Reconquista, then, even more exotically, to Byzantium, Jerusalem during the Crusades, and even thirteenth-century China.

The exponential increase in the number of books set in the last three centuries of the Middle Ages may be related to the greater number of sources available then. Mostly, they are placed in periods associated with major events, the kinds of memories that one might be expected to recall from one's school days: war, political crises, or other forms of civil or religious turmoil such as the Norman Conquest, the Crusades, the Hundred Years War and the Black Death. In the same way, most novels are situated in suggestive places such as London (the court at Westminster, the City), Oxford (the university), York (the Minster), Cambridge, Moorish Spain, Venice, Byzantium, and Jerusalem. They often center on well-remembered names of kings or writers like Chaucer. The purpose is that of appealing to the reader by drawing them into the plot through a surface familiarity with the events and places, particularly if these places have both historical and aesthetic connotations and can be visited today. The reader is hooked by being made to recognize elements vaguely familiar but still sufficiently alien to be seen as colorful and slightly mysterious.

The clergy in all its forms is predominant, to add specific color to a period regarded as dominated by the Church, and to contribute to the *otherness* in relation to our time, while still remaining in not totally unfamiliar ground. Even detectives who do not apparently belong directly to the clergy display such *otherness*, which is made up of social position or profession: they hold positions, such as royal officials (bailiff, sheriff) or doctors and rich merchants, that give them access to knowledge, writing and law, and hence reasoning and deductive powers commensurate with their role as detectives, and are thus associated, through work or personal friendships, with the clerical group.

Other elements contribute to the known-yet-exotic factor, for example the English–foreign issue, inherited mostly from Walter Scott, which translates into hostility between the "native" Saxons and the Norman "conquerors."[8] This issue has renewed appeal in the late twentieth century, in a multiethnic and multicultural society preoccupied with immigration and integration problems, just as the growing role of the Crusades in historical fiction is linked with the post-2001 crisis in the West's relations with Islam. The importance of emancipated women doing the same jobs as men, for example as lawyers and doctors, and being their equal socially and intellectually, is an interpretation partly commensurate with the writers' own wishes to perceive medieval society as more egalitarian than later periods, and hence a clear precursor of our own. At the very least, presenting it in such a way is a good ploy to ensure popular success for the book, by tuning into contemporary feeling and prompting the readers' surprise and pleasure as they are led to experience the medieval as being so "modern." Similarly, the choice of the Middle Ages for eco-friendly attitudes is part of the attraction for both readers and writers. Here, as with the "Celtic spirit," what appeals is the perceived common ground between the medieval and the contemporary, such as natural medicine, organic food, animal welfare, while nostalgia for values perceived as good but now gone forever, such as social solidarity or a sense of the sacred to be found in nature, are evoked as models for our own time.

Some writers may make mistakes on factual matters, and many are taken in by clichés, or deliberately cultivate those because they make a better story, or rather one with which the audience is already slightly familiar. The "Celtic Church" and the English, the Saxon and Norman divide, the Crusades, the Inquisition, are themes that reappear regularly, precisely because they tap into already familiar areas, a key factor for ensuring popularity by reinforcing already existent preconceptions among the readers. So-called historical accuracy is not only unachievable, but misplaced because the writers' perception, even when real, has to be overruled to make the book palatable and interesting. This inevitably means projecting twentieth-century attitudes and moral issues onto medieval characters. While modern perception is that of a medieval world of cruelty, injustice, violence, intolerance, poverty, and filth, its characters are made to hold values seen now as lost, such as solidarity and a way of life attuned to nature. The reader can feel at the same time superior, nostalgic, and plunged into a world both strange but not totally unfamiliar through collective memory, and places still visible and enhanced by the Heritage world.

The Heritage industry itself includes both tangible and intangible elements. The tangible are historic sites, many belonging to English Heritage, and artifacts sold by commercial retailers or museums. The intangible comes in the form of the "experience" of the Middle Ages, in either specific reconstituted spaces like theme parks, or as living-history experiences through re-enactment and living history groups.

English Heritage's advertising literature is illuminating: whenever possible, England is divided, not into modern administrative units, but into historic regions with evocative names, such as Wessex and Northumbria.[9] The Castles of Devon leaflets, *Mighty Fortresses and Romantic Ruins*, offers the area as one of "Ghostly legends and medieval chivalry." Wessex's offers "Great castles and abbeys," Northumbria's "battles for survival, saints preserved," and Cornwall's *Castles, Celts and Kings* "mystery, myth and magic." Descriptions follow of, for example, the site of the battle of Hastings, the "most famous date in English history," where the whole family is invited to "let King Harold's mistress tell you what really happened – and stand on the very spot where Harold fell." Lindisfarne Priory is the "cradle of Christianity, one of the holiest Anglo-Saxon sites in England."

Heritage providers offer interactive audio-visual displays and exhibitions. A whole range of events is set up every year: medieval entertainment with jousting, displays of falconry, archery, the arming of a knight, the dressing of a court lady, a "strolling medieval minstrel," a medieval Christmas (or rather Yule Fayre), "life in a medieval castle," and re-enactments of battles such as Maldon, Hastings, or Bosworth. English Heritage in particular also regards its brief as educational in terms of the daily life of the past: "Come and see medieval knights fighting for their honour at the castle," and "William versus Harold, who was the hero? Find out about the battle which changed England's history forever," and "Brother Oswald and Sister Septima share with us their spooky tales." Also available were a portrayal of "life during the reign of King Edwin of Northumberland, 627 AD," "the lavish social life of a royal court on tour as Richard III returns to his childhood home [with] entertainment staged for the monarch," "meet Ragnor Svensson the Viking and learn about Viking life,"[10] and an invitation to "recreate the Arthurian legends on this magical day out. Become a knight of the round table and embark on the quest for the Holy Grail. Hear mythical tales of old about the great King Arthur and maybe learn a bit of magic!" The combination of Arthur, knights, Grail, quest, tales of old, magic and myth, perfectly demonstrates what it is that maintains the prominence of the Middle Ages in the popular imagination.

In history-book-club catalogues, the Medieval World and Celtic History together usually take up the greatest amount of space, often placed into categories introduced by an overarching sentence: "Medieval Images of Faith and Piety" (the Church and pilgrimages) and "Champions and Chatelaines of the Middle Ages" (the Crusades and knights). Heritage theme parks like Shrewsbury Quest offer workshops in manuscript illumination or the cultivation of medicinal herbs, both associated with monks. The Jorvik Centre in York enables visitors to experience the "sounds, sights and smells" of Viking York. Medieval feasts and banquets are so popular that they have become part of corporate entertainment.

The Heritage industry's retail arm is a big earner.[11] Reproductions of medieval-style furniture are matched by reproductions of medieval artifacts from museums and art collections across Europe and the US: Virgin-and-Child statuettes, jewelry, tapestries like the Lady with the Unicorn, ivories, stained glass, and other objects sold especially at Christmas. In addition to appearing on illuminated-manuscript Christmas cards and wrapping paper, medieval motifs and designs such as fleur-de-lys, mille-fleurs, and tassels are reproduced on table mats, ties, scarves, candles, umbrellas, bags, cushions, paper goods, jewelry, and clothing. The main UK retailer *Past Times* usually heads its medieval sections "a realm of fair maidens, troubadours and courtly love" or "the age of cathedrals" or the "medieval lady: the graceful maiden of Arthurian myth and legend," each highlighting apparently relevant objects, for example gothic-shaped mirrors, caskets, or illuminated-manuscript cushions. Even objects associated with Christianity are more acceptable under a medieval cover. Compilations of prayers, psalms, icons, and monastic offices are rendered palatable by being disguised as history, and are especially successful when sold under the umbrella of "Celtic spirituality." Every retail catalogue has had a section entitled "Celtic Treasures" or "Celtic Art," including brooches, rings, or crosses, sold as reflections of "interwoven Celtic motifs […] thought to symbolise the eternal thread of life," and "a joyous Celtic blessing." Thus a throw "decorated with a traditional knotwork design […] the warm blues evok[ing] the colour of early Celtic fabrics produced using natural dyes such as woad," since "in Celtic symbolism the fine knotwork designs […] represent unity and eternity" – through buying this product rather than something made of modern materialistic non-ecological materials, you [the buyer] too can benefit, through the association with natural fabrics, colors, stones, which have the magical properties of nature and age-recognized value, and by implication, share in the blessings they would bring to you, as your ancestors did in their time – the message is everywhere. Special pages are consecrated to the "Celtic Christmas: a mystical midwinter celebration of fire and light," a "traditional" festival of a pre-Christian period (meaning in opposition to the modern-day commercialized festival.)

The association between the Middle Ages and "Celticism" today is paramount. From the reclaiming of Arthurian myths of chivalry and the Holy Grail for a pre-Christian pagan world,[12] to the link of anything Celtic with the world of New Age paganism, wicca, druidism, and magic, all relate to the message of worship of nature and the feminine principle.[13] This in turn has led to the association of this imagined past with an "anti-Establishment" attitude, the religious Establishment being described as oppressive and repressive,[14] to the extent of concealing major metaphysical and historical truths from seekers who try to bring them to light.[15] Such are the roots of the fascination with the myths of secret or allegedly secret societies, Knights Templars, Freemasons, Rosicrucians, and the numerous others taken on by the authors of conspiracy-theory thrillers that have exploded in the wake of Dan Brown's *Da Vinci Code*.

Re-enactment societies represent the more intangible aspect of Heritage. On a major website serving the international community of re-enactors, the medieval period, by far the most popular in number of active societies, is divided into Dark Ages (400–1066), Vikings (800–1150), and Medieval (1066–1599).[16] The first includes fifty societies and the second sixty, though quite a few recoup each other, and in each case the respective number of UK-based ones is much higher than in any other country. The Medieval category includes 178 names, of which only a few are the same as previously. Among them, the UK-based number is nearly 115, while the US moves up to twenty-one; Australia, Canada and New Zealand are represented for the English-speaking world, but other countries also appear, France in the lead with seven groups, followed in much smaller numbers by Italy, Germany, the Czech Republic, Portugal, Scandinavia, Poland, Switzerland, Spain, Belgium, and Mexico. Re-enactment has become a worldwide activity, regardless of nationality, but English-speaking countries, and the UK in particular, have the lion's share of the activity. The names and activities of these societies go some way towards explaining this popularity. Leaving out the purely descriptive,[17] and the humorous ones,[18] most groups' names fall into these categories:

1. those reminiscent of the romantic fantasy world of the Middle Ages (Sword of Pendragon, Kingdom of Gryphons, Paladins of Chivalry)

2. those using medieval words: Anglo-Saxon (Angelcyn, Cestrecire, Wryngwyrm), Welsh (Milwr Morganwg, Gwerin Y Gwyr), Irish (Mogh Raith and Na Degad), Scandinavian (Hrafnanir, Odir Hundar), Al-Andaluz

3. those that imitate medieval associations of aristocratic house-holds, orders of knights, or merchants groups: Households (Boteler, Clarence, Neville), Retinues (Deveraux, Erpyngham), Companies (Compagnie des feu-vetus, Companions of the Crows), Orders of Knights (Knights of Jerusalem, Knights of Royal England, Ordem de Calavaria do Sagrado Portugal), guilds and town associations (Gylda Cinque Ports, York City Levy, The Yorkshire Yeomen).

Several key trends can be identified. First and foremost is the purely escapist, with its fantasy element, appealing to those who want a fun day out, especially if it involves fighting ("safe combat and fun are more important than hand-stitched authentic underwear").[19] Second comes the ethnically conscious, which takes pride in its roots ("We didn't have a 'Dark Age', it was our 'Golden Age' "),[20] have a pride in their ancestors (the Lithuanian group Vilkatakai) or in being "Italys [sic] sole Military order born in Italy the Order of Santo Stefano,"[21] which is, however, an American and more specifically Cali-fornian-based group. A third, the perfect-accuracy-seeking trend, can itself be divided into two strands. The first focuses on battle re-enactment, with either jousting, sieges, or whole battles, as in the Wars of the Roses. The group names evoke the romance of chivalry, such as the Knights of the Order of the Lion Rampant, or the Order of the Black Pryns. They put on sponsored shows and local events, visit other countries, and have regular training sessions. The second strand, concerned with "living history," regarded as primarily educa-tional, is less concerned with major events and warfare than with displays of everyday life at court, in the households of aristocrats, merchants or peasants. Some go as far as to acquire, not just costumes, tools, and weapons, but a whole physical area ("we have our own 7-acre site with a re-created ring fort that is now fully pallisaded").[22]

The success of medieval re-enactment seems to go against con-temporary political, social, and spiritual norms of behavior. Re-enactment gives official permission to have a good fight, with the only allowed use of real weapons in public, and many re-enactors cite this as the real reason for their involvement.[23] It gives expression to the desire to belong to a nation and to express pride in it and in one's roots, on the Celtic fringes in the British Isles or in countries newly emerged from communism like Poland and Lithuania, but also in countries where such manifestations, unless they take place within the limits of the Last Night of the Proms or a football match, are regarded as politically sensitive and only carried out by the likes of the British National Party (BNP) or the Front National. In the US, Australia, and Canada, it allows a feeling of return to the distant roots of one's family. It recreates a sense of present community too, through Living History Fairs, websites, and international exchanges. It leads to the fulfillment of more or less acceptable social dreams, such as being a member of the aristocracy, or of returning to a traditionally-gendered role, of women doing women's things and men fighting (less rigorous groups, notably those affiliated with the Society for Creative Anachronism [SCA], may allow their members to choose their persona and gender in costume, but groups that lay claim to strict historical accuracy often do not).[24] The western world's freedom from war, disease, and lack of food for several decades may enable a vicarious enjoyment of periods when life was much harsher in practical terms, but it also leads to an idealization of a lifestyle perceived to be closer to nature, when one had direct control over food and clothing production, reconstructed today for fun or educational purposes. Another sought-for purpose is a desire to retrieve social cohesion, belonging to a community that helps its members, and to exercise some greater degree of control over one's immediate life and environment, which appears lost within the less stable modern world.[25] Some of these themes, already discussed in crime fiction, also explain the success of Internet games.

The fastest developing area in twenty-first-century historical recreation is the Internet, with its new generation of war and strategy games. The first kind is the fantasy game, creating a new virtual world (e.g., Azeroth), with its own peoples and geography, in the manner of Tolkien's *Lord of the Rings*, which serves as its universal model; its main themes are battling against enemies and an overall quest (*World of Warcraft: The Burning Crusade* or *Rune: Viking Warlord*). The second focuses on recreating a "real" medieval world centered on familiar themes: castles, lords, peasants, sieges, popes, Crusades (*Total War: Medieval II*; *Stronghold: Crusades*; *Lords of the Realm*; *Crusader Kings*).[26]

The best introduction to the success of these games is provided by the promotional text on their cover, and the direct comments made by players.[27] Key themes are:

1. The pleasure of fighting (being in the middle of the action on the battlefield), with war as a great adventure in its immediacy and the feeling of power as the player belongs to the elite in charge, dominating events:

> "NOW WE GET TO USE OUR BIG BAD WEAPONS HOW COOL!!!"

> "Total War series is returning to the most turbulent era in Western history **as you take control** of the country of **your** choice in the golden age of chivalry and really big battles."

> "You will be thrilled at the sound of **your men** marching, their cheers as they hack their opponents to bits."

> "You can hang **your citizens** or dunk them in boiling hot water."

> "The sound of an arrow puncturing the flesh is perfect in every aspect."

2. The feeling of community with other players, both as virtual friends and sometimes as a family-building time:

> "It's not all about fighting, there are plenty of things to do. Its excellent for socializing, I have made lots of friends around Europe via this game. Its also a great game for couples [...] you are both too busy to make the tea."

> "Both me and my husband play it, along with friends, nephews and nieces [...] if you live alone then even more reason to buy this game, there's loads of people out there to make friends with."

3. The ability to immerse oneself in a period that is vaguely familiar, especially as one can pick and choose only the nice bits of it and leave out the nasty ones:

> "For those of you who want the splendour of the Dark Ages with none of the side effects – scurvy, the Black Death, being burnt at the stake."

> "Anyone with an interest in the middle ages will *adore* this game for its ability to immerse you in the sights and sounds (but thankfully not smells) of the time."

> "The brutish reality of medieval England proves to be a great gaming experience (You definitely wouldn't want to live there.)"

4. The acceptance of traditional gendering of roles in a way that might seem unacceptable in real life:

> "Women have the role they would mostly have had at the time, as princesses producing heirs, or being married off to cement an alliance."

5. The ability to control the world and use one's skills and intelligence to make it work:

> "I love the sieges in this version, they do mean that you have to really use your head and not just brute force in order to win with a minimum of casualties."

6. The nostalgia for a time when one could be closer to the land and able to manage the basic needs of life, especially food, and know how they were brought into existence:

> "If you want to make bread you need to grow wheat, get it milled into flour and then build some bakeries to make the bread."

7. In addition, people have the thrill of exchanging news about the addiction level of the game, in which some pride is being taken: the higher that level, the better the game is supposed to be:

> "This will change your life (going out somehow doesn't seem the same anymore) [...] once you have begun you will find yourself wanting to do little else with your spare time, meaning huge savings in other areas."

and the rejection of a political-correctness culture that precludes robust discussion about weapons, the pleasure taken in the thrashing of one's enemies, and religion:

> "The developers have approached the subject of religion somewhat sensitively [...] there are disclaimers in the manual that they are making no claims or comments about the effects or desire of religion blah blah blah. It's a game, people, it's a real pity they took such a sensitive approach to what could have been a really interesting 3rd element."

To a society that, on the whole, has lived in a safe world with no recent wars, food shortages, or major epidemics, in which much is done to create a safe environment (whether people want it or not, Health and Safety rules enforce it), when people live longer and, unless they belong to high-risk professions like the army, rarely see death, the excitement of danger, risk-taking, and fighting, as long as it is virtual, is most attractive. In an increasingly dispersed, specialized, internationalized society, the ability to control a small world and make it work, when so much of the large world seems out of control; to mete out immediate and visible punishment, when in real life government and law seem increasingly remote; to reaffirm gender roles now blurred, are all prized for re-establishing apparent certainties now gone. Nostalgia for a return to the land, which appears to allow players to control their environment, the familiarity with the clichés of medieval history (knights and castles, crusades, princesses, priests), which allows for a sense of vaguely known territory, and national pride, which can find an outlet not always openly available to western Europeans today, also contribute to the success. Last but certainly not least is the sense of community and belonging, both virtual and real, for which the game is a means of bonding around similar needs and pleasures.

However different in other respects, some patterns other than escapism are common to game players and to re-enactors: belonging to a community, the need for the apparent reality of fighting and brutality of living, the acceptance of conventional gender roles, and the enthusiasm at being able to wield real (or virtual real) big bad weapons. While the constituencies of the two are by no means equivalent (games are for individual pleasure, while re-enactment can be for educational purposes; one is clean, while the other implies exposure to dirt, mud, scratchy clothing, heavy armor, and perhaps physical injury), some features work for both, as they do for popular fiction and Heritage. In one respect, medievalism has not changed in its main function since the sixteenth century: it remains one of the key forms of escapism from modern life, with outlets that are not always so much about "loving the [whatever historical] Age as about escaping from the Plastic Age."[28]

NOTES

1. This essay will be further expanded into two longer ones, currently in progress. In view of the relatively short bibliography on most of the topics discussed here, I have used several times material presented in Veronica Ortenberg, *In Search of the Holy Grail: The Quest for the Middle Ages* (London: Hambledon-Continuum, 2006).

2. One major form of popular culture not discussed here at all is film and television, partly because it is a vast topic, and partly because a lot of work has already been done on medievalism and film.

3. *The Story of the Glittering Plain* (1891) and *The Well at the World's End* (1894) are the two best examples.

4. Philip Pullman, *His Dark Materials*, now renamed *The Northern Lights* trilogy; on the genre, see Edmund Little, *The Fantasts: Studies in J. R. R. Tolkien, Lewis Carroll, Mervyn Peake, Nikolay Gogol and Kenneth Grahame* (Amersham: Avebury, 1984), 1–12, 31–38; Mark R. Hillegas, ed., *Shadows of Imagination* (Carbondale, IL: Southern Illinois University Press, 1969), 68–69, 100–6; Jane Chance, *Tolkien's Art: A Mythology for England* (Lexington: University Press of Kentucky, 2001), 42–43, 77–79 and 162–83; Tom Shippey, *The Road to Middle Earth* (London: Allen & Unwin, 1982; rev. ed. London: HarperCollins, 2005), 189; Jane Chance, ed., *Tolkien the Medievalist* (London: Routledge, 2003); Humphrey Carpenter, *Tolkien: A Biography* (New York: Ballantine Books, 1977), 77, 101–2, 136–40; Ortenberg, *In Search*, chap. 7.

5. Ortenberg, *In Search*, chaps. 4 and 5.

6. Ortenberg, *In Search*, chap. 7.

7. Eric E. Christian and Bernard Lindsay, "The Habit of Detection: The Medieval Monk as Detective in the Novels of Ellis Peters," *Studies in Medievalism* 4 (1992): 276–89.

8. On the Norman Yoke theory in political thought, see Christopher Hill, "The Norman Yoke," in his *Puritanism and Revolution: Studies in Interpretation of the English Revolution of the Seventeenth Century* (London: Secker & Warburg, 1958), 50–122; David Underdown, *A Freeborn People: Politics and the Nation in Seventeenth-Century England* (Oxford: Clarendon Press, 1996); Michael Wood, "The Norman Yoke," in his *In Search of England: Journeys into the English Past* (Berkeley: University of California Press, 1999), 3–22; John G. A. Pocock, *The Ancient Constitution and the Feudal Law* (Cambridge: Cambridge University Press, 1957), 124–47; Clare A. Simmons, "Absent Presence: The Romantic Era Magna Charta and the English Constitution," in Richard Utz and Tom Shippey, ed., (Turnhout: Brepols Publishers, 1998), 72–75; on Walter Scott's role in popularizing the

notion, see Nicholas Rance, *The Historical Novel and Popular Politics in Nineteenth-Century England* (London: Vision Press, 1975); Alice Chandler, *A Dream of Order: The Medieval Ideal in Nineteenth-Century Literature* (London: Routledge & Kegan Paul, 1970), 12–51, and "Sir Walter Scott and the Medieval Revival," *Nineteenth-Century Fiction* 19 (1964): 315–32; Mark Girouard, *The Return to Camelot: Chivalry and the English Gentleman* (New Haven, CT: Yale University Press, 1981), 30–38; Jerome Mitchell, *Scott, Chaucer and Medieval Romance: A Study of Sir Walter Scott's Indebtedness to the Literature of the Middle Ages* (Lexington: University Press of Kentucky, 1987); and summaries for these, as well as for the continuation of the theme in Hollywood filmography, in Ortenberg, *In Search*, chaps.1, 3, 4, and 8.

9. Most of my examples are extracted from the English Heritage activities brochures from 2003 onwards, on-site English Heritage and other museums leaflets, and some relevant websites, e.g., <www.battle-of-hastings-1066.org.uk>; <www.suttonhoo.org>; <www.kingarthurslabyrinth.com>; <www.bbc.co.uk/history/british/middle_ages>. Significantly, there are very few such non-personal websites of this kind outside the UK.

10. Several of the above names are themselves references to other medievalist material that visitors may already know from other sources such as crime fiction and film, for example Ragnor who recalls Ragnar in the film *The Vikings*, or Sister Septima who recalls Sister Fidelma – another way of making the visitor both comfortable and pleased with their own recognition of the material.

11. Examples come from *Past Times*, individual museum bookshops, e.g., British Museum and Victoria and Albert Museum in London, the Metropolitan Museum in New York, the Louvre in Paris, museums in Italy, Spain, and northern Europe; and from Christmas mail-order catalogues from outlets like *Museum Selection*; see Ortenberg, *In Search*, chaps. 5, 6, and 9.

12. Girouard, *Return to Camelot*; Debra N. Mancoff, *The Return to Camelot of King Arthur: The Legend through Victorian Eyes* (London: Pavilion, 1995); Juliette Wood, *Eternal Chalice: The Enduring Legend of the Holy Grail* (London: I. B. Taurus, 2007); Ronald Hutton, *Witches, Druids and King Arthur* (London: Hambledon, 2003).

13. The literature on this subject is so vast that it would be impossible to cover here. The most one can do is name a few among the most relevant titles on each subject, such as Neville Drury, *Magic and Witchcraft: From Shamanism to the Techno-Pagans* (London: Thames & Hudson, 2004); Philip Carr-Gomm, ed., *Druidcraft: The Magic of Wicca and Druidry* (London: Thorsons, 2006); Daphne Brooke, *Saints and Goddesses: The Interface with Celtic Paganism* (Whithorn: Friends of the Whithorn Trust, 1999); Vivienne

Crowley, *Wicca* (London: Thorsons, 2000); Paul Heelas, *The New Age Movement: The Celebration of the Self and the Sacralization of Modernity* (Oxford: Blackwell, 1996); see Ortenberg, *In Search*, chap. 5.

14. The identification of the Catholic and/or Anglican Church with the Establishment and therefore repression and oppression versus the "native Celtic Church" representing individual religious freedom is a very old one, going back to at least the sixteenth century and the Reformation, and taken up again from the eighteenth century onwards by nonconformists; see, for example, Oliver Davies, "Celtic Christianity: Texts and Representations," in Mark Atherton, et al., ed., *Celts and Christians: New Approaches to the Religious Traditions of Britain and Ireland* (Cardiff: University of Wales Press, 2002), 23–38; and, in the first instance, Kathleen Hughes, "The Celtic Church: Is This a Valid Concept?," *Cambridge Medieval Celtic Studies* 1 (1981): 1–20; Wendy Davies, "The Myth of the Celtic Church," in Nancy Edwards and Alan Lane, ed., *The Early Church in Wales and the West* (Oxford: Oxbow Books, 1992), 12–21; Peter Morgan, "From a Death to a View: The Hunt for the Welsh Past in the Romantic Period," in Eric J. Hobsbawm and Terence Ranger, ed., *The Invention of Tradition* (Cambridge: Cambridge University Press, 1983), 43–100; Ortenberg, *In Search*, chap. 5. Scholarly debate has not had any impact on popular perception, however, as the success of many books such as Donald E. Meek, *The Quest for Celtic Christianity* (Edinburgh: Handsel Press, 2000); Michael Mitton, *Restoring the Woven Cord: Strands of Celtic Christianity for the Church Today* (London: Darton, Longman & Todd, 1995); J. Philip Newell, *Listening for the Heartbeat of God: A Celtic Spirituality* (London: SPCK, 1997) proves.

15. Wood, *Eternal Chalice*, 167–80.

16. <www.histrenact.co.uk>.

17. The Anglo-Saxons, Colchester Historical Enactment Society.

18. Rent-a-Peasant, Scabius Corpus who "by popular demand, will infect villages etc with Black Death, Leprosy and anything else we can catch."

19. The Company of St. Jude.

20. Mogh Roith, <www.moghroith.org>.

21. Cavalieri della [sic] Ordine dei [sic] Santo Stefano.

22. Dark Ages Charitable Trust, <www.darkagestrust.org.uk>.

23. This has generally been ascribed primarily to Viking groups, but seems to be fairly general: see for example Tim Moore, *I Believe in Yesterday: My Adventures in Living History* (London: Jonathan Cape, 2008), 92, 104.

24. <www.sca.org>.

25. Moore, *I Believe in Yesterday*, 138–44, 149.

26. I have left out the *Age of Empires* game, which involves some of the same issues discussed here but is slightly different in using the Middle Ages

as a staging post rather than a self-contained unit; it is looked at in detail by Daniel T. Kline, "Virtually Medieval: The *Age of Kings* Interprets the Middle Ages," in David W. Marshall, ed., *Mass Market Medieval: Essays on the Middle Ages in Popular Culture* (Jefferson, NC: McFarland, 2008), 154–70.

27. I have used extensively the comments made by players on the relevant Amazon websites – it has rarely been possible to have such direct access to the makers and consumers of popular culture, since these comments are unprompted and freely offered, in everyday language, without restraint or censorship. The embolding is mine, and I have tacitly corrected the spelling in most cases, but not the grammar.

28. Moore, *I Believe in Yesterday*, 22.

Medievalism and Excluded Middles

Nickolas Haydock

In an uncharacteristic breach of Aristotelian *ordo*, Umberto Eco remarked that before we can speak about medievalism we have the "cultural duty" first to specify what kind of medievalism we're talking about.[1] Of course this puts the cart in front of the horse, the species ahead of the genus: before we identify sub-categories of medievalism we first need to define medievalism itself – something Eco's famous essay "Dreaming of the Middle Ages" never does.[2] Without delimiting the genus we run the risk – as indeed has tended to occur, in part because of the popularity of Eco's piece – of multiplying sub-categories willy-nilly and failing to exclude what doesn't fit within the general definition or neglecting to revise this definition to bring wayward sub-categories into the fold. For me, central to any definition of medievalism should be the concepts of *alterity* and *continuity*, each the product of a complex array of *contingencies*. Such contingencies include medium and genre-specific influences (e.g., the historical novel or action-adventure films, church ornaments or popular music), as well as those contingencies brought to bear by the particular time, place, and situation of a maker and particular audiences. Indeed, adjectives or substantives qualifying the noun *medievalism* offered as sub-categories often represent attempts to identify just such contingencies: romantic medievalism, futurist, New Age, or postmodern medievalism, Spenserian medievalism, the medievalism of Alfred Lord Tennyson or T. S. Eliot, J. R. R. Tolkien or Seamus Heaney. Many kinds of medievalism breed oppositional forms: romantic medievalism certainly represents a concerted response to neoclassical views of the Middle Ages, Tolkien's medievalism is in part a reaction to that of Spenser and Tennyson, Heaney's to Eliot's.

Regarding cinema, it would be useful to anatomize action-adventure medievalism, medievalism in the woman's film, *auteur* or biopic medievalism. Stylizations of *auteur* medievalism play a crucial role in postmodern and popular cinémedievalism: Antoine Fuqua's *King Arthur* is a pastiche of Kurosawa and Eisenstein; Ridley Scott's *Kingdom of Heaven* (2005) represents a stylization of Hollywood spectacle (pioneered by DeMille and perfected by David Lean) and famous *mises en scène* from the historical films of Bergman and Kurosawa. In a forthcoming book, *Hollywood in the Holy Land*, E. L. Risden and I have assembled a collection of essays that treat the painfully relevant sub-category of orientalist medievalism in film.[3]

Yet the narrowing of reference is also a slippery slope: the danger of a certain hyper-taxonomy looms, whereby every work (or even a number of elements within a work) potentially becomes *sui generis* medievalism.

You'll notice that I have avoided mentioning any dates – something many definitions of medievalism make a point of including at the outset. The phrase "Chaucer's medievalism" (or better, Chaucer's Dark Age medievalism) is not the contradiction in terms that the "medievalism of Statius" would be. Even "the medievalism of *Beowulf*" is not a patent absurdity. Speaking of Chaucer's or the *Beowulf*-poet's medievalism can be more than a gratuitous exercise if we concede that the worlds represented in *Beowulf* and, say, the Canterbury tales of the Man of Law, the Wife of Bath, and Chaucer's own "Tale of Sir Thopas" are contingent constructions set in a period within the traditional dates for the Middle Ages, understood by the author and his audience to be a time radically different from the world in which they live yet mysteriously continuous with it, such that all the fairies have been well and truly banished by the friars, though rapacious warriors and magical women still have their representatives in *aller compaignye*. Chaucer's "Thopas" launches a strain (perhaps the dominant strain) of fantasy medievalism running right through English literature, from Spenser to William Morris through Tolkien and his epigones. Moreover, if we accept C. S. Lewis's well-known characterization of *Troilus and Criseyde*, we might reasonably treat Chaucer's medievalization of Boccaccio's *Il Filostrato* as a thoroughgoing example of medievalism. It is unfortunate Chaucer's medievalization of the archaic world has found few takers in recent times among classicizing or medievalizing writers. Sir Thomas Malory's widespread influence on later forms of medievalism need not prevent us from nominating his works – and especially the Caxton redaction published in the watershed year 1485 – as a classic of medievalism. My definition, then, would characterize medievalism as a discourse of contingent representations derived from the historical Middle Ages, composed of marked alterities to and continuities with the present. Contingencies will also influence the relations between continuities and alterities in any particular evocation of the medieval.[4]

What I suggest we call *medievalistics* identifies, analyzes, and theorizes particular constellations of these contingencies, especially their influence on the cultural production of alterities and continuities in relation to a distant but not necessarily remote past. This thoroughly contingent, multivalent, and multi-leveled negotiation between the pastness of the past and its presentist applications, the exotic and the immediate, is a proper concern of academic medievalistic studies. *Medievalistics* has exploded in recent decades, perhaps on the verge of becoming a full-fledged academic discipline in its own right, yet I would argue that it is still poor in theory and (largely as a result of this) continues to occupy a marginal place within medieval studies as a whole.[5] The call to historicize our practices and read critically the genealogies of our disciplines is being widely heeded across medieval studies, yet many medievalists continue to believe that their expertise in a particular specialty will somehow render their work inviolable to future archaeologies. This certainly isn't a question of who is likely to produce the more accurate, nuanced assertions about the Middle Ages: academic research is dedicated to the production of such statements and does so with a much greater consistency than History Channel documentaries, major motion pictures, popular novels, "Renaissance" fairs, or video games. The point is to avoid the temptation to define medievalism as error and to recognize that in the long view medieval studies is a sub-set of medievalism. Medievalism is contingency and to contingency everything must submit – even the work of scholars – a fact nowhere more obvious than in the chagrin of medievalists acting as advisors or consultants when they experience the translation of their subject to big-screen films, small-screen documentaries, museum exhibitions, or historical recreations.[6] The differences between popular medievalism and academic medieval studies are those of degree – not of kind – and these differences in degree erode quite precipitously with the passage of time. When eminent scholars of the Crusades like Jonathan Riley-Smith and Thomas F. Madden entered the fray of post-9/11 politics, chiefly to combat what they deemed the deleterious influence of medievalism on contemporary foreign policy, the contingencies of their own neoconservative brand of medievalism became readily apparent.[7] Can any scholar of today rest assured that his or her work will not come to exemplify turn-of-the-century medievalism in three or four decades? In increasingly shorter periods of time, scholarship – if it survives in a general way at all – survives in medievalistic histories of scholarship. If Auerbach and Curtius, Tolkien and Lewis, Huizinga and Bloch have ultimately become practitioners of medievalism, can even the finest among us reasonably expect a different fate?[8] "May your work become medievalism" should become for us the blessing we bestow on those whose work we admire. This is certainly not to say that what in some sectors is derisively called "traditional medieval studies" does not advance. Traditional medieval studies remain the source of the most exciting and momentous insights achieved in the field. It is rather to insist that these insights occur within the context of particular cultural avenues and constraints whose influence on what we are looking at/for, on how our insights are disseminated, on what matters and what doesn't, to whom it matters and why grow increasingly apparent with the passage of time.

To adapt Julia Kristeva's phrase, medievalism contributes to the reciprocal psychosocial process whereby we make "strangers of ourselves." Yet this very estrangement also initiates the interplay of fear and desire that defines the limits of the self. These limits constitute a destabilizing borderland of abjections and introjections. Yet even that medievalism determined to arouse disgust or horror in audiences will provide compensations in the form of analogies, allegories, or *figurae* that work to stitch the wound opened up between chronological others and ourselves. And if alterity is doomed to this *limited* success in medievalism, so too is continuity.

Imaginary identifications and genealogies, conspiracies and time travel appeal to continuities within increasingly assailed constructs like race, gender, and nationality. Pure, unbroken lines of descent can only emerge from the racist and sexist, homophobic and xenophobic, utopian and apocalyptic substrata that forged these links in the first place. Returning to the present, uncovering the hidden secret, tracing or identifying with your medieval ancestors will not, cannot make any real difference. If it could, the cycle of desire and frustration in the endless, aching need for origins would grind to a halt. Continuity can never pin down the protean otherness of the Middle Ages; alterity can never stifle the desire for connection. Both alterity and continuity are powerful mechanisms for the channeling of desire, but each functions to block the other, preventing satisfaction. The perfect machine, medievalism both manufactures and harnesses the perpetual oscillations of desire in relation to ever-changing objects, fashioned by contingency.

The triangular nature of my definition is no accident. The Middle Ages themselves were first identified as the middle element in a threefold division of history, and such triads recur repeatedly in medievalistic attempts to define medievalism, as we will see. Medievalism as the desire for the other also guarantees that the distant past will always be a function of mediation and therefore a product of what Rene Girard calls "mimetic rivalry," which functions through the triangulation of desire. This position as mediator and model, conduit and barrier accounts for the fact that our projections of the Middle Ages will always vacillate between contempt and emulation, fear and admiration. Medievalism is the supreme instance in historiographic terms of the problem of excluded middles. We should perhaps trace its genesis not from the nineteenth but rather from the twelfth-century controversy that pitted *Antiqui et Moderni*. Yet, in our terms there can have been no twelfth-century "Renaissance" because the debate between the ancients and the moderns adhered faithfully to the Aristotelian law of the excluded middle. The Renaissance, in a move continually repeated in later ages, defines itself against the Aristotelian principle of contradiction by the invention of a middle term, the Middle Ages, thereby casting the twelfth-century dyad as a false dichotomy and launching the dialectic of abjection and identification that continues to structure both medievalism and medievalistics. The Renaissance invention of a *medium aevum* as that which inhibits renewal, then, establishes the possibility of identity with the ancient world through the introduction of a middle. The underlying logic of this move can be expressed formulaically, where **a**=ancient culture, **b**=the medieval period, and **c**=modern (i.e., early modern) times:

That ancient is not modern can be resolved by the addition of a third term, such that:

b both is and is not **a**
b both is and is not **c**
c is composed of what **b** is with relation to **a**
and of what **b** is not with relation to **a** and **c**

With the introduction of **b** the (quasi) identity of **a** and **c** becomes possible, without the appearance of violating the law of excluded middles. False logic certainly, but a logic that assumes a necessary continuity between ancient and modern – provided by the middle term – that can be transcended through that characteristic amalgam of philological reconstruction and emotional identification we associate with the Renaissance. The twelfth-century *Antiqui et Moderni* is then a false dichotomy; the insertion of a middle age between ancient and modern makes possible the contention that two ages widely separated in time are fundamentally one. Two contradictory models of history, continuity and rupture, create an almost magical prolepsis whereby the present is brought into intimate relation with its origins.

In one sense the response of romantic medievalism accepted to a degree the putative identity of the ancient and the early modern or Enlightenment world, but ultimately offered its own triad. It reversed the valences, construing, for instance, the blight of industrialization or the sterility of neoclassical prescriptions in art and literature as evidence of a fractured continuity between the medieval and modern worlds in need of repair. An anti-modern, specular triad is also composed whereby the "modern" itself assumes the central position between the Middle Ages and the present. This present beyond the modern struggling to be born engages in utopian and nostalgic attempts to achieve a "renaissance" of the formerly "Middle" Ages now posed as the real origin of the contemporary world.[9]

The famous, almost Olympian, pronouncement of Lord Acton needs to be seen as a response to this tradition of proleptic triads:

> Two great principles divide the world, and contend for the mastery, antiquity and the middle ages. These are the two civilizations that have preceded us, the two elements of which ours is composed. All political as well as religious questions reduce themselves practically to this. This is the great dualism that runs through our society.[10]

These remarks, unpublished in this now famous form in Acton's lifetime, from their position above the fray would seem to offer an ideal banner for *Studies in Medievalism*. Yet the sentence redacting all political and religious questions "practically" to classicism or medievalism hints at a politics to which I imagine few of us would subscribe. As his two essays, "The History of Freedom in Antiquity" and "The History of Freedom in Christianity" make plain, Acton is searching for a modern world in which the ancient and the medieval are held in equipoise.[11] In law and in politics the quest is for a reason informed by faith and tradition; in religion an ethics buffered by reason. What Acton hopes to achieve by this balance are religious checks on the power of the state and legal curbs on the power of religion. Little wonder then that he takes his stand firmly against "American barbarism"!:

> In ancient times the state absorbed authorities not its own, and intruded on the domain of personal freedom. In the middle ages it possessed too little authority, and suffered others to intrude. Modern states fall habitually into both excesses [...]. Nor is the medieval revival of which we speak the enemy of classical culture. The classical world remains one great element of our civilization, as it was already in the M[iddle] A[ges]. It is as inconsistent with the law of continuity to dispense with the ancient as with the Medieval world. Antiquity is as indispensable to us as the M[iddle] A[ges]. But it is not our foundation in the same way, it does not influence us through the same things. It will always be at the bottom of our education. We should otherwise sink into the one-sided partiality of the M[iddle] A[ges] or into American barbarism. We should lose the memory of human virtues, and the idea of beauty in form. Classical literature will always teach men the form and method of things, not the substance. That is the error and danger of classical education. If it prevails alone, without counterpart or equipoise, we must look to it for substance as well as for form.[12]

If the Enlightenment led to the desire for a definitive break with the medieval past, "the last king strangled with the entrails of the last priest," that for Acton is going way too far. But equally dangerous is the separation of church and state in the American Constitution, as well as calls for the abolition of the British monarchy. Doubtless, Lord

Acton would have viewed recent events in American history more favorably, including: the wholesale erosion of legal boundaries between church and state, the abrogation to the American presidency of an almost unchecked power to suspend constitutional rights and international laws, as well as – in perfect harmony with the Vatican – the identification of Muslim enemies of civilization as those who harbor a "medieval" faith uninformed by reason. American barbarism indeed!

For Acton classicism is form and medievalism content, whose ideal synthesis in law is logic and precedent, in politics constitutional monarchy. His ideal modern world blends classicism and medievalism, each a check on the excesses of the other. Two moves here track important concepts in medievalistics, yet these moves reflect different, even mutually exclusive historiographies. In the first Acton re-emphasizes the continuous and cumulative nature of history; in the second he argues for a Hegelian synthesis of classicism and medievalism in the modern world.[13] Yet such new syntheses ultimately (perhaps inevitably?) return us to something remarkably like the master–slave dialectic: classicism must look to medievalism for its "substance," just as the latter must look to the former for its "form and method." The form and content dichotomy hopes to reproduce in the microcosm of the present exactly the shape of the original classical–medieval–modern trilogy, an envelop pattern in which form embraces and protects substance. What the example of Acton does make abundantly clear, however, is the interdependent contingency of classicism and medievalism. Tell me what you mean by classicism, and I can probably guess what you mean by medievalism. Tell me honestly which for you is slave and which master, and I'll tell you how you view the contemporary world. To discuss either -ism in isolation risks fatally distorting our understanding of both.

Yet if any position one takes with respect to classicism also implies a concomitant position with respect to medievalism, this is still only two-thirds of the story. For identities are composed in relation to alterities and continuities contingently fashioned in reference to space as well as time. Both classicism and medievalism are inextricably implicated in the discourse of orientalism, which spans ancient, medieval, and modern times with a well-nigh remarkable degree of uniformity. There was certainly an ancient orientalism: think of Plato's Egypt or Homer's Troy – or Virgil's Carthage. So too is there a long and complex post-classical tradition of orientalist classicism, evident most recently in the film *300* (dir. Zack Snyder, 2006) and the forthcoming *Hannibal the Conqueror*, inspired by Ross Leckie's novel.[14] In *300* the Persian Xerxes and his hordes represent all that is most abject to a West then as now defining itself in the protection of a border. Leckie's Hannibal valorizes the opposing principle of continuity. Dubbed by Livy "the father of strategy," Hannibal's innovations in battle tactics (thoroughly assimilated by Scipio Africanus) become yet another example of the *translatio studii et imperii* from East to West.[15] Recent years have witnessed a notable rise in the study of medieval orientalism,[16] while orientalist medievalism is already a widely studied element in the epics of Tasso, Ariosto, and Spenser. Contemporary films such as Youssef Chahine's *Destiny* (alt. title *al-Massir*, 1997) and Scott's *Kingdom of Heaven* abject the continuities of religious fundamentalisms in both the Middle East and the West, while introjecting fragile continuities of reason and inter-faith tolerance. The sweet reason of Chahine's Averroës is a testament to the continuity of ancient, medieval, and modern, as well as that between East and West. However, the abject specter of religious fanaticism not only is something shared by the medieval East and West, but also serves as an enduring cultural inheritance in both modern hemispheres.

The relationships among classicism, medievalism, and orientalism could profitably be conceptualized as a Venn diagram, the central overlap of the three circles representing those characteristics that are most perdurable in western representations of the East, that is to say those abjections and introjections least subject to contingency. The stability of these representations across time and discourses is indeed remarkable: little disturbed by the rise of Islam, the Enlightenment, or even mass communications.[17] Indeed, were we to design a second Venn diagram composed of three circles representing western ancient, medieval, and modern cultures, the central portion in which all three overlap would need to dedicate a large proportion of this shared space to orientalism, an enduring modern inheritance of ancient and medieval civilizations. Thus, the discourse of medievalism should be viewed as a product of its continuous relation with the discourses of classicism and orientalism.

While Acton's famous words have served as the banner under which medievalistics rides, providing the misleading impression that Acton equates the importance of classicism and medievalism (he doesn't), Umberto Eco's little essay "Dreaming of the Middle Ages" has become the most widely cited work in medievalistic studies. One suspects that this has as much to do with Eco's popularity as the essay's portability. It is polemical but also grossly accurate to say that Eco's essay is what medievalistics has had in lieu of a theory. But Eco himself has a middle to impose and overcome: that middle is medievalism itself. The triad runs Middle Ages – Medievalism – "Philological Reconstruction." Medievalism is posed as that which must be transcended to allow the kind of intimate encounters with the Middle Ages that early humanists dreamed of experiencing with the ancient world. The Middle Ages of philological reconstruction can "help us to criticize all the other Middle Ages that at one time or another arouse our enthusiasm."[18]

A more deeply ingrained Platonism that wants to expose the lies of the poets quickly belies the Aristotelian trappings of Eco's anatomy, determined to exclude medievalism from the republic of philologist kings. A Thomist turn if there ever was one. Eco is clearing the ground for his own astonishing forays into medievalism.[19] He does not provide a viable theory but rather a kind of Borgesian catalogue. And indeed this is how I suggest the essay itself should be read – as an advertisement for Eco's own brand of medievalism, not as a program for medievalistic studies. In fact it's really more of a pogrom than a program. There is a certain imp of the perverse lurking everywhere in the essay, most apparently in "the ten little Middle Ages" set to the tune of a racist nursery rhyme that celebrates cultural genocide. Eco's references elsewhere to Agatha Christie's *And Then There Were None* make plain that he knew a complete form of the lyrics, rather than just the truncated version I learned as a child. In Christie's novel the song runs thus:

> Ten little Indian boys went out to dine
> One choked his little self and then there were nine
> Nine little Indian boys sat up very late
> One overslept himself and then there were eight
> Eight little Indian boys traveling in Devon
> One got left behind and then there were seven
> Seven little Indian boys chopping up sticks
> One chopped himself in half and then there were six
> Six little Indian boys playing with a hive
> A bumblebee stung one and then there were five

Five little Indian boys going in for law
One got into Chancery and then there were four
Four little Indian boys going out to sea
A red herring swallowed one and then there were three
Three little Indian boys walking in the zoo
A big bear hugged one and then there were two
Two little Indian boys playing with a gun
One shot the other and then there was one
One little Indian boy left all alone
He went out and hanged himself
And then there were none.[20]

Various long versions of the song are extant, the earliest apparently dating back to an American minstrel show in 1868. Later variants exist that substitute "Nigger" or "Soldier" for "Injun" in the war of attrition. Even supposing a wish to tweak the nose of what would come to be called "political correctness," this is unacceptably bad behavior. Yet perhaps Eco is tweaking his own nose as well, mocking the process of winnowing out his predecessors in a realm he hopes to colonize with a "reliable Middle Ages" set against romance and fantasy "escapism à la Tolkien."

Besides the humor in desperately bad taste, there are other reasons why Eco's essay finally needs to go the way of all the Indians in the song. Its Platonist rejection of mimesis posing as a poetics is bad theory, starkly in contrast to the combination of philology and pastiche in superb novels like *The Name of the Rose* and *Baudolino*. Both novels are richly textured combinations of a "reliable Middle Ages" and the "Middle Ages as *pretext*," designed to address contemporary concerns. Eco's theory of medievalism valorizes continuity, a concern his fiction also displays in abundance. But the success of these novels is due as much to far-flung analogies and allegories, to the *unheimlich*, the abject, and the strange, as to the continuous. The "Dreaming" essay equates classicism with "philological reconstruction" and medievalism with "utilitarian bricolage."[21] In fact the kind of a return to the Middle Ages Eco wants to champion is not medievalism at all, but rather classicism as he defines it, that is an Aristotelianism of the Thomist ilk with little patience for the bricolage of, say, Averroës. In the *Name of the Rose*, revealingly, Eco's own dream of miraculous continuity is enabled by perhaps the foundational trope of romantic medievalism, the found manuscript, and crushed by the boogeyman of the gothic, the Inquisition.

With Eco's anatomy of medievalism we're back at one remove to the Renaissance triad and its prolepsis, but what is both transsumed and traduced here is medievalism *tout court*. There are a number of problems with this. The classicism of the Middle Ages certainly included philological reconstruction, but even that was more in keeping with what Eco calls "utilitarian bricolage." Indeed, bricolage not only dominates the poetics of medievalism but arguably the poetics of the Middle Ages as well. Yet I certainly don't wish to set up another excluded middle: philology and bricolage each play an important role in medievalism, and medievalism, Eco's and everyone else's, falls somewhere in between.

In closing it is precisely what comes in between that I want to underline, in contrast to the proleptic leaps I have identified in these different versions of medievalistic historiography. The Middle Ages as a period, however misleading and unwieldy, foregrounds the obstacle of a contingency that resists sublimation. Whether we long for direct access to the ancient or the medieval world, the Middle Ages stand for – as shell or kernel – everything that stands in our way. If for many the ancient world has evoked the immediacy of the past, the Middle Ages is a historiographic trope for mediacy itself, whether cast as a long, enduring tradition, a yawning gulf of otherness, or a mystery to be solved by the scientific method. Medievalism has its own traditions, and it is from these as much as from historical subjects and subtexts that new works arise. We really are only at the beginning of theorizing this remarkably influential form of cultural production. Let's not allow our reservations about medievalism and dreams of a "reliable Middle Ages" to goad us into narrowing the genetic pool.

NOTES

1. Umberto Eco, *Travels in Hyperreality*, trans. William Weaver (New York: Harcourt, Brace, 1986), 72.
2. Eco, *Travels*, 61–72.
3. Nickolas Haydock and E. L. Risden, ed., *Hollywood in the Holy Land: Essays on Film Depictions of the Crusades and Christian–Muslim Clashes* (Jefferson, NC: McFarland, 2009).

4. Perhaps the supreme instance of this is also the greatest work of medievalism, *Don Quixote*. Cervantes makes room within the novel for nostalgia as well as satire, that is to say, continuity as well as abjection. That modern is not medieval is an indictment of the contemporary world, as well as a stimulus for nostalgia. Medievalism is madness, but realism sterile, threadbare, and hopeless. At the beginning the Don's embrace of continuity is countered by Sancho's stubborn insistence on alterity. Yet contingencies – economic, inter-individual, as well as his own history – lead Sancho to share the Don's illusions, if not his madness. Once he recovers, Quixote can identify much of what has happened on his quests as the result of errors induced by his illness, but of course it is errancy that defines a quest, and his madness has transformed the world around him in ways that endure beyond the persistence of the illusion.

5. Important inroads have been made recently and indirectly through studies of medievalism in the works of major twentieth-century theorists. See especially Bruce Holsinger, *The Premodern Condition: Medievalism and the Making of Theory* (Chicago: University of Chicago Press, 2005); and Erin Felicia Labbie, *Lacan's Medievalism* (Minneapolis: University of Minnesota Press, 2006).

6. See for instance Richard Burt, "Getting Schmedieval: Of Manuscript and Film Prologues, Paratexts, and Parodies," *Exemplaria* 19.2, co-guest editors Richard Burt and Nickolas Haydock (2007): 230–33.

7. See Nickolas Haydock, *Movie Medievalism: The Imaginary Middle Ages* (Jefferson, NC: McFarland, 2008), 134–64.

8. See, for instance, Norman Cantor, *Inventing the Middle Ages: The Lives, Works, and Ideas of the Great Medievalists of the Twentieth Century* (New York: Harper Perennial, 1991).

9. For what Lord Acton revealingly dubs a "renaissance of the Christian ages," see below.

10. From Cambridge MS Add. 5528, 170b–173a, c. 1859, as transcribed in Herbert Butterfield, *Man on his Past: A Study of the History of Historical Scholarship* (Cambridge: Cambridge University Press, 1955), 212–14 (212).

11. John Emerich Edward Dalberg-Acton, First Baron Acton, *Essays on Freedom and Power*, ed. Gertrude Himmelfarb (Boston: Beacon Press, 1948), 30–87.

12. Acton, quoted in Butterfield, ed., *Man on His Past*, 213–14.

13. "The nineteenth century is a period of reaction not against the 18th merely, but against all since the fifteenth. But it has this advantage over the Renaissance, that it does not exclude one world in order to adopt another. It does not reject the accumulated progress and treasures of the last 3 centuries, as of old the work of 1000 years was condemned as a failure and

wholly worthless. It is not for the sake of the good which is in the M[iddle] A[ges] only, but for the sake of continuity, that we require this return – not because the Revival of paganism was wrong in its origin, but because it was wrong in its excess" (Acton, quoted in Butterfield, ed., *Man on His Past*, 213).

14. See Ross Leckie, *Hannibal: A Novel* (Edinburgh: Canongate, 1995); and the forthcoming film *Hannibal the Conqueror*, in production and due out in 2011, with Vin Diesel directing and in the starring role of Hannibal Barca.

15. See Leckie's *Hannibal* and the second novel in his Carthage–Rome trilogy, *Scipio: A Novel* (Edinburgh: Canongate, 1998).

16. For instance, Sylvia Heng's splendid and illuminating study, *Empire of Magic: Medieval Romance and the Politics of Cultural Fantasy* (New York: Columbia University Press, 2004); and Siobhain Bly Calkin's rewarding *Saracens and the Making of English Identity: The Auchinleck Manuscript* (New York: Routledge, 2005). For a more general introduction to medieval orientalism, see John V. Tolan, *Saracens: Islam in the Medieval Imagination* (New York: Columbia University Press, 2002).

17. For a survey of the medieval tradition and its survivals, see Norman Daniel, *Islam and the West: The Making of a Tradition* (Oxford: Oneworld, 1960, 1993), and for a collection of essays relating current conflicts to the tradition of orientalism, I recommend Emran Quereshi and Michael A. Sellis, *The New Crusades: Constructing the Muslim Enemy* (New York: Columbia University Press, 2003).

18. Eco, *Travels in Hyperreality*, 71.

19. Eco's most extensive foray into medievalistics is his book *The Aesthetics of Chaosmos: The Middle Ages of James Joyce*, trans. Ellen Esrock (Cambridge, MA: Harvard University Press, 1989). Here, fascinatingly, Joyce's apparent classicism is shown to take its form from the aesthetics of Thomas Aquinas.

20. Agatha Christie, *And Then There Were None* (New York: St. Martin's Griffin, 2004), 28–29. Originally published in Britain by Collins Crime Club under the title *Ten Little Niggers* in 1939, the novel has also been released and filmed under the title *Ten Little Indians*. It sold over 100 million copies, making it the best selling mystery of all time, according to Publications International, Ltd., as cited on Wikipedia, <http://en.wikipedia.org/wiki/And_Then_There_Were_None> [retrieved 28 February 2009].

21. Eco, *Travels*, 67–68.

Medievalitas Fugit: Medievalism and Temporality

Richard Utz

At the beginning of his influential monograph *Futures Past* Reinhart Kosellek compares two distinct moments in the reception history of the famous battle of Issus, in which Alexander the Great's Greek army defeated the Persians in 333 BCE. One, Albrecht Altdorfer's widely known historical painting, *Alexanderschlacht*, unites on a canvas of 1.5 square meters everything that was known, in the early sixteenth century, about the impressive military victory that ushered in Hellenism. Noting various kinds of anachronism employed by Altdorfer, Kosellek remarks:

> Viewing the painting in the Pinakothek, we think we see before us the last knights of Maximilian [scil. Maximilian I, Holy Roman Emperor of the Habsburg empire, 1493–1519] or the serf-army at the Battle of Pavia. From their feet to their turbans, most of the Persians resemble the Turks who, in the same year the picture was painted (1529), unsuccessfully laid siege to Vienna. In other words, the event that Altdorfer captured was for him at once historical and contemporary. Alexander and Maximilian, for whom Altdorfer had prepared drawings, merge in an exemplary manner; the space of historical experience enjoys the profundity of generational unity. The state of contemporary military technology still did not in principle offer any obstacle to the representation of the Battle of Issus as a current event. Machiavelli had only just devoted an entire chapter of his *Discourses* to the thesis that modern firearms had had little impact on the conduct of wars. The belief that the invention of the gun eclipsed the exemplary power of Antiquity was quite erroneous, argued Machiavelli. Those who

followed the Ancients could only smile at such a view. The present and the past were enclosed within a common historical plane.[1]

If for Altdorfer temporal difference between the year 333 BCE and his own historical moment was not apparent, Karl Wilhelm Friedrich Schlegel (1772–1829), who described his impressions of the painting in the early nineteenth century, "was seized 'upon sighting this marvel,' as he wrote, by a boundless 'astonishment.' Schlegel praised the work in long sparkling cascades of words, recognizing in it 'the greatest feat of the age of chivalry.'"[2] Although Schlegel appears to conflate Antiquity and the Middle Ages in the term "chivalry":

> he had [...] gained a critical historical distance with respect to Altdorfer's masterpiece. Schlegel was able to distinguish the painting from his own time, as well as from that of the Antiquity it strove to represent. For him, history had in this way gained a specifically temporal dimension, which is clearly absent for Altdorfer. Formulated schematically, there was for Schlegel, in the three hundred years separating him from Altdorfer, more time (or perhaps a different mode of time) than appeared to have passed for Altdorfer in the eighteen hundred years or so that lay between the Battle of Issus and his painting.[3]

Kosellek's conclusion is that in the three centuries that separate the reactions to the Battle of Issus by Altdorfer and Schlegel, a period commonly referred to as early modernity (*frühe Neuzeit*), history underwent a process of temporalization (*Verzeitlichung*), one that finally accelerated toward the concept of historical development that informs modernity and the modern university.

I am going to posit that, for the most part, work in Medieval Studies, that is, the scholarly investigation meant to elucidate the "real" Middle Ages, is informed by the modern temporality becoming accepted in Friedrich Schlegel's early nineteenth century. Science-like methodologies, especially those generally subsumed under the term "philology" or academic "history," enabled modern scholars of the Middle Ages to date and attribute medieval texts to authors or at least regions and social strata and to build an imposing historical narrative to describe and compartmentalize in more and more detail the roughly one thousand years between the end of the Roman empire and the fall of Constantinople. At the center of this science-like endeavor, whose origins may be said to commence with Petrarch's definition of the Middle Ages as a mere transitional age, have always been questions of temporality and periodicity, questions uniquely indicative of the difficulty of conceptualizing historical occurrences through the medium of language. Again in the words of Kosellek:

> Concepts within which experiences collect and in which expecta-tions are bound up are, as linguistic performances, no mere epiphenomena of so-called real history. Historical concepts, espe-cially political and social concepts, are minted for the registration and embodiment of the elements and forces of history. This is what marks them out within a language. They do, however, possess [...] their own mode of existence within the language. It is on this basis that they affect or react to particular situations and occurrences.[4]

The term "Medievalism" can be said to be such a linguistic perfor-mance responding to particular pressures in and outside the academy as well as to the existence of competing terms and practices such as "Medieval Philology," "Medieval History," and "Medieval Studies." The accelerating (and sometimes willfully accelerated) sense of histori-cal and methodological distance between modern academic medieval-ists and medieval culture becomes obvious in the scholarly insistence on establishing strict boundaries between pastist research of the "real" Middle Ages ("philology," "history," "studies") and the various non-academic *presentist reimaginations* of the medieval past. *The Oxford English Dictionary*'s tripartite definition of "medievalism" – "[b]eliefs and practices (regarded as) characteristic of the Middle Ages; medieval thought, religion, art, etc. Also: the adoption of, adherence to, or interest in medieval ideals, styles, or usages" – indicates that nineteenth-century voices like John Ruskin, Dante Gabriel Rossetti, or John Addington Symonds employed the term simply as a synonym for the medieval period, equivalent to other abstract period descriptors such as "classicalism," "orientalism," or "feudalism." Academic scholars of the Middle Ages, eager to present their subject matter as demanding much more serious intellectual rigor and solid academic *Sitzfleisch* than the popular reception of medieval culture, saw the polysemous quality of "medievalism" as an opportunity for better defining their own social relevance and status as experts and critics.

Consequently, the semantic narrowing of "medievalism," especially by English-speaking medievalists, into just another Victorian whim, turned out to be an essential part of the process of academizing and institutionalizing the reception of the Middle Ages.[5] "Medieval Studies," the early twentieth-century interdisciplinary North American amalgamation of nineteenth-century European medieval philology and history, increasingly defined itself as exclusive of any self-reflexive, subjective, empathic, or playfully non-scientific work on medieval culture. As Kathleen Biddick summarizes, medieval studies became a discipline "based on expulsion and abjection and bound in rigid alterity."[6]

It is fascinating to observe how the academic history of the Studies in Medievalism movement repeats, *in nuce*, the general process sketched above. In the late 1970s and early 1980s, when Leslie J. Workman (1927–2001) organized the first Kalamazoo conference sessions and founded the journals, *Studies in Medievalism* and *The Year's Work in Medievalism*, he was, while certainly not an amateur, a private scholar without the institutional support of an academic college or university and with few published credentials. Keenly aware that he embodied the very definition of a "colleague" medieval scholars would relegate to their negative definition of "medievalism," he engaged in an impressive series of rhetorical and organizational moves to make "medievalism" acceptable. He included all the necessary discursive markers in the journals (e.g., *Studies*; *Year's Work*) and conference titles (Annual International Conference on Medievalism), discouraged the submission of what he generically called "nice little papers on Tennyson," linked his enterprise with established or emerging academic organizations (e.g., International Medieval Congresses at Kalamazoo and Leeds; *Medieval Feminist Newsletter*; Annual Arizona Center for Medieval and Renaissance Studies), and made sure that all official publications and communication (*Medievalism Newsletter*, annual calls for papers) upheld the existing demarcations between a scientific/academic study and so-called "popular" forms of reception.[7] Only by the mid-1990s did Workman signal a move away from the binary distinction between medieval studies and medievalism and acknowledge, albeit not as radically as Norman Cantor in his *Inventing the Middle Ages* (1991), that all forms of medieval reception participated in the ever-developing images of medieval culture in post-medieval times.

Most medievalists were not ready to follow Workman and Cantor on what they considered a slippery slope toward a reunification of what academic custom's rigid rings had set apart.[8] However, the "New Medievalists," a group of North American scholars in Romance literatures and languages independent of the Studies in Medievalism movement, advocated for a radical inclusion of contemporary critical theory to bring about a new temporality for medieval scholarship, one not exclusively founded in unbending pastism/alterity.[9] As a revisionist movement with strong poststructuralist leanings, the "New Medievalists" reached a relatively large audience of younger colleagues and were able to demonstrate how many scholarly practices in the study of medieval literature and culture were influenced by the early modern and modern founders of their respective academic disciplines and their nationalistic and gendered agendas. While this inclusion of theory clearly contributed to a discipline more aware of its own origins, it did little to break down the modern distance between medievalia and medievalists. In fact, the greater theoretical sophistication of the "New Medievalism" may have increased the temporal chasm between investigating subjects and their medieval subjects under investigation. Thus, while the "irruption of a personalized subject in the otherwise dispassionate discourse of medievalism" was one of the principal goals of "New Medievalist" practice, the approach failed to bring about a truly innovative shift in how scholars may speak of the Middle Ages.[10] Minted by its founders to embody and register the ever-quickening need for something "New" in the competitive North American academy, the "New Medievalism" fell victim to the same accelerating temporalization that had brought it about. A little over a decade after its invention it has proven ephemeral.

Most recently, "Neomedievalism" has been growing into a new and exciting subfield that focuses on the reception of medievalia as they appear in all forms of contemporary media. As with "medievalism," this "unscholarly" area has met with a tepid response by those intent on defending scholarliness against the onslaught of the tech-savvy hordes who would make forms of contemporary entertainment their academic specialty.[11] Undeterred by this resistance, neomedievalists continue to reveal how the most recent generations of readers/viewers/gamers have added a level of understanding to the study of the myriad existing reinventions of the medieval past.

Informed by sources that have had considerably less impact on the academic medievalism of the late twentieth century, for example Umberto Eco and Terry Jones and Terry Gilliam's *Monty Python and the Holy Grail*, scholars of Neomedievalism demonstrate how "the art and technology of special effects and other video technology have been able to catch up to, perhaps even out-do, the printed word in generating the most ultimate of fantasy dream-states."[12] Neomedieval texts no longer need to strive for the authenticity of original manuscripts, castles, or cathedrals, but create pseudo-medieval worlds that playfully obliterate history and historical accuracy and replace history-based narratives with simulacra of the medieval, employing images that are neither an original nor the copy of an original, but altogether "New/Neo." Traditional approaches to the reception of the medieval have yet to develop the descriptive and diagnostic tools to recognize the revolutionary change such a commodifying attitude toward history is bound to engender.

The emergence of concepts such as the "New Medievalism" and "Neomedievalism" is more than a simple epiphenomenon of so-called "real" history, but rather responds to new medievalizing modes and technologies as well as the continued discontent with the limiting ways in which allegedly disinterested and objectivist scholarship has approached the temporal gap between various contemporaneities and the medieval past. In what follows, I would recommend future work on medievalism to consider the creative approaches exemplified by the editors, Louise D'Arcens and Juanita Feros Ruys, and many of the contributors to *"Maistresse of My Wit": Medieval Women, Modern Scholars*, a volume published in *Making the Middle Ages*, the University of Sydney Center for Medieval Studies book series, in 2004.[13] D'Arcens and Ruys specifically set out to propose to readers a variety of ways in which the ever-increasing temporalization between the medieval and the contemporary might be mended so that the academic study of medieval culture might regain what it lost along its path toward professionalization. In what follows, I will discuss some of these approaches as paradigmatic possibilities for innovative future work in medievalism.

Philippa Maddern frames her essay "A Woman and Her Letters: The Documentary World of Elizabeth Clere" (pp. 27–74) with a self-reflexive (edited) e-mail exchange with her colleague, Wendy Harding ("Ex epistolis duarum magistrarum"). The first exchange, positioned before the scholarly essay, reflects on the advantages and disadvantages of "agreeing to expose our relatively unedited thoughts to the public gaze" (28). The second exchange follows the essay and deepens the discussion. And finally, Harding continues with her own scholarly investigation of "Mapping Masculine and Feminine Domains in the Paston Letters," which is followed in another (fifteen-page) exchange in which both intimately related essays and topics can now be revisited and in which both authors reveal how scholarly communication should work, namely as a process during which ideas are being tested, refined, and finally written down. While almost all of this process is usually hidden and happens in various locations and over extended periods of time, Harding and Maddern allow us to "listen" in on the vast variety of voices, imaginings, and scholarly positionalities that we could never gather from the finished, polished, uninflected, and thus often hermeneutically one-dimensional academic essay. After reflecting questions about the difference it would make to read medieval women as a woman, an Australian, an Australian of Anglo origins, or as a child of the 1950s, the authors follow Petrarch's lead to build an even better bridge to their medieval "maistresses" by addressing letters to them (one of them in Middle English). This process reveals the hopes, fears, disap-pointments, and joys during the different developmental stages of scholarly endeavors and provides an attractive admission ticket to various kinds of readers.

In "Her Own *Maistresse*?: Christine de Pizan the Professional Amateur" (pp. 119–45) Louise D'Arcens finds in the reception of Christine's dual reputation as professional writer and autodidactic amateur a fascinating parallel for rethinking our discipline's own autodidactic past and (overly?) professionalized present. She argues compellingly that Christine's example of a "professional amateurism" might offer "contemporary medievalists a thought-provoking model of intellectual and professional authority in which passion and reason are not mutually exclusive" (p. 124), a suggestion that reminded me of Clare Simmons's challenging questions about some of the false premises still dominating the discourse of exclusivist medieval scholars: "Were the founders of the Early English Text Series amateurs or professionals? Does a professional appointment in a research insti-tution prove that a scholar's reading of the medieval past is not based on cultural preconceptions?"[14] And, as I would like to continue, are

Umberto Eco's *Il nome della Rosa* (1980) or Jürgen Lodemann's *Siegfried und Krimhild* (2002) not based on painstaking research?

Nicholas Watson's article, "Desire for the Past" (pp. 149–88) was originally published in the 1999 edition of *Studies in the Age of Chaucer*. Watson had used his own reading of Carolyn Walker Bynum's *Holy Feast and Holy Fast* (1987) and the critique of Bynum's study by Kathleen Biddick ("Gender, Bodies, Borders," *Speculum*, 1993) to argue for a systematic investigation of the role desire plays in historical scholarship and moved toward such an investigation in his discussion of Hadewijch of Antwerp's and Julian of Norwich's insights about the relationship between desire and knowledge in the realm of religion. For this reprint, Watson provided an "Afterword" in which he wonders, from a temporal distance of almost five years, if the impetus for his earlier text had not been that of "a mere defence of my own right to be, as a male scholar of women's spirituality" (p. 186) and warns that medieval studies might not be able to defend its existence as a discipline of academic inquiry unless it were to theorize the role of empathy and affect in scholarship.

Diane Watt, in "Critics, Communities, Compassionate Criticism: Learning from *The Book of Margery Kempe*" (pp. 191–210) makes a plea for readings of medieval literature that not only render perceptible their authors' stakes in the work that engages them (something she aptly terms their "ethical signature"), but also consider who constitutes their community of readers. She discusses how the recent reception *of The Book of Margery Kempe* (Carolyn Dinshaw's *Getting Medieval* [1999] and Robert Glück's *Margery Kempe* [1994]) offers fully engaged readings of the medieval text but, in an effort to address the queer community, appropriates the text to emphasize "the queer over the feminine" and "the sexual over the maternal," thereby silencing, for example, the debt queer theory owes to feminist politics and practice.

Juanita Feros Ruys, in "Playing Alterity: Heloise, Rhetoric, and *Memoria*" (pp. 211–43) is concerned with the dangers of both "presentism" and "pastism." As her cogent discussion of the reception history of Heloise's writings demonstrates, both these practices may imply, on the one hand, overly appropriative gestures toward the medieval writer or, on the other, the dehumanizing and complete silencing of these writers' human past. The possible solution to avoid the pitfalls involved in either perspective Ruys gleans from the scholarly role-playing (*memoria*) practiced by medieval women. Thus, the fictionalized dialogue ("Interrogating Heloise"), which follows Ruys's formal essay, signifies both her "empathic investment in the issue of Heloise's mothering" as well as her "acknowledged distance from (non-identification with) the historical figure of Heloise" (p. 234). Displaying on the bottom of every page the learned footnote, paragon of scholarly paratexts, this playful interrogation of Heloise by an officer from a department of youth and community services presents an intriguing symbiosis of the academic with the affective/literary.

Marea Mitchell, in her essay "Uncanny Dialogues: 'Journal of Mistress Joan Martyn' and *The Book of Margery Kempe*" (pp. 247–66), successfully applies Freud's category of the "uncanny" – that which is both familiar, recognizable, and safe, and at the same time unfamiliar, alien, and threatening – to a comparison between one of Virginia Woolf's short stories and the late medieval *Book*. Acknowledging the "real differences" (265) between both texts evolving from such a comparison, Mitchell argues, suggests the recognition of the various interests with which modern scholarship often approaches medieval texts. While the manifold resonances between medieval women and modern scholars will be helpful for a full understanding of medieval women's voices, a text like Margery Kempe's should never be subjected to an all-encompassing "assimilation" since there will always be "unfamiliar" or "undesirable" elements in her *Book* that, for example "do not fit the pictures and stories that modern feminism needs in order to make sense of its past and suggest its future" (265).

Shawn Madison Krahmer, in "Redemptive Suffering: The Life of Alice of Schaerbeck in a Contemporary Context" (pp. 267–93) approaches the vita of a thirteenth-century Cistercian nun from the often mutually exclusive perspectives of "a feminist medievalist, a friend of contemporary religious, a Christian theologian, and the survivor of a marriage" she found "emotionally abusive" (269). Krahmer holds that the foundation of any study of medieval women's spirituality is to first understand their "actions and lives within their own context. Only then can we ask what we might learn from them that is applicable in our own time and our own lives" (274). Her solution is that, while contemporary scholars need to continue a dialogue with figures like Alice, the nun's redemptive suffering should not be adopted as a model for our contemporary lives but must be rejected as a relic of the past.

Jacqueline Jenkins's essay on "Reading Women Reading: Feminism, Culture, and Memory" (pp. 317–34) first debates the intriguing possibility of a cultural memory, a number of shared common norms, conventions, and practices that would link the otherwise non-contiguous reading experiences of medieval and contemporary women. Drawing on the results of modern romance studies, she speculates if the otherwise forbidden self-realization of women through the reading of romances could not also be the cause of the popularity of vernacular devotional literature among high-status women in the Middle Ages. Ultimately, however, she entertains the sobering possibility that she might have embraced the results of modern romance studies expressly because of her desire to attribute resistance to the medieval women readers of devotional texts.

What is most attractive about the various approaches chosen by these essays in "*Maistresse of My Wit*" is their openly experimental and playful character. Empathy, memory, subjectivity, resonance, affection, desire, passion, speculation, fiction, imagination, positionality, etc. are employed in readings that, while unapologetically presentist, are not reductionist or dismissive of pastist reason, professionalism, distance, and research. The approaches sketched above successfully counterbalance the consequences of accelerating "temporalization" (*Verzeitlichung*) that Reinhard Kosellek identified as the salient feature of modern historical modes. I understand that many scholars cherish traditional hermeneutical alterity as the best protection against the complete and utter identification with the medieval past governing certain totalitarian medievalisms. However, the careful (postmodern?) "detemporalization" (*Entzeitlichung*) proposed by D'Arcens, Ruys, etc., may be our best chance at avoiding the potential dehumanizing of the medieval past as the eternal "other." Intelligent mélanges of presentist and pastist thought should assist practitioners of medievalism to be inclusive of the "contra-temporal" reception of Bernard of Clairvaux by seventeenth-century Cistercian monks, some of whom thought of the revitalization of Bernard's texts in their own time not as the revitalization of a medieval (historical) monk, but "of a set of ideas synchronically present."[15] In this case, but also in those cases that do not specifically challenge modern academic conceptual and temporal modes, a demonstrated awareness of one's own and one's subject's correlation with temporality should be one of the admission tickets to getting published in *Studies in Medievalism*.[16]

NOTES

1. Reinhard Kosellek, *Futures Past: On the Semantics of Historical Time* (New York: Columbia University Press, 2004), 9–10.
2. Kosellek, *Futures Past*, 10.
3. Kosellek, *Futures Past*, 10.
4. Kosellek, *Futures Past*, 223.
5. By 1908, as the public altercation between the former English Jesuit, George Tyrell, and Cardinal Mercier of Malines, Belgium, about the medieval or modern orientation of the Catholic Church reveals, Medievalism had turned into an umbrella term for everything retrograde and unsophisticated (George Tyrell, *Medievalism. A Reply to Cardinal Mercier* [London, New York, Bombay, Calcutta: Longmans, Green, and Co., 1908]). As any web search will demonstrate, this negative semantic shading has remained prevalent, especially in the political discourse of countries that, like India, are caught in an ongoing national argument about their (allegedly medieval) heritage and their swiftly growing global economic importance. See, for example, K. M. Shrimali's review, entitled "Medievalism Defined" (*Frontline* 18/13, 23 June – 6 July 2001:
<http://www.hinduonnet.com/fline/fl1813/18130740.htm>
[accessed 15 May 2007]), of R. S. Sharma's 2001 monograph on *Early Medieval Indian Society: A Study in Feudalisation* (Delhi: Orient Longman).
6. *The Shock of Medievalism* (Durham, NC: Duke University Press, 1998), 16. While other cultural, linguistic, and national traditions may not know the English terminological division between "medievalism" and "medieval studies," the division between a popular/writerly/artistic and a scholarly reception of the Middle Ages exists in similar or even more pronounced form. For the history of medievalist practices and terminological development in the German-speaking world, into which the term "medie[a]valism" entered as a loan translation, see Richard Utz, "Resistance to (The New) Medievalism? Comparative Deliberations on (National) Philology, *Mediävalismus*, and *Mittelalter-Rezeption* in Germany and North America," in Roger Dahood, ed., *The Future of the Middle Ages and the Renaissance: Problems, Trends, and Opportunities for Research* (Turnhout: Brepols, 1998), 151–70. See Jaume Aurell, "El Nuevo Medievalismo y la Interpretación de los Textos Históricas," *Hispania. Revista Española de Historia* 66 (2006): 809–32, and Richard Utz, " 'Mes souvenirs sont peut-être reconstruits': Medieval Studies, Medievalism, and the Scholarly and Popular Memories of the 'Right of the Lord's First Night'," *Philologie im Netz* 31 (2005): 49–59, for the terminological discussions in the Spanish- and French-speaking world.

7. On the process of Workman's establishing of the "medievalism" disciplinary field, see Richard Utz and Tom Shippey, "Introduction," in Richard Utz and Tom Shippey, ed., *Medievalism in the Modern World: Essays in Honour of Leslie Workman* (Turnhout: Brepols, 1998), 1–13; Richard Utz, "Speaking of Medievalism: An Interview with Leslie J. Workman," in *Medievalism and the Modern World*, 433–49; Clare A. Simmons, "Introduction," in Clare A. Simmons, ed., *Medievalism and the Quest for the 'Real' Middle Ages* (London and Portland, OR: Frank Cass, 2001), 1–28, especially 14–22; and Kathleen Verduin, "The Founding and the Founder: Medievalism and the Legacy of Leslie J. Workman," *Studies in Medievalism* 17 (2009): 1–27.

8. For examples of scholars upholding the binary opposition, see Allen Frantzen, *Desire for Origins: New Language, Old English, and Teaching the Tradition* (New Brunswick, NJ: Rutgers University Press, 1990), xi; Francis C. Gentry and Ulrich Müller, "The Reception of the Middle Ages in Germany: An Overview," *Studies in Medievalism* 3/4 (1991): 399–422; and, most recently, Michael Alexander, *Medievalism: The Middle Ages in Modern England* (New Haven and London: Yale University Press, 2007).

9. See, for example, the contributions to *Medievalism and the Modernist Temper*, ed. R. Howard Bloch and Stephen Nichols (Baltimore, MD: Johns Hopkins University Press, 1996).

10. R. Howard Bloch and Stephen Nichols, "Introduction," in Bloch and Nichols, ed., *Medievalism and the Modernist Temper*, 6.

11. I would hope that this attitude might change with the broader reception of Volume 16 of *Studies in Medievalism*, entitled *Medievalism in Technology Old and New* (2007), and I have discussed this issue further in "A Moveable Feast: Repositionings of 'The Medieval' in Medieval Studies, Medievalism, and Neomedievalism," a preface to the forthcoming essay collection, *The Medieval in Motion: Neomedievalism in Film, Television and Electronic Games*, ed. Carol L. Robinson and Pamela Clements (Lewiston, NY: Edwin Mellen Press, 2009).

12. Carol Robinson, "Beyond That 'It's Just a Flesh Wound …' Kind of Feeling: A Medieval Game Proposal," in Anne Lair and Richard Utz, ed., *Falling into Medievalism* (UNIversitas: The University of Northern Iowa Journal of Research, Scholarship, and Creative Activity, Special Forum Section, Spring 2006, <http://www.uni.edu/universitas/spring06/carolrobinson0306.htm> [accessed 31 March 2009]).

13. Louise D'Arcens and Juanita Feros Ruys, ed., *"Maistresse of My Wit": Medieval Women, Modern Scholars* (Turnhout: Brepols, 2004). My thoughts on the refreshingly innovative approaches in this volume are based on my own 2005 review essay published in *The Medieval Review*,

<http://quod.lib.umich.edu/cgi/t/text/text-idx?c=tmr;cc=tmr;q1=utz;rgn=main;view=text;idno=baj9928.0502.016>.

14. Simmons, "Introduction," 12.

15. Mette Birkedal-Bruun, "A Case in which a Revitalization of Something Medieval Turned out not to be Medievalism," in Utz and Lair, ed., *Falling into Medievalism,* <http://www.uni.edu/universitas/spring06/mettebruun0306.htm> [accessed 31 March 2009]. See also Nils Holger Petersen's discussion of this Birkedal-Bruun essay and its relation to modes of medieval reception in *Studies in Medievalism* 17 (2009): 36–44, esp. 37–38.

16. Perhaps a similar awareness could also extend existing readings of the *Alexanderschlacht* to tease out views that render the battle's human figures more than merely incidental to the natural and cosmic forces that dominate them and intimate that being part of an event this memorable is well worth an individual's life.

Medievalists, Medievalism, and Medievalismists: The Middle Ages, Protean Thinking, and the Opportunistic Teacher-Scholar

E. L. Risden

We live in an academic time/space occupied by an increasingly varie-gated tapestry of "Studies": American Studies, Women's Studies, Gender Studies, Classical Studies, Medieval Studies. Many academi-cians, I observe, feel less than ever inclined to call ourselves members of English or History or Art Departments – too confining, too firmly circumscribing, too incriminating, too frighteningly definitive, too, well, old-fashioned. If we do "Medieval Studies," rather than "English," we feel freer to incorporate bits of history, literature, linguistics, religion, and aesthetics into our courses with a degree of nonchalance that may seem like dilettantism except that we already have so much to learn and teach and say in such a short time that adding a new and often exciting twist does little harm (and can accomplish much good).

Of course we still love *Beowulf*, Dante, Hildegard, Marie, Julian, sagas, the *Libro de Buen Amor*, and the *Chanson de Roland*. We teach them and write about them regularly (if we're lucky) and joyfully. Then "my own work" rears its eager head, so now let's move on to the professional development step of conferences and publishing: given typically increasing administrative duties, sometimes we have an easier task dashing off a quick paper on a new favorite art film recom-mended by a friend, or the new Harry Potter that one's children are reading, or, God forgive us, *The Da Vinci Code* (some readers, to my continuing astonishment, apparently do find that book interesting). As long as a paper still counts for tenure or promotion, why not? If it doesn't follow our courses, our dissertations, or our publishing history in traditional topics, we'll just call it *medievalism* and hope no one notices, since no one knows what that means.

One of the big difficulties with defining medievalism, my nominal duty in this essay, is the tacit problem that, as current practitioners, we don't really want to define it – not too exactly, anyway. For now we desire aggressive inclusivity, legitimization as a discipline through expansion. We want to permit ourselves and our colleagues scholarly space so that we can teach and write about whatever we want in whatever means we please, from real *medieval* texts that we approach by means of the newest theoretical whiz-bangs to fantasy trilogies to movies to anything that pop culture produces in which somebody swings a broadsword or wears a broad-brimmed, pointed hat, a long, flowing gown, or a jerkin.[1] The more definitions we have, the more plums we can swipe from someone's icebox – so sweet, so cool – to add a bit of new fun to the glorious old stuff. Like many of us, I came to medieval literature as much through the influence of Tolkien as of Chaucer, and both offer plenty of Horation substance and pleasure no matter how many times we return to them. A few years back at the Medieval Congress at Kalamazoo, after I had given a paper on Tolkien, a well-respected older scholar asked me (I think disgustedly) what I thought *The Lord of the Rings* has to do with things medieval or even with medievalism: the culture of Middle-earth in many ways mirrors the eighteenth century more than it does the Middle Ages, he said. Sword and Sorcery doesn't inevitably mean medieval, and one has the particular anachronism of dealing with the pipe tobacco. My facts are that I study Tolkien because he was not only a medievalist but also a true philologist, and therefore he remains to me particularly instructive (and fun) on linguistic as well as narrative levels, because I enjoy living for a time in his world, and because I think he has much to say to our time that we haven't yet fully sorted out. I can't call that a very good argument for *medievalism*, perhaps, but I hope it sufficient that I can get away with it, especially since medievalists have a means of approaching Tolkien that illuminates his work more fully than do those of other critical persuasions. That Tolkien was by trade a medievalist, and a good one, if not as productive in that field as his colleagues would have wished him, and that his scholarship so fully infiltrated his fiction allow us the right at least to approach his work, despite its setting far from the medieval world, as medievalism: work that follows but responds creatively to the Middle Ages.

In medievalism we're dealing with joint sensibilities: something nominally from a time past that we see through a modern or contemporary lens, something mimetic, but not fully so. As we read work from different times, we may discern differences in style, concerns, and worldviews, and with persistent study we may posit that those differences exemplify, represent, typify not just the literature of their time, but also the mind of their time. Erich Auerbach observes of the *Chanson de Roland* that "[t]he poet explains nothing; and yet the things which happen are stated with a paratactic bluntness which says that everything must happen as it does happen" with "no argument, no explanatory discussion."[2] Such historical-fictional worlds, bent on "encouraging rigidification of all categories" permit "but a small, extremely narrow portion of reality to assume visual plasticity" – an author will use that small portion to connect to both past and future; the tendency to "type," though, that, "[c]onfronting the reality of life [...] is neither able nor willing to deal with its breadths and depths. [...] It simplifies the events of the past by stylizing and idealizing them."[3] What differentiates the Renaissance from that tendency to establish and affirm types is that "in Italy especially [...] the concept of nobility became ever more personal, and as such it was actually often contrasted polemically with the other concept of nobility based solely on lineage."[4] The Renaissance begins the turn to a focus on and later an obsession with individuality. As we reach the modern, writes Auerbach, working on Virginia Woolf, "The writer of objective facts has almost completely vanished; almost everything stated appears by way of reflection in the consciousness of the dramatis personae. [...] It is all, then, a matter of the author's attitude toward the reality of the world he [sic] represents," a "design of a close approach to objective reality by means of numerous subjective impressions received by various individuals (and at various times)."[5] Auerbach argues that our notions and methods of representing reality change; the medieval world created definitive registers of expression and represented experience according to those accepted registers; the modern world horizontalizes registers and provides multiple perspectives to allow an event to come into (axiomatically inexact) focus gradually. One critical charge against modern medievalist fantasy, that it provides nothing but adolescent escapism, has met its counterargument in medievalism's offer of additional/alternative perspectives and in the greater "realizability" of its objective correlative: it can manage effects that simple, "direct" realism can't. So medievalism emerges as not just what Northrop Frye might characterize as a subsidiary of the Romantic mode, but also as a palatable (and palpable to an audience steeled by documentaries) means of addressing the horrors of two World Wars and the often terrifying globalization that followed: medieval*ism* means not a hearkening back, certainly nothing nostalgic, but instead a way of schematizing political, social, and technological problems in a parallel world where authors may play them out and posit their futures.

Since Leslie Workman got things going, many scholars have attempted to define medievalism; *SiM 17* offers a garden of essays that provide the perfect ground on which I may till my own anonymous plants, since they supply both learned and viable graftings. Tom Shippey begins appropriately with the *Oxford English Dictionary* definition of *mediaevalism* as " 'The system of belief and practice characteristic of the Middle Ages' " or " 'the adoption of or devotion to mediaeval ideals or usages' "; this *official* definition, as Shippey observes, "remains standard and in a sense authoritative," even "familiar," but also incomplete.[6] Shippey adds then the definition applied to submissions, if ambiguously, by *SiM* as an academic outlet: "Any post-medieval attempt to re-imagine the Middle Ages, or some aspect of the Middle Ages, for the modern world, in any of many different media; especially in academic usage, the study of the development and significance of such attempts."[7] *SiM* after all is but one organ, and the world of medievalism grows continually, but even that definition, aimed at guiding would-be contributors, (intentionally) opens up operations for nearly any genre or medium (and the broadest possible subject matter). We have in medievalism, even in a time of economic recession, a "growth industry": lots of persons from lots of disciplines want in, and we want to encourage them. If Tolkien, Lewis, LeGuin, and Rowling get children reading, and then get them eventually to read *Beowulf, Piers Plowman,* the *Decameron,* and the *Book of Margery Kempe,* then the world will become a better place for their labors (I still believe Philip Sidney about the value of literature).

They too may grow into medievalists and medievalismists, not just consumers (not of course their only two options).[8]

Gwendolyn Morgan adds further specifics to the flowering definition: *medievalism* "may describe the use of medieval themes, stories, characters, or even styles in the fiction, art, or film in any period following the close of the Middle Ages."[9] She adds, "Politically, [medievalism] frequently denotes the recreation or refashioning of historical figures or events to justify the ideologies or national identities of a subsequent age," but it always implies a "reliance on the medieval past to lend authority to contemporary thought" (allowing as much space for recreation as re-creation).[10] The term, thus politicized, reverses the polarity of many contemporary applications of the word *medieval* that imply something not just past, but bizzarely barbaric, illiterate, generally backward, and especially *violent*; the *ism* of the disfavored parent now, having achieved academic status, grants (especially fiscally) legitimacy and some degree of influence. Plus, it may often enough have a "G" or "PG" rating that we can share it with our children. We agree not to abuse our creative power to en-thrall, but to use it to liberate; for example, we may assign something like this: *Students, find something you like in our study of the Middle Ages and create/compose/choreograph/program a story of your own from it. Most importantly have fun doing it!*

Clare Simmons raises the problem that not only *medievalism* but even *medieval* is a relatively recent coinage; she suggests that "the English word 'medieval' is a Romantic-era invention that reflects a new attitude to the past."[11] She traces the history of the word *medieval* to suggest why, "when historians had at least fairly comfortably managed without it," Victorian writers who found a need for the term "are themselves medievalists."[12] The term *medieval* has at least had its fair vetting, but medievalism has so far barely got space, weeding, and watering to grow until recently – and in the last generation it has learned to thrive. Given the recentness of the term, we have another reason to suspend definition to allow ourselves to grow into the new patch of garden.

Nils Holger Petersen aptly warns of the difficulty not only in defining medievalism, but also in establishing even the boundaries of the Middle Ages. We must first consider what constitutes a true part of a historical period versus our continuing construction and reconstruction of it:

I would argue that medievalism should not be restricted to features in which a historical consciousness is explicitly at work, primarily because all practices are received in a culture where manifold attitudes will be or have been at work. Thus, regardless of the intentions or the consciousness behind a particular practice or artifact, it will form part of a general reception in which it may play a part as an element in the construction or recreation of the Middle Ages. Certainly, the eighteenth-century San Marco liturgy and, broadly speaking, pre-1960s Catholic liturgy as a whole and even Mozart's music contribute to such a continued construction of the Middle Ages and thereby make the question of when the Middle Ages ended obsolete.[13]

Petersen specifically counsels us to move slowly. Does the continuation of a practice of the Middle Ages make that practice medieval or medievalism? Any more recent study, given that humanity may have experienced a substantial change in consciousness since the Middle Ages, reconstructs but through a glass darkly: we see that past as if we were looking at a funhouse mirror.

Jane Toswell adds as an additional caveat the problem of the "double or triple lens of the study of medievalism: always a medievalist trope is perceived first through the sceptical modern eye of the twenty-first-century scholar, second (though not invariably) through the romanticizing eye of nineteenth-century medievalist scholarship [...] that is the foundation of the medievalizing impulse in the contemporary world" and, to the degree that we can recapitulate it, "through the variable (reaching towards 'authentic') eye of the creator(s) of the text."[14] A pair of spectacles over a pair of spectacles over a pair of spectacles: even Alice would have hesitated to follow a rabbit down such a hole.

Elizabeth Emery argues that Medievalism understood (in Leslie Workman's terms) as an "active process" allows us to include under our broad scholarly umbrella what we may otherwise consider "shocking" examples. She adds:

In their attempt to capture aspects of the artificially constructed period known as the "Middle Ages," both "high" and "low" cultures perpetuate images that correspond to the dreams, beliefs, or needs of the individual producing them. Ultimately, then, medievalism is a constantly evolving and self-referential process of defining an always fictional Middle Ages.[15]

I would say *fictionalized* rather than *fictional*, but I concur that medievalism has become almost anything we wish, even temporarily, to call it, as long as we may nominally, even dubiously, connect it, by whatever gossamer thread, to the Middle Ages. And, given a possible goal of inclusiveness, that variability and idiosyncrasy, for a time at least, isn't such a bad thing.

How far, then, do we go toward inclusiveness? Do we accept Tolkien and Lewis because they studied, taught, and alluded to and drew from medieval influences consistently? I would say yes. Do we include *The Seventh Seal* and *Kingdom of Heaven*, though their sensibilities are modern and their history loose, because they claim a (fictionalized) medieval present as their milieux? I would say certainly. Do we include Harry Potter novels because many readers (and, recently, critics) who like medievalism like them also and because we hope children who read Rowling will grow up to read real medieval literature? I would say no, because there we find no pretense to connections to anything medieval (though we may see that some medieval texts influenced Rowling's imagination). Such an assertion casts no aesthetic or value judgment on Rowling's work; I aim to say only that there we may be trying too hard to include something that in all its themes, methods, and components belongs under a different rubric. I certainly would feel happy to hear the contrary argument (not because I like those novels or the films, but for the sake of understanding and inclusiveness.)

Medievalism deliberately constructs an in-between: it celebrates the medieval and critiques the present – or vice versa, or both at once. But that pattern, the attempt to fill the *aporia*, characterizes many of our critical principles: grotesque (the creature, event, or architectural device poised in the midst of a metamorphosis, lost and yet fixed between two states of being, two ages, two worlds), fantastic (suspended – or uncertainly toggling – between the imaginary and the real), carnivalesque (experience of the lived-in spectacle that temporarily suspends and nominally removes the "real" world outside it).[16] All imply a level of uncertainty and a degree of uneasiness or at least edginess, the idea that we have ascended some pinnacle from which to view in relative safety something astonishing. That perspective medievalism specifically aims to grant us.

Now that I have prophesied (in the old sense, diagnosed the

present issue of defining *medievalism*), I shall indulge in a bit of fore-telling: here lurks the shrouded spirit of medievalism yet to come. ...

One subfield I expect to grow rapidly, movie medievalism, fills two of our desires (or obsessions) at once: our wish for strange, compelling, alternative worlds and our fetish for the visually piquant, something that strikes the eye powerfully but freshly, even if that freshness delivers a new fabrication of decay. In *Movie Medievalism: The Imaginary Middle Ages* Nickolas Haydock describes this phenomenon as "an intriguing mélange, which by turns fetishizes the alterity of the Middle Ages as a temporal Other while compulsively retooling imagined continuities to fit the rapidly changing priorities of the contemporary world. [...] [I]t is as much about making the past gone as it is about the endlessly renewable surprises inherent in finding it again."[17] A great number of films use elements "medieval" without even a tip of the chapeau to historical accuracy; we need not, as Haydock argues, trouble too much over that fact if we can manage to recognize and appreciate them for what they do rather than to expect them to do something the filmmakers never intended.

In a recent phone conversation, a representative from a publisher that produces books on language study told me that in many of their textbooks they now replace discussions of literature (an old staple) with discussion of films: they find that students understand the lessons better because of their greater familiarity with the examples and enjoy them more because of the growing cultural preference for visually enhanced learning experience. I find that idea at once practical and appalling. I hope that while movie medievalism will continue to grow, so will literary/print medievalism (whatever it is), and I even more sincerely hope that the growth of both will enliven rather than replace the enjoyment, appreciation, and knowledge of medieval studies.

NOTES

1. Anyone who has tried to write fantasy fiction (or, I suspect, any other sort of fiction) will tell you that "creative writing" also constitutes scholarship: one must do a fair amount of research to carry it off, and the act itself involves a response to and dialogue with other works that we love or to which we feel moved to respond.

2. Erich Auerbach, *Mimesis: The Representation of Reality in Western Literature*, trans. Willard R. Trask (Princeton, NJ: Princeton University Press, 1953), 101.

3. Auerbach, *Mimesis*, 116 and 120–21.

4. Auerbach, *Mimesis*, 139.

5. Auerbach, *Mimesis*, 534–36. Auerbach observes the "distinctive traits of the realistic novel of the era between the two great wars" as "multipersonal representation of consciousness, time strata, disintegration of the continuity of exterior events, shifting of the narrative viewpoint" (546); they derive largely from the "widening of man's [sic] horizon, and the increase of his experiences" [...] which "continued through the nineteenth [century] at an ever faster tempo – with such a tremendous acceleration at the beginning of the twentieth [...]." (549). Those vastly changing perceptions of the world created a gulf both enticing and unfathomable from which, I suspect, the increasing desire for medievalism comes. The Romantics showed it in the Gothic; the Victorians showed it in the beginnings of modern medievalism; the twentieth century needed it not so much to escape from as to provide a means of triangulating new realities too diverse and difficult to describe directly – a genre or a mode grew to face an increasingly incumbent objective correlative, a world capable of destroying itself and perhaps willing to try.

6. Tom Shippey, "Medievalisms and Why They Matter," *Studies in Medievalism* 17 (2009): 45–54 (45).

7. Shippey, "Medievalisms and Why They Matter," 45.

8. In *Roots and Branches: Selected Papers on Tolkien by Shippey* ([n.p.] Walking Tree Publishers, 2007), Shippey writes, "My former colleague John Carey, like Tolkien once a Merton Professor of Oxford University, has argued caustically [see *The Intellectuals and the Masses: Pride and Prejudice Among the Literary Intelligentsia, 1880–1939* (London: Faber & Faber, 1992)] [...] that the drive for literary 'modernism' in the twentieth century was created by the *haute bourgeoisie* to differentiate themselves from a new, literate, lower middle-class readership and authorship whom they felt to be usurping their places and privileges," and "twenty-first century 'post-modernism' has just been raising the stakes" (20). While philology and the

number of English majors at colleges and universities have declined over the last generation, "things do not have to be that way, and Tolkien and associated studies are one way of reversing the trend" (21). Medievalism serves, then, as a counteractivity to elitist exclusion and as a means to reintroduce philology, an old essential, to the curriculum.

9. Gwendolyn A. Morgan, "Medievalism, Authority, and the Academy," *Studies in Medievalism* 17 (2009): 55–67 (55).

10. Morgan, "Medievalism, Authority, and the Academy," 55.

11. Clare A. Simmons, "Medievalism: Its Linguistic History in Nineteenth-Century Britain," *Studies in Medievalism* 17 (2009): 28–35 (29).

12. Simmons, "Medievalism: Its Linguistic History," 29.

13. Nils Holger Petersen, "Medievalism and Medieval Reception: A Terminological Question," *Studies in Medievalism* 17 (2009): 36–44 (42).

14. M. J. Toswell, "The Tropes of Medievalism," *Studies in Medievalism* 17 (2009): 68–76 (74).

15. Elizabeth Emery, "Medievalism and the Middle Ages," *Studies in Medievalism* 17 (2009): 77–85 (85).

16. Tzvetan Todorov describes the fantastic so: "In a world which is indeed our own [...] occurs an event which cannot be explained by the laws of this same familiar world," so that we must see the event as either "an illusion of the senses" or a "product of the imagination. [...] The fantastic occupies the duration of this uncertainty" (*The Fantastic: A Structural Approach to a Literary Genre*, trans. Richard Howard [Ithaca, NY: Cornell University Press, 1975], 25). Mikhail Bakhtin provides insight to the other terms in *Rabelais and His World*, trans. Hélène Iswolsky (Bloomington: Indiana University Press, 1984): "The grotesque body [...] is a body in the act of becoming" (317), an expression of "deep ambivalence" (304), displeasing because of the impossible and improbable nature of the image" (305); "medieval spectacles often tended toward carnival folk culture. [...] [T]he basic carnival nucleus [...] belongs to a borderline between art and life. In reality, it is life itself, but shaped according to a certain pattern of play. [...] While carnival lasts, there is no other life outside it" (7). That explanantion also pretty well describes the experience of the "fantasy" of nearly any good novel, of the reader's participation in it. In *The Fold: Leibnitz and the Baroque* (trans. Tom Conley [Minneapolis: University of Minnesota Press, 1992]), Gilles DeLeuze uses the metaphor of the fold, as in a piece of cloth, to express spontaneity and reciprocity, the space between inside and outside, both at once – the similarity to medievalism lies in the fact that though the text has corporeal reality, it is neither truly modern nor truly contemporary: it borrows from and links worlds. Jacques Derrida makes a similar point in *The Truth About Painting* (trans. Geoff Bennington and Ian McLeod [Chicago, IL: University of Chicago Press, 1987]) about the *frame*: "Where

does the frame take place. Does it take place. Where does it begin. Where does it end. What is its internal limit. Its external limit. And its surface between the two limits" (63). Similarly the idea of analogy and the specific power of the *bridge* as analogy: "The recourse to analogy, the concept and effect of analogy are to make the *bridge*. [...] The analogy of the abyss and of the bridge over the abyss [...] must surely be an analogy between two absolutely heterogeneous worlds, a third term to cross the abyss [...] a *symbol*" (36) – medievalism forms a metaphorical, narrative (but not necessarily allegorical) bridge between the medieval and the contemporary.

17. Nickolas Haydock, *Movie Medievalism: The Imaginary Middle Ages* (Jefferson, NC: McFarland, 2008), 5. One may say the same about medievalism in literature and art and to some extent about spirituality as well.

Living with Neomedievalism

Carol L. Robinson and Pamela Clements

Two great principles divide the world, and contend for the mastery, antiquity and the middle ages. These are the two civilizations that have preceded us, the two elements of which ours is composed. All political as well as religious questions reduce themselves practically to this. This is the great dualism that runs through our society.   (Lord Acton)

"You have to understand, most of these people are not ready to be unplugged. And many of them are so inured, so hopelessly dependent on the system, that they will fight to protect it."
(Morpheus in *The Matrix*[1])

The epigraph by Lord Acton, to be found in nearly *every* edition of *Studies in Medievalism*, points to a great dualism of political and religious proportions between "antiquity and the middle ages" that still today "runs through our society"; however, the fact that this quote is from a work written in the mid-nineteenth century underscores the transition from a dualism to a multiplicity of thought in increasingly globalized philosophies that have been developing since not long before Leslie J. Workman's founding of medievalism studies. Indeed, in "Medievalisms and Why They Matter," Tom Shippey points to the enormity, all-encompassing and thus *apparent* vagueness of the field of medievalism, observing that:

> [...] already the subject goes beyond any one person's competence even to survey. "Medievalism" is a very broad field, much less capable of definition than, for instance, "modernism." One is tempted to say that a better term would be "medievalisms

[plural]," and that a natural academic approach is to single out just one of them. But at the same time one has to remember that though its many manifestations may develop separately, they are all capable at any point of interacting, and have always done so.[2]

As with *medievalism*, there have been many uses of the word *neomedievalism*, and for diverse purposes, which has resulted in a confusing plethora of understandings. For example, Leslie Workman argues, "As a term, 'new medievalism' denotes a revisionist movement in romance medieval studies [...] a disposition to interrogate and reformulate assumptions about the discipline of medieval studies broadly conceived."[3] M. J. Toswell writes, "There remain those who study the Middle Ages who do at times further confuse the issue by the use of such collocations as 'new medievalism(s),' which appears to mean new approaches to the study of the medieval period (and particularly approaches using new theoretical paradigms)."[4] *Neo* means "new" or "recent": what was once old can never be new again; it becomes (instead) *new, recent*, for the first time. "New medievalism" is a strain upon logic unless it is, like the imaginary number *i*, perceived as an alternative universe ideology (overt or subliminal), ranging from the reactionary to the revolutionary.

For our purposes, neomedievalism is, indeed, like the imaginary number *i*, a new type of medievalism that is born of postmodernist, increasingly globalized values that include an appreciation for the absurd. Thus, it is not *anti*-romantic (as Workman argues of medievalism), but simply *non*-romantic in an anti-nostalgic and decreasingly Euro-centric, and clearly anti-historical sort of way. The type of neomedievalism we are discussing is a medievalism that seems to be a direct and unromantic response to the general matrix of medievalisms from which people are partially "unplugged" and thus not at all "so inured, so hopelessly dependent on the system, that they will fight to protect it." Much like its "parent" – medievalism – neomedievalism represents a complexity of ideologies that, like any truly complex theory (such as feminism, Marxism, and ultimately, other types of medievalism), holds both extremes of ideologies (conservative to liberal, destructive to constructive). In particular, neomedievalism is further independent, further detached, and thus consciously, purposefully, and perhaps even laughingly reshaping itself into an alternate universe of medievalisms, a fantasy of medievalisms, a meta-medievalism.

Since the mid-1970s, the field of medievalism studies has grown dramatically (thanks to the great efforts of Leslie Workman, Kathleen Verduin, and other groundbreakers), taking on both academic earnestness and significance. Because of this, scholars are beginning to use the toolbox of aesthetic theories to examine works of medievalism and the impulses that create them. Theory, of course, has been one of the defining characteristics of the study of medievalism. (After all, the very attempt to describe what it is we are talking about is indeed a theoretical stance.) Identifying the way in which medieval "matter" is used in post-medieval literature, music, film, economics, politics, religion, and other disciplines is itself a theoretical stance – or rather, a series of *stances*.

Several of these stances seem to struggle with taking a firm hold of the term medievalism, a term that Gwendolyn Morgan wryly identifies as remaining "somewhat slippery."[5] Use of the term medievalism has both increased and broadened (sometimes simultaneously with, sometimes because of) the *Studies in Medievalism* circle, for better and also for worse, and this has added to the slippery conceptions and perceptions of medievalism. This slipperiness is perhaps due to the fact that, while *medievalism* may have been originally coined in the early nineteenth century and later picked up by Workman and others in the late twentieth century to depict a phenomenon that is both about the medieval and yet also post-medieval, the phenomenon itself has both evolved (carefully used) and de-evolved (carelessly abused) over the years.[6] While we appreciate the concept that the study of medievalism(s) is not anything like a chronological movement, we would like to argue that some types of medievalisms are indeed tied to chronology.[7] Another example *might* be found in neomedievalism, which is directly reflective of and yet loosely tied to particular strands of medievalism of the late twentieth and early twenty-first century.

Medieval Electronic Multimedia Organization, greatly influenced by previous medievalism analyses, such as those published in *Studies in Medievalism*, has attempted such a structuring of twentieth- and twenty-first-century medievalisms in glossarial terminology that is less (in Shippey's words) "the *OED*'s magisterial style,"[8] and more akin to a literary handbook.[9] The most recently posted definition of neomedievalism includes the following:

Angst becomes aggression. Histories are purposely fragmented. The illusion of control is made through changes of the illusion, rather than attempted changes of reality. There is no longer a sense of the futile, or at least it is second-staged by an illusionary sense of power and a denial of reality. Medieval concepts and values are purposely rewritten as a conscious vision of an alternative universe (a fantasy of the medieval that is created with forethought). Furthermore, this vision lacks the nostalgia of earlier medievalisms in that it denies history. Contemporary values (feminism, gay rights, modern technological warfare tactics, democracy, capitalism, …) dominate and rewrite the traditional perceptions of the European Middle Ages, even infusing other medieval cultures, such as that of Japan.[10]

However, terminology, of course, is just the beginning. For example, *Studies in Medievalism XIII: Postmodern Medievalisms* demonstrates that, as Richard Utz and Jesse G. Swan declare in their Editorial Note, "relaxing disciplinary constraints between historiographies that centralize either medievalism or postmodernity yields, at once, a deeper critique of the modern as well as several possible ontological states for realizing knowledge in ways other than those of the last several hundred years."[11] Utz and Swan seem to be taking advantage of Workman's conception of medievalism as a philosophical approach to history. "The brilliance of Workman's definition," writes Elizabeth Emery, "lies less in identifying medievalism as a method (the *OED* also does this), than in acknowledging the extent to which the 'Middle Ages' is itself an artificial construct, changing in accordance with the individual or the society imagining it."[12] Workman identified medievalism as being, according to Kathleen Verduin, "'the continuing process of creating the Middle Ages',"[13] which, in its eloquent simplicity (like a finely tuned mathematical equation) allows for a history of the process. It soon became apparent that chronology fails to account fully for the many strands of twentieth- and twenty-first-century medievalism, for neomedievalism (like its parent, medievalism) crosses definitions nearly as much as it crosses disciplines – from aesthetics to pop-culture, to economics, to government, to perhaps beyond – as a brief examination of its origins demonstrates.

Origins of the term *neomedievalism* are clear, though multiple. *Neomedievalism*'s first apparent uses, by Italian semiotician, novelist, and literary critic Umberto Eco (1973 in "Dreaming of the Middle

Ages") and by British political theorist Hedley Bull (1977 in *The Anarchical Society: A Study of Order in World Politics*) anticipates the ways in which neomedievalism has developed in both its lexicographical complexity as a term and its philosophical sophistication as a theory, for, clearly, Eco and Bull are each using the term neomedievalism to address a phenomenon in entirely different fields that just happened to arise at about the same time, as well as parallel to the rise of Workman's recognition of medievalism.

According to Eco, neomedievalism is an intentional rewriting of medieval social codes and ethics into contemporary aesthetics.[14] It is derived from careful thought, developed into a theory (about more than mere motifs, themes, or genres) that attempts to dissect and explain the psycho-socio-economical phenomenon of looking back to illusions of the medieval past for solutions to the problems of the present and the future. It would seem, therefore that Eco's definition of neomedievalism is not much different from Leslie Workman's definition of medievalism. Indeed, Domenico Pietropaolo argues that Umberto Eco was unaware of the concerted efforts of the organization behind *Studies in Medievalism* to generate "a systematic effort to define the parameters of the study of medievalism as a new discipline of scholarship and, simultaneously, gain acceptance for it in the academic establishment" through conference work, just as it was "also likely that these conferences were then organized in total independence of Eco's effort to elucidate the concept of medievalism. There was no crossover."[15] In other words, both Eco's *neomedievalism* and Workman's *medievalism* seem to describe similar phenomena.

However, there is another – distinctly different – concept of neomedievalism. At about the same time as Workman argued for the multi-disciplinary existence of a medievalism and Eco generated a more pop-cultural coinage of *neomedievalism*, Hedley Bull also coined the term *neomedievalism* for political theorists in his 1977 book, *The Anarchical Society: A Study of Order in World Politics*. For Bull, neomedievalism is an anarchical placement of the state over the individual ruler (a replacement of contemporary state-ruled systems by a type of resurgent feudalism). Writes Tanja E. Aalberts:

> Indeed, when Bull was providently discussing a qualified return to medieval structures of political organization, he conceived such a system of overlapping authorities as signifying the end of

sovereignty. He defines a neo-medieval form of universal political order as one where states share their authority to such an extent that "the concept of sovereignty cease[s] to be applicable," and is "recognised to be irrelevant."[16]

As noted by many political and economic analysts, Bull's concept of neomedievalism has inspired much discussion of the effects of globalization upon both state governmental rule and economy. Caleb Gallenmore argues that government has changed because communications have changed with the development of the World Wide Web, and he calls this new style of rule "eGovernment," arguing that it "will reconfigure several political relationships within the EU, fostering the development of a neomedieval polity similar to that first described by Hedley Bull, where government is multi-layered and overlapping and mobility among certain individuals is very high."[17] A more linguistic and rhetorical analysis of recent uses, actually misuses, of the term "medieval" in recent politics was conducted by Bruce Holsinger, who redefined the political and economic analysts' use of Bull's concept of neomedievalism to suit his own agenda. Evaluating the George W. Bush administration's Patriot Acts and Gulf War policies, Holsinger declares [his italics], "*In its current form, neomedievalism is above all a paradigm for neoconservative intellectual renewal.*"[18]

With regard to this rewrite of Bull's concept of neomedievalism, Shippey writes, "There is a medievalism still at work in the world, and it is a dangerous one: which is why scholars, having set the bomb ticking, have a duty not to distance themselves from any possible explosion."[19] Shippey acknowledges that Bruce Holsinger makes an argument "much more forcibly" with regard to the dangers of American neomedievalism and its current stance on the Gulf Wars. Holsinger would seem to agree in identifying this as a type of medievalism, but unlike Shippey, does not seem to see it as a phenomenon occurring beyond the United States, and does not seem to agree with Shippey's latter declaration about academic responsibility.[20] "For medievalism," writes Holsinger, "in this climate has become the historical handmaiden of a renewed anti-intellectualism that casts suspicion on any politically-minded utterance from within the American university as the sign of a debased leftism that flirts with outright treason."[21]

We respectfully disagree. First, it must be made clear that this

argument is neither new nor singularly tied to the American events of
9/11/2001. Several decades earlier, Eco contended, "Nothing more
closely resembles a monastery (lost in the countryside, walled, flanked
by alien, barbarian hordes, inhabited by monks who have nothing to
do with the world and devote themselves to their private researches)
than the American university campus."[22] Therefore, these are really
two sides of the same thing – where you have the academy isolated
from the mainstream of society and living in an insular world of their
own, it is easy for anti-intellectualism to flourish. Furthermore, this
seems to parallel what Shippey is alluding to when he writes that
"scholars, having set the bomb ticking, have a duty not to distance
themselves from any possible explosion." If there is a menacing medievalism in the world, it is the responsibility of universities and its
scholars to fight it with knowledge and example.[23] Second, to paraphrase Holsinger, in its current form, neomedievalism is above all a
paradigm for a reinventing of self, government, and culture; more
specifically, it is a reinventing of the modern (if modern is equivalent
to Enlightenment) ideas about self, government, and society. It ranges
from the most conservative to the most liberal extremes of state, religious, scientific, and artistic expressions. It is a post-postmodernist
medievalism: fragmentary, fluid, attempting to encompass all truths,
yet also brazenly fictionalizing these apparent truths. Furthermore,
while the overtly political neomedievalism of Bull and Holsinger
would seem to have little to do with the works of art or entertainment
we might call neomedieval, some connections can be made. A sense of
anarchy is a key to this type of neomedievalism; it is a medievalism
full of anachronisms, from the joyfully constructive (for good or for
bad) to the aggressively destructive (for better or for worse), fully
aware and celebratory of the constructed nature of its world(s). This
type of politico-economic analysis might prove very interesting, especially if applied to massive multi-player online role-playing games
(MMORPGs), such as *Lord of the Rings Online* or *World of Warcraft*.

Clearly, Eco's, Bull's, and even Holsinger's definitions of
neomedievalism are not the type of neomedievalism with which we
are currently concerned. Truthfully, just as Eco, Workman, and Bull
developed their perceptions of medievalism/neomedievalism independent of each other, we have developed a conception of neomedievalism that is clearly an alternative to previous uses.[24] For our
purposes, neomedievalism is a post-postmodern ideology of

medievalism that has perhaps taken its cue from the French theorists and other postmodernist thinkers (Eco included) who, as Bruce Holsinger eloquently observes, "found in the thousand years before the Renaissance an extraordinary cultural variety and an enabling source of heuristic models for their own critical practice."[25] For better or for worse, neomedievalism draws from the Middle Ages (European, but more recently also from non-European sources, such as Japanese).[26] Unlike in postmodernism, however, neomedievalism does not look to the Middle Ages to use, to study, to copy, or even to learn; the perception of the Middle Ages is more filtered, perceptions of perceptions (and of distortions), done without a concern for facts of reality, such as the fact that The Knights Who Say "Ni" never existed. This lack of concern for historical accuracy, however, is not the same as that held in more traditional fantasy works: the difference is a degree of self-awareness and self-reflexivity. Nor is it the same as what we conceive to be medievalism.

The matter of medievalism, including that of neomedievalism, includes thousands of collectively owned tropes: recognizably "medieval" costume and settings, certain common plots and plot devices (the quest, the damsel rescued, the dragon slain); "archaic" language also incorporates values and value systems assumed to be medieval, such as honor, courtly love, religiosity. In addition, many works of medievalism subscribe to one of two views of the Middle Ages: either the Merrye Olde England version, or the "life is filthy, brutal and short" version, neither of which provides anything like a realistic picture of the era. Some medievalist works manage to combine the two views – think Hobbiton vs. Saruman's orcs – but most choose to depict the medievalist Middle Ages either *in bonum* or *in malum*.

There are many medievalist films that, in aiming, however successfully or unsuccessfully, for "authenticity," we would not categorize as neomedieval. For instance, *Knights of the Round Table* (1953), which includes numerous opportunities for medieval scholars to shake their heads in dismay over the inaccuracies, is not neomedievalist because such inaccuracies are the result of carelessness, but *King Arthur* (2004) which is clearly just as erroneous, if not clearly even more erroneous, is neomedievalist because the inaccuracies are the result of careful carelessness: an act of taking care to consciously impose contemporary ideology and comprehension (no matter how inaccurate) of Arthurian history. *Knights of the Round Table* was re-imagined, for better or for worse, ultimately for profit. *King Arthur* was re-digitalized, ultimately for the same capitalistic gain, but in response to an audience that would willingly pay for strong, warrior-women characters and other contemporizations.[27]

Another characteristic that seems to distinguish our concept of neomedievalism from other forms of medievalism/neomedievalism is its very self-consciousness or self-reflexivity. It is assumed that the reader, viewer, or player knows that the "medieval" world of the work is a construct, and a not necessarily accurate construct at that. There is no attempt at verisimilitude. In these works, "medieval" equals simply "other," in the same way that alternative realities allow science fiction to inhabit "the other." An aspect of such self-reflexivity is the way in which neomedievalist works reflect, or pass through, earlier medievalist works, rather than looking directly to the Middle Ages. Just as the Middle Ages of the musical *Camelot* is more informed by White's *Once and Future King* than it is by Geoffrey of Monmouth or by the archeological work of Geoffrey Ashe (though apparently Warner Bros. did call him to find out where Camelot might have been located),[28] so does C. J. Cherryh's *Port Eternity* model its genetically designed characters on key players in *Idylls of the King* rather than on Malory. In both of these works, the reader or viewer is assumed to know, and appreciate, how many levels of literary artifice are being employed.

In fact, neomedieval works will playfully revel in blatant anachronisms. Deaf storyteller Peter S. Cook's adaptation of a blending of "The Wedding of Sir Gawain and Dame Ragnell" and "The Marriage of Sir Gawain" into a contemporized story done in gesture and mime (with supplemental communication in American Sign Language) also demonstrates the creation of an informed reader, but one who purposely and self-reflexively defies history: in this adaptation, he pulls in Pythonesque humor: King Arthur, in all his medieval armor and while on his horse, uses a cell phone to call over the "celebrity" Sir Gawain.[29] Such adaptations are not always light in their humorous tone, as another work by another Deaf artist, Willy Conley, will testify: in his complete modernization and politicization of *Everyman* into a blending of American Sign Language and English, Conley "corrects" the play's limited human-rights parameters, bringing in a diversity of beliefs as well as re-naming the play "For Every Man, Woman and Child."[30] Clearly, the audience is not only expected to pick up on these jokes on medievalism, but to revel in them, be they intended as a light poke (Cook) or a serious jab (Conley).

It is in this elaborate artifice, its self-conscious remaking of a new "medieval" world, that there is room for different, sometimes opposite, ideologies to play. Neomedieval constructs of the medieval lack the medieval sense of solidarity and finiteness – all is fragmentary, fluid, either susceptible or conducive (depending upon one's values) to constant change. In this way, neomedieval constructs participate in the postmodern techniques of fragmentation: anachronism, pastiche, bricolage. Holsinger is right in judging that there is a neomedievalist menacing, destructive political faction. That is one extreme. The other extreme is a kind of neomedievalism that is simply aesthetic silliness. Either way, it is anachronistic anarchy. A few small examples might further illustrate the seeming permutation of this attitude into current ideology (within and without the United States and Europe). One example is the rise in Viking mascots named Erik (after the postmodernist medievalist and Monty Pythoner film, *Erik the Viking*).[31] Several examples may be found in *A Knight's Tale*: the use of the Nike athletic shoe logo on medieval armor, Chaucer presenting his champion knight as if he were a WWF all-star wrestler, and the use of music by Queen, both as a surrounding context for the narrative as well as within the narrative by the "audience" characters (who stomp their feet and clap their hands in the same rhythm as done in "We Will Rock You").[32] Martha W. Driver observes of medieval-themed films:

> Issues of gender, periodicity, and appropriation are endemic and central to medieval film. Behavior is codified and ways of thinking are imposed, not only by the films themselves but also by critics of those films. The distance between the medieval period and the cinematic era is vast, allowing ample space for distortion about the medieval idea of history and the classical past.[33]

However, it is not just the distortion of the medieval that makes a work neomedieval *but the nature of that distortion*. As Driver also observes, "The tendency to recast an older story in light of current tastes or to address contemporary issues under the guise of historical representation is not, in fact, new."[34] Some scholars seem to limit the parameters to historicism in defining medievalism in video games. For example, Oliver M. Traxel writes of medieval-themed video games that to his knowledge, "no games set during the Middle Ages feature such ubiquitous modern innovations as electricity, radiators, or running water."[35] But Nils Holger Petersen rightly argues that:

> [...] medievalism should not be restricted to features in which a historical consciousness is explicitly at work, primarily because all practices are received in a culture where manifold attitudes will be or have been at work. Thus, regardless of the intentions or the consciousness behind a particular practice or artifact, it will form part of a general reception in which it may play a part as an element in the construction or recreation of the Middle Ages.[36]

As Petersen points out, the question as to when the Middle Ages stopped is obsolete. "The only alternative I see," he writes, "would be to actually have to define when the Middle Ages ended, a historiographic project partly without end and partly at odds with the history of the concept itself."[37] While it may have only developed in recent times, neomedievalism plays "a part as an element in the construction or recreation of the Middle Ages" that is anti-historical; it does not define when the Middle Ages ended (or began); it simply moves it off the timeline entirely, a phenomenon of distortion that steps outside of historical consciousness but also changes the very nature of that consciousness, thereby restricting medievalism to historical consciousness by default.

One might, for example, argue that Geoffrey Chaucer was a pre-Feminist – an immediate moot point of observation since the Feminist lens is rooted in contemporary philosophy. And yet, in BBC One's production of six of *The Canterbury Tales*, "The Wife of Bath, for example, is a wonderful, feisty, bawdy, independent woman who is very much alive and living in the 21st century. Society might have changed, but human emotions and characters have not."[38] Ideas happen all the time, sometimes progressively, sometimes regressively, and anything that strikes us as being derived from the Middle Ages into later times has to be acknowledged as having been, in that derivation: repossessed, rewritten, remanufactured, re-philosophized, manufactured, mass produced, mass marketed, and (in the case of neomedieval constructs in particular, though not always) digitalized.

Leslie Workman has also cited "the 'cultural revolt of the 1960s,' the search for alternative lifestyles that led inevitably to models of a pre-industrial society."[39] Yet, digital technology has greatly influenced the shape of both medieval studies and studies in medievalism(s) in the past twenty years. Now, supplements to both teaching and research are globally available.[40] In a sense, whenever one reads, writes, speaks, listens, shows, and/or views items and performances of medievalism in cyberspace, one is automatically inviting a cyberpunk science-fiction virtual reality that is only going to become increasingly "real" as technology improves. There are significant differences, for example, between the experiences of holding *The Exeter Book* in (gloved) hands, looking at photographs of it in a textbook that also has transcribed and/or translated it, and seeing it on the internet (in video, still image, transcription and/or translation, read aloud in an audio file). The differences are not just of convenience in travel, but also in distance of space (in addition to the distance in time from the Middle Ages that the book already provides), both from the actual item and in terms of the perception of that item (the three-dimensional book vs. an image of it on a computer screen or the printed words vs. those read aloud for an audio file online). The Digital Age has provided works, from the fictional to the scholarly, with an alternate "reality" of perception and conception: ready-access information, nearly immediate feedback, virtual representations: easily downloaded audio/video recordings and colorful still images of authentic, "authentic," and blatantly inauthentic manuscripts, castles, weaponry, armor, dresses, jewels, crowns, rituals, … In this sense, neomedievalism is the type of medievalism that has gone global.

As stated above, it is the blatantly inauthentic in which we are currently most interested: the overtly, even celebrated, "new and improved" alternate universe that we call neomedievalism. One may find, for example, several pages of information on the Internet regarding a Canadian who has "retro-fitted" Geoffrey Chaucer's *The Canterbury Tales* to rap music, intended to draw adolescent audiences into Chaucer's stories but (therefore?) censored of "offensive" language and translated into contemporary, even "hip" English – a well-intended "modernization" of what Chaucer's poetry would be like if he were a rapper.[41] The point is that Geoffrey Chaucer was never a rapper, but in this alternate neomedieval universe he becomes a rapper. One may also find a web page promoting The Wife of Bath restaurant with rooms in Wye, Kent (United Kingdom) that features "imaginative menus" "created from the finest local and seasonal produce" and "wines from new, old and emerging regions, classic cocktails, premium spirits and memorable malts." ("The Wife of Bath. Wye go anywhere else?" they advertise).[42] Mel Brooks's *Robin Hood: Men in Tights* may parody lousy portrayals of the history and stories of Robin Hood, but *Star Trek: The Next Generation* turned a lousy portrayal into a good, science-fiction story set in an alternate universe in which an already alternate universe science-fiction character (Captain Picard) becomes further altered into Robin Hood, and his staff are also altered to fit into this medieval tale.[43] Both *Men in Tights* and the *Star Trek* episode are examples of medievalism; however, the episode of *Star Trek* is also an example of neomedievalism because the medieval fantasy/history of the Robin Hood tale has been moved to the science-fiction fantasy future of an alternate universe, though the joke in this case is on the *Star Trek* characters who become these medieval characters.

Neomedievalism is also influenced by the appeal of medieval tropes and images to the scientists themselves who created the computer science that fuels our electronic entertainments today. Still more examples may be found within the narrative structures of electronic games. The vast majority of Massive Multiplayer Online Role Playing Games (MMORPGs) are games dominated by medieval-themed tropes, narratives, and iconography, but not all MMORPGs are demonstrative of medievalism, much less neomedievalism. Or rather, many fantasy games contain medievalism elements; some of these games, in turn, seem to embrace neomedievalism. The gothic version of cyberpunk science fiction[44] (a fiction focused upon characters who "live" in the virtual universe of cyberspace, abandoning their real bodies for avatar identities) is a type of neomedievalism, but so is an individual who is role-playing through an avatar within an online medievalist video game (even if the game itself is not actually *neo*medievalist). "Perhaps," suggests Amy S. Kaufman with regard to *Neverwinter Nights*, "programmers, whose own encoded language seems mysterious and inaccessible, and who act as the invisible yet omnipotent force behind a game, have a certain affinity for magic-users, whose enchantments, encrypted texts, and need for secrecy are not unlike their own."[45] Indeed, neo-Tolkienist elements (fantasies of J. R. R. Tolkien's fantasy that is of and from the Middle Ages) abound in such games as *Arcanum, Dungeon Siege, World of Warcraft, Dungeons and Dragons Online* – not to mention all the *Lord of the Rings* games adapted both from the Peter Jackson film adaptations of

Tolkien's works as well as more directly from Tolkien's fantasy world. Regardless, it is clear that a strong bond exists between the culture of computers and the culture of medieval fantasy and that culture is conducive to juxtapositions of tropes between both worlds, and this bond is usually based upon filtered experiences of the medieval, be it Tolkien's fantasy novels and Jackson's adaptation of those novels into fantasy films, or Monty Python's parody of Arthurian medieval films and the Broadway musical adaptation of *Monty Python and the Holy Grail* into *Spamalot*.

Indeed, some types of neomedievalism overflow with purposely juxtaposed elements of both the medieval and the non-medieval. For example, *Dungeon Siege*'s narrative setting and characterization are both medieval; it is a medievalist fiction fantasy that becomes neomedievalist as more contemporary technology is introduced, until it all ends with the player battling a space alien disguised as a medieval trope, a goblin. The reverse is also possible: a science-fiction fantasy that becomes neomedievalist as medieval tropes and other elements are introduced. The Moberly Brothers observe that a video game, *Star Wars: Knights of the Old Republic*:

> presents players with a "new" version of the *Star Wars* intraverse that is repackaged from the tried and true elements of the *Star Wars* movies and from what are, arguably, the tried and true tropes of the medieval romance – tropes that are the bread and butter of pen-and-paper and computer-enabled role-playing games like *Dungeons and Dragons* and *Neverwinter Nights*.[46]

One additional aspect of neomedieval entertainments is the dissolution of single authorship. Electronic entertainments, from the loftiest art film to the simplest of video games, are the creation of multiple authors and creators. In terms of interactive gaming, the player also takes part as an "author," helping to create the narrative as the play progresses. "Scrolling through the character-creation options in many of these games," observes Lauryn S. Mayer, "one can hear a voice explicitly stating what comes across incessantly and often silently through a whole nexus of cultural codes: our identities are largely constructs."[47] Evidence points to a dominance of anonymity of single authorship in the European Middle Ages, which is different from an anonymity of multiple authorship of these games. Furthermore, narrative structural changes from writer–reader interaction to writer–

player–apparent co-creation interaction also affects the power over character creation and narrative development. It suggests a movement from identity of narrative creator(s) through characterization (such as one seeks through the *Gawain, Pearl,* and *Cleanliness* poems) to identities of creators imposed upon the reader/player. The illusion of control seems to be on the end of the player as she develops her character and moves through the narrative structure of the game; however, just as is the case with most Hollywood studio films, the actual control is that of the corporation (the programmers, designers, marketers, …) that produces the film.

So, in terms of aesthetics, what does neomedievalism have in common with other medievalisms? Obviously, a fascination with the Middle Ages, seen as distinctively alterior to the present time. Scholars have argued both *against* and *for* the otherness of the Middle Ages, beginning perhaps with Jauss' "The Alterity and Modernity of the Middle Ages."[48] Bettina Bildhauer and Robert Mills provide a brief summary of this movement in the introduction to their recent book *The Monstrous Middle Ages*:

> The Middle Ages as a period continually threatens to disrupt modernity from its position on the edges of history; if the Middle Ages is popularly imagined as a time full of monsters, then it can also be said to operate itself as a kind of historiographic monster, challenging ideas of modernity as radically different [...].[49]
> One of the boundaries that a focus on monstrosity arguably disrupts is that between past and present; and whereas a renewed emphasis on "marginal" phenomena like monsters in medieval scholarship is lamented by scholars like Paul Freedman and Gabrielle Spiegel as contributing to an emerging view of the Middle Ages as inherently "pathological," a recent wave of literary medieval scholarship by the likes of Kathleen Biddick, Carolyn Dinshaw, and L. O. Aranye Fradenburg has pursued the possibility of a partial connection with the past, of *becoming* medieval in a way that produces neither hard-edged alterity nor complete identification.[50]

Neomedievalism allows us to have it both ways: to appreciate simultaneously the modernity of the Middle Ages and its very difference from the world we readers or viewers inhabit. In a constructive sense, aesthetic neomedievalism reminds us, forcefully and playfully, that all medievalisms are constructs, made from prefabricated materials.

Gwendolyn Morgan argues that many of us "have fallen prey to introducing false medievalism into our examination of the state of the [academic] profession. Nowhere is this more apparent than in our rebellion against the model of the so-called 'corporate university.' "[51] She is referring to those disgruntled faculty who nostalgically look back to the medieval university as a glorious model from which current institutions have fallen. Certainly, she rightly points to an abusively romanticized conception of medievalism. A neomedievalist academe would not look to a romantic illusion of the medieval university as an alternative to "today's" increasingly "corporate" education system. A neomedievalist academe would consciously and unabashedly play a re-created video game of an alternate medieval university on her office computer! We believe that neomedievalism is a type of medievalism that is more than just a genre or motif to be found in books, paintings, plays, movies, video games, and other media; it is certainly more than a weak political agenda for disgruntled faculty or neoconservatives. However, as with any philosophy or critical theory, it needs refinement and development. More work remains to be done exploring the implications of assigning the term neomedievalism to any work of medievalism. As Lesley Coote concludes in her piece on violence in medievalist films:

> Our gazes, however, are informed by multiple literacies deriving not only from the book and the spoken word, but from the World Wide Web, cyberspace and the cellphone. We read not "medievally", but "*neo*-medievally". In order to catch glimpses of the Middle Ages beyond the text, we need to realize, to explore, and to utilize, this ability.[52]

Neomedievalism works from a postmodernist stance of multiplicity in our thinking about medievalism. What we like about Tom Shippey's thesis is its emphasis on the multiplicity of medievalisms, for as we wrote this work together, we often found ourselves struggling to embrace small points of disagreement. (We were even struggling to agree to disagree.) But there is no doubt in our minds that what we refer to as neomedievalism is significant change in process, clearly a self-reflexive and often humorous twist upon medievalism in works prior to the 1990s. All of this makes Robinson think of T. C. Chamberlin's "The Method of Multiple Working Hypotheses" theory (1890), which essentially states that one must approach a problem with multiple possibilities. All of this makes Clements think that there is much more than the eye can see.

NOTES

1. *The Matrix*. Dir. Andy Wachowski and Larry Wachowski. Perf. Laurence Fishburne, Keanu Reeves, Carrie-Anne Moss, and Hugo Weaving. Groucho II Film Partnership; Silver Pictures; Village Roadshow Pictures; Warner Bros. Pictures. 1999.

2. Tom Shippey, "Medievalisms and Why They Matter," *Studies in Medievalism* 17 (2009): 45–54 (47–48).

3. Quoted in Kathleen Verduin, "The Founding and the Founder: Medievalism and the Legacy of Leslie J. Workman," *Studies in Medievalism* 17 (2009): 1–27 (16), from "Review: *Medievalism and the Modernist Temper*, *Arthuriana* 7 (1997): 1.

4. M. J. Toswell, "The Tropes of Medievalism," *Studies in Medievalism* 17 (2009): 68–76 (68–69).

5. Gwendolyn A. Morgan, "Medievalism, Authority, and the Academy," *Studies in Medievalism* 17 (2009): 55–67 (55). "Moreover," writes Morgan, "the Middle Ages have been and continue to be deliberately manipulated and appropriated by those in various positions of influence to further their agendas, be it Nazi ideology, feminism, various nationalistic movements, theories of art, or religious systems, producing a view palatable to the general population. This latter practice provides the material for Norman Cantor's *Inventing the Middle Ages* and the numerous studies that follow his lead. Still others, such as Ronald Hutton in *Witches, Druids and King Arthur* or Michael Cramer's recent examination of the Society for Creative Anachronism, celebrate the medievalism in popular culture as a positive, creative force allowing for the development of effective responses to contemporary problems and ideologies. That their connection to the Middle Ages is all but completely fictional is, in their view, inconsequential" (56).

6. Some of the confusion is that medievalism describes both what medieval scholars *do* and post-medieval works in many genres that employ medieval themes and images.

7. For example, Romanticism is a medievalism tied to chronology. As Clare Simmons writes, "'Romantic'" in the sense of partaking of the qualities of medieval romance, that is, depicting a world of more heroic figures, grander actions, and more marvelous occurrences than those that limit the reader's own, remains a term commonly found in Romantic-era accounts of the Middle Ages, and is unquestionably a crucial reason why the Romantics found the Middle Ages more to their taste than eighteenth-century

rationalists had done. But here lies the final paradox for Romantic-era history. A romance is by definition a made-up story, yet part of the romantic appeal of medieval history is that it is true. According to those medievalists who attempted to recuperate the Middle Ages – figures such as Kenelm Digby, the members of the Young England movement, and A. N. W. Pugin – there really was a time when human beings would sacrifice all for religion or for love or for honor, when those who sought power always lived on the brink of danger, and where society was in many respects governed by the cycles of nature. Too real to be romance, too romantic to be dismissed as the murky Dark Ages or prosaic Middle Ages, it needed to be medieval and to pave the way for the medievalism of the High Victorian period." "Medievalism: Its Linguistic History in Nineteenth-Century Britain," *Studies in Medievalism* 17 (2009): 28–35 (34).

8. Shippey, "Medievalisms and Why They Matter," 45.

9. MEMO has a forthcoming anthology of essays that explore and debate attributes of both medievalism and neomedievalism.

10. <http://medievalelectronicmultimedia.org/definitions.html>.

11. Richard Utz and Jesse G. Swan, "Editorial Note," *Studies in Medievalism* 13 (2004): 1.

12. Elizabeth Emery, "Medievalism and the Middle Ages," *Studies in Medievalism* 17 (2009): 77–85 (79).

13. Verduin, "The Founding and the Founder," 20, and epigram.

14. For example, Eco writes, "In the general crisis of universities and the plan of uncoordinated student grants, the students are turning to vagantes, and they look always and only to unofficial masters, rejecting their 'natural educators'." "Living in the Middle Ages," in *Travels in Hyperreality*, trans. William Weaver (San Diego, New York, and London: Harcourt Brace Jovanovich, 1973, 1976, 1983), 80.

15. Domenico Pietropaolo, "Eco on Medievalism," *Studies in Medievalism* 5 (1993): 129.

16. Tanja E. Aalberts, "The Future of Sovereignty in Multilevel Governance Europe – A Constructivist Reading," *Journal of Common Market Studies* 42.1 (March 2004): 33. She is referring to Hedley Bull, *The Anarchical Society: A Study of Order in World Politics* (1977; 2nd ed. London: Macmillan, 1995), 246, 256.

17. Caleb Gallenmore, "Of Lords and (Cyber)Serfs: eGovernment and Postructuralism in a Neomedieval Europe," *Millennium – Journal of International Studies* 34.1 (2005), abstract:
<http://mil.sagepub.com/cgi/content/abstract/34/1/27>.

18. Bruce Holsinger, *Neomedievalism, Neoconservatism, and the War on Terror* (Chicago: Prickly Paradigm Press, 2007), 65.

19. Shippey, "Medievalisms and Why They Matter," 50.

20. In light of Holsinger's declaration, however, it is significant to note that *some* (not all) neomedieval video games may entertain such neoconservative regards to the appeal of a simplified moral world where force need not be hampered by the need to obey the law.

21. Holsinger, *Neomedievalism, Neoconservatism*, 14.

22. Eco, "Living in the New Middle Ages," 83.

23. Some argue that it is not just American anti-intellectualism that serves as neomedieval in the political arena: the fundamentalist Islamist movement is also a rejection of modernism (though the Arab Middle Ages were not at all like today's reimagining of them).

24. We did so unwittingly. As is testified on the home page for Medieval Electronic Multimedia Organization (MEMO), several of us nicknamed this type of medievalism that we were identifying after the character Neo of *The Matrix*. It was done as a sort of joke because our email discussions (Spring 2002) were constantly interrupted by viruses and worms at the time. Neo, we joked, was getting in the way of our discussions of types of medievalisms (including the anticipated volume of *Studies in Medievalism* on postmodernist medievalism), and since a significant aspect of this newly perceived medievalism seemed to hold the same sort of self-reflexivity themed in the movie, we named this type of medievalism in honor of this character.

25. Bruce Holsinger, *The Premodern Condition: Medievalism and the Making of Theory* (Chicago and London: The University of Chicago Press, 2005), 13–14.

26. For example, the Japanese video-game industry, influenced by its manga and anime industries, has generated thousands of medievalist games that are, for the most part, rooted in a Japanese conception of the European Middle Ages.

27. These motives are actually quite similar – is it just that the expectations of the audience have changed? So in the 1950s you have bullet-breasted meek women, and in the 2000s you have (well, one) scantily-clad warrior woman. We think the biggest difference is less in the female characterizations than in the K of the RT insistence that it is "historical."

28. Geoffrey Ashe explains: "One evening, my telephone rang and a voice said: 'This is Warner Brothers. Where is Camelot?' I asked why they wanted to know. The voice at the other end explained that Warner Brothers was filming a musical and wanted to include a map showing Camelot. I said Camelot was in Somerset. In the movie, there actually is an almost subliminal moment when a weird-looking map of England is displayed […] and Camelot is in Somerset," as quoted in Mary Flowers Braswell and John Bugge, ed., *The Arthurian Tradition: Essays in Convergence* (Tuscaloosa: University of Alabama Press, 1988), 22.

29. Peter S. Cook, "Sir Gawain & Lady Ragnelle," in *Sir Gawain and Other Finger-licious Stories*. DVD (Chicago: PC Production, 2007). <http://www.deafpetercookonline.com>

30. Willy Conley, "For Every Man, Woman, and Child." First Performed at Elstad Theatre, Washington, DC, Gallaudet University Theatre Arts Department; 12–20 November 1999 (A full-length modern adaptation based on Everyman; 31 characters: deaf or hearing, unisex; doubling possible.) Forthcoming in an anthology of his plays, Gallaudet University Press (2009).

31. See the following websites as small proof: <http://www.roadsideamerica.com/story/4051>; <http://www.ohio.com/news/37444314.html>; <http://www.family-ancestry.co.uk/history/vikings/popular_culture/>; <http://www.churchie.com.au/content/?id=397>; <http://www.visityork.org/media/factsheets/McarthurGlen.asp>.

32. Pamela Clements argues that any visual (cinematic) adaptation of *The Canterbury Tales* will suffer "severe trauma," for the *Tales* is "a work that is self-reflective about the nature of its own medium, essentially a metatext, must suffer critical trauma when expressed in a primarily visual, not exclusively verbal, medium." "Neomedieval Trauma: The Cinematic Hyperreality of Chaucer's *Canterbury Tales*," in Carol L. Robinson and Daniel T. Kline, ed., *The Medieval in Motion* (Lewiston, Queenston, Lampeter: The Edwin Mellen Press, forthcoming).

33. Martha W. Driver, "Preface," to Martha W. Driver and Sid Ray, ed., *The Medieval Hero on Screen; Representations from Beowulf to Buffy* (Jefferson, NC: McFarland, 2004), 9.

34. Martha W. Driver, "What's Accuracy Got to Do with It?" in Martha W. Driver and Sid Ray, ed., *The Medieval Hero*, 20.

35. Oliver M. Traxel. "Medieval and Pseudo-Medieval Elements in Computer Role-Playing Games: Use and Interactivity," *Studies in Medievalism* 16 (2008): 131.

36. Nils Holger Petersen, "Medievalism and Medieval Reception: A Terminological Question," *Studies in Medievalism* 17 (2009): 36–44 (42).

37. Petersen, "Medievalism and Medieval Reception," 42.

38. BBC Press Office. Press Release. "Stars line up for modern retelling of The Canterbury Tales for BBC ONE." 8 June 2003: <http://www.bbc.co.uk/pressoffice/pressreleases/stories/2003/08_august/06/canterbury_tales.shtml>

39. Verduin, "The Founding and the Founder," 22.

40. The Chaucer Metapage (http://www.unc.edu/depts/chaucer/), The Camelot Project (http://www.lib.rochester.edu/camelot/cphome.stm), Internet Medieval Sourcebook (http://www.fordham.edu/halsall/Sbook.

html), Medieval and Early Modern Data Bank
(http://www2.scc. rutgers.edu/memdb/),
Digital Scriptorium (http://www.scriptorium. columbia.edu/), and
The Labyrinth (http://labyrinth.georgetown.edu/), are just a few of the data-bases housed by Internet-savvy medieval scholars on servers in North America alone.

41. Baba Brinkman, *The Rap Canterbury Tales.* Audio CD (11 December 2007). MP3 available at *Babasword* <http://www.babasword.com/>. You can listen to samples of this music there or in the program, "Modern Chaucer: Street Talk and a Dance Beat," *All Things Considered.* National Public Radio, 28 July 2005. <http://www.npr.org/templates/story/story.php?storyId=4775661>.

42. <http://www.thewifeofbath.com/>.

43. *Star Trek: The Next Generation.* "Qpid." Season 4. Episode 20. Orig. broadcast 20 April 1991.

44. Carol Robinson argues that the gothic elements to be found in the science fiction of cyberpunk writer William Gibson is a form of neo-medievalism. "Cyber Babes and Byte Dudes: The Environment and Body as Fluid Media for Sexual and Gender Identity in Neomedieval and Postmodern Matrices," in Carl B. Yoke and Carol L. Robinson, ed., *The Cultural Influences of William Gibson, the "Father" of Cyberpunk Science Fiction: Critical and Interpretive Essays* (Lewiston, Queenston, Lampeter: The Edwin Mellen Press, 2007), 187–206.

45. Amy S. Kaufman, "Romancing the Game: Magic, Writing, and the Feminine in *Neverwinter Nights*," *Studies in Medievalism* 16 (2008): 147.

46. Brent Moberly and Kevin Moberly, "Revising the Future: The Medieval Self and the Sovereign Ethics of *Empire* in *Star Wars: Knights of the Old Republic*," *Studies in Medievalism* 16 (2008): 163.

47. Lauryn S. Mayer, "Promises of Monsters: The Rethinking of Gender in MMORPGs," *Studies in Medievalism* 16 (2008): 193.

48. Hans Robert Jauss, "The Alterity and Modernity of Medieval Literature," *New Literary History* 10 (1979): 181–232.

49. Bettina Bildhauer and Robert Mills, *The Monstrous Middle Ages* (Toronto: University of Toronto Press, 2003), 3.

50. Bildhauer and Mills, *The Monstrous Middle Ages*, 5.

51. Morgan, "Medievalism, Authority, and the Academy," 82.

52. Lesley Coote, "Remembering Dismembering: Reading the Violated Body Medievally," in Carol L. Robinson and Daniel T. Kline, ed., *The Medieval in Motion*, forthcoming.

Tough Love:
Teaching the New Medievalisms[1]

Jane Chance

Those of us who teach the Middle Ages today are likely to be familiar with Medievalism, namely, the appropriation of beliefs, ideas, methods, styles, and worldviews common to the period roughly between 500 and 1500 CE in western Europe in any later historical period except what has been designated as "the Middle Ages," denoting, according to Petrarch, the period between classical antiquity and its alleged Renaissance in Italy and England. The *OED* defines Medievalism as "The system of belief and practice characteristic of the Middle Ages [...] the adoption of or devotion to mediaeval ideals or usages; *occas*. An instance of this." The journal *Studies in Medievalism* has for some thirty years published individual issues that traced specific aspects of medievalism in the later literature, music, art and architecture, etc., of specific countries or languages. In the previous annual volume, Tom Shippey – who followed Leslie Workman as editor of *Studies in Medievalism* – described medievalism in his new essay "Medievalisms and Why They Matter" as "Any post-medieval attempt to re-imagine the Middle Ages, or some aspect of the Middle Ages, for the modern world, in any of many different media; especially in academic usage, the study of the development and significance of such attempts."[2] According to French medievalist Elizabeth Emery in her essay in the same volume of *Studies in Medievalism* in which various scholars puzzle over what Workman's concept of "Medievalism" means now, Shippey's plural – "Medievalisms" – constitutes a necessary emendation because of the multiple forms in which medievalism has appeared over time, that is:

[…] different scholarly interpretations over periods of time (Jules Michelet's, Joseph Bédier's, and Ernst Curtius'), different artistic representations in varying media (Walter Scott, the Pre-Raphaelites, Richard Wagner, and Ridley Scott), different political or religious claims (Joan of Arc claimed by the Catholic Church, the secular French Republic, the Action Française, and Le Front National), "medieval" analysis of the Middle Ages (François Villon's fifteenth-century ballad "en viel langage françois," written in Old French), and even scholarly studies of the way individuals have been influenced by other uses of the Middle Ages (analysis of Hugo's debt to Sir Walter Scott in imagining the medieval world)[…].

Emery concludes that "the brilliance of Workman's definition lies less in identifying medievalism as a method (the *OED* also does this), than in acknowledging the extent to which the 'Middle Ages' is itself an artificial construct, changing in accordance with the individual or society imagining it."[3]

Given the varieties of the "Middle Ages" that now exist, should those often inaccurate and artificial characterizations found in popular culture – chiefly, in Hollywood films, but also fantasy works and video games – receive the same respect as the high-culture and academic incarnations? Kim Selling offers one cultural justification for the seriousness of some of these medievalisms in her argument that "fantastic literature can in many ways be seen as a reaction against the rationalistic, anti-heroic, materialist and empiricist discourses upon which Western Culture and society are founded."[4] And the medievalist Milton McGatch long ago valorized fantasy's "imaginative adoption of what are conceived to be the ideals of that era" because "Honour, courage, and faithfulness in all things are as necessary to the fantasy hero as to the ideal medieval knight.[5]

If "medievalism," then, covers the multiplicity of subjective recasting of the Middle Ages by later interpreters, both in high (academic) culture and low (popular) cultures, why has the practice of medievalism also seemingly and so suddenly become a way to teach (for example) our traditional medieval English courses on *Beowulf,* Old English, Chaucer, Arthurian Literature, Middle English Literature, Epic and Romance, Mythology/Mythology, Dante, and many others?

Why Teach Medievalism

Medieval reception has formed an integral part of the teaching and, therefore, the study of the Middle Ages for two reasons related to the contemporary status of Medieval Studies in American universities and how that status represents a change in what we have practiced over the past thirty or forty years. First, both new (and established) medievalists these days often confront dwindling enrollments in the traditional medieval courses they are required to teach, along with reduced departmental and university support for the study of the medieval. This is largely related to changes in requirements for the major in English and other languages and literatures and to what our colleagues perceive as requisites for the understanding of our field, which no longer depends (in the case of English Departments) on literary history and genre so much as methodology and theory. This change has occurred because of the advent of postmodern theory and the concept of deconstruction that resulted from the birth of existentialism as a postwar form of nihilistic, neo-nominalist philosophy in western Europe during the earlier part of the twentieth century, all of which, over the past twenty-five years, have diminished the importance of the value of authority, knowledge, and objectivity and, therefore, forms of structured knowledge in the humanities. What this change has meant nationwide is a cutback on medieval staff in many departments, a resulting loss in jobs for graduate students, and a decrease, therefore, in the number of graduate students interested in the traditional study of the Middle Ages and/or admitted into graduate study at research institutions.

The second reason for the rise in importance of the teaching and study of medieval reception is related to the first: new medievalist Ph.Ds have had to become conversant with contemporary theory, multiculturalism, and interdisciplinarity if they intend to publish and thereby attract teaching positions and receive tenure. By "interdisciplinarity" I mean, minimally, the interrelationship between the Middle Ages and the Renaissance, because in many departments these two separate fields have become conflated into one larger field for which there is only one position available; but also I mean the interrelationship between, say, the medieval and those thematic and topical program areas such as Women, Gender, and Sexuality, or African-American Studies, or Neocolonialism, or Geopolitics, or Media

Relations, or a host of others with whose names we are likely familiar from our own institution's incarnations.

New Medievalisms

This explanation for the rise of medieval reception recently brings us back to my title "New Medievalisms": What, then, is the *New* Medievalism (or, "Medievalisms"), unless it is what *is* "new" in the past two or three decades or so, that is, the implicitly or explicitly *theorized* study of multiple and subjective (individually authorized) characterizations or interpretations of the medieval? As postmodernist medievalists, can we even know whose "medieval" is the most accurate – how would we ascertain the veracity of any one abstraction? Indeed, has not the New Historical methodology taught us that the study of the thirteenth century in France – or, more accurately, Paris, in the 1270s – is not the same as study of the city of Meun in the next decade? Further, is not "New" also appropriate in a second sense? Because the modes and media of the production of medievalism have changed so radically in this era of New Technology, blending together the print media of books and poems with visual illustrations in hybrids such as graphic novels and video games and adding the new blended audio and visual media of feature-length films, YouTube, cell phone, and music videos ("Mediaeval Baebes"), commercials, blogs, and websites, does not "New" refer as equally to production by "artists" as to interpretation?

     In such a small space I cannot begin to explore all of these, although those of us who have attended the annual medieval conference in Kalamazoo the past year or two may have noticed the arrival of one of the New Medievalisms in what is now called "Neomedievalism." The Medieval Electronic Multimedia Organization (MEMO) offered a workshop and poster session on 9 May 2008 on "Medieval Video Gaming" that focused on: "Medievalist Teaching with Neomedievalist Computer Games," "Neomedievalism MMORPG Games *Dungeon Siege, Morrowind,* and *World of Warcraft*," "Medievalism in the Computer Game *Syberia*," "Neomedievalism Gone Global: *Lord of the Rings Online* and *World of Warcraft*," "*King's Quest* (Computer Game)," "*Legend of Zelda: Twilight Princess* (Wii)," "*Tales of Symphonia* (Wii)," and "*King Arthur* (Wii)," "*Buffy the Vampire*

Slayer on Xbox," and "Space Opera Medievalism: The *Xenosaga* Trilogy for the Playstation 2."[6]

What I would like to do, instead of cataloging the New Medievalisms, is to suggest one way in which they might be used in the classroom. However limited my example, what I hope will emerge from this essay is the New Medievalism's dependence on methodology – juxtaposition and comparison, intertextuality, intervisuality, and the cross-theoretical – all the while that it continually redefines the specific historical "Medieval" in its overlaying of its "texts" with an overarching interrogation of the essential idea of the medieval. In this respect we might take a note from Bruce Holsinger in *The Premodern Condition*, who notes that:

> historicizing the medievalism of the theoretical avant garde entails an awareness of the pressures exerted on these writers by contemporaneous institutions and schools of thought (French Thomism, the *Annales* school) as well as an approach to intellectual history that recognizes strands of influence between thinkers separated by as little as a decade (Panofsky and Bourdieu) and as many as sixteen centuries (Augustine and Derrida).[7]

While I am less interested in the medievalization of a historicized contemporary theory than in the teaching practice of theorizing medievalism, the methods Holsinger and I both might use can be seen as analogous in various ways.

My example involves the similar but distinct homosocial bonds evident in the feudalism and/or chivalry of four medieval (or medievalized) "texts" whose very overlay reveals their cultural and historical differences as much as the distillation of the idea of a queer medieval. These texts include the twelfth-century Anglo-Norman Breton lai *Lanval* by Marie de France, the fourteenth-century anonymous Middle English romance *Sir Gawain and the Green Knight*, the twentieth-century epic-romance novels of *The Lord of the Rings* by British medievalist J. R. R. Tolkien, and the twenty-first-century film of *The Return of the King* directed by New Zealand filmmaker Peter Jackson. What interests me is the critique of and interrogation of masculinity and male bonding that occurs in each one through the relationship between vassal and overlord or between knight and king/host. How might we teach the theorization of a queer medieval? How does queerness become embedded in questions of medievalized feminism and misogyny, issues that have become much more readily accessible to students today? How, in short, do we use contemporary pedagogy and theory to retrieve a historicized cultural difference?

Tough Love

Marie de France constructs a feminized and powerless male hero, Lanval, in her vernacular lai of the same name, recently added to the medieval section of the *Norton Anthology of British Literature*. Lanval's alien nature – he is from a foreign land – matches his similar unconventional inability to manage the chivalric and masculine duties of valor and the indoor and courtly virtues of courtesy and feudal homage to a lady. That is, practicing generosity in giving out gifts to his own men, the beautiful knight runs out of money, which his feudal lord Arthur fails to replenish; he wanders away from the court, dismounts, and in a quasi-dream state is visited by an equally beautiful fairy queen who recognizes his true worth and grants him both her love and her money as long as he does not reveal her existence/name. After he returns to court and renews his gifts to his men, Queen Guinevere becomes infatuated with him one midsummer night, even though he refuses her advances. She then privately accuses him of being gay but publicly charges him – through Arthur – with having made a pass at her, and, therefore, with having committed treason. During his trial in front of the Barons, Lanval is rescued by the evidence offered by the Fairy Queen, who then transports him to her own world. If his foreign overlord Arthur is uncharitable and unsupportive of his vassal, and his liege lady Guinevere is herself disloyal to liege, husband, and king, and, therefore, also treacherous to king, then feminized Lanval is, perhaps, right to reject the masculine world of chivalric values for the more virtuous, even noble realm of faërie led by a true queen.

To encourage students to tease out this queer *Lanval*, I include specific questions, some examples of which follow, each of which might build a foundation for either a feminist or queer reading: Who is Lanval?[8] What factors constitute this Breton's subject position or identity? Does his subject position or identity change throughout the course of the *lais*? How is the British King Arthur portrayed in *Lanval*? How does Marie de France reshape and gloss the Arthur in Geoffrey of Monmouth's *The History of the Kings of Britain*? What does the opening and ending tell us about Arthur, his court, and its judicial system? What does the way knights are rewarded tell us about the social status of women in the twelfth century? What is the role of Arthur's queen in the depiction of the court of Arthur? How is male bonding disrupted by the females? What is the role of the fairy mistress in *Lanval*? Do you think *Lanval* offers proto-feminist viewpoints or is it just the ultimate male fantasy come true? What are some of the thematic parallels and contrasts in *Lanval*? How do they contribute to a "feminist" or "non-feminist" reading of *Lanval*? What does love come to mean in *Lanval*? What are the connections between love, property, loyalty, and identity?

My second example, *Sir Gawain and the Green Knight*, perhaps is better known today because of Carolyn Dinshaw's well-known interpretation of the poem in "A Kiss is Just a Kiss" as an interrogation of heteronormative sexualities in which homosexuality does not belong.[9] Here, Sir Gawain's temporary feudal allegiance to his new lord, Bertilak, as symbolized by the mercantile exchange of daily winnings, is complicated most especially by the third day's test involving the green girdle. Of course anything sexual that Bertilak's wife has given him – a kiss, two kisses, and the imagined physical favors she might have given – would require Gawain to offer the same to Bertilak. This is one of the reasons he never reveals to his new lord the gift of the green girdle, given its nature as a gesture of either sexual or amorous conquest of the lady (and, therefore, of course, by implication suggestive of the adulterous and treasonable, as was the possibility in *Lanval*). Dinshaw's clever analysis unpins the queer threat implied by the temptation and necessity for exchange with Bertilak's winnings during all three days of kisses, one that students readily understand in discussions of what is at stake in each exchange between Gawain and Bertilak's lady and Gawain and Bertilak.

Tolkien, of course, famously discusses *Sir Gawain and the Green Knight* in two separate works, first, his essay "Ofermod" that introduces his verse drama, "The Homecoming of Beorhtnoth Beorthelm's Son" (a continuation of the tenth-century Old English chronicle entry known today as *The Battle of Maldon*), and, second, his W. O. Ker Memorial Lecture on *Sir Gawain and the Green Knight*, delivered at the University of Glasgow on 15 April 1953 and published in *The Monsters and the Critics and Other Essays*.[10] Tolkien's two works touch on two different but related aspects of the poem: the pride (or *ofermod*, in the Old English of *The Battle of Maldon*) of Arthur's nephew and best knight, which (according to Tolkien) stems from the chivalric necessity for fame in prowess and valor, in contrast to the retainer's heroic obligation of sacrifice of life in battle to serve his lord in *The Battle of Maldon*. In this regard, Sir Gawain most obviously keeps the girdle to save his neck (and, therefore, his reputation for valor) in the contest with the Green Knight at the Green Chapel. In the long essay on *Sir Gawain*, Tolkien zeros in on the temptation of Gawain in the third fitt, in which the lady tempts the knight through her advances and gifts, as a particularization in fact of what most troubles the Oxford medievalist about what appears to be "chivalric" rather than "heroic" – that is, given Gawain's sexual attraction to the lady from the beginning, the conflict between moral law and the requisites of courtesy and the code of honor.[11] But because Gawain has confessed, presumably he has confessed all his sins and (according to Tolkien) as a Christian may view the alleged magic of the green girdle as a trifle not worthy of confession.[12] For Tolkien, however, the Green Knight most faults Gawain for not surrendering the green girdle as a gain on the third night. Tolkien actually acknowledges the gendered nature of the fault: "It is as *man to man*, as *opponents in a game*, that he is challenging Gawain. And I think that it is plain that in this he expresses the opinion of the author" (my emphasis).[13]

Of course Tolkien nowhere considers the possibility that Gawain might actually succumb to the lady's advances and consequently need to offer similar embraces to his lord, the implication of which would be that Gawain had committed both adultery and treason to his lord. And, of course, Tolkien never mentions the absurd possibility of sodomy between the two men, although that is the logical consequence of a sexual gift exchange between the Lady and the knight. The unspoken issue of a gay Gawain that underlies the temptation scenes is made more vivid when, in the classroom, we juxtapose the English Arthurian romance with the French Arthurian lay of *Lanval*, in which the Breton knight, so uninterested in Guinivere's charms, is accused by Arthur's queen of being homosexual:

> "Lanval," fet ele, "bien le quit,
> Vuz n'amez gueres cel delit;
> Asez le m'ad hum dit sovent
> Que des femmes n'avez talent.

Vallez avez bien afeitiez,
Ensemble od eus vus deduiez.
Vileins cuarz, mauveis failliz,
Mut est mi sires maubailliz
Que pres de lui vus ad suffert."

["Lanval," she said, "I am sure
you don't care for such pleasure;
people have often told me
that you have no interest in women.
You have fine-looking boys
With whom you enjoy {or pleasure} yourself.
Base coward, lousy cripple,
my lord made a bad mistake
when he let you stay with him."][14]   (lines 277–85)

By accusing Lanval of being a "Vileins cuars" (Base coward) and also a
"mauveis failliz" (lousy cripple) (line 283), Guinevere strips him of his
manhood, in medieval cultural as well as in sexual terms. He likes
good-looking boys, and he is not much of a knight in terms of his
valor and physical prowess, in the poem as we have it (indeed, from
the beginning when Lanval dismounts and lets loose his horse so that
he can take a nap, the fairy queen appears and seduces him, an equiva-
lence by which Marie de France deconstructs *chevalerie* and the injustice of its demands).

In an Arthurian literature course, it is possible to read these two
works concurrently to open up discussion of a queer medieval within
the homosocial practice of chivalry. One way I instigate this is to list
the segment in the syllabus on *Sir Gawain and the Green Knight* as
"Gay Gawain?" Providing a hand-out of discussion topics also introduces the topic of queerness; my hand-out also pinpoints the
Heinleinian concept of "The Stranger in a Strange Land" to under-
score the alterity of these two knights, given the Green Knight's
abrupt transgression of the merry and civilized mood of the English
court and its holy festival (the feast of Circumcision, as it is New Year's
Day), coming as he does from a realm possibly that of faërie, and in
English Sir Gawain's more courteous progression over the various
liminal thresholds into Bertilak's faërie-like castle, despite wind and
snow, in his bedraggled finery. Their alterity, their individual difference, is marked by physical and cultural differences from all others, in

Lanval's case, a difference in origin, in that he is from Brittany, and one of great physical beauty, and in the Green Knight's case, a difference in color and size, both markings that can easily invite negative and stereotypical characterizations from those in power, and in Gawain's case, a difference in valor and in courtesy toward women. Interestingly, both the Breton knight Lanval and the Green Knight while in the Arthurian court in England, and Gawain while at Bertilak's court and the Green Knight's chapel, are, indeed, "strangers in a strange land."

Tolkien's focus on the "man to man" contest or question, if you will, in his *Sir Gawain and the Green Knight* essay easily leads us (and students) into discussion of the feudal relationship of Sam to his "lord" Frodo in *The Lord of the Rings* and, in general, of discussion of other male–male engagements throughout Tolkien's medievalized epic-romance. From the very beginning, Sam's service to his master represents a backdrop against which more minor relationships involving service are replayed. Sam initially serves as gardener before the quest begins, but he becomes a squire to his lord in *The Two Towers* after they are separated from the Fellowship and, eventually, in *The Return of the King*, evolves into a deeply compassionate friend whose love transcends the ordinary. Gollum, also a Hobbit, if degenerate in form, represents a parody of Sam as servant, as Frodo parodies the Dark Lord, Sauron, in Tolkien's version of how self-aggrandizement, greed, and pride pervert masculine relationships. Tolkien portrays their mutual emotional enslavement by the Ring (called the "Precious" by Gollum in an ironic reference both to valuable items and the beloved) in the most medieval, feudal, scene of oath-swearing in the epic, in "The Taming of Sméagol," when Gollum swears to the Master – Frodo – by the Precious, or tries to: "Sméagol will swear never, never, to let Him have it. Never! Sméagol will save it. But he must swear on the Precious."[15] At the moment Frodo insists Gollum swear instead *by* the Ring, Sam imagines that "his master had grown and Gollum had shrunk: *a tall stern shadow, a mighty lord who hid his brightness in grey cloud,* and at his feet a little whining dog. Yet the two were in some way akin and not *alien*: they could reach one another's minds" (LOTR, 4:1, 618; my emphasis).

Tolkien fully rehearses homosocial relationships in scenes that involve the Hobbits as medieval vassals or thanes who serve some lord or master, willingly or no, as a means of suggesting the possibility of the misuse of domination and, therefore, to hint at exaggerated masculinity. In *The Return of the King*, this scene of feudal domination is varied by Hobbit Pippin, who, like Gollum attempting to swear on the Ring, similarly swears to the House of Denethor his allegiance as vassal, but as compensation for the loss of Denethor's son Boromir while defending the Hobbits, in "Minas Tirith": "Here do I swear fealty and service to Gondor, and to the Lord and Steward of the realm, to speak and to be silent, to do and to let be, to come and to go, in need or plenty, in peace or war, in living or dying, from this hour henceforth, until my lord release me, or death take me, or the world end" (LOTR, 5:1, 756). After constructing these contrasting scenes of medieval fealty, Tolkien provides a tertium quid when Hobbit Merry willingly and joyfully offers his service to King Théoden of Rohan in "The Passing of the Grey Company": "Filled suddenly with love for this old man, he knelt on one knee, and took his hand and kissed it: 'May I lay the sword of Meriadoc of the Shire on your lap, Théoden King?' he cried. 'Receive my service, if you will!'" (LOTR, 5:2, 777).

Throughout *The Lord of the Rings*, Tolkien defines Hobbits in relation to Men, whose masculinity represents, according to Holly A. Crocker, an invisible standard of heteronormativity. The ideal of masculinity epitomized by Aragorn is evidenced by the support that he receives from the Free Peoples, yet in what does it inhere, if not in his refusal of dominion over others through "visible gestures?"[16] Hobbits, smaller than Men, the Black Númenóreans, the Ringwraiths, and the Lieutenant of the Tower of Barad-dûr – the Mouth of Sauron – identified as a "living man" [LOTR, 5:10, 888], are defined as inversions of Men; so also Orcs, as mutations of Elves, provide what Crocker calls "the distinctions that divide groups."[17] Crocker argues that, "By positing kind as a racializing geography that exceeds the human, Tolkien's trilogy calls attention to the status of masculinity as 'the apparatus of cultural difference,' as Homi K. Bhabha puts it [1995: 8]."[18]

Tolkien's Orcs differ from Men in their broad flat faces, coal-black eyes, and red tongue; they speak their own language, which further isolates them (LOTR, 2:5, 325). Bearing yellow fangs, Orcs have "no time to play," meaning that they must work, that is, kill and torture, and they are quarrelsome, dominating, disloyal, and vengeful, differentiated only by a military chain-of-command, not individual personal or temperamental characteristics (LOTR, 3:3, 445–46). Cruel – they jeer at Merry when he puts "medicine" on his wound and promise that "We shall have some fun later" (LOTR, 3:3, 448) – they are regularly abusive and sadistic verbally, physically, and even sexually. For example, Uglúk, leader of the Uruk-hai of Saruman's Isengard (who have been further mutated so they can march by day), insults Grishnákh of Sauron's Lugbúrz by calling his Orcs swine and maggots: "Don't stand slavering there! Get your rabble together! The other swine are legging it to the forest" (LOTR, 3:3, 452). Further, when Grishnákh steals Merry and Pippin away from the other Orcs because he thinks they have the Ring, Tolkien portrays his search for it as disturbingly sexualized. Grishnákh's "long hairy arm" and "foul breath" are apparent when "He began to paw them and feel them. Pippin shuddered as hard cold fingers groped down his back [...]. His fingers continued to grope" (LOTR, 3:3, 455). Grishnákh, angry that he has not found the Ring, threatens the Hobbits with torture if he does not find it: "I'll cut you both to quivering shreds" (LOTR, 3:3, 457).[19] Ironically, after Sauron's Orc leader is killed by an arrow, Pippin locates Grishnákh's Orc knife and cuts Merry and his bonds. Pippin's acquisition of this phallic weapon – the carved handle of an Orc blade is shaped like a hideous head with "squinting eyes" and "leering mouth" (LOTR, 3:3, 489) – represents both his re-arming and masculinization, for it is after this escape that Pippin generously offers his indenture as servant to tyrannical and mad King Denethor of Gondor as compensation for the loss of his son Boromir defending the two Hobbits against the Orcs.

Within this context, Tolkien invests both Orcs and Hobbits with cultural difference. The epithet most descriptive of their mutual alterity is "queer," that is, not like Men. The Orc chieftain is described in *The Two Towers* as "almost manhigh," a phrase Tolkien uses to differentiate the Orc from the human norm (LOTR, 2:5, 325); interestingly, when Men are corrupted they look more like Orcs (LOTR, 2:5, 566). The Orcs – mutants bred by Sauron from captured Elves – represent the Other, like the "queer" Hobbits who isolate themselves geographically from Men and all other races.[20] As Alexander Doty argues, "queerness has been set up to challenge and break apart conventional categories."[21] Indeed, "The term 'queer,'" for Tison Pugh:

need not be limited to the sexual, as it also describes relations of
power predicated upon relations of sexuality [...]. "[T]o queer"
means to disrupt a character's and/or the reader's sense of self by
undermining his or her sense of heteronormatively inscribed sexuality, whereas "homosexual" and "homosexuality" are used to
describe sexual relationships between members of the same sex (of
whatever degree, from kissing to intercourse). Thus, heteronormative identity stands at stake in the queer as much as any
specific sexual act.[22]

How this identity stake works depends upon a kind of queer gender
parallaxis. Doty observes that "gender" within the queer either mirrors
conventional forms of "feminine" and "masculine," parodies external
behaviors without complete identification with straight ideology, or
resists (or combines) gender codes to transcend straight formulations
of female and male; only in the latter two instances does a queer
gender identification exist.[23] The Orc, as repressed sexuality amid
brute animality, in queer terms represents the hypermasculine polar
opposite of the Hobbit as a form of desexualized and even idealized
feminine.

Just as Tolkien uses the Orc re-arming of Pippin with Grishnákh's
knife in *The Two Towers* to signal the Hobbit's metamorphosis into a
being more masculinized and military, his bonds having been cut, our
medievalist also changes the costume of Sam and Frodo throughout
the epic in their conflicts with other beings, most especially Orcs, to
signal the breaking of Hobbit boundaries and borders in their epic
quest. Indeed, *who* they are, as they evolve, confuses the enemy, who
rely on external signs for racial identity: one small black-skinned
tracker Orc quarrels with a larger warrior Orc who bears the sign of
the Eye over the object of their search, the two Hobbits: "First they say
it's a great Elf in bright armour, then it's a sort of small dwarf-man,
then it must be a pack of rebel Uruk-hai; or maybe it's all the lot
together" (LOTR 6:2, 925). But the Hobbits are all three: Frodo's
dwarf mithril-coat, given to him by Bilbo, not only protects this
newly heroic Hobbit from death in the attack by the Orcs at the
Dwarves' abandoned mine at Khazad-dûm[24] but also reveals him, in a
sense, *as* a Dwarf defending his ancient home: he valiantly stabs the
foot of an Orc who is attempting to break down the door (LOTR,
2:5, 324). Later, in Lothlórien, the grey-green and silver Elven hood
and cloak Galadriel gives to the Hobbits offer camouflage in any forest

setting, near-invisibility from enemies, and lightness and warmth in wearing, but also mark them more symbolically as Elven in their song-making and wisdom (LOTR, 2:8, 370).[25] So also when Sam and Frodo put on Orc armor to disguise themselves from Saruman's searching Orcs, the Orcs themselves think Sam is a big Orc. For Frodo, this assumption of Orc armor is necessary because the Orcs who captured him have stripped him of all clothing, including the garments and "armor" given to him by others – the coat of mithril mail from Bilbo and the Elven cloak with the elven-brooch; for Sam, the Elven blade he uses against Shelob has failed (LOTR, 4:10, 728), and the short sword he carries has been taken by the Orcs (LOTR, 5:10, 889).

This stripping and queered epic re-arming of the hero(es) in *The Return of the King* alerts us to an important stage in their journey together – what might be called a defensive identification of the Other with the Other for self-protection as they cross Mordor, which is indi-cated by the donning of Orc apparel. The Orc clothing they put on includes long hairy breeches, a dirty leather tunic, a coat of ring mail, a belt with a sword, and, for Frodo, a black cap on which a red Evil Eye has been painted with iron rim and "beaklike nose-guard" (LOTR, 5:1, 913). So effective is this garb that both Hobbits appear to be Orcs: captured Frodo, dazed and dreaming in "The Tower of Cirith Ungol," in anticipation of Sam's appropriation of Orc costume saw "an orc with a whip, and then it turns into Sam" (LOTR, 6:1, 910). After they don the clothing, Sam calls Frodo "a perfect little orc" or would be, if he would cover his face with a mask and if he were longer in arm and bow-legged (LOTR, 6:2, 913). Tolkien implies that they have in some way been symbolically transformed into Orcs, but what that means is not explicitly indicated. Further, in "The Land of Shadow," *before* they meet the Orc company, they divest themselves of some of the armor because Sam is too big and cannot wear Orc-mail over his clothing (he just wears an Orc-helm and a black cloak) and because the Orc-mail is too heavy for Frodo (he borrows Sam's Elven cloak, which he wears over the "orc-rag") (LOTR, 6:2, 918).

That director and screenplay-writer Jackson understands this mutual difference of Orcs and Hobbits as "queer" is clear from the way both are cast in the filmic trilogy. The all-male group of Orcs, with their Neanderthal, bulked-up forms, long hairy arms, low brows, incisor-like teeth, phallic-snouted helmets, and bestial rage, project a campy, monstrous masculinity at odds with that of the ideal and nonauthoritarian Aragorn (Viggo Mortensen in the film) or the more gentle, even childlike (feminized) Halflings.[26] Barely post-adolescent, Frodo Baggins (Elijah Wood), Sam Gamgee (Sean Astin), Merry Brandybuck (Dominic Monaghan), and Pippin Took (Billy Boyd) hardly resemble the middle-aged Hobbits (and Men) of Tolkien's medievalized epic (Frodo is over fifty when he begins his adventure in *The Fellowship of the Ring*, as is Aragorn). Yet Jackson keeps Frodo permanently queer throughout the film – perpetually youthful, if scarred, and childlike, if not infantilized.[27]

Interestingly, Jackson adds one crucial scene (62) in the special extended edition of *The Return of the King* – not a chapter in Tolkien's book – in which Jackson "queers" Tolkien: that is, the director there makes explicit the underlying heteronormative gender polarity of Orc and Hobbit through their mutual ontological alterity. Jackson simultaneously uses the scene, "In the Company of Orcs," to parody the three other medieval comitatus or feudal indenture scenes that I have just described from *The Two Towers* and *The Return of the King* between Hobbit and Hobbit or Hobbit and Man. This scene, when compared with the events preceding it in Tolkien, becomes a gloss on the text that can be used in the classroom to reveal the queer underpinnings of the feudal/chivalric bond between lord and thane or knight.

What actually occurs in Tolkien's version of the encounter of the Orc company and the Hobbits? This encounter happens at night, when the Orcs are moving very quickly to reposition themselves for battle. Smaller "breeds" of Orcs who want to get the trip over, even if it means joining Sauron's wars, constitute the group, which is guided by very large "uruks" (slave-drivers) with whips (LOTR, 6:2, 930). Dressed as Orcs, Sam and Frodo do not try to escape – they merely hope they will not be noticed, but of course they are, not as Hobbit imposters, but as deserters. One of the slave-drivers whips and harasses these "slugs" into joining the front of the phalanx:

> Now and again the orc-driver fell back and jeered at them. "There now!" he laughed, flicking at their legs. "Where there's a whip there's a will, my slugs. Hold up! I'd give you a nice freshener now, only you'll get as much lash as your skins will carry when you come in late to your camp. Do you good." (LOTR 6:2, 931)

When the company later meets several Orc companies that converge at the road intersection, during further whippings, scuffles, and confusion Sam falls to the ground with Frodo so that Orcs fall on top and they are able to crawl off in the dark (LOTR, 6:2, 932). This is all there is in Tolkien's text.

Unlike Tolkien, Jackson portrays both Hobbits as wearing their Orc armor throughout "In the Company of Orcs," which underscores the relationship between the intertextuality of book and film and how Jackson may be queering Tolkien. In Jackson's parodic treatment of the scene, "Company" suggests that Frodo and Sam join (and intend to fight) the band of Orcs – the queer Other – in a medieval military sense, but "company" (a business) also suggests entertainment and companionship, that which might be provided by a "fellowship." Frodo and Sam in their snouted black armor (it is not explained in the film where they have found it) are similarly beaten and called slugs, but instead of a chance meeting with other Orc troops and the confusion that results, which allows the Hobbits to escape, Jackson emphasizes the Orc-like sadomasochism of the two – abuse and violence that enable them to survive in Orc-company. Just as the Orcs in Jackson's scene whip their inferiors and slaves into moving faster – both captain and soldier serving the ultimate purpose of Sauron, who has bred these mutants from Elven captives[28] – so also when the two Hobbits halt for inspection, Frodo, wearing what looks like an S & M dog collar tearing into his neck, almost falls and it is Sam who insists that he "stand up!" while a guard snarls "no speech." Yet it is Frodo, not Sam, who begs, "Hit me, Sam! Start fighting!" as a ruse to distract the Orcs so they can escape. Only in the following scene 63, "The Land of Shadow," do the Hobbits strip off the heavy Orc armor to expose just their shirts underneath, momentarily returning to truer selves when Frodo, with his head on Sam's shoulder, admits there is beauty in the light.

That Sam and Frodo have acquired an Orcish hypermasculinity in Jackson's film (but not in Tolkien) is mirrored both in their violent and abusive treatment of Hobbit alter-ego Gollum, the "Precious" and in their later homoerotic relationship at the end of the film. Earlier, in scene 3 of *The Two Towers*, "The Taming of Sméagol," Frodo has exhibited pity toward the fallen Hobbit, although both Frodo and Sam grapple with him while he scratches, hits, and bites. It is Frodo who threatens aggressive Sam with Sting: "Release him [Sam] or I'll cut your throat." Then, after Gollum complains of the pain when he is dragged by the rope on his neck, Frodo removes the rope after Gollum "swears to do what you wants" and "swears to serve the Master of the Precious." Further, Jackson (but not Tolkien) highlights the violent (sadomasochistic) relationship of Gollum and his higher Hobbit self, Sméagol, in scene 29, "Gollum and Sméagol," which involves the famous debate over killing his Master. Dominant and Orc-like Gollum abuses Sméagol to manipulate him into dropping his opposition to the proposal. Smeagol cries, "Master is my friend!" while Gollum replies, "No one likes you! You're a liar and a thief! Murderer!" While Sméagol resists him by telling him to go away, Gollum eats away at his self-esteem – what little he has left – by demanding, "Where would you be without me?" Although Sméagol knows he does not need Gollum now that "Master looks after us," later, in the corresponding betrayal scene of Frodo by Gollum, in scene 66, "Gollum's Plan," he loyally promises that "Sméagol will look after Master." To convince Sméagol, Gollum notes that Master broke his promise. Gollum's violence erupts in a non-Tolkienian way: "We ought to break his filthy neck! Kill him! Kill them both! Then we'll be the Master" (even "Put out his eyes"). When Sméagol answers that it is too risky to kill him, Gollum understands he has won and comes up with the possibility that "she" (Shelob) could do it, absolving them of responsibility. The violence of Jackson's last scene involving the three Hobbits, scene 68, "Mount Doom," when Gollum attempts to seize the Ring and jumps on Sam and Frodo, Sam hits Gollum with a rock, and Gollum bites Sam, has been previously foreshadowed by this violent Jacksonian psychomachia.

Jackson's scene "The Tower of Cirith Ungol," however, provides a touchstone for the blossoming of the final love relationship between Frodo and Sam – and leads to their pairing, repairing, and reuniting in at least three to four scenes of "endless endings" for Jackson's trilogy. In "The Tower of Cirith Ungol," Shagrat the Orc guard, who realizes Frodo, as a commodity, a treasure, is still alive, calls him "precious" (LOTR, 5:10, 741), in echo of the name used by Gollum to address both the Ring and himself. As a name, "Precious" reflects the endearments for the beloved in a heterosexual relationship and thus invokes the intratextual queerness of the Orc. This Orcish love climaxes in the appropriation of the conjugal "ring" by their jealous Hobbit alter-ego Gollum (and still slave of his true lord and master Sauron) at the moment of dis-consummation, or, in another sense, Gollum's "union" with the sexualized female fires of Orodruin (here it is important to note the vaginal fiery eye of Sauron with which those fires are matched). After the destruction of the Ring, in scene 70, "The Crack of Doom," when Frodo hangs from a precipice with two hands, Sam appeals to Frodo, "Don't let go," and offers his hand to him. Visually, Jackson here employs Michelangelo's "Creation of Adam" as a context, to zoom in on the entwined hands to invoke God's loving clasp of Adam's hand. In the next scene, 71, "Sauron Defeated," as the Hobbits touch hands and Mount Doom spews fire, Sam is reminded of sex and love – he would have married Rosie Cotton if he had been able to return home – while Frodo comforts and embraces him: "I'm glad to be with you, Samwise [...] here at the end of all things." "The End of All Things" is also the title of scene 72, in which the giant Eagles rescue them from fiery doom by clutching them in their talons like Jove's Eagle lifting Ganymede, the classical myth of the rape of the Cup Bearer for the gods and medieval code for gay love.[29] But it is not the end of all things, for when Frodo awakens at last, safe in bed at Rivendell, the last of the homely figures he sees, after Merry and Pippin jump into his bed like boys, embracing, and Gandalf, Gimli, Legolas, and Aragorn appear in quick succession, is beloved Sam; their eyes meet as if they were long-parted lovers (scene 73, "The Fellowship Reunited").

In his figuration of the Orcs and Orcish behavior, Jackson deploys a masculinity theorized as "queer" by Pugh and other film critics because of its exaggeration of male physical characteristics and behavior.[30] The symbolic act of Orc re-dressing by the two heroes in "In the Company of Orcs" not only enables the next step in the two Hobbits' journey to return the Ring but also situates the couple within a context of extreme and monstrous masculinization necessary for their survival in the savage and warlike world of Mordor. Jackson's Orc armor with its metal helmets bearing protective guards for noses and cheeks resembles medieval armor, even if noses and cheeks appear grotesque and deformed. Indeed, this scene parodies a medieval chivalric engagement and feudal relationship: the Orcs savage one another with emotional abuse and demeaning epithets, and their captain brutalizes them with whips and other weapons. For Frodo and Sam to join the group out of survival, even to ensure and protect their progress across Mordor, suggests that they both become – and also fail to become – one with this group. That is, they fail to embrace the ironic Orcish rupture/displacement of the feudal bond between lord and serf, which depends upon a sadomasochistic imbalance between master and slave. Thus they remove the armor afterwards because it – the armor and the Orcish masculinity – are too heavy. In a sense, they remain children, they do not "grow up" to become "men" in the bizarrely Orc parody of masculinity. They remain not-men, or women – different, queer.

While this queer-theory analysis of Tolkien and the medieval chivalric tradition extends feminist theory and cultural studies to film analysis, it also operates, I would hope, as an example of the usefulness of the popular and contemporary reception of the postmedieval. If Jackson's filmic gloss on Tolkien's modernist epic aids in the interpretation of the subtexts of a twentieth-century masterpiece and in the reinterpretation of earlier medieval Arthurian lay and romance – *Sir Lanval* and *Sir Gawain and the Green Knight* – it also facilitates an understanding of the vexations of sexual, gender, and national difference and their mirroring in media that tell us as much about ourselves and our biases as about Tolkien or the Middle Ages.

Beyond this, the New Medievalisms offer many opportunities to interrogate the traditional, "old," medieval cultures we have all been trained to teach. Whether we choose a new historical or a postmodern theoretical approach or we mix media to compare the medieval analogously with the modern, we may find our understanding of the Middle Ages – and our teaching – renewed and refreshed through this treasure-trove of New Medievalisms. Or, to use a more appropriately Tolkienesque metaphor in a more defensive context, for our own Hobbit-like survival as academics in an era when hard-earned skills in language study and understanding of a thousand years of literature, history, and art have all too often been marginalized by our institutions, we may need to open new windows in our disciplinary walls, see what lies beyond, and – like Frodo – take up the journey.

NOTES

1. This essay served in longer form as a plenary lecture delivered at the Seventeenth Annual Texas Medieval Association Conference at Texas Tech University, Lubbock, TX, on 3 October 2008. The excerpt in it relating to J. R. R. Tolkien's *The Lord of the Rings* and Peter Jackson's film version of *The Return of the King* is here reprinted in revised form from Kathleen Coyne Kelly and Tison Pugh, ed., *Queer Movie Medievalisms*, Queer Interventions Series (Farnham, Surrey: Ashgate Press, 2009), 79–96, with kind permission of Ashgate Press.

2. Tom Shippey, "Medievalisms and Why They Matter," *Studies in Medievalism* 17 (2009): 63–75 (64).

3. Elizabeth Emery, "Medievalism and the Middle Ages," *Studies in Medievalism* 17 (2009): 106–17 (108).

4. Kim Selling, "'Fantastic Neo Medievalism': The Images of the Middle Ages in Popular Fantasy," in David Ketterer, ed., *Flashes of the Fantastic: International Conference on the Fantastic in the Arts* (Westport, CT: Praeger, 2004), 216.

5. Milton McGatch, "The Medievalist and Cultural Literacy," *Speculum* 66 (1991): 591–604 (597).

6. Authors of these poster papers included, respectively, Pamela Clements, Kevin A. Moberly, Brent Addison Moberly, Carol L. Robinson, Shaina Edmondson, George Ruckman, and Brad Philips, presenting at The Forty-Third International Congress on Medieval Studies, Western Michigan University, Kalamazoo, Michigan.

7. Bruce Holsinger, *The Premodern Condition* (Chicago: University of Chicago Press, 2005), 5.

8. How I teach *Lanval* has evolved over the years, but what I believe Marie de France intended in her lai is a critique of a masculinized society in which there is no place for sexual difference, whether characterized as queer and embodied in the deviant chevalier Lanval – the knight without a horse – or identified as a male feminized by his beauty (again, Lanval) but signifying the female (that is, as a projection of Marie de France herself). See my argument in the essay "Marie de France Versus King Arthur: Lanval's Gender Inversion as Breton Subversion," chapter 3 of *The Literary Subversions of Medieval Women*, New Middle Ages Series (New York and London: Palgrave Macmillan, 2007), 41–62.

9. Carolyn Dinshaw, "A Kiss is Just a Kiss: Heterosexuality and Its Consolation in *Sir Gawain and the Green Knight*," *Diacritics* 24 (1994): 205–26. For the text from which I draw my references to *Sir Gawain and the*

Green Knight, see J. R. R. Tolkien and E. V. Gordon, ed., 2nd ed., rev. Norman Davis (Oxford: Clarendon Press, 1968).

10. See J. R. R. Tolkien, "The Homecoming of Beorhtnoth Beorhthelm's Son," *Essays and Studies by Members of the English Association*, n.s., 6 (1953):1–18. Rpt. in *The Tolkien Reader* (New York: Ballantine, 1966), and "Sir Gawain and the Green Knight," *The Monsters and the Critics and Other Essays* (London: George Allen & Unwin, 1983), 72–108.

11. Tolkien, "Sir Gawain and the Green Knight," 84, 86.

12. Tolkien, "Sir Gawain and the Green Knight," 89.

13. Tolkien, "Sir Gawain and the Green Knight," 93.

14. See *Marie de France: Lais*, ed. Alfred Ewert (1944; rpt. Bristol: Bristol Classical Press and London: Gerald Duckworth, Ltd.; Newburyport, MA: Focus Information Group, 1995), 65; and Marie de France, *The Lais*, trans. Robert Hanning and Joan Ferrante (Grand Rapids, MI: Baker Books, 1978), 196.

15. All references to *The Lord of the Rings* (cited within the text by the abbreviation *LOTR* and one book of the six, chapter, and page[s] within parentheses) derive from J. R. R. Tolkien, *The Lord of the Rings*, 2nd ed., with Note on the Text by Douglas Anderson (Boston: Houghton Mifflin, 1994). This reference is to LOTR, 4:1, 618.

16. Holly A. Crocker, "Masculinity," in Robert Eaglestone, ed., *Reading the Lord of the Rings: New Writings on Tolkien's Classic* (London and New York: Continuum, 2005), 111–23 (121). Crocker notes: "Instead, Aragorn must refashion the masculinity of his kind to avoid their missteps, ultimately by taking a role in the Fellowship that reveals his leadership through gestures of service that avoid visibility. His support of Frodo's errand, therefore, is simply the culmination of a long formation of masculinity that is fostered by contact with groups who protect Middle-earth using quiet modes of dominion" (117). She also adds, "Before he becomes king, then, the new masculinity that Aragorn realizes is enabled by its ability to pass unseen amongst those it protects" (117).

17. Crocker, "Masculinity," 111.

18. Crocker, "Masculinity," 122–23. "The central place in field of sight that Aragorn finally assumes, I suggest, asserts masculinity's invisibility by defining it as the standard of identity that will consolidate all kinds in this new reign" (122). The citation from Homi K. Bhabha comes from "Are You a Man or a Mouse?" in Maurice Berger, Brian Wallis, and Simon Watson, ed., *Constructing Masculinity* (New York: Routledge, 1995), 57–65 (58).

19. In Jackson's film *Two Towers*, scene 12, "The Fate of Merry and Pippin," compresses three different text scenes without any mention or illustration of the theft and groping of the Hobbits by Grishnákh, perhaps because the event hints at pedophilia and male rape.

20. On the queerness of Hobbits, see Jane Chance, "The Problem of Difference in 'The Birthday Party'," chapter 5 of *The Lord of the Rings: The Mythology of Power* (New York: Twayne, 1992), 27–35; recast as chapter 2, "'Queer' Hobbits: The Problem of Difference in the Shire," in the rev. ed. (Lexington: University of Kentucky Press, 2001), 26–37.

21. Alexander Doty, *Making Things Perfectly Queer: Interpreting Mass Culture* (Minneapolis and London: University of Minnesota Press, 1993), xv.

22. Tison Pugh, *Queering Medieval Genres* (New York: Palgrave Macmillan, 2004), 5.

23. Doty notes: "Generally, lesbian- and gay-specific forms of queer identities involve some degree of same-gender identification and desire or a cross-gender identification linked to same-gender desire. The understanding of what 'gender' is in these cases can range from accepting conventional straight forms, which naturalize 'feminine' and 'masculine' by conflating them with essentializing, biology-based conceptions of 'woman' and 'man'; to imitating the outward forms and behaviors of one gender or the other while not fully subscribing to the straight ideological imperatives that define that gender; to combining or ignoring traditional gender codes in order to reflect attitudes that have little or nothing to do with straight ideas about femininity/women or masculinity/men. These last two positions are the places where queerly reconfigured gender identities begin to be worked out." See Doty, *Making Things Perfectly Queer*, 5.

24. Frodo at the end of book 1 has so mastered the Ring he carries that he resists the summons of the Black Riders in "Flight to the Ford" and lifts his sword at them (LOTR 1:12, 214).

25. The leader of the Elves tells the Hobbits that "we put the thought of all that we love into all that we make. Yet they are garments, not armour, and they will not turn shaft or blade" (LOTR 2:8, 370).

26. See *The Lord of the Rings: The Fellowship of the Ring, The Two Towers, Return of the King*, Special Extended DVD Editions, dir. Peter Jackson, screenplay by Peter Jackson, Fran Walsh, and Philippa Boyens, perf. Elijah Wood, et al. (United States: New Line, 2002–4).

27. See Jane Chance, "Is There a Text in this Hobbit? Peter Jackson's *Fellowship of the Ring*," *Literature/Film Quarterly* 30:2 (2002): 79–85; and Jane Chance, "Tolkien's Women (and Men): The Film and the Book," in Janet Brennan Croft, ed., *Tolkien on Film: Essays on Peter Jackson's "The Lord of the Rings"* (Altadena, CA: The Mythopoeic Press, 2004), 175–93. In addition, Daniel Timmons, "Frodo on Film: Peter Jackson's Problematic Portrayal," in Croft, *Tolkien on Film*, 123–48, contrasts the unheroic and "witless" filmic Hobbit very specifically with Tolkien's protagonist to demonstrate Jackson's attempt to build suspense leading to the climax at Sammath Naur.

28. Within the separate context of the history of Tolkien films, note-worthy as a gloss on this scene, is the early version of scene 62's Orcization – queering – of the heroes in the campy Rank and Bass original in which Tolkien's poem "Where There's a Whip, There's a Will" is set to catchy music to dramatize the underlying sadomasochism of the Orc guards in the phalanx. See *The Return of the King*, prod. and dir. Arthur Rankin, Jr. and Jules Bass, adapted by Romeo Muller Production, perf. Orson Bean, John Huston, Roddy McDowell et al., VHS Home Video (United States: Warner, 1993). While Jackson tones down the camp of the Rank and Bass original, he retains the sadism in his creepy Jason-like main guard ("Shut this rabble down!") and its echo in the diversionary scrap between "Orc" Frodo and Sam so they can escape scrutiny and, therefore, discovery by the guards.

29. John Boswell, "The Triumph of Ganymede: Gay Literature of the High Middle Ages," *Christianity, Social Tolerance, and Homosexuality: Gay People in Western Europe from the Beginning of the Christian Era to the Four-teenth Century* (Chicago and London: University of Chicago Press, 1980), 243–66.

30. See Tison Pugh, "Queering the Medieval Dead: History, Horror, and Masculinity in Sam Raimi's *Evil Dead* Trilogy," in Lynn Ramey and Tison Pugh, ed., *Race, Class, and Gender in "Medieval" Cinema* (New York and London: Palgrave-Macmillan, 2007); also, Lee Edelman, *No Future: Queer Theory and the Death Drive* (Durham, NC: Duke University Press, 2004).

Is Medievalism Reactionary?
From between the World Wars to the
Twenty-first Century:
On the Notion of Progress in our
Perception of the Middle Ages[1]

Alain Corbellari

Today's fascination with the Middle Ages is usually attributed to Romanticism. This, however, is true only in that Romanticism marked a peak of interest in the period; the Romantics largely misunderstood the Middle Ages, and one may as well situate the crucial moment for the revival of medieval studies in the eighteenth century, when serious scholarly work on the Middle Ages began, or at the end of the nineteenth century, when scholars brought to fruition the erudition and methodology developed during the previous century. Or, as I would like to do here, one may place it still later, in the 1920s and 1930s, two decades during which our vision of the Middle Ages went through a decisive reevaluation. In this article I would like to trace a possible approach to the study of our combined representations of the Middle Ages and its literature, particularly in France, during the years between the World Wars, in order to try to show how our current vision of the Middle Ages largely depends on what happened during these important years. In order to do this, I will start with a short text dating from the very end of this period, a text that seems to me emblematic of the author's assumption that his audience is familiar with the Middle Ages. The passage also reveals a certain number of automatic responses on the part of his audience linked to the use of such a reference.

Studies in Medievalism XVIII, 2010

It is July 1940. All of France is occupied; all of it? Not yet all of it, but the intellectuals are taking sides and literary life is having a hard time bouncing back. A francophone Swiss writer, Guy de Pourtalès, author of *La Pêche miraculeuse* (*The Miraculous Catch of Fish*) and some famous composers' biographies, has the honor of inaugurating the first literary polemic of the Occupation with an article entitled "*Aprés le désastre*" ("After the disaster"), which appeared in the *Journal de Genève* on 28 July. This article is far from being his nicest piece of writing. He accuses the writers active between the two World Wars, Gide most of all, of not having done their job, that is to say, of not having provided sufficient moral guidance for the next generation.

Readers did not take long to respond to the article, and thus began what would shortly be called the "*querelle des mauvais Maîtres*" ("the dispute of the bad Masters"), the details of which do not interest us here, but which gave rise to a response from André Rousseaux, comrade of Albert Béguin at the "Cahiers du Rhône" and future member of the Resistance; someone who, for this reason, we cannot suspect of indifference towards the enemy. This article is entitled "*C'est la faute à Voltaire ou la querelle des mauvais Maîtres*" ("It's Voltaire's fault or the dispute of the bad Masters"), and it ends with the following anecdote:[2]

> And I think that, in regards to the point we are discussing, the debate is as old as the world. I fully imagine that after the battle of Crécy, two good Frenchmen like us quarreled in just the same way. The first said: "None of this would have happened if we had continued to recite the *Chanson de Roland* instead of giving in to the pathetic and morbid influence of *Tristan et Yseut*." And the second one said: "We especially should have figured out that the lance, the helmet, and chain mail were outdated weapons when the English started to give bows and arrows to their soldiers."[3]

This outburst, in 1940, naturally corresponded with cultivated readers' expectations. To mention only one representative example from the preceding decade, readers would have been familiar with a group called the *Théophiliens*: since 1934, Gustave Cohen, professor at the Sorbonne, had, almost every year, revived a different medieval play. Performances met with consistent success, and this success also perfectly illustrates the new role played by scholars in the popularization of old French literature.[4]

To mention an equally important tendency, however, that is perhaps less apparently spectacular, the preceding twenty years also saw the resurrection, in France, of an Arthurian imaginary landscape. Up until the beginning of the twentieth century, the Third Republic had, when it came to medieval literature, largely identified itself with the *chansons de geste*. Meanwhile, the Arthurian romances were left to England, as they had been in the Middle Ages (if one believes Jean Bodel's famous division between the different source materials, the *matières de France, de Rome*, and *de Bretagne*).[5] Under the double influence of closer political ties to Great Britain (the *Entente cordiale* of 1904), and the work of romance philologists, such as the renewal of the Tristan and Iseut story by Joseph Bédier in 1900, Arthurian themes made a noticeable reappearance in French culture as soon as World War I ended.[6] Important scholars, such as Ferdinand Lot, Edmond Faral, Albert Pauphilet, Gustave Cohen, and Jean Frappier, wrote seminal works on Arthurian themes; adapters such as André Mary and Jacques Boulenger offered readers modernized, popular versions of Arthurian texts; first-class writers, such as Apollinaire, Cocteau, Cendrars, and especially the Surrealists, following an author by the predestined name of Breton, allowed, through their works, a space in which this imaginary landscape could develop. France finally recognized the Arthurian romance as belonging to it as much as does the *chanson de geste*.[7]

One can thus read Rousseaux's fable on two or even three different levels: first, it is a historical narrative that reveals a striking parallel. Let us not forget that one of the most penetrating essays on the *Débâcle* of 1940, *L'Etrange défaite* (*The strange defeat*), was written by Marc Bloch, the most famous medieval historian to come out of France.[8] Though Bloch does not mention the Hundred Years War in his book, one can remark a strong tie between his style of argumentation and Alain Chartier's in the *Quadrilogue invectif*, in which the latter analyzes the defeat at Agincourt, underlining in particular the corrupt leadership, the internal tensions, and the desire for a new order.[9]

In addition, the first notable French literary dispute took place during the Hundred Years War, shortly before Agincourt; the "debate on the *Roman de la Rose*" pitted Christine de Pizan and Jean Gerson, both of whom attacked Jean de Meun's misogyny, against Jean de Montreuil, the Gontier brothers, and Pierre Col as defenders of literature's inalienable right to say whatever it pleases.[10] The modernity of this quarrel is striking. In response to Christine de Pizan's *avant la lettre* politically correct understanding, which blames the author for the ideas expressed in the *Roman de la Rose*, Jean de Meun's defenders insist that one should not confuse the author with the narrator in a work of fiction, as if they had already read Proust's *Contre Sainte-Beuve*. Even if the political context is not so much as mentioned during the debate, one should not forget that Christine de Pizan, at the same time, was attempting to bring an end to the struggles that were internally destroying the kingdom of France.[11] If one assumes that a great writer has something to say about everything, one must also admit that it would be surprising if no tie existed, however indirectly it might appear, between Christine's two concurrent battles. In fact, is it surprising that a single politically engaged understanding of literature would simultaneously recommend morality of expression and politically efficacious speech?[12]

Rousseaux probably did not think of Christine de Pizan while writing his anecdote, yet the parallel is all the more striking: the same sort of crisis brought about a similar division between writers. The menace of civil war and the risk of English intervention caused Christine de Pizan to moralize literature in the same way that the catastrophe of spring 1940 led Guy de Pourtalès to ask himself if prewar literature would not have been better off had it been more moral.

On a third level, the very terms Rousseaux chooses to transfer to the fourteenth century, the "dispute of the bad Masters," are not innocent, since the revaluing of Arthurian romance over the traditional corpus of *chansons de geste*, as we have already noted, was one of the important changes wrought to the French literary canon during the very same period criticized by Guy de Pourtalès for its pernicious influence. One must thus add a third, more literary parallel to the political and socio-literary parallels already mentioned. One of the rare discordant voices in the chorus of praise that greeted Bédier's *Roman de Tristan et Iseut* belonged to the philosopher Alain Chartier (who changed his real name, Emile Chartier, in order to take the first name of his medieval namesake). In 1922, he criticized Tristan's philter, seeing it as an artifice unworthy of the modern novel, and condemning modern adapters of medieval texts for their lack "of heart or taste, which is here the same thing."[13]

This leaves us with more than one similarity between, on the one hand, the replacement of Barrès' nationalism in the heart of intellectual youth, which inspired the *revanche* of 1914–18, by the immorality and hedonism of a Gide and a Breton, and, on the other hand, a supposed evolution in the medieval taste for the *chanson de geste* to the "pleasing" if "vain" (according to Jean Bodel) courtly romance. One may also remark a more insidious parallel between the influence of the new and supposedly bad masters, and the influence wielded by medievalists and their followers, zealots for a renewal of the spirit of the *matière de Bretagne*.[14]

This episode of the "dispute of the bad Masters" amounts to far more than a silly argument and invites us to scrutinize our love of the Middle Ages and the use that we might make of the period. At the same time, Rousseaux shows us that the Middle Ages should not be considered less modern than any other era, once we realize that they were full of sensible people who were able to recognize that one can never completely escape one's own time.

One cannot separate, however, this idea of the *modernity* of the Middle Ages from the renewal the image of this period underwent during the years between the two World Wars. Since our rediscovery of the Middle Ages in the eighteenth century, our image of it has vacillated between light and dark, changing from one to the other according to the era and sometimes combining the two. The rose-tinted Middle Ages of the Enlightenment, whose thinkers savored the fabliaux and the troubadour style, stands in sharp contrast to the shadowed Middle Ages of the Romantics, who used it as a setting for their gothic novels and chose as emblematic figures of the entire thousand-year period the late-blooming Louis XI and the Witch.[15] Nevertheless, the rose-tinted Middle Ages did not disappear. They continued to live on in Germany, through Novalis and Hoffmann, and even Wagner; they informed, in England, the imagination of the Pre-Raphaelites; and in France, they came back in force at the end of the nineteenth century amid Catholics, such as Huysmans and Léon Bloy, and with scholars, who rediscovered a subtle and refined literature.[16] One has to wait until 1918, however, to see medieval literature widely received. This description, of course, leaves room for error: no representation is monochromatic. The question of knowing whether, in this day and age, our mental representation of the Middle Ages is more rose-tinted than shadowed does not make much sense, since never before have our feelings about this period been so mixed and so ambivalent. Today, our fascination with the Middle Ages is so widely shared that the period attracts the most varied fantasies. Note how a cult movie like *The Name of the Rose* portrays at once famished beggars and superior sages, heretical burnings and an incredible library.[17] Our desire for both a rose-tinted and a shadowed Middle Ages, which is at once unsettling and desirable, is as contradictory as that for which this desire yearns.

Though perhaps unremarkable from a strictly scholarly point of view, the years between the two World Wars were above all else years of synthesis and expansion. Latin literature from the Middle Ages at last became available, after a long stay in purgatory, thanks to the work of Edmond Faral, and then Ernst Robert Curtius.[18] Scholastic philosophy regained its former glory through Gilson and the Neo-Thomist school.[19] Gothic and Romanesque art, through the work of Mâle and Focillon, broke out of the shadows to which they had been relegated by Viollet-le-Duc.[20] We have already mentioned the quantity of adaptations that flourished in the 1920s. If one had to choose a single book to summarize the spirit of this era, it would have to be *The Renaissance of the Twelfth Century*, by Charles H. Haskins, published in 1927.[21] Even though it has never been translated into French, the book perfectly relates an idea whose seed was already planted in French thought during the middle of the nineteenth century by Ernest Renan. This scholar believed in the "Greek miracle," which proves that the two ideas – a twelfth-century renaissance and a belief in Greece as the origin of all culture – are not necessarily incompatible.[22] Joseph Bédier, along with his disciples, later brought the idea to fruition. Bédier, shortly before his death in 1938, intended to write a book on "the first century of French literature."[23] All of this is to say that Haskins, rather than invent an idea, placed a catchy phrase on a paradigm that had already been in the air for a long time. This did not happen in the 1920s by chance, however. Something had indeed exploded after the first world conflict, something that suddenly allowed for the conclusion to be drawn, by the light of day, that the Middle Ages did not represent a regression of civilization. It was rather a creative, conquering, and, let us dare to use the word, *modern* period. Such an affirmation was possible because of the tidal wave of liberty that engulfed the artistic and intellectual movements of the age. There was certainly no lack of avant-garde movements during the years that directly preceded World War I, and some would argue that their radicalism was not rivaled until 1945. One could discuss at length whether or not 1918 represented, in some respects, a regression in terms of avant-garde thought, but for those like us who have lived through the incessant flight forward of the avant-garde, these very questions bring the period after World War I surprisingly close to us.

One cannot deny what the sociologists, thinkers, and especially the citizens of the period unanimously understood: the years after World War I marked a sudden break with the preceding moral order.[24] Psychoanalysis would dive into this rupture, and we would quickly call the ten years that followed 1918 the *années folles*, the "crazy years." In one of his least-known books, *Miroirs de l'amour* (*Mirrors of love*), Paul Zumthor echoes the liberation but also disorder that the period provoked in people's spirits. He sees *Lady Chatterley's Lover* by D. H. Lawrence as the symptom, and he praises novelists like Ramuz and poets like Claudel, who seem to him to be prophets of a return to the elementary. This return may represent, over other more ephemeral and transgressive wills, the real modernity of our time.[25]

One should not, however, confuse different eras. If the 1920s showed a certain taste for "primitivism," it remained a minor one. Overall, the art of this period was trying to be more careless than engaged and does not in the least resemble our era's more radical attempts to subvert Eurocentric rationalism. The forms taken by the medieval paradigm are in keeping with this. Neither the ribald and muddy Middle Ages of our contemporary "Medieval Fairs," and other more or less amusing reconstructions, nor the quasi science-fictional atmosphere of Tolkien's heroic fantasy dominated.[26] Instead, a policed Middle Ages prevailed that was settled down and sobered up, most likely marvelous, but above all else a model of courtliness. Ironically, as disrespectable as they wished to appear, André Breton's disciples had an overtly romantic side that informed how they wrote about the quest for love and which explains the fairy-like characters that haunt their works.[27]

Yet let us not be detained here. If, as I have said, the period between the two Wars played an important role in the modern rehabilitation of the Middle Ages, it is not because it exalted a rather conventional rose-tinted Middle Ages, but because it embraced the idea that the Middle Ages wanted to be, and knew how to be, resolutely modern.

The idea of a "Renaissance of the twelfth century" took so long to become well-known because it took scholars a long time to get rid of an essentially popular idea of medieval art. In the eighteenth century, readers unearthed the fabliaux and reveled in the joyous and licentious jokes of their ancestors.[28] A perception of the Middle Ages as the childhood of modern civilization thus took root. No one then suspected that the literary production of this period could have artistic qualities comparable to the works of the French classical period: the distance between the fabliaux and La Fontaine appeared to be as great as that between a child and a grown man. Romanticism, contrary to what one might suppose, did nothing to contradict this value judgment. The German Romantics, in particular the brothers Grimm, probably felt more inclined than the French to appreciate medieval works, but, essentially, they asserted that the literary production of the Middle Ages represented only the infant cries of a newborn literature.[29] If they deemed this a virtue, it was only to trump French works, which were too disciplined, too civilized, and too cold to serve as examples, but their reaction remains only that, a reaction. They elevated the primitive, but did not deny that the works themselves were primitive, or roughly written. In France, the most fanatic medievalists of the first half of the nineteenth century, such as Paulin Paris or François Génin, lived their enthusiasm practically schizo-phrenically.[30] They could not imagine going against the popular opinion that saw the history of literature as evolutionary and deemed unsurpassable the works of the seventeenth and eighteenth centuries, yet they still felt the need to consider medieval works in their own right. They realized, however, that if they upset the canon, opening up a Pandora's box of relativism, they would be severing the very branch on which they were sitting, effectively becoming the grave-diggers for the institutions they were supposed to be guarding. Tradi-tionally, only the masterpieces of antiquity enjoyed the privilege of being excluded from the literary law of evolution; putting medieval works on the same level as them would have more or less quickly signed a death sentence for the humanities, a fate that they wanted to avoid at all costs.

Scholars from the second half of the nineteenth century, led by Paul Meyer and Gaston Paris, the son of Paulin, found a way to tame this unruly enthusiasm by insisting on the rigor of their scientific approach. Seeking the *truth* behind the facts, they did not have to judge the works they were studying.[31] Originating in Germany, these norms of modern scientific research came to be practiced by the French in the middle of the century. The whole approach can be summarized by the following formula by Ernest Renan, published in 1849 in *L'Avenir de la science* (*The future of Science*): "One must not say: This is silly, this is wonderful; one must say: This comes from the human mind, thus it is valuable."[32] It is worth noting that during these same exact years, a young, still unknown, writer from Normandy wrote the following to one of his friends: "In order for a thing to be interesting, you simply need to look at it long enough." You may have recognized one of Flaubert's most famous quotations. Is this meeting of the minds between the authors of the *Vie de Jésus* (*The Life of Jesus*) and *Madame Bovary* purely coincidental? Probably not. Flaubert's quote, read in context, is less the announcement of a future stylistic credo by someone who will want to write "a book on nothing," than a general description of how he perceives reality.[33] In this way, both Renan and Flaubert, at the end of Romanticism, have the same sense of a reality that they can no longer judge but need to perceive, or even *experiment* with. Has our academic morality changed in a hundred and fifty years? Listen to the conversations of your colleagues, listen to yourself, and you may notice how the category "interesting" allows us to talk about anything without sounding ridiculous and without degrading our terribly precious status as academics!

Ferdinand Brunetière, after the death of Renan, violently attacked him for almost the same reasons that Guy de Pourtalès, fifty years later, blamed Gide and others like him for Germany's defeat of France. Renan would have confessed himself guilty of having disoriented the younger generation with an untimely relativism. [34] Today, all one can do is bury this judgment. With Renan, relativism certainly came in through the front door of the academic world; since then, it has become more radical, and it is not ready to give up its position, especially since it is the approach that permits, in one way or another, a researcher in the human sciences to find out something *new*. How do we attract attention to the obscure writer we were unlucky enough to choose to write a dissertation about if it is not by decreeing that no one before us has ever understood how to write literary history?

The academic ethical code promoted by Renan, though it seems unconcerned with value judgments, disguises the problem, because to give the same attention to a canonized work as to a work generally considered secondary is in fact to make a positive value judgment about the second. The Middle Ages would certainly come up a winner in such a redistribution of the cards.

Academic criteria alone, however, would not have sufficed to bring about this rehabilitation if there had not already been a fundamental ambivalence at the heart of our connection to the Middle Ages, which erupts like something long repressed as soon as we notice it. Here, the concept of the "Renaissance of the twelfth century" intervenes. Indeed, accepting this idea is to recognize a third element in the reassuring dialectic that sees our civilization as simply following in the steps of Antiquity.

In general, one might say that there are two main ways to consider the origins of western civilization: either we admit, in the traditional manner, that everything that is good, original, and valuable in our civilization was already present in Ancient Greece, that the Romans only copied the Greeks, and that the Renaissance (the *real* one, in the fifteenth and sixteenth centuries) brought it back to life; or we prefer a direct filiation beginning in the Middle Ages to this broken heritage. In this view, the Middle Ages certainly descended from Antiquity, but only after a radical amount of refining and re-elaborating. The rediscovery of Greek culture in the fifteenth and sixteenth centuries is then simply an epiphenomenon of this effort. In the first case, one would say that our society is *Greco-antique*, and in the second that it is *Latino- medieval*.

Now, the idea that medieval Latinity held in condensed form all that differentiates the western model of civilization from other models around the world could not have been developed prior to the period between the two World Wars because the eighteenth and nineteenth centuries totally ignored the clerical caste as a force of innovation and progress in the Middle Ages. Even for Gaston Paris, at the end of the nineteenth century, the cleric was essentially a negative character who was holding on to a dead culture while being overshadowed by a lay culture in full bloom. It was Joseph Bédier, a disobedient disciple of Gaston Paris, who would reverse this paradigm.[35] In contrast to his professor, he perceived clerics as representatives of medieval progress because they were an essential intermediary between a popular culture, whose existence he certainly did not deny, and the tools that assured this culture's survival, namely writing and scientific understanding. To quote him: "Old stones would have no history if the 'clerics' had not taken the pains to ensure that they did."[36] Formulated at the same time that the word "cleric" was taking on new meaning due to the Dreyfus affair, Bédier's rehabilitation of the clerical caste offered fans of the Middle Ages something they longed for: the missing element that allowed them to see it as the melting pot of everything we are today, instead of as a dead period, or, little better, as a friendly break during the development of western culture. The idea of the *Renaissance of the twelfth century* thus only makes sense if medieval Latinity is seen as a vector of progress instead of as a conservatory of obscurantism.

And this is exactly what the texts of the twelfth century themselves tell us. Shall we reread the very famous prologue to Marie de France's *Lais*?:

> Custume fu as ancïens,
> Ceo testimoine Precïens,
> Es livres ke jadis feseient,
> Assez oscurement diseient
> Pur ceus ki a venir esteient
> E ki aprendre les deveient,
> K'i peüssent gloser la lettre
> E de lur sen le surplus mettre.
> Li philosophe le saveient,
> Par eus meïsmes entendeient,
> Cum plus trespassereit li tens,
> Plus serreient sutil de sens
> E plus se savreient garder
> De ceo k'i ert a trespasser.[37]

This text, well known to all medievalists, nevertheless continues to add fuel to the fire because its content remains potentially problematic for partisans of the "Greco-antique" vision of western civilization. The allusion to the Ancients certainly does not refer to a classical model, absolute and unsurpassable, as it will for the humanists and after. On the contrary, the prologue invites readers to surpass them, seeking to pass on a dynamic, energizing force. Even the connection traditionally made between Marie de France's prologue and the famous saying by her contemporary that we are "dwarfs on the shoulders of giants" is partially false, because nothing proves that Marie thought of the Ancients as giants. The only thing she retains from Bernard de Chartres' translation is the fact that "we can see more things and we see further than them."[38]

Chrétien de Troyes is even more direct in the prologue to his second work, *Cligès*:

> Car des Grezois ne des Romains
> Ne dit an mes ne plus ne mains,
> D'ax est la parole remese
> Et estainte la vive brese.[39]

Ernst Robert Curtius saw in this "the opposite of a humanist's professional confession,"[40] and perhaps, despite the protests of Jean Frappier, he was not altogether mistaken. Can we still speak, if not of humanism, at least of the humanities, in the scholarly sense of the term, if we think that the works of the Ancients no longer have anything to teach us? For all intents and purposes, this first "quarrel of the Ancients and Moderns" is not even one, since the Moderns are the ones who always win, unequivocally. What a difference when compared to the petty, sententious, and ultimately hesitant polemic that would oppose, five hundred years later, Boileau and Perrault![41]

Curtius proves in two ways, however, that paradoxically he is not a partisan of the purely Medieval Latin origins of our civilization. First, he wrote a seminal work on *European Literature and the Latin Middle Ages*, which can also be considered a book from between the two World Wars since it was written primarily during the Nazi period (he chose not to publish anything while Hitler was in power). And second, he showed reserve. His "Latin Middle Ages" appears more to be a museum of antique practices than the purveyor of a new spirit. The critic Jean Frappier had no doubt of this, and reveals in the following passage the radically Hellenic and classical bias of the German scholar:

> The Greco-Latin tradition, however predominant it might have been, can neither adequately explain the genesis of Medieval Literature nor its many aspects. The Middle Ages created much more than one might think after having read Curtius. The period was not only a hyphen between Antiquity and the Europe's modern literature. To take only one famous example, courtly love in its essence cannot be reduced to Ovid's precepts and his *Art of Love*, even though medieval writers borrowed from these Latin texts. In truth, the Middle Ages were never more original then when they wrote in *vulgaire*, in the national languages. Curtius too often

forgets the fertile role played in the formation of European literature by Provençal lyricism, the *chanson de geste*, and the French
roman. Is this a simply his preconception? Is he being excessive,
overly firm in order to defend his argument? With great satisfaction, Curtius not only imagines a continuous but also an almost
immobile humanism which lasted for centuries.[42]

The formula with which Frappier ends his essay is striking and
remarkable in every way; one notices that it is lacking neither in
courage nor in daring for a man who was a professor at the Sorbonne
before May 1968: "A culture does not exist without tradition. But it
sometimes happens that a civilization is extinguished by its official
supporters."[43] One can see that Frappier hopes to find a compromise
between Chrétien de Troye's radicalism and Curtius' conservatism.
Do not forget, however, the contradicting view of him as a supporter
of the traditional and anti-intellectual thesis that thought of medieval
literature as owing nothing to the clerical caste: the affirmation that
medieval literature in the vernacular is more original than the Latin
literature of the period depends upon the currently accepted belief in
an important clerical contribution to vernacular literature. As for the
canonic example of courtly love, it obviously relies on another famous
book from between the World Wars, *L'Amour et L'Occident* by Denis
de Rougemont, published in 1939.[44] Scientifically a weak work, this
book undoubtedly did more than any other towards convincing the
public that, according to a formulation attributed to Charles
Seignobos, "Love is an invention of the twelfth century."[45] This is an
ambiguous example, however. Rougemont only wrote his book to say
that, since the twelfth century, western culture has been on the wrong
track, valuing passion for its own sake and disdaining marriage. One
might reply that the work's popularity had nothing to do with this
thesis, however clearly it is stated in the work, and though it is essentially a glorification of the era of the troubadours, the fact remains
that the author did not intend it to be one. Annoyed by its Christian
morality, Jean-Paul Sartre viciously criticized the work, which brought
down in the cultured public's eye not only Rougemont but also the
Personalist movement of which he was the most visible partisan.[46]
This cleared the intellectual terrain after Liberation, insuring the
triumph of Existentialism in France. While calling Rougement's
vision a dream, the beauty of which he cannot deny, Sartre

simultaneously criticizes the idea that passionate love was an invention of the Middle Ages and the associated assumption that Christianity has universal value. He ends the article semi-ironically by stating that the Cathars should have been listened to more closely since (and these are the last words of his article) "they were decent folk."[47] Sartre does not definitively dismiss the idea that the twelfth century could have represented one of the key moments in western civilization, but his implied reasons are the opposite of those suggested by Rougemont: his praise of the Cathars points to the idea that a certain freedom of thought, in which Sartre likes to see the distinctive mark of the western world, could have been born in the twelfth century. I will leave to others the task of evaluating the links between Catharism and Existentialism, but nevertheless, Sartre's ambiguous attitude – in which he seems, by the way, not to have considered the medieval period very highly – entertains the idea that a renaissance of western thought was still fresh at the time of the troubadours.

There are other more tangible signs, however, that the great minds from between the two Wars were able to think of the Middle Ages as a definitive beginning. Let us now turn to a book whose reference to the Middle Ages, even though it is in its title, is often dismissed as anecdotal. *When Cathedrals Were White*, written by Le Corbusier and published in 1937, is probably the most perfect example of the *tabula rasa* idea that was responsible for a vision of the twelfth century as "absolutely modern," as Rimbaud would have said. Le Corbusier clearly sets the tone from the very first pages:

> When cathedrals were white, Europe had organized the trades under the imperative request for an altogether new technique that was prodigious and completely daring, the use of which gave rise to systems of unexpected forms, to forms whose spirit disdained the heritage of a thousand years of tradition, and which were unafraid of directing civilization towards a hitherto unknown adventure. An international language reigned wherever the white race was, privileging the exchange of ideas and the movement of culture. An international style had spread from the West to the East and from the north to the south, a style that drew with it a passionate torrent of spiritual delectations: love of art, unselfishness, the joy of living while creating.
> Cathedrals were white because they were new. Cities were new;

they were being built from scratch, in an orderly and regular fashion, geometrically, after plans. [...]

The new world was beginning. White, limpid, joyful, clean, precise, and without a backwards glance, the new world bloomed like a flower growing out of the ruins. All common customs had been laid aside; we had turned our backs on them. In one hundred years, the feat was accomplished and Europe had been changed.[48]

Without a doubt, this passage owes much to fantasy. It is a veritable prose poem that projects on to the twelfth century the utopian spirit of one of the greatest visionaries of the twentieth century. Significantly, Le Corbusier writes of technique and not religion, the desire for art and not the desire for God; but is he saying anything different from what Chrétien de Troyes says in his prologue to *Cligès*? If humanism conserves a heritage out of respect for the past, then this vision is profoundly anti-humanist. It runs every risk of being too absolute, but coming from one of the most revolutionary men of the twentieth century, it sounds like liberation.

The idea that medieval art is, in contrast to the classical centuries that preceded and followed it, primarily identifiable with liberty thus gained ground. During the same period, Charles-Albert Cingria, a writer as free as he is difficult to categorize and a great admirer of Stravinsky, developed a vision of Gregorian chant and the art of the troubadours in which respectful invention predominated alongside rigorous liberty.[49] All of the music written by Monteverdi and Stravinsky thus seems to him to be the extension of an earlier tradition disfigured by what he calls "an impertinent and incessant itch for variety" that characterizes western art and culture "since the renaissance."[50] It is not my intention here to trace the prolific theories of Cingria, with all their twists and turns. I would simply like to remark that this author, whose ideas seemed reactionary in his own time, has such a modern style that he has become one of the most important reference points for many of today's best French writers.[51] His love for the Middle Ages, in particular, marks him as one of those "anti-moderns" (to use Antoine Compagnon's expression).[52] It also rhymes particularly well with the explosion of thought that has nourished the artistic and theoretical movements of our time, the beginning of the twenty-first century.

Interest in the Middle Ages and its possible modernity connects authors otherwise as different as the anti-modern Cingria and the ultra-modern Le Corbusier, or the moralist Denis de Rougement and the stolid humanist Ernst Robert Curtius. In fact, the Middle Ages imposes itself on everyone as a period in direct contact with their own, although to varying degrees. It is no longer a mere unhappy interlude on the triumphant road from the pre-Socratics to the Enlightenment, but an integral moment in the creation of our western identity. These four authors are above all else cosmopolitans who disregard national barriers and who each have something to tell us about the unified Europe that we are trying to establish today, although here again according to different modalities. Does this mean that the period between the two World Wars has continued uninterrupted until today? No one could defend that argument. On the contrary, the years that followed the end of World War II in many ways reflected a drastic reaction to the two decades that had preceded them. Abstract painters and atonal composers, whose paradigms were in the minority during the two Wars, thus made a striking come back after 1945, renewing currents that dated from before 1914. Nevertheless, this frantic avant-garde started losing from the 1970s onwards, and, in many ways, the period from 1945 to 1975 seems from our point of view today to be as dated if not more so than the period from 1918 to 1939. It is thus no surprise that the craze for all things medieval dramatically abated during the first thirty years after World War II, only to reappear in the 1970s stronger and more determined than it was before. Love for the Middle Ages, still limited to a certain cultured elite during the period between the two Wars, became the property of all. At the same time, there emerged tendencies that contributed to the extraordinary variety of references available today for those who appreciate distant and different cultures. One need only mention the surprising renewal of Baroque music, which seems to have become popular at the very moment the dogmatism of avant-garde composers was running out of steam. In fact, our current interest in the Middle Ages is a postmodern one. If the years between the two Wars offer such an abundant theoretical explanation for this, it is because this period, taking into account the ideological and moral breakdown the West felt at the end of the first worldwide conflict, carefully posed the foundations for an anxious self-questioning on the part of our civilization, a self-questioning that the three resolutely modern decades after World War II tried in vain to sublimate. This self-scrutiny comes

back to us today, more obsessively than ever, in the form of a relativism that some see as dangerously nihilist.

Of the four authors that we have mentioned (Curtius, Le
Corbusier, Rougement, and Cingria), Le Corbusier may seem,
because of his belief in progress, the most distant from us. At the same
time, of the four, he is the one who most resolutely discarded any
respect for tradition. Yet it is precisely our postmodern relativism that
has done the most harm to the sacrosanct cultural canon on which
western civilization was supposedly constructed. When answering the
question, mentioned above, of whether we are "Greco-antique" or
"Medieval-Latin," today's relativism would have a tendency to prefer
the second answer, since today the idea that the Greeks thought for all
of humanity is suspicious, while no one ever attributed such a claim to
the Middle Ages. Our relativism is apparently contradictory since it
doubts everything except for itself, and while it hopes to compare
cultures on equal footing, it perniciously threatens to close them in on
themselves.

Does the medieval period have anything to gain from this debate?
A pointless question, since the Middle Ages is only whatever we make
of it. The fact remains that we are spread out between two diametri-
cally opposed postulates: either we continue to believe in the Greek
essence and universal appeal of our civilization, and we then admit
that the Middle Ages and what it produced necessarily fade in the
light of this Hellenic sun, most influential to the Enlightenment; or
we decree that the works and ideas of the Middle Ages are equal to
others, are absolute in and of themselves, yet we remain unable to
determine whether there exists a cultural norm applicable to all of
humanity. Those who unilaterally denounce western imperialism
would say this is just as well. It could be, though, that everything
cannot be resolved by simply considering questions of power and
hegemony. Charles-Albert Cingria's axiological model, which I briefly
summarized and which consists of considering everything done by the
West between the Renaissance and the dawn of the twentieth century
as a deplorable and forgettable interlude, drew interest from thinkers
of the western decadence, such as Spengler, and had many followers
after World War II.[53] One can sense in this work Marshall McLuhan's
main thesis. He was the prophet of a "post-Gutenberg" age that would
reestablish ties with the pre-printing press world.[54] Among medievalists,
Paul Zumthor became the torch-bearer for a similar proposition, all the

while criticizing McLuhan. The current success of Tolkien's work – not to mention Harry Potter! – tells us how much a pre-rational mentality, built on certain more or less reliable "medievalisms," fascinates our contemporaries.

I will not attempt to take sides here, even though I cannot help but admit my sympathy with Jean Frappier's attempt at conciliation; yet is it really possible to plead for a "dynamic humanism," without the fear that it would get carried away and negate itself?

I have primarily tried to summarize a line of questioning based on what is for me the only obvious thing one might say about the matter: despite the different anecdotal, often funny, and apparently inoffensive forms it often takes on, our modern, or more accurately postmodern, fascination with the Middle Ages is far from innocent and raises extremely serious questions. The very definition of our civilization is at stake, as well as our relationship to culture, and especially that which we would like to do with this culture. Surely, Jean Bodel, at the dawn of the thirteenth century, was wrong – or perhaps all too right! – when he said that the tales of the *matière de Bretagne* were "vain and pleasing."[55] All entertainment has its price, and we cannot hope to master the infatuations of an entire epoch. We can certainly put the *Iliad* and the *Chanson de Roland* on the same level, Aristophanes with Adam de la Halle, Plato with William of Ockham, Sophocles with Chrétien de Troyes, but doing so more accurately reflects the ideal library than a dialectal synthesis. If what we read always says something about what we are, maybe we will be forced to recognize that it would be less reassuring to wake up as a twelfth-century knight than as an Athenian citizen at the time of Pericles.[56] It certainly might seem wise to let one imagine oneself as one will, but is there not a contradiction in realizing at the same time that the references that allow us to identify ourselves are growing blurry and that the success of the Middle Ages resembles a societal phenomenon? There is more than one nuance between the decompartmentalization of cultures and the rejection of rationality. In any case, in fifty years we shall see what will have happened to our loves …

NOTES

1. The author would like to thank Amy Heneveld for her excellent translation of this article, which was originally written in French.

2. A development all the more remarkable since Rousseaux (1896–1960) was, before the war, close to *Action française* (a royalist political party)!

3. André Rousseaux, "C'est la faute à Voltaire ou la Querelle des mauvais Maîtres," quoted in Guy de Pourtalès, *Journal 1919–1941* (Paris: Gallimard, 1991), 425: "Et je crois que sur le point qui nous occupe, la dispute est vieille comme le monde. J'imagine fort bien qu'après la bataille de Crécy, deux bons Français comme nous se sont querellés de la même façon. Le premier disait: 'Tout cela ne serait pas arrivé, si l'on avait continué à réciter la *Chanson de Roland* au lieu de s'abandonner à l'influence amollissante et morbide de *Tristan et Yseut*.' Et le second a répondu: 'On aurait dû surtout s'aviser que la lance, le heaume et la cotte de maille étaient des armes périmées, quand les Anglais eurent inventé de donner des arcs et des flèches à leurs soldats.' Unless otherwise noted, all translations are by Amy Heneveld.

4. On the *Théophiliens*, see Helen Solterer, "Jouer les morts: Gustave Cohen et l'effet théophilien," in Christopher Lucken and Alain Corbellari, ed., *Lire Le Moyen Âge?*, Equinoxe 16 (1996): 81–96. A wide range of noted intellectuals, such as Antonin Artaud, Roland Barthes, Henri Bergson, Paul Zumthor, and Jacques Chailley, were more or less involved with this venture.

5. Jean Bodel, *La Chanson des Saisnes*, ed. Annette Brasseur, Textes littéraires français, 2 vols. (Geneva: Droz, 1989), lines 6–7.

6. For more on this topic, please see my book *Joseph Bédier écrivain et philologue* (Geneva: Droz, 1997).

7. See my article, "Le Roman arthurien dans l'entre-deux-guerres: de l'édition à l'adaptation, les chemins d'une reevaluation," in Isabelle Diu, Elisabeth Parinet, and Françoise Vielliard, ed., *Mémoires des chevaliers. Edition, diffusion et réception des romans de chevalerie du XVIIe au XXe siècle*, Etudes et rencontres 25 (Paris: Ecole des Chartes, 2007), 173–85.

8. Marc Bloch, *L'Etrange défaite* (Paris: Société des Francs-Tireurs, 1946; rpt. Paris: Albin Michel, 1957, and Paris: Gallimard, 1990).

9. Alain Chartier, *Le Quadrilogue invectif*, ed. Eugénie Droz, Classiques français du Moyen Age (Paris: Champion, 1950).

10. *Le Débat sur le "Roman de la Rose"*, Eric Hicks, ed., Bibliothèque du XVe siècle (Paris: Champion, 1977; rpt. 1996). One can find in this critical edition, as well as in the following, all necessary details on the contemporariness of this debate. Eric Hicks, "De l'histoire littéraire comme

cosmogonie: la querelle du *Roman de la Rose,*" *Critique* 348 (May 1976): 510–19; reprinted in *La troublante proximité des choses lointaines* (Geneva: Slatkine, 2004), 29–38.

11. See especially Christine de Pizan, *Epitre à la Reine Isabeau,* ed. Angus J. Kennedy, *Revue des Langues Romanes* 92 (1988): 253–64.

12. On the contemporary notion of political engagement as applied to fifteenth-century authors, see Jean-Claude Mühlethaler, "Une génération d'écrivains 'embarqués': le règne de Charles VI et la naissance de l'engagement littéraire en France," in Jean Kaempfer, Sonya Florey, and Jérôme Meizoz, ed., *Formes de l'engagement littéraire (XVe–XVIe siècles)* (Lausanne: Antipodes, 2006), 15–32.

13. Alain (Emile) Chartier said this on 22 January 1922: "de cœur ou de goût, ce qui est ici la même chose." Printed in the article "Le Philtre et l'amour," and reprinted in his *Préliminaires à l'esthétique* (Paris: Gallimard, 1939), 117–19 (119).

14. Jean Bodel, *La Chanson des Saisnes,* line 8, n. 4: "Li conte de Bretaigne si sont vain et plaisant."

15. On the troubadour style, see Henri Jacoubet, *Le Comte de Tressan et les origines du genre troubadour* (Paris: PUF, 1923). On the Romantic Middle Ages, see in particular, out of an almost too abundant bibliography, Michael Glencross, *Reconstructing Camelot: French Romantic Medievalism and the Arthurian Tradition* (Cambridge: Brewer, 1995); and Christian Amalvi, *Le Goût du Moyen Age* (Paris: Plon, 1996).

16. On Bloy, see Simone Fraisse, "Le mythe du Moyen Âge chez Bloy, Péguy et Bernanos," *La Licorne* 1–2/6 (1982): 177–93. Huysmans is something of an exception, since he was one of the precursors of the rediscovery of the Latin Middle Ages. See Jacques Dupont, "Huysmans: un imaginaire medieval," *La Licorne* 1–2/6 (1982): 337–49; and Jean-Yves Tilliette, "Les décadents, les symbolistes et le Moyen Age latin," in Laura Kendrick, Francine Mora, and Martine Reid, ed., *Le Moyen Âge au miroir du XIXe siècle (1850–1900)* (Paris: L'Harmattan, 2003), 269–87.

17. Jean-Jacques Annaud, dir., *The Name of the Rose* (1986), after the book of the same name – and just as much a cult object – by Umberto Eco (1980).

18. See, in particular, Edmond Faral, *Les Arts poétiques du XIIe et XIIIe siècle* (Paris: Champion, 1925); and his *Recherches sur les sources latines des contes et romans courtois du Moyen Age* (Paris: Champion, 1925). No one has, as yet, studied the entire corpus of Faral's work. See Ernst Robert Curtius, *La Littérature européenne et le Moyen Age latin,* trans. Jean Bréjoux (Paris: PUF [Agora], 1956). The original title was *Europäische Literatur und lateinisches Mittelalter* (Bern: Francke, 1947). The bibliography dedicated to Curtius is quite abundant: see in particular Earl Jeffrey Richards, *Modernism, Medievalism and*

Humanism: A Research Bibliography on the Reception of the Works of E. R. Curtius (Tübingen: Niemeyer, 1983); Carl Landauer, "Ernst Robert Curtius and the Topos of the Literary Critic," in Ralph Howard Bloch and Stephen G. Nichols, ed., *Medievalism and the Modernist Temper* (Baltimore, MD, and London: Johns Hopkins University Press, 1996), 334–54; William Calin, "Makers of the Middle Ages: Ernst Robert Curtius," in *Miscellanea Mediaevalie: Mélanges offerts à Philippe Ménard* (Paris: Champion, 1998), 299–309; and the following collection: *Ernst Robert Curtius et l'idée d'Europe, actes du colloque de Mulhouse et Thane, 29–31 janvier 1992* (Paris: Champion, 1995).

19. See Etienne Gilson, *La Philosophie au Moyen Age*, 2nd ed. (Paris: Payot, 1944). On Gilson, see André Droz, "Etienne Gilson, historien de la philosophie médiévale," in his *Dire le Moyen Age hier et aujourd'hui* (Amiens: Université de Picardie [PUF], 1990), 211–20.

20. See, in particular, Emile Mâle, *L'Art religieux du XIIe siècle en France* (Paris: Armand Colin, 1923); and Henri Focillon, *Art d'Occident. Le Moyen Age roman et gothique* (Paris: Colin, 1938). One must mention, however, that Mâle's first important book, *L'Art religieux en France au XIIIe siècle*, had already been published in 1898. On the connection between Mâle and Bédier, school friends who are the true tutelary figures of French medievalism between the World Wars, see my article "Emile Mâle et Joseph Bédier: de la gloire de la France à l'apologie des clercs," *Gazette des Beaux-Arts* 140 (November 1998): 235–44.

21. Charles Homer Haskins, *The Renaissance of the Twelfth Century* (Cambridge, MA: Harvard University Press, 1927).

22. One may infer the popularity of this book's reception in France by the publication of the book edited by Edouard Jauneau and Maurice de Gandillac, *Entretiens sur la Renaissance du 12e siècle* (Paris and La Haye: Mouton, 1968). On Renan, see my article "Renan médiéviste," in Alain Corbellari, ed., *Ernest Renan aujourd'hui, Études de Lettres* 3 (2005): 111–25.

23. See my book *Joseph Bédier*, 465–72.

24. We will cite only one exemplary witness: Stefan Zweig, *Le Monde d'hier* (1944), translated from the German by Jean-Paul Zimmermann (Paris: Albin Michel, 1948).

25. Paul Zumthor, *Miroirs de l'amour. Tragédie et préciosité* (Paris: Plon, 1952).

26. On Tolkien, see, among many others, Jane Chance, *Tolkien's Art: A Mythology for England*, rev. ed. (Lexington: University Press of Kentucky, 2001); and by the same author *Lord of the Rings: The Mythology of Power*, rev. ed. (Lexington: University Press of Kentucky, 2001); in French, see Charles Ridoux, *Tolkien: le chant du monde* (Amiens: Encrage; and Paris: Les Belles-Lettres, 2004).

27. See my article, "Le Merveilleux Breton (Littérature médiévale et Surréalisme)," in Francis Gingras, ed., *Une étrange constance: Les motifs merveilleux dans les littératures d'expression française du Moyen Âge à nos jours*, Collection de la République des Lettres (Québec: Presses de l'Université Laval, 2006), 219–28.

28. On the medievalists of the eighteenth century, see two classic books that are already dated: Lionel Gossman, *Medievalism and The Ideologie of the Enlightenment: The World and Work of La Curne de Sainte-Palaye* (Baltimore, MD: Johns Hopkins University Press, 1968); and Geoffrey Wilson, *A Medievalist in the Eighteenth Century: Le Grand d'Aussy and the "Fabliaux ou Contes"* (La Haye: Nijhoff, 1975).

29. On the brothers Grimm, see Walter Boehlich, "Aus dem Zeughaus der Germanistik: die Brüder Grimm und der Nationalismus," *Der Monat* 18 (1966): 56–68; and Ulrich Wyss, *Die wilde Philologie: Jakob Grimm und der Historismus* (Munich: Beck, 1979).

30. We are still waiting for a work of synthesis on the medievalists from the first half of the nineteenth century, but Charles Ridoux has already supplied some valuable information in *Évolution des études médiévales, en France de 1860 à 1914* (Paris: Champion, 2001).

31. See Ursula Bähler, *Gaston Paris et la philologie romane* (Geneva: Droz, 2004).

32. "Il ne faut pas dire: Cela est absurde, cela est magnifique; il faut dire: Cela est de l'esprit humain, donc cela a son prix." Ernest Renan, *L'Avenir de la Science*, in *Œuvres complètes*, ed. H. Psichari, 10 vols. (Paris: Calmann-Lévy, 1949), 3:877.

33. See the letter of 16 September 1845 from Gustave Flaubert to Alfred Le Poitevin, in Gustave Flaubert, *Correspondance*, ed. Jean Bruneau, Bibliothèque de la Pléiade, 6 vols. (Paris: Gallimard, 1973), 1:252: "A force de vouloir tout comprendre, tout me fait rêver. Il me semble pourtant que cet ébahissement-là n'est pas de la bêtise. Le bourgeois, par exemple, est pour moi quelque chose d'infini. Tu ne peux pas t'imaginer ce que *l'affreux* désastre de Monville (n.b.: une tornade) m'a donné. Pour qu'une chose soit intéressante, il suffit de la regarder longtemps."

34. See Ferdinand Brunetière, *Cinq lettres sur Ernest Renan* (Paris: Perrin, 1904).

35. This is not to say that Bédier questioned the traditional idea of the superiority of Antiquity and the Renaissance over the Middle Ages. While introducing the Middle Ages as the melting pot of modernity, the last sentences of Bédier's thesis on the fabliaux state this clearly: "If the Renaissance was slow in coming, if one must wait another two centuries for the illumination of the Classical and Italian geniuses, one must blame the unfortunate times, the misery of the fourteenth and fifteenth centuries, and

especially the harmful influence of Flemish tastes and the court of Burgundy. But already, at the beginning of the fourteenth century, the notion of art was born, thanks to the slow effort of the *jongleurs,* the modest rhymers, and the humble tellers of the fabliaux." (Si la Renaissance fut lente à venir, s'il nous faut attendre encore pendant deux siècles le souffle du génie antique et du génie italien, c'est au malheur des temps qu'il faut l'attribuer, aux grandes misères du XIVe et du XVe siècle, et surtout à l'influence néfaste du goût flamand et de la cour de Bourgogne. Mais déjà, au début du XIVe siècle, la notion d'art est née, grâce au lent effort de nos jongleurs, les modestes rimeurs de chansons de geste, les humbles conteurs de fabliaux.) J. Bédier, *Les Fabliaux* (Paris: Bouillon, 1895), 435.

36. Joseph Bédier, *Les Légendes épiques,* 4 vols. (Paris: Champion, 1921), 4:91: "Les vieilles pierres, dit-il, n'auraient pas d'histoire si les 'clercs' n'y prenaient peine."

37. Marie de France, prologue to the *Lais,* ed. Jean Rychner, Classiques français du Moyen Age (Paris: Champion, 1968), 1–2. "It was customary for the ancients, in the books that they wrote (Priscian testifies to this), to express themselves very obscurely so that those in later generations, who had to learn them, could provide a gloss for the text and put the finishing touches to their meaning. Men of learning were aware of this, and their experience had taught them that the more time they spent studying texts, the more subtle would be their understanding of them, and they would be better able to avoid future mistakes," as translated by R. Howard Bloch in *The Anonymous Marie de France* (Chicago and London: University of Chicago Press, 2003), 33.

38. We know this very famous saying by Bernard de Chartres (died c. 1126) only through what John of Salisbury (Ioannis Sarasberiensis), his successor, tells us: "Dicebat Bernardus Carnotensis nos esse quasi nanos gigantum umeris insidientes, ut possimus plura eis et remotiora uidere, non utique proprii uisus acumine, aut eminentia corporis, sed quia in altum subuehimur et extollimur magnitudine gigantea." *Metalogicon,* ed. J. B. Hall, Corpus Christianorum Continuatio Mediaeualis, 98 III 4 (Turnhout: Brepols, 1991), 116.

39. Chrétien de Troyes, *Cligès,* in *Œuvres complètes,* ed. Daniel Poirion with d'Anne Berthelot et al., Bibliothèque de la Pléiade (Paris: Gallimard, 1994), 174: "For, as to the Greeks and Romans, we do not say any more or less today than that their words are gone and that their once bright coals are now extinguished." In the article "Penser le Moyen Age: ou du bon usage d'une terminologie abusive" (*Etudes de Lettres* 1 [1984], 3–19, reprinted in *La troublante proximité des choses lointaines* [Geneva: Slatkine, 2004], 3–18 [5–6]), Eric Hicks gives a spiritual and enlightened reading of this passage by

replacing the Greeks and the Romans with the French and the English, the Medieval people with the Americans, and the clergy with technology.

40. Curtius, *La Littérature européenne*, 2:133.

41. See *La Querelle des Anciens et des Modernes: XVIIe–XVIIIe siècles*, preceded by Marc Fumaroli's essay "Les Abeilles et les Araignées" (Paris: Gallimard, 2001).

42. "Si prédominante soit-elle, la tradition gréco-latine ne suffit à expliquer ni la genèse ni tous les aspects des littératures médiévales. Le Moyen Age a créé beaucoup plus qu'on ne pourrait le croire après avoir lu Curtius. Il n'a pas servi seulement de trait d'union entre l'Antiquité et les littératures modernes de l'Europe. Pour ne prendre qu'un exemple illustre entre tous, l'amour courtois dans son essence, ne saurait être assimilé aux préceptes d'Ovide et [de] son *Art d'aimer*, malgré des emprunts au texte latin. Au vrai, le Moyen Age littéraire ne s'est jamais montré plus original que dans des œuvres écrites en *vulgaire*, dans les langues nationales. Curtius oublie trop le rôle fécond joué dans la formation de la littérature européenne par le lyrisme provençal, la chanson de geste et le roman français. Est-ce parti pris? Excès, durcissement dans la défense de la thèse? Avec une intime satisfaction Curtius se représente un humanisme non seulement continu, mais à peu près immobile durant des siècles." In Jean Frappier, "E. R. Curtius et la littérature européenne," *Revue de Paris* (September 1957): 148–52; reprinted in *Histoire, Mythes et symboles* (Geneva: Droz, 1976), 111–15 (114).

43. Jean Frappier, "E. R. Curtius," 115: "Il n'existe pas de culture sans tradition. Mais il arrive que les civilisations périssent par leurs mandarins."

44. Denis de Rougemont, *L'Amour et L'Occident* (Paris: Plon, 1939; def. ed., 1972).

45. Seignobos never actually wrote this sentence. He explained this in a small article in *Quotidien* 749, on 27 February 1925: "Le mot que vous m'attribuez a été mis en circulation par Gustave Téry. Il lui avait été rapporté par une dame, et dans l'intervalle, il s'était déformé – comme il arrive à tous les mots 'historiques'. J'avais dit en réalité: 'L'amour date du XIIe siècle.'" ("The quotation that you have attributed to me was popularized by Gustave Téry. It had been repeated to him by a woman, and in the meantime, it had undergone a change, as happens to all 'historical' quotations. What I really said was: 'Love dates back to the twelfth century.'") Reprinted in his *Etudes de politique et d'histoire* (Paris: PUF, 1934), 286–89 (286).

46. Jean-Paul Sartre, "Denis de Rougemont, 'L'Amour et l'Occident'," summary reprinted in *Situations* 1, Idées (Paris: Gallimard, 1947), 75–84.

47. Sartre, "Denis de Rougement," 84.

48. Le Corbusier (Charles-Edouard Jeanneret-Gris), *Quand les cathédrales étaient blanches* (Paris: Plon, 1937), 3–4: "Quand les cathédrales étaient blanches, l'Europe avait organisé les métiers à la requête impérative d'une

technique toute neuve, prodigieuse, follement téméraire et dont l'emploi conduisait à des systèmes de formes inattendues – en fait à des formes dont l'esprit dédaignait le legs de mille années de tradition, n'hésitant pas à projeter la civilisation vers une aventure inconnue. Une langue internationale régnait partout où était la race blanche, favorisant l'échange des idées et le transport de la culture. Un style international s'était répandu d'Occident en Orient et du Nord au Sud – un style qui entraînait le torrent passionné des délectations spirituelles: amour de l'art, désintéressement, joie de vivre en créant.

Les cathédrales étaient blanches parce qu'elles étaient neuves. Les villes étaient neuves; on en construisait de toutes pièces, en ordre, régulières, géométriques, d'après des plans. [...]

Le monde nouveau commençait. Blanc, limpide, joyeux, propre, net et sans retours, le monde nouveau s'ouvrait comme une fleur sur les ruines. On avait tout quitté de ce qu'étaient les usages reconnus; on avait tourné le dos. En cent années, le prodige s'accomplit et l'Europe fut changée."

49. A number of studies have already been written on Cingria's Middle Ages. See Philippe Mottet, "Les Troubadours de Charles-Albert Cingria," in *Six Essais sur la littérature romande de C.-F. Ramuz à S. C. Bille*, ed. J. Roudaut (Fribourg: Éditions Universitaires, 1989), 157–92; Pierre Marie Joris, "Dante avec Joyce: Charles-Albert Cingria ou le Moyen Âge d'un poète," in *La Trace médiévale et les écrivains d'aujourd'hui*, Michèle Gally, ed., Perspectives littéraires (Paris: PUF, 2000), 55–70, and "Le Gai savoir de Charles-Albert Cingria – une poétique de la joie," in Maryjke de Courten and Doris Jakubec, ed., *Charles Albert Cingria. Érudition et liberté, L'Univers de Cingria*, Actes du Colloque de Lausanne, Les Cahiers de la NRF (Paris: Gallimard, 2000), 95–124; and Alain Corbellari, "Cingria philologue: poésie et érudition dans les écrits sur la lyrique médiévale," in de Courten and Jakubec, ed., *Charles Albert Cingria*, 144–59. On his admiration for Stravinsky, see Maureen A. Carr, "Igor Stravinsky et Charles-Albert Cingria," in *Charles Albert Cingria*, 259–80; and Alain Corbellari, "Charles-Albert Cingria et Igor Stravinsky: à la recherche de l'essence de la musique," in *Le Paris de Richard Wagner*, followed by *Correspondances entre musiciens et entre écrivains et musiciens*, Actes du colloque international des 8, 9 et 10 décembre 2004, published by Danielle Buschinger (Amiens: Presses du 'Centre d'Études médiévales,' 2005), 101–8.

50. Charles-Albert Cingria, "Ieu oc tan," *Mesures* 3/2 (April 1937), rpt. in *Œuvres completes* (Lausanne: l'Age d'homme, 1969), 4:215–35 (224).

51. See *Charles Albert Cingria*, Les Dossiers H (Lausanne: L'Âge d'Homme, 2004), collected by A. Corbellari, with the testimonies of, among others, Jacques Réda, Guy Goffette, Pierre Bergounioux, Pierre Michon,

Gérard Macé, Jacques Chessex, Nicolas Bouvier, Philippe Jaccottet, and Jean Starobinski.

52. Antoine Compagnon, *Les Antimodernes*, Bibliothèque des idées (Paris: Gallimard, 2005). One can only regret that this book, which mentions authors as varied as De Maistre, Chateaubriand, Renan, Bloy, Péguy, Benda, Thibaudet, Gracq, and Roland Barthes, does not include a chapter on Cingria, who would have perfectly illustrated the author's argument.

53. See Oswald Spengler, *Der Untergang des Abendlandes* (Munich: Beck, 1920). This is also the period when Valéry wrote: "Nous autres civilisations, nous savons maintenant que nous sommes mortelles." ("As for us other civilizations, we now know that we are mortal.") in "La Crise de l'Esprit," an article published in 1919 in the London journal *Athenaeum* and reprinted in *Variété*, in *Œuvres*, 2 vols., Bibliothèque de la Pléiade (Paris: Gallimard, 1957), 1:988–1014. This famous saying is the first sentence of the article.

54. See Marshall McLuhan, *The Gutenberg Galaxy* (Toronto: University of Toronto Press, 1962).

55. See above, note 14.

56. In this respect, the final scene of the famous movie *Les visiteurs* (*The Visitors*) (1993) in which a man from the twentieth century (Christian Clavier) falls face down in medieval mud, has all the value of a parable, thanks to its nightmarish quality.

Gustave Doré's Illustrations for Dante's *Divine Comedy*: Innovation, Influence, and Reception[1]

Aida Audeh

Gustave Doré's (1832–83) illustrations and Dante's *Divine Comedy* have become so intimately connected that even today, nearly 150 years after their initial publication, Doré's rendering of the poet's text still accompanies, or even determines, our vision of the *Commedia*. Indeed, Doré's illustrations together with Dante's text have appeared in roughly 200 editions, with translations from the poet's original Italian available in multiple languages.[2] Doré's fame as Dante's illustrator is worldwide, and the pervasiveness of his *Commedia* imagery is undeniable. Yet there was another side to Doré. He was also a prolific painter and sculptor with ambitions for acceptance in the world of the *beaux-arts* salon – ambitions he supported with substantial profits accrued from the literary illustrations for which he is best known.

The balance Doré sought to achieve – popular success with his illustrations, on the one hand, and esteem of artists and critics involved in the *beaux arts* for his painting and sculpture, on the other hand – was precarious and, ultimately, unsuccessful for him. The role Dante plays in this balance is unique, as Doré composed both popular illustrations and salon paintings based on his reading of the *Commedia*. However, it was his illustrations of *Inferno* that truly established his renown – renown which, for the most part, excluded consideration of his abilities as a fine artist. As Doré himself remarked, "My adversary is myself. I must […] kill the illustrator [to be] spoken of only as the painter."[3] Unfortunately the relegation of Doré to the category of popular illustrator, unworthy of serious attention, has persisted and, until recently, he has been given little attention in the art historical literature.[4]

Instead, it should be noted that Doré's Dante illustrations not only enjoyed critical and commercial success, but also influenced contemporaneous and later artists who sought to illustrate or interpret the *Commedia*. The influence can be seen not only at the level of popular culture (subsequent illustrated editions, film versions, and even comic books), but also in the realm of *beaux-arts* painting and sculpture. Further, Doré's work, and his Dante imagery in particular, shared in the complex matrix of issues that was the development of modernism. With Doré's work arose questions of national identity, changes in socio-economic structures of society, and the loosening grip of academic tradition in the arts and concurrent rise of popular taste as an engine of cultural production and consumption.

At the center of all this was Doré's engagement with Dante. While Doré's choice of Dante as locus of his attempt at high and low success may seem to indicate a decision on the artist's part to embrace the medieval and reject the classical, in reality it was a most strategic choice meant to transcend these divisions, as Dante was perceived as a bridge between them in nineteenth-century France.[5] Testament to Dante's liminality is found in the wide variety of artists – of all schools and working with all media – who adopted Dante and his works as subject for pieces exhibited at the official salons of nineteenth-century France.[6] Artists who chose to work with Dante as source ranged from successful *pompier*, such as Bouguereau, to those bastions of the avant-garde, Manet and Degas.[7] Landscape artists, such as Corot, as well as specialists in the female nude, such as Cabanel, also featured Dante in salon works.[8] Sculptors, such as Canova and Rodin, also worked with diverse subjects taken from the poet.[9] And illustrated editions of the *Commedia* flourished, including those of not only Flaxman and Doré but also the sculptor Etex and Yan D'Argent.[10] Evidence of Dante's acceptance as source at all these levels is also found in the absence of debate regarding Dante's position as medieval or classical, for positive and negative commentary alike focused most often on an artist's technical skill and ability to render the poet's meaning, rather than on the choice or appropriate classification of the subject as medieval or classical.

Indeed, Ingres' renowned *Apotheosis of Homer* is visual evidence of Dante's place in the French canon, as he is included there as an undisputed *grand homme*, joining, among others, Greco-Roman ancients Virgil and Homer, Renaissance artist Raphael and founders of the academic tradition in French art Poussin and Colbert.[11] As such, the French had no trouble viewing Dante as a descendant of antiquity. However, Dante could also be symbolic of the medieval when convenient. No less a representative of nineteenth- century French culture than Victor Hugo associated the grandest monument of the French Middle Ages – Paris' cathedral of Notre Dame – with the sublime complexity of Dante's *Commedia*.[12] In sum, Dante was among the "greats" of European civilization – medieval and classical – of which the French believed themselves to be the foremost heirs, and, as such, his masterpiece, the *Commedia*, was considered canonical. Thus, Doré had every reason to believe that his choice of Dante's *Inferno* as the platform from which he would launch his attempt at popular and critical success as an illustrator/fine artist would be successful. Unfortunately, Doré's confidence in Dante's ability as a liminal figure to sustain his own attempt at liminality as an illustrator/ artist was misplaced, and Doré's attempt to garner both popular and critical success failed.

As this essay seeks to demonstrate, examination of the critical response to Doré's illustrations and paintings based on Dante's works reveals that the strength of Dante's popularity among the masses and the elite alike was not enough to overcome other, deeper issues raised by Doré and his works. These issues include: Doré's lack of academic training seen in relation to the weakening power of the traditional *Académie* and its associated political- and class-power structure; Doré's association with the proliferation of a mass consumer culture and of attendant anxieties centered on issues of socio-economic class; and Doré's association with issues of construction and maintenance of French national identity in the face of the perception of non-French influences in the artist's visual works and exhibition practices.

Background

Planned by Doré as early as 1855, the artist's Dante illustrations were the first in a series he referred to as the "*chefs-d'oeuvre de la littérature*" – all of which he intended to illustrate and produce in large in-folio editions for those ready to pay the high price he envisioned for them.[13] In addition to Dante text, Doré's list of great works was broadly inclusive. Authors whose works were selected included those stereotypically favored by the Romantics, such as Byron and Goethe, alongside those associated with (Neo)Classicists, such as Corneille and Homer.[14] Thus, in selecting the *Commedia* as the first of the series as the means to launch himself as the illustrator of the literary greats of the ancient and modern worlds, Doré sought to establish his own reputation as a comprehensive talent. To position himself within the *beaux arts*, he fundamentally relied on Dante's position as figurehead of a comprehensive selection of authors deemed canonical during the mid-nineteenth century in France.

The inclusion of Dante's *Commedia* at the top of Doré's list of great literary works awaiting illustration reflects the poet's firm position within French culture by the 1850s. By this time, Dante had achieved both critical and popular appreciation in France, and many of the characters and episodes of the *Commedia*, as well as episodes of Dante's own life, were familiar to audiences both common and elite.

Traditionally, the interest in Dante and his *Commedia* in France is assumed to be a product of the early nineteenth-century Romantic fascination with anecdotal medievalism associated with the advent of the miniature *troubadour* paintings of the 1810s such as Coupin de la Couperie's *Paolo and Francesca* (Salon of 1812, #227, Musée Napoleon, Arenenberg, Switzerland) and then the literary-based painterly sublime of the 1820s typified by Delacroix's *Barque of Dante* (Salon of 1822, #309, Musée du Louvre, Paris, France). However, recent research has shown that the interest in Dante and his *Commedia* in France actually has its origins in the eighteenth century among the students of Jacques-Louis David. These students of David – Anne-Louis Girodet-Trioson, Baron Antoine-Jean Gros, Louis Gauffier, and Fortuné Dufau – first developed interest in Dante through contact with British artists in Rome influenced by Reynolds and Fuseli, who had already tapped the *Commedia* for subject matter in the 1770s.[15] Dufau, in fact, was the artist responsible for the first Dante-based work to be exhibited at the Paris salon: *La Mort d'Ugolin* (Salon of 1800, #715, Musée de Valence, France).

The eighteenth-century interest was based more on the influence of innovations in theater and portrayal of emotion, and a burgeoning interest in subjectivity occasioned by the Enlightenment, than on a kind of precocious medievalism. It must be recalled as well that developments of the eighteenth-century "Gothick" in England came about for different reasons and took different form than the French nine-teenth-century interest in the Middle Ages. And while initial interest among David's students, as influenced by English artists, particularly Reynolds, was primarily limited to the Ugolino narrative of *Inferno* 32–33, the nineteenth century saw an expansion of awareness of the poet and his work, an expansion that resulted in numerous transla-tions (annotated and otherwise) of the *Commedia* into French, critical studies in books, in newspapers, and in specialized journals too numerous to quantify, and the appearance between the years 1800 and 1930 at the official annual salons in Paris of over 200 works of painting and sculpture based on Dante's biography, legend, or works.[16]

The interest in Dante transcended the general medieval reviv-alism in France in the nineteenth century, with references to his life and texts appearing in the works of artists and writers of all schools during this period, with the interest not limited to those of Romantic affiliation as is often assumed. Doré's choice, then, of Dante's *Inferno* as the first of his proposed series of illustrated masterpieces of litera-ture marks the extent to which Dante had entered popular and critical awareness, as Doré did not seek obscure subjects of limited appeal for his commercial productions nor to align himself with a particular group or school of artists through choice of subject or genre.

In spite of the great success earlier artists had enjoyed with Dante and his works, Doré found it difficult to secure a publisher willing to take on production of the expensive folio edition he envisioned. Doré himself financed the first book of the series, *Inferno*, which ironically turned out to be among the most successful of all his artistic produc-tions. This volume appeared in a folio edition selling at 100 francs (expensive at the time) in 1861. That same year Doré exhibited at the Salon one painting and several drawings based on his Dante illustra-tions.[17] Reassured by the success of the *Inferno* illustrations, the publisher Hachette agreed to back production of *Purgatorio* and *Paradiso*, which appeared in 1868 as a single volume.

The production value of the folio editions is very high. Doré insisted on full-page illustrations – a break from previous illustrated books of the nineteenth century that afforded only in-text vignettes – that signified a shift in perception regarding the relation of text and image. In a reversal of roles, Doré's full-page images dominate each canto, and some critics have perceived Dante's words as secondary to the illustrations. As one contemporary critic noted, unfavorably, "More than Dante illustrated by Doré, it is Doré illustrated by Dante."[18]

Doré was well aware of the importance of this shift and carefully supervised the production process.[19] He worked nearly his entire career with the same group of engravers, including Pannemaker and Pisan, who developed unique methods to successfully translate the grays and fading tones of the washes and gouaches of the artist's original designs.[20] At the same time, Doré continued producing imagery for cheap daily newspapers and comic journals, inundating the print media of his day with his signature style. After some years this glut of imagery began to work against the artist, as its value shrank in relationship to its excessive availability. But at the beginning of this venture, Doré had not yet saturated the market, and he sought a high price for his planned folio edition of the *Inferno*.

Indeed, the initial skepticism of the publishers was because of the fact that the average price for an illustrated book at that time in France was nearer to ten francs than the 100 francs Doré demanded. Yet Doré was confident that the market existed, and he transformed the illustrated book into a luxury item with this series, his finger on the pulse of the rising Second Empire bourgeoisie with money to spend and library space to fill. Doré eagerly cashed in on the aspirations of those who needed cultural clout that could be purchased readily and displayed conspicuously, his primary market being the rising upper-middle-class consumer who frequented the department stores and strolled Baron Haussmann's new, wide, tree-lined boulevards. Doré himself was well acquainted with his market, as he was ensconced in the social whirl of the Second Empire and had friendships extending to Louis-Napoleon and his court.[21]

Dante Illustrations

Doré's choice of Dante as subject was shrewd. Of Doré's literary series, few enjoyed as great a success as his *Commedia* illustrations, such that even during Doré's lifetime they were considered among his crowning achievements – a perfect match of the artist's skill and temperament and the poet's intensity. As one critic wrote in 1861 upon publication of the illustrated *Inferno*: "we are inclined to believe that the conception and the interpretation come from the same source, that Dante and Gustave Doré are communicating by occult and solemn conversations the secret of this Hell plowed by their souls, traveled, explored by them in every sense."[22]

If his attempts at painting and sculpture were not recognized as significant, his achievement as an illustrator of Dante was acknowledged nearly universally. There seems to have been no question in the minds of most contemporary critics that Doré's capacity for visual realization of Dante's detailed and evocative descriptions of infernal torments and heavenly splendors surpassed those of previous illustrators such as Sandro Botticelli, who illustrated Dante in the late fifteenth century, and John Flaxman, whose highly influential engravings of the *Commedia* were created in approximately 1793.

This was no mean feat, as Flaxman's influence on Dante imagery in the first half of the nineteenth century was substantial, exerting particular strength on the students of David and, in turn, on their protégés. Doré's illustrations constituted a serious challenge to and eventual overturning of the influence of the Englishman's cool, classical style on French imagery of Dante's text.

Indeed, after the appearance of Doré's illustrations, critics began to note in Doré's favor that Flaxman's "correct and cold" line, and imagination that lacked "suppleness," did not allow him to enter the "grandiose and strange" world of the *Commedia*, while Doré, they felt, excelled in exactly such subjects.[23] Théophile Gautier (*père*), one of Doré's strongest supporters during his lifetime, provides a good example of the tone of praise given the artist for his Dante illustrations:

> There is no better artist than M. Gustave Doré to illustrate Dante. In addition to his talent for composition and drawing, he possesses the visionary eye of a poet who uncovers the secret and singular aspect of nature. He sees things from their bizarre, fantastic, and mysterious angle. His vertiginous and playful pencil creates the insensible deviations that give to men the frightfulness of ghosts, to trees the appearance of humans, to roots the hideous twisting of serpents, to plants the disquieting bifurcations of the mandrake, [and to] clouds their ambiguous and changing forms [...]. In his chimeric architectural forms he blends Anne Radcliffe and Piranesi [...] and to all this adds a feeling alive with both reality and the humorous and fierce power of caricature, of which Goya's caprices could give only an approximate idea.[24]

The comparison to Radcliffe, Piranesi, and Goya is telling, as all excelled in the type of fantastic aesthetic championed by Gautier and his art-for-art's-sake circle, which embraced Doré and his work as simultaneously visionary and sufficiently real in its abundance of detail and atmospheric effects as to make Dante's netherworld comprehensible. This same propensity for the visionary drove Emile Zola to a sustained attack on Doré's work on the grounds that it lacked adherence to nature.[25] Zola's criticism notwithstanding, the success and widespread diffusion of Doré's Dante illustrations led to attempts by other artists to mimic the style and, they hoped, commercial success of Doré. The best example of this is Yan D'Argent, who illustrated an 1879 edition of Artaud de Montor's French translation of the *Commedia*. Examples abound of D'Argent's appropriation of Doré's signature style. D'Argent mimicked the stop-action muscularity and drama of Doré's compositions, such as that of the Demons and Barrators of *Inferno* 22 (Fig. 1). D'Argent also tried to use the subtle shading and tonal variation of Doré's rendering of the Ice Hell, and to present Dante in similarly dramatic fashion as he grabs the hair of the recalcitrant sinner Bocca in *Inferno* 32 (Fig. 2). But D'Argent's pulp paper, photogravured production, and awkward combination of in-text vignettes and full-page plates were no rival to Doré's luxury *Commedia* editions, and critics noted as much.[26]

D'Argent, like Doré, aspired to be taken seriously as a painter – and, likewise, hoped to command the respect of critics, the public, and fellow artists by taking on the literary subject of Dante's *Commedia*. This was not a successful strategy, however, as the nineteenth century tended to favor painters who experimented with popular print media only after establishing themselves within the *beaux arts*. Thus, an established artist such as Eugène Delacroix could produce illustrations for Goethe's *Faust* with great success without harming his reputation as a respected painter, while Doré, as a professional illustrator, could not hope to leap the chasm that separated high and low culture to enter the elite world of the *beaux arts*.[27] The bias against those who mass produced imagery for popular consumption worked against Doré's acceptance as a painter both during his own life and in subsequent scholarship, in spite of positive critical attention given the Dante illustrations in relation to those of Flaxman and other predecessors. However, it should be pointed out that the bias against Doré's commercial success did not hinder the success of

FIGURE 1. Yan D'Argent, *Inferno* 22, 1879 (photo: collection author).

Dante and his works as subjects within the world of the *beaux arts*, as measured by the frequency with which they appeared in works of painting and sculpture at the salons of the nineteenth century.

Dante and the Beaux Arts

Ironically, then, in the realm of nineteenth-century Fine Art, the influence of Doré's Dante illustrations was also substantial, though it went largely unacknowledged by contemporaries and, sadly, unrecognized in subsequent scholarship. Yet close examination of Doré's illustrations in reference to painted and sculpted production of the later

FIGURE 2. Yan D'Argent, *Inferno* 32, 1879 (photo: collection author).

half of the nineteenth century reveals their effect. Thus, the bias that dissuaded artists from identifying Doré's illustrations as influential upon their own work came from critical rejection of Doré himself and his attempts to be both artist and illustrator, not from issues related to Doré's choice of Dante as subject.

Doré's conceptualization of Dante as the passionate yet sometimes fearful, haughty, and even vengeful protagonist began to dominate representations of the poet after publication of the illustrations, and his influence reached even the unlikely medium of sculpture. Prior to Doré's illustrations, Dante and scenes from the *Commedia* were rarely depicted in sculpted form, and on the rare occasions when Dante himself was represented, he appeared more often than not in the form of a simple and rather expressionless portrait bust or, rarely, in the form of a medallion, as in Auguste Préault's well-known piece

FIGURE 3. Jean-Paul Aubé, *Dante*, 1880, Collège de France, Paris (photo: collection author).

(Salon of 1853, #1481, Musée d'Orsay, Paris, France). After the great success of Doré's illustrations, Dante appeared in sculpture more often and, further, began to be represented as an active participant within the events of the *Commedia*, as in Jean-Paul Aubé's *Dante* (Salon of 1880, Collège de France, Paris) (Fig. 3) or Auguste Carli's *Dante aux Enfers – Combat des Démons* (Salon of 1898, #3249, Musée des Beaux-Arts, Marseille) (Fig. 4), both of which were clearly influenced by Doré's graphic conception of the poet.

In addition to changes in the characterization of Dante himself, the choice of subjects taken from his text expanded in salon art after the publication of Doré's illustrations. Before Doré entered the scene, the dominant influences on Dante-based imagery derived from the classical model of Flaxman. Ingres' well-known versions of Paolo and Francesca's fateful kiss exemplify this cleansed version of Dante based on Flaxman's illustrations.[28] Historical genre scenes based on the

FIGURE 4. Auguste Carli, *Dante aux Enfers – Combat des Démons*, 1898, Mus. des Beaux-Arts, Marseille (photo: collection author).

biographical legend of Dante were also favored prior to Doré's illustrations, and, of course, the tightly focused Romantic paintings by Delacroix (1822) and Scheffer (1822) still loomed large in France's collective memory, spawning numerous imitations of the lovers in Hell and of Dante and Virgil crossing the Styx.

After publication of Doré's illustrations, the range of subject matter based on Dante's text expanded to include those newly illustrated or conceptualized in innovative fashion by Doré. For example, after Doré's striking illustrations of the Wood of the Suicides in *Inferno* 13, Antoine-Eugène-Ernest Buttura created one of very few paintings of the nineteenth century depicting this episode, *Dante et Messer Pier delle Vigne* (Salon of 1884, #412, current location unknown) (Fig. 5). The success of Doré's illustrations of *Purgatorio* and *Paradiso* encouraged continued exploration of these volumes of the *Commedia* on the part of salon artists such as Albert Maignan. Maignan's painting *Dante rencontre Mathilda* (Salon of 1881, #1500,

FIGURE 5. Antoine-Eugène-Ernest Buttura, *Dante et Messer Pier delle Vigne*, 1884, location unknown (photo: collection author).

Musée de Picardie, Amiens) (Fig. 6) depicts a scene within *Purgatorio* 28, but is derived visually from Doré's illustration of Dante's encounter with Leah as described in *Purgatorio* 27.

In addition to shaping the portrayal of Dante and to introducing new subjects, Doré's work influenced the compositions of many *Commedia* images submitted to the salon, particularly their epic staging of massed Michelangelesque figures in dramatically rendered landscapes.[29] This influence can be seen in sculpture as well as painting.

FIGURE 6.
Albert-Pierre-René
Maignan, *Dante
rencontre Mathilda*,
1881, Mus. de
Picardie, Amiens
(photo: collection
author).

With regard to the organization of figures as it relates to sculpture, previous versions of the Paolo and Francesca episode, such as Félicie de Fauveau's *Monument to Dante* (c. 1830–36, tabernacle destroyed, marble sculpture groups now in the Cuvillier Collection, Paris), drew from Flaxman's original illustration of the embrace on earth and from early nineteenth-century troubadour paintings by Coupin de la Couperie and Ingres. In 1822 Scheffer's painting popularized the depiction of the nude lovers in hell positioned horizontally before Dante – a format that did not carry on into sculpted depictions. With Doré's influence, however, sculpture took on the nude lovers' vertical orientation, which he favored in his illustration of the scene and in a painted version shown at the Salon of 1863, and which was an innovation that characterized their love as one of quite overt sensuality. Gautier noted Doré's innovation and wrote on it at length:

The extreme popularity of Ary Scheffer's *Paolo and Francesca* [and thus of Flaxman's version from which it was derived] would have rendered this subject difficult to treat for a spirit less fecund in resources than M. Gustave Doré. He has found a way to be new with this theme, trite and seemingly fixed in definitive form. In place of laying it out transversally, his group, detached from the plaintive swarm [of the damned] offers itself to the spectator on a perpendicular line. Paolo, his head affectionately inclined, holds in the air Francesca who turns herself with love and sadness to the chest of her lover. Her torso, of bloodless whiteness, carries on her breast the scar of the wound that interrupted the voluptuous reading of Lancelot, and her bent knee betrays the feeling of eternal suffering. A floating drapery gives wings to this couple, full of grace and voluptuousness, a soft repose for the eye amidst the horror of torments.[30]

While it was difficult for him to achieve it in sculpted form, Dominique-Jean-Baptiste Hugues emulated Doré's vertical orientation of nude lovers in sculpture in the round in 1879.[31] Likewise, Auguste Rodin could not have been unfamiliar with Doré's illustrations as he created his *Porte de l'Enfer*, and particularly his Paolo and Francesca grouping known as *Fugit Amor*, which relies on a similarly complex massing of figures that projects at a ninety-degree angle from the panel of the *Porte* to which it is attached.[32]

In painting, the primary influences can be seen in the attention to the infernal landscape that artists appropriated from Doré's illustrations, the monumentalizing scale of certain figures in relation to others or the minimization of figures within landscapes, and the use of dramatic effects of light and shade.[33]

Once again, Doré's new conceptualization of the Paolo and Francesca scene in this regard, and his interest in a dramatically rendered landscape of Hell, moved painters away from Scheffer's model. Eugène Auguste François Deully's *Dante et Virgile aux Enfers* (Salon of 1897, #531, Palais des Beaux-Arts, Lille), originally exhibited as *Françoise de Rimini (Paolo et Francesca aux Enfers)* (Fig. 7), makes use of Doré's vertically oriented lovers as well as his rocky and vertiginous landscape. The extreme differentiation of scale Doré used to great success is evident in Antoine-Auguste Thivet's *Le Huitième Cercle (Thaïs)* (Salon of 1903, #1672, current location unknown) (Fig. 8), which borrows quite directly the composition of Doré's illustration

FIGURE 7. Eugène Auguste
François Deully, *Dante et
Virgile aux Enfers*, 1897,
Palais des Beaux-Arts, Lille
(photo: cf. RMN).

of *Inferno* 31. Finally, Doré's use of dramatic lighting as seen, for
example, in his illustration of *Inferno* 9 was an obvious inspiration for
Diogène-Ulysse-Napoléon Maillart's *Dante et Virgil aux Enfers* (Salon
of 1914, #1337, current location unknown) (Fig. 9). It should be
noted that these works of the early twentieth century are testament to
the longevity of both Doré's influence on Dante imagery in France
and on the very popularity of the poet as a subject of salon works.

Doré Illustrator vs. Doré Artist

While it is clear that Doré's illustrations were indeed innovative and
clearly influenced artists of the nineteenth and even early twentieth
centuries, it must be noted that these artists were, for the most part,
loath to acknowledge their debt to Doré. Clearly, if Doré himself
could not succeed as an artist owing to his position as an illustrator,
others seeking success in the realm of the *beaux arts* could not admit

FIGURE 8. Antoine-Auguste Thivet, *Le Huitième Cercle* (Thaïs), 1903, location unknown (photo: collection author).

openly to the influence of popular culture upon their work – unless, of course, they were a member of the burgeoning avant-garde. But, then, Doré's success with the bourgeois consumer in the realm of cheap newspapers and expensive folios alike would discourage such an association as not progressive. Rather than being associated with the implied rebelliousness and political radicalism of the post-1848 lower classes, which artists such as Gustave Courbet exploited to their own advantage, Doré was perceived as catering to the tastelessly gaudy and politically conservative middle class of the Second Empire. To political progressives, such as the socialist (sometimes anarchist) theorist and Courbet apologist Pierre-Joseph Proudhon, Doré was nothing but a purveyor of "expensive curiosities [and] costly knickknacks" for the idle rich.[34] And if Manet would play with the bourgeois as subject – mixing high and low references in 1863 and 1865 with his landmarks of *modernité, Déjeuner sur l'herbe* and *Olympia* – Doré had no intention to use his association with the bourgeois to critique or subvert it. Rather he played directly to its taste for extravagance and luxury. Thus, Doré's mass appeal and participation in the low culture

FIGURE 9. Diogène-Ulysse-Napoléon Maillart, *Dante et Virgile aux Enfers;
ou Le Triomphe de l'Intelligence et de la Lumière sur les Vices et les Ténèbres,*
1914, location unknown (photo: collection author).

of illustration (whether in newspapers or in expensive folio editions of
great literature) were not of the kind that would garner him respect
among the avant-garde.

Doré's association with illustration and popular media was also
problematic for those on the other end of the spectrum – those who
sought to uphold the standards and expectations of the *Académie*, the
Ecole des beaux arts, and the salons where France's officially sanctioned
cultural production was proudly displayed. Indeed, Doré's own
attempts to gain respectability as a serious artist in the terms of
France's official art establishment were thwarted by his astounding
popular and financial success as an illustrator of books, a success that
proved to be a sort of gilded cage. His works of painting and sculpture, such as his 1861 Salon entry (#904, Musée de Brou, France)
Dante et Virgile dans le neuvième cercle des enfers (depicting Dante and
Virgil in the Ice Hell of *Inferno* 32 in which the Pilgrim and his guide
confront Ugolino gnawing on the skull of Ruggieri), were routinely

denigrated by critics who urged him to put down the brush and to stick with his wood blocks and pen.

Criticism of Doré's attempts at salon painting generally was of two types: the first attacked his choice of subject matter (not the source, but the goriness of the particular scene) as inappropriate for large-scale painting, and the second associated Doré's style with techniques of engraving, which were, therefore, inadequate or inappropriate for painting. Thus, the problem for Doré was not related to Dante's position as medieval or classical, but to the threat Doré's works posed to the traditional separation between popular and elite culture and between craft and fine art. For reviewers, what might be appropriate for the former would not be so for the latter.

E. Vinet's comments in the *Revue nationale* (1861) are typical of those that challenge Doré on the grounds of his confounding of traditions of low/high and craft/fine art by choosing a scene best left to small-format illustration:

> Here a question of esthetics presents itself. Is it permissible to lower art to the point of cannibalism? Can the painter show us Ugolino shredding with his sharp teeth the bloody skull of his enemy? What does it matter that this horrible scene is offered to us by Dante? Not everything from this great poet should be reproduced in art. Lessing, in his beautiful critical analysis titled *Laocoön*, reasons that our artists always forget to reread before going to work, demonstrated well that of fifteen to twenty scenes from Homer, there are perhaps ten that should not be reproduced in painting, because of the limits established between poetry and art by good taste, that is to say, by the most delicate part of good sense.[35]

Léon Lagrange's critique in the *Gazette des beaux-arts* (June 1861) provides an example of the challenge to Doré's style and raises the specter of the artist's lack of academic training, which left him, in the view of many critics, ill-prepared to approach large-scale painting:

> As painting, it is insufficient; one would say that the habit of drawing on wood has ruined the hand of M. Doré. The abuse of small details has weakened his execution. As much as he is daring and strong when he puts himself to cover boxwood in black and white, he finds himself timid in the presence of a great canvas.[36]

Thus, whether criticized for the gruesome nature of the scene or for his technique with its abundance of detail, Doré was facing resistance to his mixing of high and low forms of art – traditions of painting and traditions of engraving.

Often called into question at the root of Doré's distasteful attempts at mixing high and low was the artist's training, or lack thereof. For, while Doré's autodidacticism was often celebrated by supporters like Gautier, the popular success of his works could be considered a tacit threat to the *Académie*, which was already faced with challenges to its authority and supremacy in France's cultural production. Some critics, even those such as Jules Castagnary who were not particularly supportive of the *Académie* and the classical traditions for which it stood, pointedly criticized Doré's lack of training as an artist:

> Do you find any pleasure in the landscapes of M. Gustave Doré? I tell you that nature and life are equally absent there; there is only a construction of mountains, ice, and pine trees in fatiguing agglomeration. Air and light are lacking, and I perceive not one small corner where my eyes can repose. M. Gustave Doré does not content himself to be a skilled draughtsman, the king of fashionable illustrators; he wants to become a painter. Can he ever succeed? Yes, perhaps, the day when he consents to study before he produces.[37]

Doré openly admitted to using the Salon to build interest in his illustrated editions, adopting the strategy of exhibiting drawings (and paintings based on them) there before they appeared in the published work.[38] The strategy seemed to work in favor of his illustrations, but diminished his chances at *beaux-arts* respectability. Doré was criticized, even denigrated, for his fecundity as an illustrator and accused of seeking the greatest possible diffusion of his works to the detriment of his serious attention of painting. His abundance of imagination and production as an illustrator saturated visual culture of late nineteenth-century France – the success of which relegated him to the domain of the much maligned "popular" and further delegitimized his attempts to achieve critical success within the *beaux arts*.[39]

Indeed, Doré's attempts to be both illustrator and artist, self-taught and self-promoting, cast him as a central figure in the critical discourse of the 1860s and 1870s regarding the relation of popular culture to the fine arts and the role of mass production in the blurring of these sacred lines. His success touched a nerve – in this case, France's ambiguous relationship with modernization exemplified by the haphazard development of commercial culture appealing to middle and lower levels of society who previously lacked power in determination of cultural forms. Doré's rapid manner of working, churning out sometimes hundreds of drawings per day for publication in all manner of periodicals, smacked of factory production.[40] Philippe Burty's important essay on engraving and lithography at the Salon of 1861 for the *Gazette des beaux-arts* attacked the standardized production associated with Doré's work, raising as well the questionable merit of wood engraving (Doré's medium) in comparison to that of metal engraving:

> The *dessinateurs*, who no longer have the time to draw, have taken the wood that the engravers, having no time to engrave, have interpreted on their behalf. There are now known formulas to translate certain rubbings of the pencil, certain washes of Chinese ink; the *dessinateur* sketches in haste on top of the background prepared for this purpose, the engraver invents some rapid procedures, and from all this mélange is born the most deplorable confusion. [...] Wood must not, can not at all, compete with metal; it has no quality but simplicity, to display contour frankly, to express broad areas of light and dark, and to suppress half-tones. [...] This criticism will be easily proved by the Dante plates of M. Gustave Doré that fill nearly all the frames of the exhibition.[41]

Burty's diatribe raised issues of nationalism as well, comparing French engraving with that of Germany and England, and criticizing what he perceived as the state's lack of support for the tradition of metal engraving:

> The burin [engraving] is essentially a national art. [...] Still today our school of engraving protests against the coldness of the Germans and the practical facility of the English with respect to form, choice of work and discreet coloration. But at the moment where photography brings [...] the terrible achievement of reproductions at low price, we show no more respect for the masters who hold themselves to the long and painful study of the art of engraving, and we do not think to encourage them further to exhibit in public, but to offer them a side gallery [...] alongside the salons completely dedicated to exhibition of the purely industrial production of our colonies.[42]

In Burty's commentary, Germany and England are presented as
exemplars of coldness and practical skill, respectively, in contrast to
France's traditionally restrained and classically based consideration of
form, subject, and coloration. Burty's desire to assert and maintain a
French cultural national identity was not uncommon during this
period, and Doré and his work were frequently discussed, to their
detriment, in these terms. Questions in the critical response to Doré
and his works regarding what were perceived to be non-French
tendencies betray anxiety over France's national identity – long a
touchy subject, particularly in relation to its neighbors across the
Channel. This sensitivity over what constituted "French" identity was
extended to include Germany and German-speaking nations in the
1870s, after France's humiliating defeat in the Franco-Prussian War.

Nationalism

If Doré's tactics of self-promotion in France were ill-received, his
efforts outside France, particularly those in England, also rubbed
contemporaries the wrong way. As Pierre Dax wrote, sarcastically, in
L'Artiste (1866):

> It is not because M. Gustave Doré is popular that we attack the
> vogue for M. Doré. Not at all. [...] After having many times
> remarked on the incessant success of M. Doré in Paris, we must
> enlarge our statistic and include other capitals, and even the other
> [new] world. London, [...] Berlin, [...] Barcelona, [...] Holland
> [...]. In some time we will see, without a doubt, the [Edgar Allan]
> Poe and the [James Fenimore] Cooper of M. Doré.[43]

Doré's success in London's Piccadilly area, where he had established a Doré Gallery that charged a shilling to view the vast tableaux
that were so ill-received at the Paris salons, only exacerbated the negative perception of Doré's popular appeal, as France had long dispar-
aged what it perceived as England's commercialization of art.[44] As
Jules Claretie, one of Doré's sympathetic early biographers, noted:

> What upset Doré was to never have, no matter how well-loved and
> popular, this incontestable renown in his own country that he
> found outside of France, in England for example, where his name
> was more celebrated than it is with us. [...] If he were a foreigner,

English or German, this Doré, with what passion we [French] would have sung his praises.[45]

Similar criticism also touching on France's love/hate relationship with England likened Doré's paintings to panoramas, dioramas, and even circus freak shows – all considered popular, low-level forms of entertainment prevalent in England (and, even worse it would seem, in America). Claretie wrote, again sympathetic to Doré's predicament:

> Doré has been the painter and illustrator of throngs; no one is better than him at holding thousands of men, or better phantoms, in a frame. But these dioramas and panoramas have seemed the opposite of the painting we want today, the opposite of intimate art, and the dantesque visions of Doré, with his hecatombs of the damned, […] all this has seemed, to our realists of décor or scene painting, made for the theater, and in this way they deny too much their real value.[46]

Jules Breton's quite vicious characterization of Doré's Piccadilly exhibition hall is typical of the type Claretie bemoans on behalf of his friend. Breton, discussing Doré's exhibitionistic behavior at parties and social occasions, added, "*Et puis, il les* [his paintings] *roulait, les envoyait en Angleterre, en Amérique, où des barnums les montraient à coups de grosse caisse, attirant la foule.*" ("And then, he rolls them up and sends them to England and America, where the 'barnums' show them, accompanied by drum rolls, attracting the crowd.")[47] For English critic Philip Gilbert Hamerton, Doré's rejection by the French beaux-arts establishment owing to his popularity with "*la foule*" evoked distinctions based on social class as well:

> And the very popularity of Doré is in itself to be noted against his chances of recognition by the highest class. True critics have such a well-grounded distrust of the popular judgment in art that if the people applaud heartily they at once conclude that the work must have some glaring abomination in it that has fascinated the vulgar world.[48]

Ernest Duvergier de Haurenne went on at length in his critique of the Salon of 1874 for the *Revue des Deux Mondes* against Doré in terms evocative not only of national difference but of the specter of modernization:

A deplorable facility put in service of an imagination that is coldly delirious, with no conscience, no respect for nature, no care for logic, no other preoccupation but that of effect. When viewing certain paintings of M. Doré, one thinks of certain theater stage sets lit by electric light. [...] These fairylands of the Porte-Saint-Martin hardly have success in France anymore, but it seems they are still popular in England.[49]

It is interesting to recall that the first French artists to show interest in Dante, the students of David, engaged with the subject of Ugolino through the interest in theater brought to their attention by English artists such as Reynolds and Fuseli. The connection between Dante, the theatrical, and the English came full circle with Doré's success as artist and illustrator on the British Isles but, ironically, worked against his achieving success in France.[50]

France's anxiety towards non-French influence within the arts, and its traditional hostility towards the arts of the northern countries, particularly Germany and German-speaking lands, also surfaced in contemporary criticism of Doré – not only in terms of Doré's popular success as an engraver, but also in relation to the influence on Doré's works of German landscape painting. Like the rivalry with England, French suspicion of Germanic forms of art and culture meant that Doré's use of German traditions of engraving and landscape to reformulate the canonical Dante smacked of anti-Gallic sentiment – particularly in the tumultuous and disastrous years of the Franco-Prussian War – an event that profoundly affected Doré.[51]

Doré's infernal landscapes were often singled out as remarkable, positively and negatively, by critics, but were not always identified overtly with Germanic traditions. Gautier's remarks are typical of those who praised them in these general terms:

What hits you at first glance of these dantesque illustrations of Gustave Doré is the atmosphere in which these scenes take place [...] and which have no relationship to our terrestrial world. The artist has invented the atmosphere of hell, the subterranean mountains, the lower landscapes, the gloomy atmosphere where sun has never shined and that is lit by the reverberations of the central fire. [...] The first plates that make the transition from reality to dream, from this world here to the other, are still somewhat earthly; little by little they darken and take on the character of a vision that cannot be escaped until Dante's return to the surface of the earth.[52]

However, the same visionary qualities of landscape and atmosphere were the subject of Zola's criticism, not unexpectedly, in complaining, "*ces paysages et ces cieux n'existent pas*" ("these landscapes and these skies do not exist").[53] Clearly, Doré's landscapes were polarizing to critics, and decidedly different from the norm. Hamerton, writing in 1864, put his finger on the quality noted by both Gautier and Zola and identified it as decidedly not French:

> Gustave Doré possesses beyond all other Frenchmen the sense of sublimity in landscape. And although Gustave Doré has not that knowledge of nature which would be necessary to entitle him to rank with the real masters of landscape, he possesses the landscape instinct in a more intense degree than any Frenchman who ever touched canvas [...]. He is capable of feeling interest in natural scenery for itself and in itself, without any help of human interest.[54]

Hamerton's reference to the "sublime" and to landscape "for itself" as non-French certainly imply adherence to northern traditions generally, and German Romantic traditions of the sublime specifically.

Doré's own Alsatian roots qualified him as "northern," and nearly German, in the eyes of many Frenchmen. Doré's evocative landscapes were associated in criticism with "*la rêveuse mélancolie du Nord*" ("the dreamy melancholy of the North").[55] Biographers, both early and recent, make much of Doré's Strasbourg origins and the supposedly German origins of his family line, even asserting that the family name had once been the Teutonic "*Dorer*."[56] Indeed, during his lifetime the artist was often referred to as "the most German of Frenchmen"[57] and was never allowed to forget his Alsatian – and, therefore somewhat dubious and provincial – roots. As the Goncourt brothers put it in one of their quite frequently cruel remarks about Doré: "An Alsatian, even one with talent, is always an inferior Frenchman or German [at best]."[58]

The connection to German traditions of landscape and even of illustration is not actually far-fetched and deserves attention. Doré's works were likely influenced by youthful exposure to the works of Josef Anton Koch (also an ardent admirer and illustrator of Dante) and Carl Wilhelm Kolbe, and he was most certainly familiar with great northern artists like Rembrandt, Altdorfer, and Dürer. It was well known, even during Doré's lifetime, that he had little interest in Italian art (with the exception of his emulation of Michelangelo) and no interest in the classicist emphasis on academic study of the nude and of antique sculpture. Doré's lack of interest in the classical tradition embraced by France's *beaux-arts* establishment implies that his interests lay elsewhere, opening the door to consideration of northern or Germanic tendencies apparent in his art, and obviously implying an interest in the medieval. However, Doré's choice of influences was far from systematic. He drew from classical and medieval sources as it suited him, resulting in an idiosyncratic style noted by critics.

Specifically, Doré's Germanic tendencies, usually associated with the visionary yet highly detailed nature of his work and often identified as sublime, were noted by hostile and supportive critics alike. Meaning to compliment Doré, Gautier likened him to Dürer by way of France's favorite poet: "*G. Doré est à la fois réaliste et chimérique. [...] Il voit avec cet oeil visionnaire dont parle Victor Hugo en s'adressant au vieil Albert Dürer*" ("G. Doré is simultaneously realistic and chimeric. [...] He sees with the same kind of visionary eye Victor Hugo spoke of in regard to old Albrecht Dürer").[59] While Gautier intended to praise his friend, he trod on thin ice with this comparison in that Dürer took on the role of national hero for German-speaking areas in the nineteenth century.

Specifically, references to Dürer in nineteenth-century criticism necessarily implicated those traits associated with him and with northern art generally, traits that were highly controversial in France at the time: the development of a middle-class market for the arts and the erosion of the power of the elite in matters pertaining to culture; the development of Protestantism and the rejection of Catholicism; and the dominance of landscape in association with religion as seen in conjunction with a return to the primitive, tribal, egalitarian, evangelical, and community values associated with Protestantism in the north.[60] Further, reference to Dürer implied challenge to the classical tradition and its insistence on universal values. Asserted in its place was the northern privileging of subjectivity and the unity of the arts whereby painting and printmaking are considered equally valid forms of artistic expression.

Thus, comparison of Doré and Dürer, even if in relatively

positive terms such as Gautier intended, was a double-edged sword for the French artist, as it implied, in toto, serious challenges to the very French art establishment that Doré sought to enter. Doré's art, when confined to graphic book illustration, was for critics reminiscent of Dürer as taking part in and even surpassing the great northern traditions of engraving and etching. But it was in this domain that the northern style properly belonged. As was often remarked at the time, Doré's Germanic-tinged creations became objectionable when they were enlarged to the scale of history painting, for they thereby became subject to the expectations of academic classicism.

However, these critical associations of Doré with Germanic tendencies focus more overtly on questions of national identity than on issues of the medieval versus the classical. For, while rejecting Germanic-tinged traditions, the French embraced what was felt to be their own medieval past to a great extent in the nineteenth century. Thus, in stated criticism of Doré's landscapes, the issue was not presented as the perceived medievalism of the northern artists who influenced Doré's landscapes, but the Germanic (i.e., non-French) nature of these influences regardless of the time period with which these artists were associated.

Ultimately, Doré's ambitions, like his paintings, were too large for his time. Today, perhaps, he would get a different reaction to his attempt to garner both commercial and critical success through his Dante illustrations and paintings. A similar attempt to gain respect as a serious artist able to take on a canonical literary source prompted modern artist Robert Rauschenberg to undertake a new illustrated edition of the *Inferno* in 1959. Rauschenberg's story provides an interesting counterpoint to Doré's and marks the extent to which the latter's chance at success as a fine artist was limited by his time and place.[61]

Exhibited in 1960 and acquired by the Museum of Modern Art in New York in 1963, Rauschenberg's Dante images were reportedly inspired by Doré's illustrations and aimed to modernize Dante. To this end, Rauschenberg used the popular media of his day – magazine advertisements and newspaper images, among other types of recognizable imagery – to represent the characters and landscape of Hell (for example, a male figure taken from a *Sports Illustrated* advertisement for golf clubs provides the image of Dante, and photos of Adlai Stevenson stand in for Virgil).[62] At that time Rauschenberg was known primarily as a painter, and, fortunately, New York of the 1960s was more tolerant of artists working in multiple media and genres than was Paris in the 1860s. In fact, Rauschenberg's Dante images have been treated by some critics as among his best works and have been given equal status with works of painting and sculpture in recent retrospectives.[63]

Given the ideological landscape of nineteenth-century France regarding the arts, Doré could not win. His autodidacticism went against mainstream academic tradition, yet his desire for commercial success and bourgeois acceptability denied him any place with self-styled artists of the avant-garde like Courbet. His relations with English patrons and the English public brought him great financial and even critical success on the island, but further diminished his respectability in his home country. Germanic tendencies in his art made his work unique and influenced later illustrations, paintings, sculptures, and even cinematic interpretations of the *Commedia*, but his popular success worked against critical and scholarly acknowledgement of the importance of his work in establishing visual prototypes that would have lasting significance. In the final analysis, then, it was exactly the success and importance of Doré's illustrations for Dante's *Divine Comedy* that prevented him from obtaining the recognition as a fine artist he so desperately wanted and sought to achieve through paintings based on the same source – a *châtiment* certainly worthy of Dante's own infernal construction.

NOTES

1. The author presented preliminary versions of this essay within a panel devoted to Doré that was sponsored by the Dahesh Museum and Wadsworth Atheneum Museum at the 95th Annual Conference of the College Art Association, New York, 2007 and within a panel devoted to the reception of Dante and his work sponsored by the Dante Society of America at the 42nd International Congress on Medieval Studies, Western Michigan University, Kalamazoo, 2007.

2. Dan Malan, *Gustave Doré: A Biography* (St. Louis, MO: MCE Publishing, 1996), 53–55.

3. Letter of Hippolyte Taine to Blanchard Jerrold dated 1883, translated into English and published in Blanchard Jerrold, *Life of Gustave Doré* (London: W. H. Allen, 1891), 102.

4. Recent publications on Doré include: Eric Zafran, ed., *Fantasy and Faith: The Art of Gustave Doré* (New York: Dahesh Museum of Art, and New Haven, CT and London: Yale University Press, 2007); and Philippe Kaenel, *Le métier d'illustrateur, Rodolphe Töpfer, J. J. Grandville, Gustave Doré* (Geneva: Librairie Droz, 2004). Kaenel's text is distinguished by providing the most thorough analysis to date of the vast critical response to Doré and his work published during the artist's lifetime. In analyzing the critical response, Kaenel identifies several tendencies or recurring themes that necessarily arise in the present essay as well. In some cases, the present essay makes use of publications of the nineteenth century also treated by Kaenel. Such instances are noted in the citations that follow.

5. For discussion of Dante's reception in nineteenth-century France, see Michael Caesar, ed., *Dante: The Critical Heritage* (London: Routledge, 2006). See also Werner P. Friedrich, *Dante's Fame Abroad* (Chapel Hill: University of North Carolina Press, 1950); Michael Pitwood, *Dante and the French Romantics* (Geneva: Droz, 1985); and Albert Counson, *Dante en France* (Paris: Fontemoing, 1906).

6. The author's dissertation discusses in detail the extent of the interest in Dante in French art of the nineteenth century based on research undertaken in archives and museums throughout the country. In all, the author found that over 200 works of art based on Dante as subject appeared in French salons between 1800 and 1930. The vast majority of these salon works were unknown prior to the author's discovery of them. The location of many of them is not known; evidence of their existence consists of records in salon *livrets* spanning 130 years, critical response to their exhibition and, in some cases, photographs or other reproductions that appeared in periodicals of the day. Given the vast quantity of works based on Dante that

appeared at the salons throughout the nineteenth century, it is not sustainable to claim that the interest in the poet is solely the result of a medieval revival. The assumption that the interest in Dante in France in the nineteenth century was limited to the Romantic movement and its interest in the Middle Ages is based on familiarity with a few well-known works by major artists such as Ingres, Delacroix, Carpeaux, and Rodin that the author has found represent only a small portion of the works that were actually produced and exhibited steadily in nineteenth-century France. See Aida Audeh, "Rodin's 'Gates of Hell' and Dante's 'Divine Comedy': An Iconographic Study" (Ph.D. dissertation, University of Iowa, 2002).

7. William-Adolphe Bouguereau exhibited his painting *L'Enfer du Dante (chant XXXe)* at the Salon of 1850 (#337). The subject of Bouguereau's work was the episode of Gianni Schicci. The current location of the painting is not known. Edgar Degas created two known works based on Dante: a painting titled *Dante and Virgil* (1858), location unknown, and an undated drawing depicting Beatrice and now in the Louvre. Edouard Manet created a small painting, undated, after Delacroix's *Barque of Dante* and now in the collection of the Musée des Beaux-Arts, Lyon.

8. Jean-Baptiste-Camille Corot exhibited his painting *Dante et Virgile; paysage* at the Salon of 1859 (#688). The painting is currently in the collection of the Museum of Fine Arts in Boston. Alexandre Cabanel exhibited his *La Mort de Francesca de Rimini et de Paolo Malatesta* at the Salon of 1870 (#437). This work is in the collection of the Musée d'Orsay in Paris. Cabanel created at least two other large-scale paintings based on Dante as source: *Poète florentin* (Salon of 1861, #496, collection unknown) and *Pia de Tolomei* (1876, collection unknown).

9. Antonio Canova created a marble sculpture titled *Madame Recamier en Béatrice* (undated, Musée des Beaux-Arts, Lyon). Antoine Etex exhibited his bas-relief marble sculpture titled *Françoise de Rimini et Paolo Malatesta* at the Exposition Universelle of 1855 (#4365). The location of this work is unknown. Auguste Rodin began his work on his monumental bronze sculpture depicting Dante's *Commedia* entitled *La Porte de l'Enfer* (more popularly known as the *Gates of Hell*) in 1880. The work was not finished during Rodin's lifetime and was cast in bronze posthumously. Numerous works derived from the piece were exhibited independently during Rodin's lifetime.

10. Flaxman's illustrations came out in numerous editions in the nineteenth century, though they were originally created in approximately 1793 during the artist's residence in Rome. Antoine Etex's Dante illustrations accompanied an edition of the *Commedia* with translation into French by Sébastien Rhéal published by J. Bry Aîné in Paris in 1854. Yan D'Argent's illustrations accompanied a translation into French by Artaud de Montor published by Garnier Frères in 1879.

11. Jean-Auguste-Dominique Ingres' *Apotheosis of Homer* was exhibited at the Salon of 1827 and again at the Salon of 1834.

12. Hugo's interest in Dante was extensive. References to Dante appear in many of the author's works. For discussion of the breadth of Hugo's interest in Dante, see Pitwood, *Dante and the French Romantics*, 175–208.

13. For discussion of Doré's plans for the "masterpieces of literature" illustrated editions, see primarily Blanche Roosevelt, *Life and Reminiscences of Gustave Doré* (New York: Cassell, 1885), 207–11. See also Nigel Gosling, *Gustave Doré* (New York: Praeger, 1973), 21–23; and Kaenel, *Le métier d'illustrateur*, 364–65.

14. While it could be said that Doré gravitated to subjects perhaps considered "medieval," it was not his practice to take positions on ideological matters pertaining to art, such as art's use in society, proper subject matter, or the relative moral or esthetic value of medieval works versus classical works, etc. Rather, the eclecticism evident in his choice of subjects suggests that Doré was primarily driven by the prospect of commercial and critical success. Materially, Doré had no difficulty combining seemingly disparate influences in his works, something for which he was roundly criticized. The eclecticism of Doré's approach, in terms of both subject matter and style of execution, does not support the suggestion that the artist rejected or embraced any particular form of art or type of subject matter.

15. See Aida Audeh, "Dante's Ugolino in 18th-century France: Reynolds, Fuseli, and Flaxman and the Students of J-L David," in Christopher Hart, ed., *Heroines and Heroes: Symbolism, Embodiment, Narratives and Identity*. Volume 1: The English (2nd ed. Kingswinford: Midrash Publishing, 2009), 38–60. See also Aida Audeh, "Englishness, Ambiguity, and Dante's Ugolino in 18th-century France," *Identity, Self & Symbolism* 1/2 (November 2006): 95–115. As explored in these publications, the author demonstrates that the interest in Dante in art in France and England was an eighteenth-century development and began largely with Joshua Reynolds whose painting depicting Dante's Ugolino (c. 1770–73) influenced subsequent artists in that century. Reynolds' interest in the Ugolino episode was not the product of an interest in medievalism generally on the part of the artist. The students of J.-L. David were the first French artists to show interest in Dante. This interest and these artists' experimentation with subject matter based on Dante occurred in Rome in the eighteenth century owing to contact with English artists there. The stimulus for this eighteenth-century interest involved the influence of theater innovations that in turn influenced the school of J.-L. David: the emotive acting style of David Garrick in performances of Shakespeare in England and France, the theories of Diderot and the *philosophes* concerning *tragédie*, and performances of Shakespeare's *Romeo and Juliet* in France based on the translations of

Jean-François Ducis wherein the character of Dante's Ugolino was grafted into that of Montaigu, *père*. The *troubadour* paintings of the 1810s of Coupin de la Couperie and Ingres depicting the earthly embrace of Paolo and Francesca were the result of different interests and were more closely related to the type of medieval revivalism in France discussed by Lionel Gossman (i.e., a superficial and anecdotal type of medievalism associated with the aspirations of the Empire and then Restoration governments, tied up with ideas of French monarchy and history).

16. See the following publications exploring manifestations of the interest in Dante in the arts of nineteenth-century France: Aida Audeh, "Rodin's Gates of Hell: Sculptural Illustration of Dante's *Divine Comedy*," *Rodin: A Magnificent Obsession* (London: Merrell Holberton Publishers, 2006; orig. 2001), 93–126; idem, "Review of Graham Smith's *The Stone of Dante and Later Florentine Celebrations of the Poet* (Olschki, 2000)," *Annali d'Italianistica* 21 (2003): 526–28; idem, "Images of Dante's Exile in 19th-century France," *Annali d'Italianistica* 20 (2002): 235–58; idem, "Rodin's Three Shades and their Origin in Medieval Illustrations of Dante's *Inferno* XV and XVI," *Dante Studies* 117 (Fall 1999): 133–69; idem, "Rodin's Gates of Hell and Aubé's Monument to Dante: Romantic Tribute to the Image of the Poet in 19th-century France," *The Journal of the Iris and B. Gerald Cantor Center for Visual Arts at Stanford University* (continuation of *The Stanford University Museum of Art Journal*) 1 (1998–99): 33–46.

17. Doré exhibited the following works related to his Dante illustrations at the Salon of 1861: *Dante et Virgile dans le neuvième cercle des enfers, visitant les traîtres condamnés au supplice de la glace, y rencontrent le comte Ugolin et l'archevêque Ruggieri* (painting, #904); *Dante et virgile, traversant le Styx, rencontrent l'ombre de Philippe Argenti* (drawing, #906); *Virgile et Dante aux enfers, devant la tombe ardente du Florentin Farinata* (drawing, #907); and *Paolo et Francesca de Rimini aux enfers* (drawing, #908). Doré also exhibited *Françoise de Rimini et Paolo (aux enfers)* at the Salon of 1863 (painting, #598) and *Dante et Virgile visitent la septiéme enceinte* at the Salon of 1875 (painting, #688).

18. Lorédan-Lachey, "Paru pour le Jour de l'An," *Le Bibliofile français* (December 1869): 202 (quoted in Kaenel, *Le métier d'illustrateur*, 253): "Il est vrai que l'éditeur peut bien me répondre qu'il n'a pas voulu fair un livre, mais une sorte d'album colossal. Et il aura raison, car le poème n'est ici qu'un prétexte trop evident. L'auteur est écrasé par le dessinateur. Plus que Dante illustré par Doré, c'est Doré illustré par Dante."

19. William Cole maintains that Doré's supervision of the production included "when to interrupt the text and confront the reader with a picture," using the artist's treatment of Caiaphas and the Hypocrites of *Inferno* 23 as an example. According to Cole, Doré teases the reader/viewer with a

cliffhanger as he/she turns the page to the image of the crucified Caiaphas. See William Cole, "Literal Art? A New Look at Doré's Illustrations for Dante's *Inferno*," *Word & Image* 10/2 (April–June 1994): 95–106.

20. For detailed discussion of the techniques used by Doré and his engravers, see Claude Bouret, "Doré, ses gravures et ses graveurs," in *Gustave Doré, 1832–1882* (Strasbourg: Musée d'Art Moderne, Cabinet des Estampes, 1983), 207–13.

21. See Samuel Clapp, "Voyage au pays des myths," in *Gustave Doré, 1832–1883*, 25–42. See also Gosling, *Gustave Doré*, 18–21.

22. L. C., "Le Dante illustré par Gustave Doré," *Revue fantaisiste* (1861): 128.

23. Emile Montégut, "Un interprétation pittoresque de Dante," *Revue des deux mondes* 15/11 (1861): 443–45. Montégut wrote, in part: "Mieux encore, on n'a qu'à restreindre le champ de la comparaison, et à mettre les dessins de M. Gustave Doré en présence de ceux d'un grand artiste, Flaxman, qui lui aussi a fait des illustrations de Dante. Je sais bien que la série de dessins que Flaxman a consacrés à l'*Enfer* de Dante est inférieure à ses autres oeuvres; mais cette série est inférieure précisément parce que son imagination manque de souplesse, et que dans ce sujet, à la fois grandiose et étrange, elle s'est trouvée dépaysée. Flaxman n'est à son aise que dans les sujets grecs, et ne comprend bien que certains caractères du génie et de l'art grecs. Sur ce terrain, il peut défier tout le monde, et quelques-uns des dessins de son Homère et surtout de son Hésiode, l'oeuvre la plus charmante, à mon avis, qui soit sortie de son crayon élégant, correct et froid, méritent toute admiration. [...] Je ne veux pas dire – notez-le bien – que Flaxman soit un artiste inférieur à M. Gustave Doré; je dis seulement que son imagination ne possède pas la souplesse de l'intelligente imagination du notre artiste français, et que par conséquent il a beaucoup moins bien compris le caractère italien de l'oeuvre de Dante, qu'il est entré moins profondément dans l'esprit du poète."

24. Théophile Gautier, "L'Enfer de Dante Alighieri avec les dessins de Gustave Doré," *Le Moniteur Universel* (30 July 1861): "Nul artiste mieux que M. Gustave Doré ne pouvait illustrer le Dante. Outre son talent de composition et de dessin, il possède cet oeil visionnaire dont parle le poëte qui sait dégager le côté secret et singulier de la nature. Il voit les choses par leur angle bizarre, fantastique et mystérieux. Son crayon vertigineux crée en se jouant ces deviations insensibles qui donnent à l'homme l'effroi du spectre, à l'arbre l'apparence humaine, aux racines le torillement hideux des serpents, aux plantes les bifurcations inquiétantes de la mandragore, aux nuages ces formes ambiguës et changeantes [...]. Dans ses architectures chimériques, il mêle Anne Ratcliff [sic] et Piranèse [...] a tout cela ajoutez une sentiment très-vif de la réalité et une puissance de caricature

humouristique et farouche, dont les caprices de Goya peuvent seuls donner une idée approximative."

25. Zola had been favorable to Doré, initially. However, as the author became involved with Cézanne and the Impressionist circle gathering at the Café Guerbois and developed his theories regarding Naturalism, he found fault with what he saw as Doré's lack of fidelity to reality. Cézanne, apologist for experimentation in formal aspects of painting, also found Doré's work much too literary and lumped it with sterile academic painting. For discussion of Zola's art criticism in relation to Doré, see Lillian R. Furst, "Zola's Art Criticism," in *French 19th Century Painting and Literature* (Manchester: Manchester University Press, 1972); and Antoinette Erhard, "Emile Zola et Gustave Doré," *Gazette des beaux-arts* (March 1972): 185–92.

26. For relatively positive reviews, see *L'Illustration* (14 December 1878): 371, and (21 December 1878): 399. For a critical assessment of Yan D'Argent's Dante illustrations, see Irène de Vasconcellos, *L'Inspiration dantesque dans l'art romantique français* (Paris: Picart, 1925), 149–50.

27. For discussion of this phenomenon, see William Cole, "The Book & the Artist: Rethinking the Traditional Order," *Word & Image* 8 (1992): 378–82; Philip Hofer, *The Artist and the Book 1860–1960 in Western Europe and the United States* (Boston: Museum of Fine Arts, 1961); Gordon N. Ray, *The Art of the French Illustrated Book, 1700–1914* (New York: Pierpont Morgan Library and Cornell University Press, 1986); and Ulrich Finke, "French Painters as Book Illustrators – from Delacroix to Bonnard," in *French 19th Century Painting and Literature*, 339–62.

28. Ingres created several versions, all based on Coupin de la Couperie's salon *troubadour* painting of 1812 and Flaxman's illustration of the scene. Ingres' versions, each only slightly different from the other, are the following: 1814 (Musée Chantilly), 1819 (Musée des Beaux Arts, Angers), 1845 (Musée Bonnat de Bayonne), and undated (Barber Institute of Fine Arts, University of Birmingham, England).

29. Gautier was evidently among the first to compare Doré and Michelangelo. See Théophile Gautier, *Abécédaire du Salon de 1861* (Paris: Dentu, 1861), 132–33; and "L'*Enfer* de Dante Alighieri," *Le Moniteur Universel* (30 July 1861). Gautier's favorable comparison of the two artists was not consistently upheld in contemporary criticism, however. Critics such as Théodore de Banville ("Salon de 1861," *Revue fantaisiste* [1 June 1861]: 74–79) and Zola ("Une exposition de tableaux à Paris," *Le Messager de l'Europe* [June 1875]) considered Doré's use of Michelangelo to be nearly caricature, employed in calculating fashion in order to get the attention of the public.

30. Théophile Gautier, "L'*Enfer* de Dante Alighieri," *Le Moniteur Universel* (30 July 1861): "L'extrême popularité de la *Francesca* et du *Paolo*

d'Ary Scheffer aurait rendu ce sujet difficile à traiter pour un esprit moins fécond en ressources que celui de M. Gustave Doré. Il a trouvé moyen d'être neuf sur ce thème rebattu et qui semblait fixé dans une forme définitive. Au lieu de filer transversalement, son groupe détaché du plaintif essaim s'offre au spectateur sur une ligne perpendiculaire. Paolo, la tête affectuesement penchée, soutient en l'air Francesca qui se renverse avec amour et douleur sur le sein de son ami. Son torse, d'une blancheur exsangue, porte à la poitrine la cicatrice toujours vive de la blessure qui interrompit la voluptueuse lecture de *Lancelot du Lac*, et son genou replié accuse un sentiment d'éternelle souffrance. Une draperie volante prête ses ailes à ce couple plein de grâce et de volupté, doux repos pour l'oeil au milieu de l'horreur des supplices."

31. Dominique-Jean-Baptiste Hugues' large plaster group *Ombres de Françoise de Rimini et de Paolo Malatesta* was exhibited at the Salon of 1879 (#5105) and was originally intended for the Villa Medici in Rome. The current location of this work is not known. A small plaster sketch for this work is in the collection of the Musée d'Orsay, Paris.

32. Interestingly, when exhibited as a separate piece, Rodin's *Fugit Amor* is displayed attached to its roughly sculpted base in horizontal position, similar to Flaxman's portrayal of the couple.

33. Emile Montégut noted this as a defect of Doré's work: "[…] il n'y a pas de proportion entre le paysage et les personnage […] un défaut trop habituel à M. Doré […]" ("Une Interprétation Pittoresque de Dante," *Revue des Deux Mondes* 15/11 [1861]: 449).

34. Pierre-Joseph Proudhon, letter to Hetzel, c. 1861 (quoted in Kaenel, *Le métier d'illustrateur*, 248): "Si c'est à moi, je vous ferai remarquer que je suis peu amateur de curiosités chères, de bibelots coûteux, et que ma bibliothèque pouilleuse, dépareillée, décousue, n'a pas de place où je puisse mettre votre in-folio [Doré's *Perrault* of 1861, sent to Proudhon by Hetzel as a gift]." Philippe Burty also criticized the fashion for expensive folio editions on the occasion of publication of Doré's illustrated Bible of 1866 in terms of the increasing industrialization of the production process: "ce formidable établissement qui possède à lui une papeterie, des ateliers de stéréotype et de reliure, des presses pour la taille-douce, des cours de dessin et de gravure sur bois, et dont la librarie peut livrer en moyenne cinq millions de volumes par an." ("La Sainte Bible éditée par la Maison Mame de Tours," *Gazette des Beaux-Arts* [March 1866]: 273.)

35. E. Vinet, *Revue nationale* (1861): "Ici une question d'esthétique se présente. Est-il permis d'abaisser l'art jusqu'à l'anthropophagie? Le peintre pouvait-il nous montrer Ugolin déchirant de ses dents aiguës le crâne ensanglanté de son ennemi? Que cette horrible scène nous soit offerte par le Dante, qu'importe? Tout dans ce grand poëte ne saurait être reproduit par

l'art. Lessing, dans cette belle analyse critique intitulée le *Laocoön*, analyse que nos artistes oublient toujours de relire avant de se mettre à l'oeuvre, a fort bien démontré que sur quinze à vingt tableaux d'Homère, il n'en est peut-être pas dix que la peinture puisse reproduire, à raison des limites établit entre la poésie et l'art par le bon goût, c'est-à-dire par la partie la plus délicate du bon sens."

36. Léon Lagrange, "Salon de 1861," *Gazette des beaux-arts* (June 1861): 267: "Comme peinture, il existe trop peu; on dirait que l'habitude de dessiner sur bois a gâté la main de M. Doré. L'abus de petits moyens a appauvri son execution. Autant on le voit hardi et fort quand il s'agit de couvrir de blanc et de noir un carré de buis [boxwood], autant il s'est trouvé timide en présence d'une grande toile."

37. Jules Castagnary, "Salons 1869," in *Salons (1857–1870)* (Paris: Charpentier, 1892), 373 (originally published in *Siècle* as a *feuilleton*): "Trouvez-vous quelque plaisir aux paysages de M. Gustave Doré? Je vous avertis que la nature en est absente et la vie également: il y a là toute une maçonnerie de montagnes, de glacier, de sapins, dont l'agglomération fatigue. L'air et la lumière manquent et je n'aperçois pas un seul petit coin juste où reposer mes yeux. M. Gustave Doré ne se contente pas d'être un crayonneur habile, le roi des illustrateurs à la mode, il voudrait devenir peintre. Le pourra-t-il jamais? Oui, peut-être, le jour où il consentira à étudier avant de produire."

38. Kaenel, *Le métier d'illustrateur*, 248–49, citing Doré's letter to editor Alfred Mame who had reproached the artist for exhibiting his drawings for the Bible before the published edition appeared. Doré countered by citing his exhibition of Dante drawings that resulted in the rapid production and diffusion of the published work.

39. E. Saglio, "Les Dessins de l'Enfer du Dante par M. Gustave Doré," *Gazette des beaux-arts* (October 1861): 362–63. Saglio wrote, in part: "Tout le monde aujourd'hui connaît l'artiste, ou croit le connaître. Il serait difficile, en effet/qu'on ne le connût pas quelque peu. [...] C'est avec cette naturelle abondance que M. Gustave Doré fait ses dessins. Il a semé, comme l'arbre en fleur, à tous les vents [...] M. Gustave Doré est donc populaire, et je pense qu'un de ses voeux les plus chers est ainsi satisfait. Il a souhaité ardemment la popularité, et, comme si, avec beaucoup de talent, ce n'était pas assez pour y atteindre de beaucoup produire, il paraît s'être préoccupé toujours du soin de multiplier ses ouvrages et des moyens de les mettre sou les yeux d'un plus grand nombre de personnes. Ainsi, pendant des mois, quelquefois pendant des années entières, il a laissé de côté la peinture, où il lui était permis d'espérer d'autres succès, mais nécessairement restreints dans un cercle de public polus étroit. Il a dessiné; le nombre des dessins qu'il a composés est vraiment prodigieux; et, pour les reproduire, il a fait choix des procédés dont

il pouvait attendre une plus large diffusion de son oeuvre." See also *Musée de Montpellier: la galerie Bruyas par Alfred Bruyas avec le concours des écrivains et des artistes contemporains* (Paris: Impr. Claye, 1876), 481.

40. Doré rarely did preliminary sketches on paper as he produced his book illustrations. Rather he drew directly on the boxwood block and then applied a quick color wash, going on to the next image with fifteen to twenty blocks of this sort before him. He would then take the lot to the engravers – this all in one morning. See Joanna Richardson, *Gustave Doré: A Biography* (London: Cassell, 1980), 78.

41. Philippe Burty, "La gravure et la lithographie à l'exposition de 1861," *Gazette des beaux-arts* (August 1861): 176–77: "Les dessinateurs, qui n'avaient plus le temps de dessiner, ont livré des bois que les graveurs, n'ayant plus le temps de graver, ont interpétés à leur guise. Il y a maintenant des recettes connues pour traduire certains frottis de crayon, certains lavis d'encre de Chine; le dessinateur croque à la hâte par-dessus des fonds préparés à l'effet, le graveur invente à son tour des procédés rapides, et de tout ce mélange naît la plus déplorable confusion. [...] Le bois ne doit pas, ne peut point lutter avec le métal; il ne porte son effet qu'à la condition d'être simple, d'accuser franchement le contour, de réserver de larges lumières, de préciser l'ombre par une vive indication et de supprimer les demi-teintes. [...] Cette critique serait facile à prouver par les planches du *Dante* de M. Gustave Doré, qui garnissent presque tous les cadres de l'exposition."

42. Burty, "La gravure et la lithographie," 172–73: "Le burin est un art essentiellement national. [...] Aujourd'hui encore notre école de gravure proteste contre la froideur des Allemands et l'habilité pratique des Anglais, par le respect de la forme, le choix des travaux et la coloration discrète. Mais au moment où la photographie porte, et nous nous en félicitons, une atteinte terrible aux reproductions à bas prix, on ne doit en montrer que plus de respect pour les maîtres que s'astreignent à la longue et pénible étude de l'art de la gravure, et nous ne pensons pas que ce soit les encourager à se manifester en public que de leur offrir une galerie accessoire, lorsque l'on réserve, à côté, des salons tout entiers pour l'exhibition des produits purement industriels de nos colonies."

43. Pierre Dax, "Chronique," *L'Artiste* (15 January 1866): 89 (quoted by Kaenel, *Le métier d'illustrateur*, 255): "Ce n'est pas parce que M. Gustave Doré est à la mode, que nous nous attaquerons à la vogue de M. Doré. Nullement. [...] Après avoir maintes fois constaté les succès incessants de M. Doré à Paris, voici qu'il faut élargir notre statistique et compter avec les autres capitales et même avec l'autre monde. A Londre, [...] Berlin, [...] Barcelone, [...] Hollande, [...]. Dans quelque temps on verra sans doute le [Edgar Allan] Poë et le [James Fenimore] Cooper de M. Doré."

44. Edward Morris notes specifically that the success of Doré's Piccadilly gallery, filled mainly with his vast paintings on religious themes such as his *Christ leaving the Praetorium*, attracted English Protestants "deprived of art in churches." See his *French Art in Nineteenth-Century Britain* (New Haven, CT: Yale University Press, 2005), 129–30.

45. Jules Claretie, "Gustave Doré," in *Peintres & Sculpteurs Contemporains: Artistes vivants en janvier 1881* (Paris: Librairie des Bibliophiles, 1884), 118–19: "Ce qui désolait Doré, c'est de n'avoir point, quoique fort aimé et populaire, dans son pays cette renommée incontestée qu'il recontrait à l'étranger, en Angleterre, par exemple, où son nom était plus célèbre que chez nous. Gustave Doré était même, peut-on dire, comme une sorte de gloire anglaise. [...] S'il eût étranger, Anglais ou Allemand, ce Doré, avec quelle passion nous aurions inventé sa gloire."

46. Claretie, "Gustave Doré," 126: "Doré était le peintre et le dessinateur des cohues; personne n'a mieux que lui fait tenir des milliers d'hommes, ou plutôt de fantômes, dans un cadre. Mais ces dioramas et ces panoramas semblaient le contraire de la peinture telle qu'on la veut auhourd'hui, le contraire de l'art intime, et les visions dantesques de Doré, avec ses hécatombes de damnés [...] tout cela semblait, à nos réalistes du décor, de la peinture d'aspect, faite pour le théâtre, et ils en niaient beaucoup trop leur valeur réelle."

47. Jules Breton, *Nos Peintres du Siècle* (Paris: Société d'edition artistique, 1899), 184–88 (quoted in Kaenel, *Le métier d'illustrateur*, 278).

48. Philip Gilbert Hamerton, "Gustave Doré's Bible," *The Fortnightly Review* 4 (1 May 1866): 669–81 (quoted in Kaenel, *Le métier d'illustrateur*, 256).

49. Ernest Duvergier de Haurenne, "Le Salon de 1874," *Revue des Deux Mondes* (1 June 1874): 661 (quoted by Kaenel, *Le métier d'illustrateur*, 257): "Une déplorable facilité mise au service d'une imagination froidement délirante, nulle conscience, nul respect de la nature, aucun souci de la logique, aucune autre préoccupation que celle de l'effet. En voyant certains tableaux de M. Doré, on songe à certains décors de théâtre éclairés par la lumière électrique. [...] Ces féeries de la Porte-Saint-Martin n'ont plus guère de succès en France, mais il paraît qu'on en trafique encore en Angleterre."

50. The association of Doré's paintings and illustrations with theater has retained its power. Early film versions of the *Commedia* relied extensively on Doré's creations to guide their staging of Dante's narrative: for example, Henry Otto's 1924 version of the *Inferno* for 20th Century Fox. More recently, the films of Walt Disney have been shown to have been greatly influenced by Doré's work, as Disney himself and many of his European artists were familiar with, and specifically looked to, Doré's work for visual source material. For discussion of Doré's influence on film versions of the

Inferno, see generally *Gustave Doré, réaliste et visionnaire, 1832–1883* (Geneva: Editions du Tricorne, 1985). See also Amilcare A. Iannucci, *Dante, Cinema, and Television* (Toronto: University of Toronto Press, 2004). For discussion of Doré's influence on Disney productions, see Bruno Girveau, ed., *Once Upon A Time: Walt Disney – The Sources of Inspiration for the Disney Studios* (Paris: RMN, and Munich: Prestel, 2006).

51. For discussion of Doré's reaction to the Franco-Prussian War, see Lisa Small, "L'Année Terrible and Political Imagery," in *Fantasy and Faith: The Art of Gustave Doré*, 32–63.

52. Gautier, "L'Enfer de Dante Alighieri," *Le Moniteur universel* (30 July 1861): "Ce qui frappe au premier coup d'oeil dans les illustrations dantesques de Gustave Doré, c'est le milieu où passent les scènes qu'il dessine et qui n'a aucun rapport avec les aspects de notre monde sublunaire. L'artiste a inventé le climat de l'enfer, les montagnes souterraines, les paysages inférieurs, l'atmosphère brune où jamais soleil n'a lui et qu'éclairent des réverbérations du feu central. [...] Les premières planches qui servent de transition de la réalité au rêve, de ce monde-ci à l'autre sont encore possibles terrestrement; peu à peu elles s'assombrissent et prennent le caractère de la vision pour ne plus le quitter au'au retour de Dante à la surface de la planète."

53. Emile Zola, "Gustave Doré," *Le Salut public* (14 December 1865) (quoted in Kaenel, *Le métier d'illustrateur*, 258–60).

54. Philip Gilbert Hamerton, "Gustave Doré," *The Fine Arts Quarterly Review* (October 1864): 22–23.

55. Claretie, "Gustave Doré," *Peintres & Sculpteurs Contemporains*, 109–10.

56. See, for example, Roosevelt, *Life and Reminiscences of Gustave Doré*; Gosling, *Gustave Doré*; and Richardson, *Gustave Doré: A Biography*. These authors make many references to Doré's "Germanic" roots as a native of Strasbourg and link this heritage to his artistic production.

57. George Thornbury, in his preface to the English edition to Doré's illustrated *Wandering Jew* of 1857 (quoted in Richardson, *Gustave Doré: A Biography*, 41–42), wrote: "Doré was the most German of Frenchmen; and [he] has something Teutonic in his width of vision. He is a broad-bowed man; and his eye is as piercing as it is microscopic. Such breadth and such depth have seldom met before in a painter of dreams."

58. *Goncourt Journal* (10 February 1880).

59. Théophile Gautier, "Gustave Doré," *L'Artiste* (12 December 1856): 17 (quoted in Kaenel, *Le métier d'illustrateur*, 243).

60. For discussion of this issue, see Giulia Bartrum, *Albrecht Dürer and his Legacy: The Graphic Work of a Renaissance Artist* (London: The British Museum Press, 2002; rpt. 2003). See also Craig Harbison, *The Mirror of the*

Artist: Northern Renaissance Art in Its Historical Context (New York: Abrams, 1995).

61. *Rauschenberg: XXXIV Drawings for Dante's "Inferno"* (New York: Abrams, 1964).

62. Calvin Tomkins, *Off the Wall: Robert Rauschenberg and the Art World of Our Time* (Garden City, NY: Doubleday, 1980), 158; also Karl Fugelso, "Robert Rauschenberg's *Inferno* Illuminations," *Studies in Medievalism* 13 (2004): 47–66.

63. See Roberta Smith, "Art: Drawings by Robert Rauschenberg, 1858–68," *The New York Times* (31 October 1986); and Walter Hopps and Susan Davidson, ed., *Robert Rauschenberg: A Retrospective* (New York: The Solomon R. Guggenheim Foundation, 1997), reviewed by Catherine Craft in *Art Journal* 57/2 (Summer 1998): 108–11.

Soundscapes of Middle Earth: The Question of Medievalist Music in Peter Jackson's *Lord of the Rings* Films

Stephen Meyer

I

The highly popular combination of cinema and medievalism has produced a plethora of ironies and contradictions, but none is more curious than that which attends the notions of authenticity and historical accuracy. The latest cinematic version of the Arthurian legend – Antoine Fuqua's *King Arthur* – exemplifies the ways in which these notions may suffuse both the creation and the interpretation of a medievalist film. Keira Knightley's voice-over for the theatrical trailer sets the tone of the movie. "For centuries," she begins, "countless tales have been told of the legend of King Arthur. But the only story you've never heard is the true story that inspired the legend." This realistic aesthetic – at least to a certain degree – informs the movie's plot, which jettisons much of the familiar mythos in favor of a rationalist explanation of the legend. Drawing on the work of C. Scott Littleton and Linda A. Malcor, Fuqua presents Arthur and his knights as a contingent of Sarmatian cavalry, attempting to defend the last vestiges of Roman rule in Britain from the advancing Saxons.[1] Fuqua thus frames his film as a realist response to the centuries of legend that have encrusted the historical events of the fifth century. Ironically, much of the negative criticism of the film is couched in precisely the same terms. A review from the webpage of *Decent Films Guide* by Steven D. Greydanus, for instance, takes issue with the historical and geopolitical inaccuracies of the script:

[The scriptwriter] Franzoni and [the director] Fuqua jettison even the most basic facts about Arthur's historical setting, relocating him from post-Roman Britain to Britain at the time of Rome's withdrawal. In one fell swoop, they eliminate Arthur's predecessor Vortigern, who was responsible for inviting the Saxons into Britain to help fight against the Picts and Scots in the wake of Roman withdrawal. As a result, the Saxons are thus no longer entrenched in East Anglia, pushing their way west and north, but instead invade Britain north of Hadrian's Wall and fight their way south.[2]

Allen Johnson is equally critical of the film's historical inaccuracies, but focuses instead on props and costumes. Johnson is particularly troubled by the hex nut that appears prominently on the pommel of one of the swords: "Another, absolutely revolting display of inaccuracy," he continues, occurs "when one of Arthur's knights, Tristan, carries a Chinese Dao sword! Really? In 5th century Britain? Someone should have been fired for that."[3] Johnson's language may be unsophisticated, but his sentiments are widely shared. Medievalist movies – like other historical films – are routinely praised or attacked on the basis of historical veracity, and this veracity is defined primarily in terms of plot and what we might call the visual materiality of the film: costumes, sets, and props.

Although notions of authenticity and realism frame much of the discourse surrounding the plot and visual aspects of medievalist film, they are largely absent from discussions of film music.[4] No one, at least to my knowledge, has criticized Fuqua for using twenty-first-century film scoring techniques rather than fifth-century musical instruments and/or vocal styles – instruments and styles that, in any case, would be extraordinarily difficult to reconstruct. Indeed, the score for *King Arthur* has little to do with what we commonly understand to be early medieval music. It seems rather to belong to a cluster of film scores by Hans Zimmer – *Crimson Tide, Backdraft, Gladiator* – films concerned with male heroism and/or epic themes. Like the scores to these other films, *King Arthur* underscoring features broad, sweeping diatonic or modal themes that guide and direct viewers' emotional responses to the visual material. The music for *King Arthur,* in short, can be located in the center of the late twentieth-/early twenty-first-century fantasy-epic genre. The fountainhead of this film music genre is almost certainly John Williams's *Star Wars* score; more recent examples include not only the Zimmer film scores cited above, but also James Horner's score for *Troy* (2004). These later scores evoke the music for earlier epic films, but combine rich orchestral textures with new sounds derived from global pop. The idea of authenticity is not wholly absent from these film scores, but it takes second place to other dramatic needs. Relying on digital processing and carefully crafted by sound engineers, these scores are full of the audio equivalent of hex nuts: markers of modernity that – at least potentially – might interfere with the suspension of disbelief. And yet they do not. Hex nuts and Chinese swords can have no place in an ersatz medieval world, but synthesizers and symphony orchestras are freely admitted.

All of this suggests that the idea of authenticity does not apply to cinematic music in the same way as it does to the visual aspects of film. Music in medievalist films seems to function primarily as what Claudia Gorbman famously called an "unheard melody" – subliminally manipulating our emotional responses to the moving image without ever fully rising to the level of analytical consciousness.[5] Following this argument, we might argue that most cinematic music contributes to the medievalism of a movie only indirectly. It might amplify, direct, or manipulate our emotional identification with the film's characters as they move through a more or less medieval world, but it contributes nothing by itself. Music – to use a metaphor developed by Carolyn Abbate – is inherently "sticky."[6] It might cling to medievalist images or ideas; it might even take on some of the properties associated with the visual elements of a film. But it is not intrinsically or inherently medievalist. It becomes so only insofar as it partakes of the historical authenticity of the film's visual elements.

While this model may describe the bulk of music for medievalist films, I would like to focus in this essay on those instances in which medievalism appears to flow from the music into the film's visual elements rather than the other way around. My interest will be in the interpretation of film music rather than its production: questions about the extent to which a film music composer was inspired by or attempting to recreate authentic medieval music will therefore not enter into my argument. Instead, I will be concerned with ways in which film music might invoke, utilize, or reference a cluster of musical topoi that have come to be associated with the Middle Ages. These topoi include monophonic chant or chant-like singing; harmonization in parallel fifths or octaves (supposedly replicating organum practice); drones and/or ostinato patterns; a particular "straight tone" vocal style; modal harmonies; as well as certain instrumental timbres associated with Renaissance or medieval instruments. These musical characteristics may be found – to a greater or lesser degree – in the medieval or medievalist music that has penetrated the popular imagination in the late twentieth and early twenty-first centuries: the *Chant* phenomenon of the early 1990s (now being revived); certain early music musical ensembles (New York Pro Musica, The Hilliard Ensemble, Sequentia, Anonymous Four, etc.); medievalist works such as *Carmina burana*; as well as the music of medievalist groups such as Qntal and Highland.

Cinematic musical medievalism – at least in the terms in which I will define it – is by necessity active: it points at or articulates the cluster of medievalist topoi that are part of the audience's general frame of reference. But in order for music to function in this way, the soundtrack must become analytically audible to the audience; it must itself be "pointed out." Cinematic musical medievalism, in this sense, depends on a gesture of articulation, through which the medievalist associations of the soundtrack become accessible. It is clear that we can make no universal claims about these gestures of articulation or about the possible meanings that might emerge from them. The group of medievalist topoi that I described above is a moving target that never coheres into a unified style. It shifts as the audiences for medievalist films shift, evolving as the consequence of some of the very types of associations I will be discussing. Disparate, even (on occasion) mutually incompatible, these topoi emerged from the metaphor-like processes whereby certain musical gestures adhere to the idea of the medieval. I will therefore treat musical medievalism not as a quality or aspect of certain films, but rather as a process: a process in which new associations are continually emerging through reference to the associations of the past. The twofold gesture of articulation is the framework through which this medievalizing process is set into motion.

In this essay, I will examine this medievalizing process at work in three examples from Peter Jackson's *The Lord of the Rings* trilogy. Howard Shore's score for these films is very much a part of the fantasy-epic-film music genre to which *King Arthur* and *Gladiator* also belong, differing from these films mainly in its length and complexity rather than in its fundamental style. Like other fantasy-epic films, the

Lord of the Rings films rely heavily on underscoring (roughly 80 percent of the footage is accompanied by nondiegetic music) and an extraordinarily developed arsenal of sound effects. Like Zimmer and Horner, Shore freely combines conventional orchestral textures with those derived from non-Western traditions. If Shore's music stands apart from that for other fantasy-epic films, it is in the extent to which it is spun out from a complex web of leitmotivs, almost in the manner of a Wagnerian music drama. Only a few of these motives may be regarded as specifically medievalist. Their appearance in the score illustrates not only the diverse ways in which music might articulate the medieval, but also some of the new kinds of cinematic musical medievalism that are emerging in the twenty-first century. They also raise questions about how cinematic musical medievalism blends with other musical referents and styles, and, consequently, about the meaning of medievalism in an increasingly globalized and postmodern cinema.

II

The gesture of articulation through which cinematic musical medievalism becomes potentially accessible to the audience occasionally occurs in the most direct way: as part of the film dialogue. We may find an example of this strategy early in Jackson's *The Fellowship of the Ring*. As Frodo and Sam are preparing dinner underneath a spreading oak, they hear the faint sound of singing. "Sam," says Frodo in a moment of recognition, "Wood Elves!"[7] Frodo's exclamation articulates and sets apart the scene that follows, in which we see the Elves on their way to the Grey Havens. These Elven sounds occupy an indeterminate space between source music and underscoring. Frodo and Sam hear music emanating from the Elves, but we never see them singing or playing instruments. Noble, serene, suffused with silvery light, they appear as visitors from another realm.

In both Tolkien's novel and Jackson's film, Frodo and Sam experience the singing of the Elves as what I am tempted to call a medievalist moment. The Elves, after all, are at least potentially immortal, and they bear memories of events that happened centuries, even millennia, before the chronological present of the cinematic diegesis. For the hobbits, the Elves are "living fossils," and the Elvish music is for them a marker of "olden days," chronologically and aesthetically distinct from the world that they inhabit. In this sense, the position of Frodo and Sam with regard to the Elves is analogous to the position of the viewer or reader with regard to the entirety of Middle Earth. Tolkien's strategy in this regard, as Tom Shippey points out:

> engage[s] a problem faced and solved in not dissimilar ways by several writers of historical novels. In setting a work in some distant time, an author may well find that the gap between that time and reader's modern awareness is too wide to be easily bridged; and accordingly a figure essentially modern in attitudes and sentiment is imported into the historical world, to guide the reader's reactions, to help the reader feel "what it would be like" to be there.[8]

The soundtrack for this scene might be interpreted as an aural analogue of this process. Immediately before the moment in which Frodo hears the Wood Elves, there is a close-up shot of a skillet over an open flame, a skillet in which Sam is cooking a meal of bacon, sausages, and potatoes. The underscoring ceases, or rather, is replaced by the sounds of sizzling bacon fat. Quotidian cooking sounds, we might say, help to establish the hobbits (at least in this scene) as "essentially modern," and their presence in the aural environment of the film helps to bridge the gap between acoustic normalcy and the exotic soundscape of the Elves.

Although the diegetic structure of the scene in certain ways parallels that of a historical novel, it is more difficult to find evidence of medievalism – or any type of historicism, for that matter – in the music. Certain features, especially the drone accompaniment and the vocal timbres, do seem to fit into a medievalist paradigm. In other respects, however, Shore's Elven music seems quite distant from any medievalist reference. Its most prominent melodic characteristic, for example, is the presence of both the natural and flatted third scale degree, along with a flatted seventh. It might be possible to interpret these modal characteristics as a sub-species of medievalism: evoking the North African and Middle Eastern influences on European medieval music that performers like Thomas Binkley did so much to foreground. Such an esoteric reading, however, seems wide of the mark. Like so much of the music for the other Elven scenes, that for the Wood Elves seems to evoke not so much the European Middle Ages as traditional music either of the Middle East or Southeast Asia. The

Elven music in *The Lord of the Rings* is certainly exotic, but it is not particularly medievalist.

III

A more specific type of medievalism might be found in the music that Shore uses for the Ringwraiths, particularly as it appears in the first movie of Jackson's trilogy. The nine Ringwraiths are the most fearsome servants of the Dark Lord. Once mortal men, they were trapped by magic rings given to them by Sauron: rings that ultimately transformed them into shadowy beings wholly enslaved to his will. Their musical motive is characterized by choral textures, cluster chords built up from major and minor seconds, and an ostinato-like motoristic bass. In *The Two Towers* and *The Return of the King*, Shore uses these elements in other contexts, and the association between the Nazgul and this particular sound complex is less secure. In *The Fellowship of the Ring*, however, it forms a clearly recognizable motive. Its dramatic function is clearest, perhaps, in the nighttime scenes that take place in Bree. As Verlyn Flieger points out, this scene begins with a moment of cinematic intertextuality that has no counterpart in Tolkien's novel. In Tolkien, the entrance to Bree is barred by an iron gate. When the four hobbits approach, the gatekeeper looks at them from *over* the top of this gate. In Jackson's film, by contrast, the gatekeeper opens a small rectangular peep door in the gate itself, referencing the famous moment in *The Wizard of Oz* in which Dorothy and her companions are questioned as they try to enter the Emerald City.[9] Another striking moment of cinematic intertextuality, I would argue, occurs about six minutes further into the film, when the Ringwraiths break down the town gate (*The Fellowship of the Ring*, disc 1, 1:03:27). As the riders gallop into Bree, we hear a fully developed iteration of their motive. This particular visual context evokes a famous scene from another medievalist film: John Boorman's Arthurian epic *Excalibur* (1981). A turning point in Boorman's film comes after Arthur drinks from the Holy Grail offered to him by Perceval. The king decides to end his indolent decadence and ride out to meet the rebellion of his son Mordred (*Excalibur*, 1:55:22), and as he does so, we hear the "O fortuna" opening movement from Carl Orff's *Carmina burana* (shorn of its grandiose opening section). Arthur and his knights gallop out of the castle gate – not in through it, as the Ringwraiths do in *The*

Add women's voices only on repeat.

EXAMPLE 1: Ringwraiths motive from Peter Jackson's *The Fellowship of the*

Fellowship of the Ring – but the effect is similar. In this visual context the similarities between "O fortuna" and the Ringwraiths music are foregrounded. Both feature stepwise melodies, short phrases that seem almost to be truncated or abbreviated, and motoristic ostinato accompanimental patterns. Both "O fortuna" and the Ringwraiths music are cast in the minor mode, and in each, repetition with doubling at the octave creates a sense of dramatic intensification. Not all audience members, of course, will interpret the Bree scene as a reference to *Excalibur*. Even those unfamiliar with Boorman's film, however, are likely to feel the resonance between the Ringwraiths' music and the popular-culture meanings that have become associated with "O fortuna" over the past thirty or forty years.

This intertextuality, of course, is another sort of articulation: pointing at the Middle Ages through the lens of Boorman's film. But it also sets the Ringwraiths' music apart from the rest of the soundtrack, marking it for special attention. In this case, then, the two kinds of articulation that I have described as the framework for the medievalizing process collapse into a single gesture.

IV

The third example that I wish to discuss comes from *The Two Towers*, in a scene that appears only in the extended edition version of the film and not in the original theatrical release. In this scene, Théodred (the son of Théoden King of Rohan) is being laid to rest in his howe. Éowyn (the king's niece) is depicted as the principal mourner, singing (perhaps "declaiming" is a better word) a lament for her dead cousin. What brings this lament to the attention of the audience, of course, is not only its status as source music (music, it should be noted, that is relatively rare in the *Lord of the Rings* films), but also the fact that it is sung in Old English.

Of all the lands of Tolkien's Middle Earth, it is the Mark of Rohan that is most closely modeled on a specific medieval culture (in this case, Anglo-Saxon England), and Éowyn's lament strongly evokes this world. The text, by Philippa Boyens, was translated into Old English by David Salo in an explicit imitation of *Beowulf*.[10] The music for Éowyn's lament is by Plan 9 (David Donaldson, Stephen Roche, and Janet Roddick), and some commentators have suggested a connection between the lament and the track "Senn Voro Aesir Allir A Thingi" from Cologne Sequentia Ensemble for Medieval Music's "Edda" album (1999). Such a direct path of influence is difficult to establish. What is important for my purposes here is not the inspiration for the lament, but rather the ways in which its monophonic texture, archaic text, and free metrical structure suggest the Middle Ages. Éowyn's lament clearly stands apart from its surrounding musical context, appearing very much like a relic from the distant past. All in all, it is probably the most purely medievalist moment in the entire *Lord of the Rings* soundtrack.

Placing this in the context of the *King Arthur* criticism with which I began this essay, we might say that the sonic hex nuts have receded into the background, leaving music that can make claim to a certain kind of authenticity. And yet this authenticity – in my opinion – does not make Éowyn's lament more effective. Indeed, I would argue that the scene comes dangerously close to being *too* medievalist, or rather, that the realism of the lament threatens to undermine the suspension of disbelief essential to the fantasy genre. Precisely by virtue of its authenticity (or "quasi-authenticity"), the lament may call attention to the artificiality of the surrounding soundtrack, exposing the "irrevocable staginess" that Siegfried Kracauer thought was an essential characteristic of all historical or fantasy films.[11] By approaching realism, in other words, the lament threatens to open up an aesthetic gap between the real and the fantastic, a gap that is (at least potentially) as jarring as the sight of a hex nut in the pommel of Lancelot's sword. Indeed, the aesthetic gap created by the dangerous authenticity of the lament may have been partly responsible for the decision to cut this scene from the theatrical-release version of *The Two Towers*. In a broader sense, however, we may regard this aesthetic

gap as a perennial problem of cinematic musical medievalism. For in
"setting things apart," the twofold gesture of articulation that I have
claimed as a necessary part of this medievalism also – at least potentially – calls the authenticity and realism of the rest of the film into
question.

In a broad sense, my metaphor of the opening gap alludes to a
phenomenon that has been a central concern of film criticism for
nearly fifty years. I refer to the concept of "suture." The term first
appeared during the 1970s, as a way of describing the shot/counter-
shot procedure that seemed to be such a common cinematic practice.
"Suture" has been the subject of an extensive literature, but for the
purposes of my argument, it will be enough to reference the description given by Slavoj Žižek in his book *The Fright of Real Tears*:

> Firstly, the spectator is confronted with a shot, finds pleasure in it
> in an immediate, imaginary way, and is absorbed by it. Then, this
> full immersion is undermined by the awareness of the frame as
> such: what I see is only a part, and I do not master what I see. I am
> in a passive position, the show is run by the Absent One (or,
> rather, Other) who manipulates images behind my back. What
> then follows is a complementary shot which renders the place from
> which the Absent One is looking, allocating this place to its
> fictional owner, one of the protagonist.[12]

Thinking metaphorically, we could say that the "awareness of the
frame" creates a gap that must be closed, or – more specifically – a
wound that must be sutured. In this sense, the diegetic music of
Éowyn's lament undermines full immersion by drawing attention to
musical manipulation. If we are to accept the lament as the genuine
(medievalist) music of the Mark, how is it that the rest of the Rohan
music sounds so different? If Éowyn sings in the authentic language of
Rohan, why does she use modern English in the rest of the film?
These questions cast the lament as a destructive agent, creating the
psychic wound that then demands suture. Music, in this particular
case, brings about a damaging awareness of artificiality. Placing
Éowyn's lament into this theoretical frame, we could say that it is
precisely its markers of authenticity – Old English text, declamatory
vocal style, simple tonal materials, etc. – that (at least potentially)
create an awareness not so much of the frame, but of the fictionality or
artificiality of the underscoring.

Speaking of music's "wounding authenticity" casts it in a very different role vis-à-vis suture than that which it usually holds. In my reading, the lament creates the need for suture. More typical is a concentration on the ability of music to contribute to the suturing process. Claudia Gorbman's discussion of music and suture from *Unheard Melodies* may provide an example of this – perhaps more normative – notion about the function of music. "Music," she writes:

> may act as a "suturing" device, aiding the process of turning enunciation into fiction, lessening awareness of the technological nature of film discourse. Music gives a "for-me-ness" to the soundtrack and to the cine-narrative complex. I hear (not very consciously) this music which the characters don't hear; I exist in this bath or gel of affect; this is my story, my fantasy, unrolling before me and for me on the screen (and out of the loudspeakers).
>
> Music lessens defenses against the fantasy structures to which narrative provides access.[13]

Merging these ideas about music and suture – or about wounding and suturing – approximates music to the position of the Holy Lance in the Parsifal legend: it creates the wound that it alone can heal.

In a certain sense, the aesthetic problem of Éowyn's lament attends all films that employ both underscoring and source music. Composers and directors suture this potential contradiction by a number of strategies. The simplest of these is purely visual. Directors may begin a sequence with a shot establishing the source of music, then continue the music as the camera focuses on other scenes. Or, inversely, music that seems to function as underscoring at the beginning of a sequence is subsequently shown to be source music. When Ilsa Lund and Victor Laszlo enter Rick's Café Américain – to use a famous example from *Casablanca* – we hear music that might conceivably be understood as underscoring. Later, we see a shot of the house band, retrospectively establishing the music as diegetic sound. More relevant for a discussion of music in the *Lord of the Rings* films is a second strategy, whereby the source music and the underscoring are compositionally integrated with one another. *Casablanca* also provides an example of this. The underscoring to the famous flashback sequence, in which Rick remembers his Parisian idyll with Ilsa, begins with an orchestral quote of "As Time Goes By," the same tune that has appeared diegetically in the previous scene. The musical gesture sutures the aesthetic gap between source music and underscoring. But it also creates or accentuates a narrative connection between the cinematic present (i.e., Rick's Café Américain in *Casablanca*) and the cinematic past (Paris in the days leading up to the German occupation), suturing, we might say, a chronological gap and making the past present.[14]

The soundtrack to *The Lord of the Rings* is replete with examples of this kind of musical suturing. The modal mixture and basically triadic structure of Wood Elves' melody, for instance, is closely related to one of the score's central motives: a major triad with a flatted sixth neighbor tone. This motive appears prominently not only (as we might expect) in other Elven scenes, but also as a bass pattern in the "Lighting of the Beacons" sequence from *The Return of the King*. Initially marked as diegetic sound, the Wood Elves' music is quickly absorbed into the motivic network of the underscoring. Just as the dual presence of "As Time Goes By" (as source music and as part of the underscoring to the flashback sequence) illustrates the enduring love between Rick and Ilsa, so too does the integration of the Elven motives into the texture of the soundtrack suggest their importance to the chronological and physical space that the hobbits inhabit. Like "As Time Goes By," the Elven music is the sonic marker for the present-ness of the past.

However much the aesthetic gap opened by Éowyn's lament might resemble – in purely structural terms – the gaps between diegetic and non-diegetic sound surmounted by Max Steiner (or by Howard Shore in other sections of *The Lord of the Rings* films), I would like to emphasize its differences from these other examples. In contrast to "As Time Goes By" or the Rivendell motive, Éowyn's lament is singularly ill-suited for integration into the musical *habitus* of the surrounding non-diegetic music. Her chant-like declamation lacks the clear rhythmic and/or melodic character that typifies most film-music leitmotifs, and its texture is quite distant from most of the rest of *The Lord of the Rings* soundtrack. Indeed, nothing very much like Éowyn's lament occurs anywhere else in *The Lord of the Rings* movies; even the other diegetic songs – Gandalf's "The Road Goes Ever On and On" or the snippet from the lay of Beren and Lúthien that Aragorn sings in the Midgewater Marshes – seem more closely related to the musical styles of Howard Shore's score. As distinct and unusual as this music is, however, it is nevertheless carefully linked to a particular musical-cultural sphere, namely, what we might call the pseudo-Germanic soundscape of Rohan. Indeed, it is precisely these links – these markers of authenticity – that make the lament so difficult to absorb. By confronting this specific problem, Shore confronts the characteristic issue of cinematic musical medievalism: how to reconcile the demand for authenticity with the essential "suturing" or "immersing" function of film music.

In order to understand Shore's response to this problem, we must open up our field of vision to glance briefly at the dramatic context for the lament, namely the sequence of scenes indexed as "The Funeral of Théodred" on the DVD release of *The Two Towers*. The scene begins with Théodred being carried on a litter to his final rest. The underscoring at first features a noble horn melody (#1 in the musical example), a motive first heard during the scene in which Théoden recognizes Éowyn after he awakens from Saruman's spell. This motive soon gives way, however, to a brief trumpet melody, outlining a descending tetrachord and establishing E as a tonal center (#2). As the camera shifts to a close-up of Éowyn, we hear a wordless choir, and the "masculine" brass instruments are temporarily silenced. A wordless choir momentarily shifts the tonal center, and seems to suggest a distinct, perhaps anti-heroic emotional space for the king's niece. When Éowyn begins her lament, however, she re-establishes the tonal center of E. Indeed, E functions essentially like a reciting tone for the lament, helping to establish a connection back to the heroic world suggested by the trumpet theme. At first, the source music – Éowyn's singing – stands alone. But a faint F-sharp sounds in the lower register after "onsended," and on the penultimate syllable of "sorgiende" we hear a distinct D. As the lament continues, a tone cluster is built up, step by step, adding the four notes that Éowyn sings to the initial D. The underscoring grows more prominent as more tones are added, until by the end of the lament it is nearly as loud as the diegetic sound.

The increasing volume and tonal density of the underscoring creates a sense of mounting tension, but it also places the lament itself in a meaningful harmonic context, suggesting D – or more specifically, D major – as a subsidiary tonal center. In the following scene – the dialogue between Gandalf and Théoden over Théodred's grave – this E/D tonal axis will play a central role. After Gandalf voices his elegiac consolation "his spirit will find its way to the halls of your

1. THEODRED'S PROCESSION ----------------->   2.

EOWYN CLOSE - UP

Beal   -   o - cwealm   ha - fath   fre - o - ne   fre - can   forth   on - sen - ded

3.

Giedd   scu - lon   sing - an   gle - o - menn   sor - gien - de   on   Me - du - sel - de   thaet

fathers," we hear another trumpet theme (#4). Recalling both the low register and the tonal center of the trumpet theme at #2, this underscoring helps to re-establish the mood of noble mourning that characterized the procession. And yet this is more than a simple recapitulation. The trumpet is now accompanied – I am tempted to say "enriched" – by a wordless choir, alternating between sustained D major and E minor chords. In this way, the E/D tonal axis of the lament is carried forward into the underscoring of the following scene,

EXAMPLE 2: Musical outline of "The Funeral of Théodred" sequence
from Peter Jackson's *The Two Towers*

subtly enmeshing Éowyn's music into the more general heroic
soundscape of Rohan. The recitational style, archaic text, and monophonic texture of the lament – to sum up – clearly articulate the
lament from its musical context and suggest alternate, possibly medievalist worlds. The harmonic materials, on the other hand, integrate
the lament into the rest of the soundtrack, linking the problematic
authenticity of the lament to the "sonic gel" of the underscoring.

V

Shore's music for this scene represents a specific solution to the
problem of the "aesthetic gap," but it may also stand more broadly for
an essential part of the process of cinematic musical medievalism. I

have offered up two metaphors to describe this process: the idea of bridging an aesthetic gap and the idea of suturing a psychic wound. In place of these, I would like to suggest a third: namely the idea of estrangement and assimilation. Estrangement corresponds to the first moment of cinematic musical medievalism: the twofold gesture of articulation that I have claimed as the *sine qua non* of the phenomenon. In order for music to participate fully in the medievalist fantasy, however, this twofold moment of articulation must be met by a response, a second gesture of bridging, suturing, or – as I would have it here – of assimilation.[15] It is perhaps not coincidental that Tolkien himself provides a very close analogue of this dialectic between estrangement and assimilation. I refer to the numerous inserted lyrics that he uses in both *The Hobbit* and *The Lord of the Rings*, or rather, to the way in which they appear within these texts. The vast number and range of these lyrics is one of the many extraordinary things about these most extraordinary novels, and many of them exhibit the same twofold gesture of articulation that characterizes the moments of musical medievalism in Jackson's *Lord of the Rings* movies. In the third chapter of *The Return of the King*, for example, Tolkien presents a song from the future, commemorating the events that we see unfolding in the present tense of the narrative. The final lines of the poem describe the Riders' approach to Minas Tirith, an event that in the main narrative occurs only several pages later:

> Mundburg the mighty under Mindolluin,
> Sea-king's city in the South-kingdom
> foe-beleaguered, fire-encircled.
> Doom drove them on. Darkness took them,
> horse and horseman; hoofbeats afar
> sank into silence: so the songs tell us.[16]

With its alliterative, bipartite lines, compound adjectives ("foe-beleaguered, fire-encircled") and insistent trochaic meter, Tolkien's poem is a marvelous imitation of Anglo-Saxon heroic poetry. It creates a particular sense of time and space; of a rich and distant culture distinct from the one inhabited by the audience. In terms of mood, character, and function, it is quite similar to the Éowyn's lament scene in *The Two Towers* film. By recreating Anglo-Saxon poetry in what at least approximates modern English, Tolkien is engaging in a process similar to the naturalization or assimilation of the cinematic lament that I described above. Tolkien's poem – at least potentially – bridges not only the linguistic gap between the modern and early forms of English, but also the aesthetic gap between the twentieth- (or twenty-first-) century reader and the idealized heroic medievalism embodied by the Riders of Rohan.

A more fully developed example of this process of estrangement and assimilation occurs in a group of scenes from *The Fellowship of the Ring* that Fran Walsh and Peter Jackson (co-writers of the cinematic screenplay) chose not to include in the film, namely, the Old Forest/Barrow Downs section of Tolkien's *The Fellowship of the Ring*. Although some fans have taken issue with the decision to eliminate this sequence of scenes from the screenplay, the choice was a logical one. While these chapters ("The Old Forest," "In the House of Tom Bombadil," and "Fog on the Barrow Downs") enrich our understanding of Middle Earth, they do little to advance the plot of the novel.[17] Tom Bombadil, moreover, is the only character in the novel who seems to be immune from the power of the Ring, and if he had appeared in the movies he might have distracted audiences from what Jackson clearly understands as the central theme of the plot, namely, the malevolent power of the Ring. It is precisely the quasi-independent, episodic nature of the Tom Bombadil passages, however, that makes them such a good analogue for the phenomenon of cinematic musical medievalism that I have been discussing.

Tom Bombadil is introduced as a kind of *deus ex machina*, who rescues the hobbits from what – in the context of my argument – we can only regard as an "inverse assimilation." The junior hobbits (Pippin and Merry) are in the process of being swallowed by Old Man Willow, assimilated, quite against their will, into the body of the tree. The following scenes rectify this situation, replacing the negative assimilation by a positive one. Through Bombadil's agency, the hobbits are able to assimilate at least a part of the forest's strangeness. It is not incidental that this process of assimilation is mediated by music.

Tom Bombadil is perhaps the most enigmatic figure in Tolkien's novel, and one of the most peculiar things about him is the extent to which he is characterized by song. Indeed, Bombadil is probably the most musical creature in all of Middle Earth. The hobbits hear him singing before they see him, and singing seems more comfortable and natural to him than speech. Tolkien casts all of Bombadil's songs in the same – highly flexible – meter. Each line has seven accents, and breaks naturally into two verses: a tailless trochaic tetrameter followed by a verse in trochaic trimeter.[18] The first and second trochees are often replaced by accented monosyllables, as in the repeated lines that function almost like a chorus in Tom Bombadil's songs:

> Old Tom Bombadil is a merry fellow;
> Bright blue his jacket is, and his boots are yellow.[19]

With its simple, direct diction and alternating pattern of four and three-foot verses, Bombadil's meter clearly alludes to the English folk ballad. Like every other aspect of his character, it evokes the rustic, unspoiled natural world of which he is the chief representative and embodiment.

Tolkien tells us of Tom's tendency to break into song at any moment, but he also demonstrates what we might call the "musicalization" of everyday life by echoing the "Bombadil meter" in the prose sections of the "In the House of Tom Bombadil" chapter. It appears, for instance, in a passage that occurs near the end of the chapter, after Frodo has slipped the Ring onto his finger. With the Ring on his finger, Frodo is invisible to the other hobbits, but Tom Bombadil seems to be unaffected by its power. Bombadil is able to see Frodo, and admonishes him with the following words:

> Hey, Come Frodo there! Where be you a-going? Old Tom Bombadil's not as blind as that yet. Take off your golden ring! Your hand's more fair without it. Come back! Leave your game and sit down beside me! We must talk a while more, and think about the morning. Tom must teach the right road, and keep your feet from wandering.

Although Tolkien does not do so, we might rewrite this passage as a poem, one that would follow very closely the accentual patterns (although not the rhyme scheme) of the songs that Bombadil sings:

> Hey, Come Frodo there! Where be you a-going?
> Old Tom Bombadil's not as blind as that yet.
> Take off your golden ring! Your hand's more fair without it.
> Come back! Leave your game and sit down beside me!
> We must talk a while more, and think about the morning.

> Tom must teach the right road, and keep your feet from
> wandering.

Bombadil's speech patterns – like those of the other characters in *The Lord of the Rings* novel – reveal his essence. The fact that his speech is perpetually on the cusp of music places Bombadil in that magical, liminal space between the wildness of the Old Forest and the comforts of the Shire, between nature and culture. More interesting for our purposes is the subtle ways in which Bombadil's particular diction seems to infuse Tolkien's own narrative voice. Here, for instance, is Tolkien's description of the first morning of the hobbits' stay in Bombadil's house:

> It was a pale morning: in the East, behind long clouds like lines of soiled wool stained red at the edges, lay glimmering deeps of yellow. The sky spoke of rain to come; but the light was broadening quickly, and the red flowers on the beans began to glow against the wet green leaves.[20]

It is perhaps unsurprising that the bucolic imagery and homely simile of soiled wool evoke Tom's rustic vocabulary – the author, after all, is describing Bombadil's garden. But in the insistent double accents – "soiled wool," "stained red," "sky spoke," "red flowers," and finally the triple "wet green leaves" – we also hear an echo of the "tailless trochees" that typify Tom Bombadil's poetic meter. Certain phrases – such as "The sky spoke of rain to come; but the light was broadening quickly" – employ the same basic meter that informs Bombadil's poetry and prose. Bombadil's strangeness, we might say, is partially assimilated into the novel's central narrative voice.

The play of styles in Tolkien's Tom Bombadil scenes may provide a structural analogue of estrangement and assimilation in the Jackson films, but this process also becomes a central element of the novel's plot, at least in the scenes under consideration here. The hobbits are fundamentally – perhaps even magically – transformed by the encounter with Tom Bombadil. When Frodo first meets Goldberry (Tom Bombadil's wife), for instance, he spontaneously utters an improvised poem, falling naturally into the "Bombadil meter" described above. Immersed in the magical beauty of Bombadil's world, Frodo unconsciously assimilates his voice and – to some degree – his character. Later in the chapter, this process affects the other hobbits as well. As they share a meal with Tom Bombadil and Gold-berry, Tolkien writes, "[t]he drink in their drinking-bowls seemed to be clear cold water, yet it went to their hearts like wine and set free their voices. The guests became suddenly aware that they were singing merrily, as if it was easier and more natural than talking." [21]

The analogy with cinematic musical medievalism becomes clear if we imagine Tolkien's third-person narrative voice as film underscoring and Tom Bombadil's poems as source music. As in the examples from (Jackson's) *Lord of the Rings* described above, Tom Bombadil's songs are set apart or pointed out by their unusual meter and diction. If they are not as explicitly medievalist as the "Ride to Mundburg" lyric quoted above, they nevertheless evoke an ageless, pastoral world: not specifically medieval, perhaps, but distinct from the bourgeois comforts of the Shire. Like the Wood Elves' music or Éowyn's lament, Tom Bombadil's songs manifest a double gesture of articulation. The hobbits, like the contemporary reader, perhaps, are initially estranged from them. But like the lament and the Wood Elves' music, Bombadil's spirit is ultimately integrated or assimilated: first into the speech and behavior of the hobbits, and ultimately into the narrative voice of the novel. If we accept Shippey's description of the hobbits as to some extent proxies for the contemporary reader, then the scenes might be read as an idealized description of the reading process, and by extension, of the experience of viewing the *Lord of the Rings* films. Just as the hobbits/readers are unconsciously transformed by the reading experience; so too are the hobbits/viewers unconsciously transformed by the viewing experience. In this sense, the Tom Bombadil scenes narrate in microcosm the assimilating process that operates in the novel – and in the film – as a whole.

VI

The fact that Tolkien's narrative of estrangement and assimilation should take place in the context of the Tom Bombadil scenes – and not in some other part of the novel – is central to their meaning. For the Bombadil sequence has no direct implications for the main plot (this is part of the reason that Jackson could so easily excise it). Although a few characters refer sporadically to Bombadil, he himself does not appear in any other part of *The Lord of the Rings*. Indeed, his presence as an anomalous character over whom the Ring has no power raises more questions than it answers. Fans and critics of Tolkien's novel have speculated about who or what precisely Tom Bombadil is, but surely his primary function in the work is to contribute to what Barry Langford has called the "unusual density of Tolkien's wholly imaginary fictive world."[22] What entrances and beguiles the reader is not merely the plot of the novel, but precisely this sense of density: the cultural diversity of Middle-earth and the vast chronologies that Tolkien sets into play. The hobbits – and the readers of the novel – are continually encountering ruins, legends, and lore of distant peoples and cultures that they only dimly understand. We have the feeling that Middle Earth contains – at least potentially – a multitude of stories as complex and deeply moving as *The Lord of the Rings*. It is into this complex multitude of stories – and not merely the specific plot of *The Lord of the Rings* – that the hobbits (and the readers) are being assimilated.

As Tom Shippey points out, it is this quality of plenitude or density that distinguished *The Lord of the Rings* from other works, and that transformed the genre of epic fantasy fiction. "When Tolkien drew his maps and covered them with names," Shippey writes:

> he felt no need to bring all the names into the story. They do their work by suggesting that there is a world outside the story, that the story is only a selection; and the same goes for the hints of other creatures unaffected by and uninterested in the main plot. Middle-earth is different from its many imitators in its density, its redundancy, and consequently its depth.[23]

Music is clearly one of the primary ways through which this sense of plenitude is translated from the novel to the cinematic screen. The soundtrack employs an impressive number of different musical instruments and references a diverse array of musical styles, and in this sense it functions like the names on the map, creating "density" and "depth." Cinematic musical medievalism is a part of this postmodern referential matrix, but it is by no means dominant or even particularly prominent. Like other musical referents in *The Lord of the Rings*, moreover, medievalism is slippery and unstable. Musical timbres and motives – as we have seen – acquire new meanings in the course of the film. By its very nature, music does not have the stable geography of Tolkien's cartography. What music provides is not so much the equivalent of the names on the map, but rather the cinematic analogue for the nuances of meter and diction that Tolkien uses in the Bombadil scenes (and indeed, throughout the novel). Music in the *Lord of the Rings* film trilogy is continually at work, articulating strange worlds and then assimilating them into the narrative flow. The *Lord of the Rings* soundtrack – to put this another way – is a pathway into the density of Middle Earth, but it is not the density itself. It is not so much the medievalist object, as part of the process that makes medievalism possible.

NOTES

1. The scholarly background for this idea comes from C. Scott Littleton and Linda A. Malcor, *From Scythia to Camelot* (New York: Garland, 2000).

2. Steven D. Greydanus, online review, *Decent Films Guide* <http://decentfilms.com/sections/reviews/1691> [accessed 18 August 2008].

3. Allen Johnson, "King Arthur Historically Fails its Audience" <http://media.www.slccglobelink.com/media/storage/paper442/news/2004/08/03/Entertainment/king-Arthur.Historically.Fails.Its.Audience-696098.html>, issued 3 August 2004 [accessed 23 June 2008].

4. In this sense, non-diegetic music is similar to dialogue. We are not troubled when Arthur and Guinevere do not speak early medieval Gaelic or Latin on screen.

5. Claudia Gorbman, *Unheard Melodies* (Bloomington and Indianapolis: Indiana University Press, 1987).

6. Abbate develops this idea in "Music: Drastic or Gnostic," *Critical Inquiry* 30/3 (Spring 2004): 505–36.

7. Jackson, *The Fellowship of the Ring* (Extended edition), disc 1, 45:01.

8. Tom Shippey, *J. R. R. Tolkien: Author of the Century* (Boston and New York: Houghton Mifflin, 2000), 6–7.

9. Jackson, *The Fellowship of the Ring* (Extended edition), disc 1, 57:38. Flieger's discussion of this connection may be found on pp. 72–73 of Verlyn Flieger, "A Distant Mirror: Tolkien and Jackson in the Looking-glass," *Studies in Medievalism* 13 (2005): 67–78.

10. The specific passage from *Beowulf* that seems to have inspired Boyens begins with line 2265 of the poem.

11. Siegfried Kracauer, *Theory of Film: The Redemption of Physical Reality* (New York: Oxford University Press, 1960), 77.

12. Slavoj Žižek, *The Fright of Real Tears: Krzysztof Kieslowski Between Theory and Post-theory* (London: BFI Publishing, 2001), 32.

13. Gorbman, *Unheard Melodies*, 5. Psychoanalytic theories of film music – such as those articulated by Gorbman, Kalinak, Žižek, and others – have been rigorously critiqued. See Jeff Smith, "Unheard Melodies? A Critique of Psychoanalytic Theories of Film Music," in David Bordwell and Noël E. Carroll, ed., *Post-Theory: Reconstructing Film Studies* (Madison: University of Wisconsin Press, 1996), 230–47.

14. Smith uses precisely this example in his critique psychoanalytic approaches to film music. See "Unheard Melodies?," 244.

15. The idea of assimilation plays a large role in Anahid Kassabian's analysis of film music in *Hearing Film Tracking Identifications in Contemporary Film Music* (New York: Routledge, 2001).

16. J. R. R. Tolkien, *The Return of the King* (New York: Ballantine Books, 1965), chap. 3 ("The Muster of Rohan"), 92.

17. It should be noted that the extended version of *The Two Towers* (although not the theatrical version) contains a scene in Fangorn clearly modeled on the Old Man Willow episode from Tolkien's *The Fellowship of the Ring*. In the scene from Jackson's *The Two Towers*, Treebeard more or less stands in for Tom Bombadil.

18. For a discussion of Bombadil's poetic meter, see Geoffrey Russom, "Tolkien's Versecraft in *The Hobbit* and *the Lord of the Rings*," in George Clark and Daniel Timmons, ed., *J. R. R. Tolkien and His Literary Resonances: Views of Middle-earth* (Westport, CT and London: Greenwood Press, 2000), 63.

19. Tolkien, *The Fellowship of the Ring*, 173.

20. Tolkien, *The Fellowship of the Ring*, 178.

21. Tolkien, *The Fellowship of the Ring*, 175.

22. Barry Langford, "Time," in Robert Eaglestone, ed., *Reading "The Lord of the Rings": New Writings on Tolkien's Classic* (London and New York: Continuum, 2005), 29–46 (30).

23. Shippey, *J. R. R. Tolkien: Author of the Century*, 68.

Now You Don't See It, Now You Do: Recognizing the Grail *as* the Grail

Roberta Davidson

Every director who makes a film depicting the Holy Grail faces the same challenge: the audience assumes it knows what the Grail looks like. Contemporary representations of the Grail have uniformly shown a glowing chalice, and for audiences this chalice is immediately recognizable as the Grail.[1] Accordingly, every director who makes a film depicting the Grail has the same problem: how to avoid cliché and anticlimax when an object the audience has already recognized before it appears on screen is finally seen.

To put the problem in its most basic terms – film is a visual medium. When we see an object in a film we recognize it, or we are told what it is, or we are conscious of not knowing what that thing on the screen is supposed to be. If, in order for the Grail to be visually accepted *as* the Grail it must conform to the popular expectation of a glowing chalice, it also, presumably, cannot be other than that when revealed. The audience must not need to ask the question, "what is it?" Therefore, the director and the screenwriter must address a crucial creative question: how a film, in which the familiarity of the object is a prerequisite of the narrative, can nonetheless surprise the audience when the already recognized object is found?

Traditionally, the history of both the representation and identification of the Grail was far less iconic than our contemporary perception of it. Its association with a holy cup does not occur until the late twelfth or early thirteenth century, in Robert de Boron's verse romance, *Joseph d'Arimathie*, or *Le Roman de l'Estoire du Graal*. Previous versions of the Grail or Grail-like objects included a serving platter (*Perceval*), a cauldron that brought the dead back to life

(*Branwen, Daughter of Llyr*), and one that would only cook food for the brave (*Spoils of Annwn*).² However, the chalice and its identification as the cup from which Jesus drank at The Last Supper has dominated modern popular culture. In that sense, then, the actual history of multiple Grail representations does not provide the filmmaker with any viable alternative image.

It does, however, provide a strategy. Traditionally, the quest for the Grail was not so much one of finding, but one of recognizing. In order to "achieve" the Grail, the seeker needed to ask the appropriate question. This tradition may have begun with Chrétien de Troyes' *Conte del Graal*, composed sometime between 1175 and 1190. The Grail's appearance in Chrétien's poem is in a procession, following a spear with a drop of blood running from the tip. Because the poem's hero, Perceval, had been advised against asking so many questions in a previous adventure, he refrains from comment:

> The youth watched them pass, but he did not dare to ask concerning the grail and whom one served with it, for he kept in his heart the words of the wise nobleman. I fear that harm will come of this, because I have heard say that one can be too silent as well as be too loquacious. But, for better or for worse, the youth put no questions.³

While Perceval clearly sees the object itself (an object that is apparently shaped like a serving dish), neither the hero nor the reader understands its identity or its function until much later in the poem. Indeed, it is not even immediately evident that the Grail has a holy, as opposed to a magical, nature. It is not until five years later in the narrative that Perceval encounters a hermit who is able to explain to him that the Grail, though large enough to hold a fish, contained only a single communion wafer, to serve the father of the Fisher King. It has been noted that, far from constituting a complete narrative resolution, this is an explanation that raises more questions than it answers.⁴

In Sir Thomas Malory's *Morte Darthur* (1486), which is the source of the Grail story most frequently utilized by contemporary filmmakers, questions must also be asked to "achieve" the Grail and, additionally, the Grail requires a great effort to be seen. The Grail enters the hall where the knights are feasting, covered in white samite, its bearer invisible. The hall is filled with good odors, and all the knights eat and drink their favorite foods. Gawayne subsequently initiates a Grail Quest with the intent of seeing it more openly, a motivation easily transferable to film.[5] When the Grail is finally found, by Galahad, its sighting is associated with the visually miraculous, when a man comes out of the Grail, bearing the signs of the passion, presumably Christ himself. He approaches Galahad with a series of questions:

> "Sonne, wotyst thou what I holde betweyste my hondis?"
> "Nay," seyde he, "but if ye telle me."
> "Thys ys," seyde He, "the holy dysshe wherein I ete the lambe on Estir Day, and now hast thou sene that thou moste desired to se. But yet hast thou nat sene hit so opynly as thou shalt se hit in the cite of Sarras, in the spirituall paleyse."[6]

Significantly, even when Galahad looks directly at the Grail, he still requires an explanation of the object's true identity. It is further implied that, though he is in the actual presence of the Grail, he may not even then be fully seeing it, as his perception is limited by the location in which he sees it. As in Chrétien's version, the narrative's answers to questions concerning the Grail raise even more questions. But, although this may cause some frustration for both knight and reader alike, from a purely artistic viewpoint it is a wise authorial choice. The reader both does and does not want the Grail to be fully explained. Complete cognition would also circumscribe the Grail's mystery. A factor in an audience's fascination with the Grail – and hence a part of its enduring box-office appeal – is, that although the hero may "achieve" it, it can never be fully possessed.

Inherent in this narrative tradition of the Grail's ambiguity, then, are the seeds of a solution for film directors who wish to sustain the audience's sense of surprise and mystery beyond the moment at which the Grail is seen. Even as the answers the medieval Grail Knight receives to his questions may open up new avenues of inquiry rather than entirely resolving the old, filmmakers use disinformation and misrepresentation to deliberately confuse the film's viewers about what they are seeing. The presumed visual familiarity of the Grail as an object actually gives filmmakers the opportunity to defamiliarize it perceptually, along the lines of Wittgenstein's "duck-rabbit."[7]

As Wittgenstein describes it in *Philosophical Investigations*, the picture of a duck-rabbit is neither a picture of a duck nor of a rabbit. It is a duck when one is looking for the picture of a duck, and a rabbit when looking for the picture of a rabbit. It is both duck and rabbit, and neither:

> Imagine the duck-rabbit hidden in a tangle of lines. Now I suddenly notice it in the picture, and notice it simply as the head of a rabbit. At some later time I look at the same picture and notice the same figure, but see it as the duck, without necessarily realizing that it was the same figure both times. – If I later see the aspect change – can I say that the duck and the rabbit aspects are now seen quite differently from when I recognized them separately in the tangle of lines? No. But the change produces a surprise not produced by the recognition.[8]

This experience of surprise concerns Wittgenstein, as it reveals the intersection between seeing and interpretation. However, this same intersection provides a filmmaker with an opportunity to restore surprise to the visual narrative of the Grail Quest. Although not a Grail film, this well-known dialogue from *The Court Jester* (1955) demonstrates the technique:

> **Hawkins:** I've got it! I've got it! *The pellet with the poison's in the vessel with the pestle; the chalice from the palace has the brew that is true!* Right?
> **Griselda:** Right. But there's been a change: they broke the chalice from the palace!
> **Hawkins:** They *broke* the chalice from the palace?
> **Griselda:** And replaced it with a flagon.
> **Hawkins:** A flagon […]?
> **Griselda:** With the figure of a dragon.
> **Hawkins:** Flagon with a dragon.
> **Griselda:** Right.
> **Hawkins:** But did you put the pellet with the poison in the vessel with the pestle?
> **Griselda:** No!!! The pellet with the poison's in the flagon with the dragon! The vessel with the pestle has the brew that is true!
> **Hawkins:** The pellet with the poison's in the flagon with the dragon; the vessel with the pestle has the brew that is true.
> **Griselda:** Just remember that.[9]

The script of *The Court Jester* cleverly de-distinguishes three otherwise obviously, visually discrete vessels, leaving the audience nearly as unsure as Danny Kaye and his opponent (who approach their contest desperately trying to remember the correct mantra) which cup holds the true brew. As Freud pointed out in *Jokes and Their Relation to the Unconscious*, "Words are a plastic material with which one can do all kinds of things."[10] It is a common cultural assumption that pictures are less plastic – hence the cliché, "a picture is worth a thousand words" – but, as W. J. T. Mitchell explains in *Picture Theory*, images are also subject to

> a complex interplay between visuality, apparatus, institutions, discourse, bodies, and figurality. It is [necessary to] realize that *spectatorship* (the look, the gaze, the glance, the practices of observation, surveillance, and visual pleasure) may be as deep a problem as various forms of *reading* (decipherment, decoding, interpretation, etc.).[11]

Critical iconology reveals perspective as a historical, cultural formulation that masquerades as a universal, natural code.[12] Accordingly, Althusser describes ideology as a process that "hails or interpolates concrete individuals as concrete subjects [...] a *(mis)recognition* function."[13] This misrecognition function is what destabilizes perspective when we turn to metapictures, "a class of pictures whose primary function is to illustrate the co-existence of contrary or simply different readings in a single image, a phenomenon sometimes called 'multistability.'"[14] Hence, one generic feature of the metapicture is its role as a scene of interpretation.[15]

Metapictures make the boundary between first- and second-order representations ambiguous. Again, to quote Mitchell:

> [...] they do not refer to themselves, or to a class of pictures, but employ a single gestalt to shift from one reference to another. The ambiguity of their referentiality produces a kind of secondary effect of auto-reference to the drawing as drawing, an invitation to the spectator to return with fascination to the mysterious object whose identity seems so mutable and yet so absolutely singular and definite.[16]

For example, we may only be able to perceive Wittgenstein's duck-rabbit as alternating between its representations as a duck and then a rabbit, but we recognize it as a third thing altogether, a hybrid picture, a duck-rabbit.

It is this combination of fascination, mutability, misrecognition, and singularity that places the Grail squarely in the category of a metaimage. It is also what both allows and impels directors to represent the Grail as simultaneously both itself and other, which, in the most practical terms, becomes a strategy, one of avoiding anticlimax through promoting misperception. And, as already noted, the medieval tradition of Grail narratives provides filmmakers with the plot device that it is necessary to ask questions before full recognition is possible, even when the familiar object is on the screen.

In four films – *Monty Python and the Holy Grail* (1975), *The Fisher King* (1991), *Excalibur* (1985), and *Indiana Jones and The Last Crusade* (1989) – the director begins with the premise of representing the Grail, but deliberately *misrepresents* it at some point in the narrative in order to create surprise. It is interesting to note, for example, that the original script for *Monty Python and The Holy Grail* called for the Grail to be found by Arthur and his knights at Harrods's, at The Holy Grail Counter (because they have everything at Harrods's).[17] In the final version of the film, however, the Grail, as concrete object, is seen but never found. We are shown images of it that turn out either to be intangible and unobtainable (as when a cartoon God displays a cartoon Grail), or simply false, like the grail-shaped beacon at Castle Anthrax. Near the end of the film, a group of French knights claims to possess it, but this is a practical joke played on the English. Similarly it is the practice of Terry Gilliam and Terry Jones, the film's directors, to poke fun at all established images and icons.

"We love all this stuff," Gilliam avows in the Director's Commentary to the film. "I love the Middle Ages; Terry and I are just mad about it, but take the thing you love most and rip it apart and see what happens." Interestingly, Gilliam follows this statement with one shortly afterwards: "I've become a pagan, a total pagan […]," as though this were the logical end result of the "ripping apart" of a beloved icon. "Most of the episodes we tell you really came from medieval stories and lore," he informs the audience during the commentary on Castle Anthrax. "There were always these places in all the grail quests; there was always a castle with beautiful maidens in it, and they had secrets […] maybe the only way you can deal with the medieval dialogue and the medieval references is to treat them as silly as this." The end behind Gilliam's and Jones's loving deconstruction of the medieval Grail quest is not solely to be silly, however. Even as there is an association, if only of spoken proximity, between Gilliam's mockery of traditional institutions and his own professed "paganism," there is a similar association between an audience's discomfort and, oddly enough, hope. *Holy Grail*, Gilliam recalls, affected the audience by surprising, confusing, and angering them. They found it funny, but did not know why. The film "made them think in ways they hadn't." This recollection, however, leads him to the different memory of showing *The Meaning of Life* to UCLA students:

> I remember years later when the world had changed a bit from the early seventies, when people were still committed and fighting for different things and trying to change the world, to later when we came around to doing *The Meaning of Life* and we showed it at Universal to basically UCLA students; at the end people were saying why did you do the scenes with the vomiting, why were you doing these ugly disturbing scenes; and by then students didn't want to be disturbed, they didn't want to be shocked and made to think, they wanted to know that if they went their four years and got their diploma they'd have a job at the end of it. The change in those ten years was phenomenal. There was still a bit of hope when we made *Grail*.[18]

Gilliam makes his association of materialism with the desire for comfort and the failure of the audience to ask the right questions – in essence, failing the Grail Quest – even more explicit in his film *The Fisher King*.

As Susan Aronstein has pointed out:

> Gilliam plays out a narrative that, as do all good Arthurian legends, calls its audience to a definition of ideal subjectivity, centering this call, as do all good Grail legends, on a redefinition of the "valuable" that teaches its audience to reread the world around them, offering the truth of the Grail – a truth capable of restoring fertility and meaning to a lost generation.[19]

Indeed, the Grail is almost more of a concept than an object in *The Fisher King*. It represents any number of desired consequences, but, most essentially, the healing potential of human relationships. It does also, however, appear in the film as a chalice. Perry, one of several Wounded Kings in the film, has seen a picture of it in a magazine. He shows the picture to Jack, a former radio celebrity who, like a modern-day Balyn, has destroyed lives, including his own, through his inability to foresee the consequences of his actions. Later in the film, when Perry lies in a coma, partly induced by the tragedy Jack inadvertently brought about, Jack dresses himself as a medieval outlaw and breaks into the home of the millionaire where the chalice Perry "recognized" as the Grail is housed.

When Jack finds the chalice, it is revealed as a cup awarded at a school Christmas play, in what initially appears to be another kind of practical joke. Jack's response to the inscription, "To Little Lannie Carmichael for all his hard work [...] P.S. 247 Christmas Pageant 1932," like the audience's, is cynical. The chalice seems trivialized by its mundane context. However, despite Jack's whimsical expression, he does not discard the Grail when it turns out to be something other than what both he and we had expected. This is fortunate, as Gilliam first visually devalues the Grail, in order subsequently to restore its value by proving its effectiveness as an object of healing. This blends with the film's recurring theme of recycling – of garbage, of men, and of myths. Perry awakens from his coma the next morning, after Jack has spent the night at his bedside, and leads a celebratory choir of "angels" in singing "How About You." Moreover, in saving Perry, Jack also saves the life of Langdon Carmichael, who has apparently attempted suicide, even as Perry earlier saved Jack from his own suicide attempt. Jack, who has suffered from a corrosive materialism that has kept him from sustaining meaningful relationships with others, is arguably healed himself of his mercenary values in the performance of an unselfish act. It is noteworthy that it was the original unselfish act of the young Carmichael in helping others that caused him to receive the chalice. (Despite Rebecca and Samuel Umland's suggestion that the number 247 represents the score for a sporting event,[20] it is more likely that the audience is meant to recognize P.S. as standing for Public School. There is, indeed, a Public School 247 in Brooklyn.) It is probable that the character's name, "Little Lannie," is an oblique reference to Lancelot, the knight who, in Malory, received a partial glimpse of the chalice, but could not achieve it totally.[21] Lancelot, in Malory, is spiritually enlightened and partially transformed through his quest for the Grail, but falls back into his sinful relationship with Gwenyvere over time. Similarly, Carmichael, at one point in his past, recognized the chalice's value enough to keep and display it but, perhaps owing to his own increased wealth and materialism, failed to benefit lastingly from its influence.

The activity for which Little Lannie was rewarded with a cup involved helping others in some fashion, perhaps even in the staging of the Christmas Pageant at which he received the chalice. Because at one point in the past Lannie did something for others, years later Perry recognizes the chalice in a photograph as "the Grail," which inspires Jack to steal it to heal Perry, and so causes him to be on the spot when Carmichael's own life needs to be saved. Even salvation is recyclable in *The Fisher King*.

Achievement of the Grail requires more than one stage for Jack – he must reject his idea of relationships as based in economic exchange (although, even at the end, he tells Perry "I've done my part."). He must recognize his place in the world in relation to others as organic. Finally, he must accept that it is perception that dictates experienced reality, and to trust others' perceptions, which may be invested with a different but equal truth to his own. Similarly, the audience experiences the Grail in the film in stages. First, it is a recognizable picture in a magazine. We understand why Perry believes it is the Grail when he sees it, as we see a Grail-like object as well. Then it is made unrecognizable as the Grail by its inscription (which, nonetheless, with its reference to Christmas, as well as to Little Lannie/Launcelot, associates the object with the values of sacrifice, healing, and quest). Finally, in viewing the Grail's effectiveness, we once again see "the Grail" as the Grail. It is not the object itself that is transformed; it is our perceptions of it.

In *Excalibur*, John Boorman goes even further in playing with our perceptions. It is the object itself that transforms, before our eyes. "Boorman," as Kevin Harty notes with understatement, "has been free with his sources [...]."[22] Indeed, although the credits cite Malory as the film's source, the Grail sequence in the film appears more strongly to reflect Chrétien's *Perceval*. Boorman's is also the least Christian of contemporary film Grails, having more in common with a healing cauldron than the cup from which Christ drank. This is in line with Boorman's attitude toward the whole of Arthurian legend. His vision of the Grail is not solely a reflection of his admiration of a pagan past, but also of his quarrel with Ireland's modern political history. (Ireland was where the film was made, and where Boorman owns property that was used as one of the film's backgrounds.) Christianity is one of the "foreign" overlays Boorman would like to remove from the Arthurian narrative. The Christian faith, he has declared, is "alien" to his understanding of British myth, born from olive groves and deserts rather than oak trees.[23] Correspondingly, it is when Arthur turns away from the primal forces that made him king to Christianity for protection from Mordred that he is struck by the lightning that turns him into a Wounded King.

This is the event that precipitates the Grail Quest in the film, one in which the character Morgana represents a far more potent threat to the Grail Knights than the ladies of Castle Anthrax. Interestingly, it is the knights' materialism that she appeals to, in terms reminiscent of Satan's temptation of Christ. The principal Grail Knight, Perceval, the one who finally succeeds, must draw upon both purity of heart and willingness to sacrifice everything, even his own life. Although Gilliam's Jack and Boorman's Perceval could not be more different as characters, the persistent motif of gain (of the Grail, and its healing potential) at the price of the Grail knight's willingness to sacrifice both his ego and his body, runs through both films.

Boorman transposes one reality for another – a stripping away of a false (Christian) system in order to restore a native (pagan) one – and he treats his cinematic Grail in similar fashion. In the scene in which Percival finally comes into the presence of the Grail, he participates in the following dialogue, reminiscent of the conversation Chrétien's medieval Perceval failed to have:

> **Grail:** What is the secret of the Grail? Whom does it serve?
> **Perceval:** You, my lord.
> **Grail:** Who am I?
> **Perceval:** You are my lord and king.

There is a significant pause, into which the audience inevitably projects their expectation that Perceval will identify his "lord and king" as "Jesus Christ." Therefore, the name that Perceval speaks comes as a surprise:

> **Perceval:** You're Arthur.

Coinciding with this verbal exchange with the Grail, the audience watches the familiar image of the chalice change into a shining image of Arthur in full armor. The Grail then once again becomes a chalice and, in the process, is also visually transformed from an image the size of a man into a cup that Perceval holds in his hand. However, even when the chalice is reintroduced as visual object – the cup from which Arthur drinks – we no longer believe it is limited by concrete reality.

As Norris Lacy explains:

> the filmmaker [Boorman], all the while forging dialogue and images to encourage [Christian] associations, manages to subvert them. Everything in the scene seems to have pointed toward a traditionally religious interpretation of the events surrounding the Grail [...]. This substitution [of Arthur's name and image] is a stunning and daring innovation, one of the larger shocks of the film.[24]

Boorman's visual strategy, therefore, has a twofold effect – it restores an image he believes was co-opted by Christianity to its "authentic" meaning, and it surprises the audience, preventing them from experiencing anticlimax when the familiar object is found. Indeed, Boorman's representation of the Grail is almost a literal demonstration of the "duck-rabbit" effect upon the audience.

If Boorman seems most affected by the narrative version of Grail Quest found in Chrétien de Troyes', Steven Spielberg's Grail Quest incorporates multiple traditions; from the need to question to gain understanding, to the physical challenge involved in "achieving" the Grail. In "Whom Does the Grail Serve? Wagner, Spielberg, and the Issue of Jewish Appropriation," Martin Shichtman reveals how in *Indiana Jones and the Last Crusade*, Spielberg:

> deploys visual imagery often taking the form of traditional Christian symbols – crosses, in particular, abound. The movie's theme, though weakly reinforced, invokes traditional Christian theology [...]. With *Indiana Jones and the Last Crusade*, Spielberg seems to raise the stakes in his ideological war against Nazism. He means to suggest that the Third Reich threatened not just Judaism but all that is holy.[25]

This supposition is borne out throughout the film, but it may also be suggestive that the true Grail is most closely linked with Jesus as a man, not as a God. Once the medieval accretions of gold, and by analogy Christianity, are pared away, we are left with a cup made by a

Jewish carpenter. It is an implicit reminder that under Christianity's golden plating is Judaism.

We, in the audience, experience the now-familiar defamiliariz-ation of the expected image. Indiana Jones, having followed a series of archaeological clues, arrives at the crescent-shaped valley where the Grail is hidden (clearly a reference to Islam as one of those aspects of holiness that the Grail incorporates). Once there, however, he discovers a false Grail knight, the archaeologist Donovan, and the Morgana equivalent in the film, Elsa. In order to motivate Jones to retrieve the Grail for him, Donovan wounds Jones' father, the one who truly believes in the existence of the Grail. This sets up a dynamic similar to that in *The Fisher King*, in which true-believer Perry is "wounded," and needs to rely upon the cynical Jack to act as his proxy in the quest. Jones, to reach the Grail, must traverse three tests – very much constructed as a potentially fatal short answer quiz – in order to reach the room in which the Grail is kept. (It is worth recalling that even *Monty Python* incorporates this pattern of question and answer, until Arthur disrupts it by requesting specifics concerning the *kind* of swallow whose air-speed velocity he is required to know. At this point, the questioner himself is thrown off the bridge.)

Once Indiana Jones has reached the chamber where the Grail is kept and has easily subdued the centuries-old knight who guards it, we are shown a table covered with chalices, any one of which could be the authentic Grail. The variety of grails is unsettling. Presumably we, the audience, expected the Grail to be instantly recognizable. What we discover, instead, is that there are multiple versions of the Grail that are equally recognizable, although different from one another. We expected to be shown an object naturally linked to its meaning without any need for interpretation. What we discover, instead, is a metaimage (a whole table of them, in fact), foregrounding the subjec-tivity of perception and disrupting our certainty of the seamlessness of the space between seeing and knowing. As Wittgenstein realized with the duck-rabbit, "the change produces a surprise not produced by the recognition."[26] Accordingly, like the villain Donovan, we realize that we are going to have to depend upon someone else to tell us which is the real Grail. And, like him, we are initially misled.

Aronstein has pointed out that this technique reflects the film's emphasis on the correct reading of texts and the recovery of lost wisdom, situating that wisdom in the figure of the Father as the true

hero of the film.[27] Aronstein's reading (no pun intended) works well
with my own suggestion that the correct interpretation of The New
Testament, in Spielberg's eyes, requires the recognition of its origins
in the Tanahk. Although Judaism is never referred to directly in the
film, as Shichtman notes, it is implicit as a necessary component for
recognition – the asking of the right question so integral to Grail
Quests. The Nazis, who burn Jewish books, cannot possibly read the
Grail correctly, as they have destroyed the very reference texts they
need.

Ultimately, Spielberg confirms the authenticity of the Grail that
Jones chooses. Water poured from the Grail not only kills the
unworthy, but heals the good man (Jones, Sr.). Spielberg then seemingly destroys the Grail when villains attempt to remove it from its
proper sphere, taking it across a "Great Seal," an image that resonates
with Solomon's magic and reflects the danger of perceiving the Grail
primarily as a material object to be possessed. Again, this suggests the
problem of a superficial reading of Christianity that attempts to deny
its Jewish origins and mystical significance. In removing the Grail
chalice from future "achievement," Spielberg implies that all further
Grail Quests will need to be performed on an immaterial plane.
Possibly, this narrative choice reflects the filmmaker's desire that no
one produce a future rendering of the Grail that would read it in a
different fashion than Spielberg had; in his article, Shichtman tracks
some of the ideological struggles that have underlain representations
of the Grail. Conversely, it may simply have been Spielberg's way of
resolving the problem that, if Jones is to be true to his mantra, the
Grail would end up displayed in a museum, like any normal artifact.
Whatever lay behind Spielberg's directorial decision to bury the Grail
at the bottom of a chasm, it is nonetheless unlikely that *Indiana Jones
and The Last Crusade* will be the last in the line of cinematic Grail
Quests.

The visual nature of filmmaking, and the perceptual possibilities
of the metaimage, combine in such a way as to bring many contemporary Grail films full circle to the medieval romances of the past, in
which the Grail's characteristics of being both hard to see and needing
to be recognized were originally established. Moreover, the challenge
of visually reimagining the Grail is linked to its qualities as metaimage
and its narrative appeal. To paraphrase Freud in reference to another
inanimate object filled with interpretive possibilities, the Grail is never

just a Grail. The Grail's narrative potential allows it to be endlessly reenvisioned, while remaining always unique. No matter how often sought and found, it is achieved but never entirely possessed. That, of course, is one reason why it has remained so endlessly desirable, so artistically challenging, and so engaging for an audience's imagination, for so long.

NOTES

1. Perhaps the most iconic version of this familiar image is M. L. Kirk's 1912 "And Down the Long Beam Stole The Holy Grail," which depicts a radiant vessel with sun-like rays of light extending from it.

2. Indeed, this is only the tip of the iceberg, as is clear from any number of works, including Richard Cavendish, *King Arthur and the Grail: The Arthurian Legends and their Meanings* (New York: Taplinger, 1985); Roger Sherman Loomis, ed., *The Grail: From Celtic Myth to Christian Symbol* (Princeton, NJ: Princeton University Press, 1991); and John Matthews, ed., *Sources of the Grail: An Anthology* (Hudson, NY: Lindisfarne Press, 1997).

3. Loomis, *The Grail*, 33.

4. Loomis, *The Grail*, 46.

5. Eugene Vinaver, ed., *The Works of Sir Thomas Malory* (Oxford: Clarendon Press, 1947), 866.

6. Vinaver, *Works*, 1030.

7. Ludwig Wittgenstein, *Philosophical Investigations* II (Oxford: Oxford University Press, 1953), 194.

8. Wittgenstein, *Philosophical Investigations* II, 199.

9. *The Court Jester*, Dena Enterprises, 1955.

10. James Strachey, trans., *The Standard Edition of the Complete Psychological Works of Sigmund Freud, Vol. VIII* (London: The Hogarth Press, 1905), 34.

11. W. J. T. Mitchell, *Picture Theory* (Chicago: University of Chicago Press, 1994), 16.

12. Mitchell, *Picture Theory*, 31.

13. Mitchell, *Picture Theory*, 29.

14. Mitchell, *Picture Theory*, 45.

15. Mitchell, *Picture Theory*, 76.

16. Mitchell, *Picture Theory*, 48.

17. Director's Commentary, *Monty Python and The Holy Grail*, National Film Trustee Company Limited, Python (Monty) Pictures, Ltd., 1974.

18. Director's Commentary, *Monty Python and The Holy Grail.*

19. Susan Aronstein, *Hollywood Knights: Arthurian Cinema and the Politics of Nostalgia* (New York: Palgrave Macmillan, 2005), 160.

20. Rebecca and Samuel Umland, *The Use of Arthurian Legend in Hollywood Film: From Connecticut Yankees to Fisher Kings* (Westport, CT: Greenwood Press, 1996).

21. I am indebted to the anonymous *Studies in Medievalism* reader who pointed out the probable relationship between the two names.

22. Kevin Harty, ed., *Cinema Arthuriana: Twenty Essays* (Jefferson, NC: McFarland, 2002), 21.

23. Charles Taylor, 'Safe Haven,' 1998, <www.salon.com/ent/movies/int/1998/12/17int2.html> [accessed 15 March 2006]. See also Roberta Davidson, "The *Reel* Arthur: Politics and Truth Claims in *Camelot, Excalibur* and *King Arthur*," *Arthuriana: Journal of the International Arthurian Society*, 17.2 (2007), <http://faculty.smu.edu/arthuriana/>, for a more extensive discussion of Boorman's attempt to restore pagan "authenticity" to the Arthurian legend.

24. Norris Lacy, "Mythopoeia in *Excalibur*," in *Cinema Arthuriana*, 39.

25. Martin Shichtman, "Whom Does the Grail Serve? Wagner, Spielberg, and the Issues of Jewish Appropriation," in Debra Mancoff, ed., *The Arthurian Revival: Essays on Form, Tradition, and Transformation* (New York and London: Garland Reference Library of the Humanities, 1992), 292.

26. Wittgenstein, *Philosophical Investigations* II, 199.

27. Aronstein, *Hollywood Knights*, 129–33.

From the Middle Ages to the Internet Age: The Medieval Courtly Love Tradition in Jeanette Winterson's *The Passion* and *The.Powerbook*

Carla A. Arnell

The contemporary British novelist Jeanette Winterson (b. 1959) is well known for her fantastical autobiography of life among a zealous group of Pentecostal Evangelicals, her gender-bending fictional narratives, her spare but seductive prose style, and even her shameless self-promotion. But she is less well known for the medievalism that has subtly and persistently shaped her works of fiction. A quick survey of the scholarship that has proliferated about Winterson in the last two decades reveals essay titles replete with permutations of the prefix "post": post-humanist, post-realist, post-Enlightenment, and of course "postmodern." What rarely merits mention are Winterson's pre-modern and, indeed, medieval affiliations.[1] Recently, Jean-Michel Ganteau has come closest to focusing on this medieval strand in Winterson's fiction, but his criticism positions her work within the context of romance as a transhistorical mode ranging from Malory to Hawthorne and Woolf rather than to romance as a specifically medieval literary tradition.[2] Yet Winterson's works of fiction are rich in allusions to and rehearsals of medieval romance in particular.

As an illustration of this debt to medieval literature, Winterson's first published fiction, the quasi-autobiographical novel *Oranges Are Not the Only Fruit* (1985), featured interpolated stories from the medieval Perceval legend. And most of her works of fiction published since 1985 have drawn more or less heavily on medieval textual traditions. Even her most recent novels illustrate that magnetic attraction to medieval material: the 2004 novel *Lighthousekeeping*, though set primarily in northwest Scotland in the nineteenth and twentieth centuries, includes a character named Tristan as well as brief reflections on Arthurian romance,[3] and her 2005 novel *Weight* plays with Boethian ideas about freedom and destiny, albeit in a story about the classical Atlas myth.[4]

The prevalence of medieval influences in Winterson's fiction can be explained in part by her childhood reading: Arthurian romance tales were one of the few non-biblical forms of literature Winterson was permitted to read during her rigidly religious upbringing. In fact, Malory's *Morte d'Arthur* was one of just six books her family owned during her growing-up years, in a small collection that included three explicitly religious texts.[5] Winterson's official website biography singles out Malory's text as the central one that "started her life quest of reading and writing."[6] And she has remarked that the medieval quest pattern, as modeled in Malory's *Morte d'Arthur*, provides a basic paradigm for understanding her life: "Life for me is a quest and that is how I must interpret it."[7] Even more significantly, Winterson has claimed that "the medieval world vision" contains an openness to the mysterious – a sense of the wonderful and miraculous – that the novel's characteristic literary mode traditionally forecloses; therefore, in drawing upon medieval literature throughout her novels, Winterson sees herself as restoring art to its proper "visionary role."[8]

In Winterson novels such as *The Passion* (1987) and *The. Powerbook* (2000), however, readers are reminded of another dimension of her medievalism: her use of the courtly love tradition.[9] Although *The Passion* is set in nineteenth-century Europe rather than during the Middle Ages, that novel's central character Henri becomes a tower-bound knightly lover, whose love for the mercurial and unattainable Villanelle is resolved only through the formal patterns of a courtly love relationship. Contrasting his gentle, refined love for Villanelle to other inferior forms of love in the story, Winterson portrays courtly love as a meaningful alternative to the novel's deadening domestic marriages and downright villainous obsessions. She also implies that Henri's courtly love for Villanelle is a model of the ideal relationship between author and character, a metafictional allegory that is developed in a different direction in *The.Powerbook*. In that novel, which weaves throughout its love story re-angled tales of

Lancelot and Guenevere and Paolo and Francesca, Winterson flirts with the courtly love tradition as an allegory for the relationship between author and reader, using that metafictional allegory to challenge conventional ideas about the relationship between language (narrative, poetry) and reality.

Nevertheless, to assert that Winterson participates in a medieval tradition of courtly love writing immediately invites controversy from critics of both contemporary and medieval literature. On the one hand, a contemporary critic of Winterson's work, Marian Eide, has claimed, "Unlike the classic model of courtly love, in which love is heightened by the pain of absence, negligence, or desertion, the passion in Winterson's texts emulates the Biblical model in narrating extreme devotion and radical union."[10] On the other hand, critics of medieval literature have long questioned whether or not such a thing as courtly love even existed in the Middle Ages, with arguments for and against courtly love creating one of the most enduring debates about medieval love literature.

The French scholar Gaston Paris introduced the term *amour courtois* in 1883, based on his analysis of Chrétien de Troyes's Lancelot romance. In that essay, he defined courtly love according to four key features: its illegitimacy and secrecy, its emphasis on the servantship of love, its ennobling and refining character, and its character as a ritualized art with certain rules and laws.[11] In response to that seminal essay, many critics have developed and elaborated upon Paris's definition of courtly love. For instance, in a classic compilation of medieval love literature from the troubadours to Dante, Bernard O'Donoghue identifies recognizable "courtly love" features as including "a feudal respect for the dominant loved lady; the figures of jealous husband, tale-bearer, votive and lady; the cult of joy from love; ideas such as *mesura, solace, pretz, valors*."[12] But since Paris's coining of the term "courtly love," medievalists have also persistently debated the value and authenticity of it. E. Talbot Donaldson was one of the first to argue that courtly love is simply a "myth." Noting that the specific phrase "*amour courtois*" makes just a single appearance in Provençal, Donaldson concluded that a "definition of courtly love based on all the literature of the Middle Ages is too broad to be useful, while one derived from only selected primary documents fits well only those documents from which it has been derived."[13] Henry Ansgar Kelly proposed "burying" the term on the grounds that Paris's own use of *amour courtois* evolved and changed so much throughout his extensive writings that such variability renders the term too imprecise to be useful.[14] As James Schultz summarizes the history of critical commentary about "courtly love":

> [Courtly love] has been the subject of controversy ever since [1883]. Some have tried to replace it with medieval terms like *fin' amor* or *hôhiu minne*. D. W. Robertson would have gotten rid of it altogether as "an impediment to the understanding of medieval texts." Rudiger Schnell finds it so embarrassing that, in a book of over five hundred pages and a number of lengthy articles, he puts *höfische Liebe* "courtly love" in scare quotes every time it appears.[15]

Joachim Bumke adds, "Every detail and the very concept itself are disputed. It has even been argued that courtly love is merely a figment of scholarly imagination."[16]

Thus, the term "courtly love," like a kind of beleaguered romance heroine, has suffered numerous fortunes and misfortunes in the sea of criticism written during the past century. In 1980, as a direct rebuttal of Donaldson's argument, Joan Ferrante sought to reclothe the term in respectability by challenging the notion that courtly love is a "modern invention"; to the contrary, she claimed that "courtliness and love are commonly associated in medieval texts in Provençal, French, Italian, and even Middle English, from the earliest vernacular poets through the fourteenth century,"[17] making courtly love "not a figment of a nineteenth-century imagination, not simply a useful term which we choose to preserve, but a perfectly valid medieval concept."[18] More recently, courtly love has been rehabilitated by at least two other medievalists. In a study of courtly love and the history of sexuality, Schultz launches his argument about medieval German love-literature by asserting that he wants to "embrace the term [courtly love]."[19] He justifies the term for three key reasons: an identifiable phenomenon of love literature during the Middle Ages; the preoccupation of that literature with love rather than with sex or desire;[20] and the identification of love with a "love of courtliness" – the aristocratic manners and mores found in a specifically courtly milieu.[21] And even though Schultz asserts that courtly love should not be reduced to formulaic definitions, he is still able to define those who created themselves as courtly lovers: "They are men who serve a lady who does not respond, who suffer since she is inaccessible or disdainful, who speculate about the nature of love, and who sing themselves into existence as courtly lovers before a courtly audience."[22] Thus, Schultz finds the term "courtly love" both fitting and useful.

Recently, Sarah Kay has also defended courtly love as a term appropriate for analyzing the love poetry and romance narratives of the High Middle Ages. She agrees that problems with past definitions of courtly love have arisen from their formulaic nature, a problem that leads her to view courtly love "more broadly as a series of questions which are debated across large numbers of texts."[23] As she explains, "representations of love in courtly texts do not constitute a doctrine, but rather an agenda which reflects the preoccupations of medieval courts: their concern with decorum, elegance, display, and afflu- ence,"[24] and she traces those debates to "tensions within medieval court life."[25] In this sense, both Schultz and Kay reject rigid and simplified definitions of courtly love and try to locate the concept within the cultural debates of the medieval courtly world, even as they acknowledge that courtly love was a "literary fiction,"[26] not a lived reality.

Neither *The Passion* nor *The.Powerbook* is set specifically in the medieval courtly world. Winterson's novel *The Passion* takes place not during the Middle Ages but in early nineteenth-century Europe during the Napoleonic Wars, and the fictional characters' lives even intersect from time to time with the life of Napoleon.[27] Likewise, *The.Powerbook* does not have a medieval setting in the traditional sense. Although the time-travelling lovers in *The.Powerbook* suggest the Middle Ages as an appropriate meeting place for their tryst, the e-writer Ali(x) playfully rejects that place because "[t]he food isn't that good."[28] Instead, *The.Powerbook* begins in 1591 and flits from era to era in the fashion of Woolf's *Orlando*, looping back to the Middle Ages only through the interpolated tales of Lancelot and Guinevere and Paolo and Francesca.

For Winterson, then, the attraction of the courtly love tradition is not its link to the historical reality of the medieval courts. Indeed, from Winterson's perspective, courtly love's status as a literary *fiction* about love is precisely its attraction, for she uses this decidedly literary trope to elide fiction and reality. To imply that courtly love is a literary fiction, in her interpretation of it, is not to deny its reality. Quite the opposite. In *The Passion* and *The.Powerbook*, she uses the courtly love tradition to illustrate how language – narrative and poetry – confers identity, creates relationships, and constructs a golden world better than the brazen one her lovers would otherwise inhabit.

I

In *The Passion*, Winterson draws upon the traditional definition of courtly love in portraying courtly love through two different but interlaced love stories – Villanelle's love for an unnamed lady in a large house and Henri's love for Villanelle. Throughout that novel, Winterson divides the task of narration between two characters, Henri, a young French soldier, and Villanelle, a web-footed prostitute. Part One follows Henri's early enchantment with Napoleon and his own career in the imperial army as Napoleon's cook. Part Two traces Villanelle's origins and her life of gambling and passion in Venice. Part Three interweaves the two narratives as the characters meet on Napoleon's Russian expedition and their lives come to intersect through love as well as politics. And Part Four takes place more than twenty years after Henri's enlistment in the army; he is on an island in a safe place called San Servelo – an institution for the mentally insane.

The love relationship at the heart of the story is Henri's love for Villanelle, a relationship that ends rather than begins in courtly love fashion. For, in the beginning, Henri often has sex with Villanelle and passionately wants to marry her and make her his wife; only later, when he chooses to remain imprisoned in San Servelo does he become Villanelle's distant, refined "courtly lover." To explain that evolution in their relationship, I would suggest that Henri's eventual role as a courtly lover rather than a husband evolves from his observation of other inferior relationships and forms of love. As such, Henri's courtly-lover role is best understood against the background of other lovers in the novel, particularly married lovers whose relationships are characterized by convenience or necessity, rather than authentic passion.

Of the married lovers in the story, one of the most glamorous is Napoleon Bonaparte. Yet Winterson's portrayal of that famous married lover is notable for the absence of his marital counterpart, Josephine, from the story. Indeed, Napoleon's role as a lover in the novel is significant because he models the narcissistic, self-refracting love the novel comes to criticize. We learn little about Napoleon in the novel except that he has a particular passion for chickens and a certain monocular stare. Whenever Henri goes into Napoleon's tent to deliver a new cooked chicken, he finds Napoleon "sitting alone with a globe in front of him. He doesn't notice me, he goes on turning the globe round, holding it tenderly with both hands as if it were a breast."[29] The globe is of course an image of the world itself – a model of Napoleon's future empire. And when he was not looking at the globe itself, he was presumably studying his own image reflected back to him. Henri explains:

> [Napoleon] believed he was the centre of the world and for a long time there was nothing to change him from this belief. [...] *He was in love with himself* and France joined in. It was a romance. Perhaps all romance is like that; not a contract between equal parties but an explosion of dreams and desires that can find no outlet in everyday life. Only a drama will do and while the fireworks last the sky is a different colour.
> [italics mine] (13)

For Napoleon, the only true "beloved" is the world he wants to conquer, as his romancing of the globe suggests. His wife – the flesh-and-blood Josephine – is nothing more than a name and an allusion in the novel; she is not even a vivid presence in the world of his imagination, as she would be were he her courtly lover.

The drama connected to Napoleon's romantic passion for himself is sharply contrasted to the daily dullness and sometimes shocking crudeness of the many other mismatched marriage partners the novel depicts. Henri's own mother, a passionately religious woman who would prefer convent life to conventional marriage, ends up married to a "slow-witted but kindly" older man named Claude (10). At first, she thought to find in him a temporary escape from her father, who was intent upon thwarting her religious aspirations, but she ends up being tied down by home and then their son, Henri, in just the kind of ordinary domestic life she had sought to escape (10–11). Through this relationship, Winterson presents marriage as a loveless fate forced upon Georgette because her parents prohibited her from entering a convent, and town gossip shamed her into legitimizing her living arrangement with Claude (11).

A third marriage in the novel – Villanelle's marriage – is equally loveless, but in this case the husband possesses none of Claude's slow-witted kindness. Indeed, because Villanelle's husband is crass and cruel, his marriage to Villanelle positions her within the stock *malmariée* role so common in medieval romances. Marie de France's *Laustic* offers a classic example of that *malmariée* type insofar as that tale's wife is unhappily married to a husband who is possessive, jealous, and indeed violent. In that story, when the husband discovers his wife awakening to hear a nightingale sing, he "kill[s] it out of spite,/ he br[eaks] its neck in his hands – / too vicious an act."[30] In *The Passion*, Villanelle marries a man who is no less vicious or possessive; also known as Napoleon's cook, he is a violent man who subjects women to sex as brutally as he chops chickens. As Villanelle describes him, "There was a man who had wanted me for some time, a man I had refused, cursed. A man I despised. A rich man with fat fingers" (96), but despite her strong independent streak, Villanelle marries him anyway. This "greasy, cock-sucking husband," as Villanelle later calls him, pursues and tries to control her (126), having become enraged when Villanelle took his money and tried to abandon him (98). He is the ultimate bad husband of medieval romance tradition, and one whom Villanelle is savvy enough to escape for much of the novel through wit and trickery and finally her love for a rich Venetian lady in a large house.

Villanelle's relationship with that lady serves as a positive alternative to the negative marriages Henri sees. As Lisa Moore notes, this lesbian relationship "exemplif[ies] the kind of passion for which he is searching."[31] Indeed, that relationship is itself a form of courtly love, one that illustrates how courtly love provides a vehicle for exploring relationships deemed transgressive within conventional society. In medieval stories such as Lancelot and Guinevere, romance writers chronicled the pursuit of love in "illegitimate" ways – that is, through relationships outside the boundaries of marriage, in a world where marriages often served politics or economics rather than love. In Winterson's novel, the "illegitimacy" and secrecy of the courtly love relationship arise not just because the woman is married, but also because the lovers are both women. In the historical world of the novel where marriage is the norm only for opposite-sex relationships, a courtly love relationship provides the vehicle for fulfilling passion between same-sex lovers. And notably, this "courtly" relationship between two women takes place not in the section of the novel devoted to Napoleon's historical expeditions, but in Venice, the imaginary city, where "all things are possible" (49) – as if the relationship is an imaginative exploration of Villanelle's question, "Could a woman love a woman for more than one night?" (69). Although Villanelle savors the pleasure of standing outside the lady's house, looking for her beloved with longing, the two arrange secret trysts when the woman's husband is away. During those trysts, their encounters consist of cultured conversation about "opera and the theatre and the visitors and the weather and ourselves" (66) and sweetly refined kissing (67). It is a ritualized kind of game for Villanelle, one that brings her both passion and pleasure; as Villanelle describes the kissing that falls short of full consummation, it was "sweet and precise torture" (67). Their ritual conversation and lovemaking serve as a refined contrast to the cook's brutal behavior towards Villanelle and other women.

The brutal conduct of Villanelle's husband is in fact representative of the villainous values that Winterson contrasts to more admirable courtly ones exemplified by the two women's relationship and by Henri himself. For instance, in Henri's early days of war service, he must innocently watch the lewdness, vulgarity, violence, and indeed villainy of the cook's treatment of women in a brothel (14). By contrast, Henri is established as a gentle man – one who, though a soldier, is himself as meek as a girl. Having been reared by a "priest and a pious mother," Henri is a "young man who," according to his friend Domino, "can't pick up a musket to shoot a rabbit" (28). And later, when Henri recounts how his father would trap blind moles back home, Henri admits, "I've killed them myself since, but only by looking the other way" (31). This gentle behavior helps to explain the courtly conduct we later see in Henri's treatment of Villanelle.

Henri's gentle conduct, however, is the exception rather than the norm in Napoleon's wartime world, and Winterson demonstrates the psychological schism created by "chivalric" military duties (good soldiering) and courtly ones, with the former tragically supplanting the latter. Indeed, in the thick of war, Henri contrasts the "country way" in which French men used to court their sweethearts and the way men regard women in the wartime world: "Here, without women, with only our imaginations and a handful of whores, we can't remember what it is about women that can turn a man through passion into something holy" (27). Henri's reflection suggests that passion for women can in fact be ennobling, as the troubadours of courtly love tradition implied, but the villainy and violence of war as well as the utilitarian role of women (whores) make such a "courtly" world impracticable. As a consequence, "mothers and sweethearts" no longer occupy a presence in their lives or mental universes: "We never think of them here. We think of their bodies and now and then we talk about home but we don't think of them as they are; the most solid, the best loved, the well known" (27). Absent from Winterson's fiction is any portrait of a "parfit, gentil knight" who can perfectly integrate violence on the battlefield and the courtesy characteristic of civilized society.

It is perhaps for this reason that Patrick the Priest preaches an eccentric sermon on the famous Annunciation story as a failure of courtesy and a critique of male conduct towards women. Rather than viewing the Virgin Mary's unexpected impregnation as a gracious gift, Patrick irreverently interprets it as a fault of divine manners:

> "See, women like you to treat them with respect. To ask before you touch. Now I've never thought it was right and proper of God to send his angel with no by your leave and then have his way before she'd even had time to comb her hair. I don't think she ever forgave him for that. He was too hasty. So I don't blame her that she's so haughty now." (40)

This heretical exegesis prompts Henri to adopt a different attitude towards the Virgin Mary, the ultimate courtly lady. And although Henri does not consider himself a believer, the next time he attends Church, he genuflects before the Virgin: "Despite myself I made her a little bow" (41). In doing so, Henri shows the kind of reverence for women so rare in what he witnesses of the war.

It is against this background, where, for men, prostitution or marriage is the norm for fulfilling love relationships and Napoleon seems to offer the only outlet for any other kind of love, that Henri's relationship with Villanelle develops. The relationship is from the start a physical one, with the innocent Henri seeking a fleshly fulfillment he had not hitherto known and Villanelle affectionately obliging. She is content simply to have sex with him, loving him in what she calls a "brotherly incestuous way" (146). Henri, however, becomes dead set on marrying Villanelle, a prospect that is not only impossible given her marriage to the cook, but also undesirable given her freewheeling ways and desire to remain free. Despite her independent bent, Henri believes that marriage would bring both of them joy. He says, "though I know it's nonsense I really believe we would always be happy and that our children would change the world" (123). As these words imply, his passion begets false fantasies that alienate him from the real Villanelle, who lives the rootless life of a gambler and harbors a passion for a beautiful woman in a big house. Moreover, such marriage fantasies threaten to make his own life a lie, for he acknowledges, "If I give in to this passion, my real life, the most solid, the best known, will disappear and I will feed on shadows again like those sad spirits whom Orpheus fled" (146). But as a person who loves security and safety as much as passion, Henri fears the prospect of seeing Villanelle only "by chance" (122–3); thus he persists in his quest to make her his wife.

The crisis of the novel, precipitated equally by the horrors of the war and Henri's increasingly possessed passion for Villanelle, occurs when Henri murders Villanelle's husband, the cook, tearing the cook's heart from his chest in a fit of rage.[32] This act results in Henri's imprisonment on the island San Servelo, which is where he comes to terms with a new relationship to Villanelle. He is imprisoned in a tiny room, haunted by voices and visions from his past. From his tower room he observes Villanelle pass on her Venetian boat, much as Chaucer's Palamon and Arcite once gazed at Emily in the garden beneath them during their imprisonment. Villanelle offers to help Henri escape, but he refuses, preferring certain "freedoms" of his island imprisonment. Villanelle's narration suggests that he is immured in a world of illusion, still vainly believing that he is "her husband" (148). Henri, however, describes his new state locked in San Servelo not as imprisonment, but as a form of freedom – indeed, as the freest way to love:

> Bonaparte taught us that freedom lay in our fighting arm, but in the legends of the Holy Grail no one won it by force. It was Perceval, the gentle knight, who came to a ruined chapel and found what the others had overlooked, simply by sitting still. I think now that being free is not being powerful or rich or well regarded or without obligations but being able to love. To love someone else enough to forget about yourself even for one moment is to be free. The mystics and the churchmen talk about throwing off this body and its desires, being no longer a slave to the flesh. They don't say that through the flesh we are set free. That our desire for another will lift us out of ourselves more cleanly than anything divine. (154)

Paradoxically, though, it is not through the flesh, but through a distant relationship facilitated by the imagination and its capacity for empathy, wherein Henri merely waves to Villanelle from the tower and observes her silently from his prison vantage, that he is made free. In Winterson's fiction, love and passion issue in a new ethic; according to Jean-Michel Ganteau "They are expected to make the subject push away his/her own boundaries as far as possible so as to achieve an encounter with the radical otherness of the beloved object."[33] Henri stands by the tower window with a mirror "and if the sun is shining [he] can catch the reflection of her hair. It lights up the straw on the floor and [he] think[s] the holy stable must have looked this way; glorious and humble and unlikely" (152–53). Here, then, Henri's passion blooms, like the unlikely rose garden he imagines flourishing in the rocky hard soil outside his window. And it is from this vantage that, as he asserts, he is able to love Villanelle "not a fantasy or a myth or a creature of [his] own making" (157). As Susana Onega concludes, "Henri's rejection of Napoleon and his revelation of what true love is signifies the end of his quest."[34]

These final passages from *The Passion* illustrate one prominent motif from the courtly love tradition of the troubadours: the mirror image. In many of the French troubadour lyrics and in *Romance of the Rose*, the mirror is linked to the courtly lady herself. For instance in one poem, Bernart de Ventadorn observes:

> Never have I had power over myself, nor have I to this day been mine, since the hour when she let me look into her eyes, into a mirror which pleases me greatly. Mirror, since I gazed at myself in you, sighs from deep down have killed me; and so I lost myself, just as the beautiful Narcissus lost himself in the fountain.[35]

Here the mirror is an image of self-reflexive, even narcissistic love. The lover adores the woman because she reflects his own image back to him, a process that paradoxically "kills" the lover. Winterson borrows this traditional mirror image but reverses its meaning within Henri's modern courtly love relationship. The mirror, which I shall later argue represents Henri's art, through the interaction of his own agency and the "sun" (perhaps a Platonic image of the truth) allows him to create a real picture of Villanelle *and* preserve his own self-identity. Neither he nor the beloved is destroyed through this love relationship, and indeed something new is even created in the art that issues from it.

In *The Passion*, therefore, a courtly love relationship resolves the passion between Henri and Villanelle, redeeming their broken relationship and offering a healthier alternative to the unhappy marriages and perverted passions chronicled in the novel. For, Winterson seems to suggest that even the formal constraints of courtly love allow the lover greater moral and spiritual freedom than the imprisonment of marriage or the degradation of prostitution.[36] Yet courtly love functions on a metafictional level, too, in *The Passion*. Henri's act of "mirroring" Villanelle offers one piece of evidence for that interpretation as does the metafictional mantra "Trust me. I'm telling you stories," which is repeatedly invoked throughout the novel, providing a refrain variously attributed to Henri, Villanelle, and the author of the novel. In key places, however, Winterson hints that Henri himself is the sole author of the dually narrated novel, making Henri not just lover and lunatic, but poet, too. For instance, just in passing, Henri mentions that he "kept working on [his] little book" (29), and later he refers to how he needs to rest from writing and take some exercise (81). Both passages suggest the possibility that Henri is the novel's author, and the voices and visions he hears are the inspiration for his characters. Bengtson supports this view by asserting, "Villanelle *is* poetry (hence her name) and in a sense Henri's muse; Henri the writer who grapples with the natures of passion and obsession as illustrated in his progress from an immature worship of Napoleon to an adult, selfless love for Villanelle."[37]

Read at a metafictional level, Henri's story proposes the courtly love paradigm as the perfect vehicle for relating author and character. For it is only through the author's distanced yet loving gaze that his characters can freely flourish in their own world, not merged with another in marriage but merely watched, observed, and admired. So, when Henri asserts from his prison window, "I will have a rose garden" on this rocky island, in this harsh climate, his claim makes sense only if he is the fictional author of *The Passion*, using language to create a love story out of the rubble of history and its hard facts. The power of the lover/author to create beauty where an objective observer might see none is foreshadowed in strikingly similar imagery by the medieval troubadour Raimbaut D'Aurenga. Self-conscious of both his love and his imaginative power, D'Aurenga claims:

Because I invert things for myself, so that hills seem to me beautiful plains and I regard the frost as a flower, and the heat seems to
me to cut though the cold, and the thunder is songs and whistlings
for me, and the dry sticks are leaved to me. I am so wholly taken
up in Joy that I can see nothing which is miserable in my eyes —[38]

Henri is similarly buoyed by joy and hope, confident that he "will
have red roses next year. A forest of red roses" (160), despite the frost,
the rocky land, and the bitter salt water (155). In this sense, the
garden of roses is the story of his flame-haired beauty; it is the imaginative issue of an author's love for a character and the ultimate gift
that he offers his inaccessible beloved.

II

Winterson's novel *The.Powerbook* moves her use of the courtly love
tradition more clearly in a metafictional direction. *The.Powerbook* is
an "Internet novel,"[39] structured according to a menu of computer
commands: Open Hard Drive, New Document, Search, View, and so
forth, with an e-writer named Ali (or Alix) willing to write anything
you, the reader, like, as long as you will respond to her *demande
d'amour* and enter her domain – that is, the fiction itself. The novel
shifts, with Ovidian fluidity, from story to story, metamorphosing
direct conversations with the reader into fairy tales, thinly-veiled auto-
biographical stories, and even medieval romances reaccented for a
contemporary audience. In her retelling of such tales, the e-writer Ali
slips into the role of lovers like Lancelot and Francesca, often imagining the reader as her famous romantic counterpart. As Jeannine
DeLombard puts it, "Paring proper names down to a simple 'I' and
'You,' Winterson reduces all such stories to the elemental pairing of
the lover and the beloved."[40]

    As part of this unfolding of romance, the reader becomes as much
a character as the narrator Ali is. According to the novel, what the
reader wants is "Freedom for a night" and transformation (4). That
transformation of identity is achieved within the linguistic space of
the novel itself; as Ali explains, "People arrive as themselves and leave
as someone else" (3). Moreover, the vehicle for creating and fulfilling
the reader's quest is language itself, which is introduced as a form of
costuming in the novel's first chapter (or "computer command"). The

fiction is a costume shop (3–4), and each of its stories is a fashion that "fits" someone and is sold to wear (235). However, there is a disembodied nature to the reclothing of participants in this relationship – one that links it to the idealized self-fashioning of the courtly love poets. After all, the narrator's first command is paradoxically sexual and disembodied: "Undress. Take off your clothes. Take off your body. Hang them up behind the door. Tonight we can go deeper than disguise" (4). The true essence of things, Ali claims, is story: "It's only a story, you say. So it is, and the rest of life with it" (4). Ali later ponders the possibility that the body itself is a disguise, "But what if my body is the disguise? What if skin, bone, liver, veins, are the things I use to hide myself? I have put them on and I can't take them off. Does that trap me or free me?" (15). In answer to those questions, she claims that language – story – frees her even from the constraints of the body, for "there is always a new beginning, a different end. I can change the story. I am the story" (4–5). In the narrator's view, identity is synonymous with story because story creates identity. Thus, "[f]or Winterson," as Jan Rosemergy observes, "the very act of creating fiction is a means of liberation."[41] But of all the stories Winterson plays with in this quest for identity, it is medieval ones that are especially prominent. When Winterson introduces readers to the apparel available in the shop, at least two items distinctly recall the medieval era, suggesting that her fiction is at least partly a reclothing of the reader in the trappings of medievalia: "At the tinkle of the bell you would have found yourself alone for a moment in the empty shop, looking at the suits of armour, the wimples, the field boots [...]" (3). Ali's statement hints that narrator and reader will try on identities and become themselves through and in response to medieval characters and story patterns, and such an idea is affirmed by the medieval narratives interpolated within the novel's "plot."

The medieval tales Winterson rewrites – the *Romance of the Rose*, Lancelot and Guinevere, Paolo and Francesca – are particularly tales of courtly love. In the novel's opening story, which one might call "Romance of the Tulip," the narrator Ali describes her quest to carry a tulip from Turkey to Holland in 1591; in good medieval allegorical fashion, the tulip is called "Key of Pleasure" and "Lover's Dream" (9). This initial story focuses on how Ali uses a flower for gender concealment during her journey – the "embalmed" tulip becomes a penis by which Ali can masquerade as a man. In an ironic inversion of the

Romance of the Rose (the medieval allegory about a male lover's quest to pluck the rose lying at the heart of a pleasurable garden), it is not a rose that essentially defines the sought-after female, but rather an artificially grafted tulip that allows her to perform another gender. Ali explains:

> This was my centerpiece. About eight inches long, plump, with a nice weight to it. [My mother and I] secured it to my person and inspected the results. There are many legends of men being turned into beasts and women into trees, but none I think, till now, of a woman who becomes a man by means of a little horticultural grafting. (12)

The Ovidian reference to metamorphosis becomes clear – however, it refers not only to a woman changed to a man, but also to a medieval tale transmuted into a modern one as *Romance of the Rose* becomes Romance of the Tulip. Thus, artifice lies at the heart of Ali's gender identity as well as at the heart of the retold romance story.

The romantic dimensions of Ali's story become clear when, along the quest to Holland, s/he encounters a Princess; at first, the story between Ali and an otherwise nameless Princess is described in typical courtly fashion. The Princess is "beautiful, young, haughty" (20). She possesses great power, in that she can "behead" her lover, Ali, if he behaves in a way that is not "gentle" (20). She is to be married to another person but, at her husband's request, needs someone to teach her the "arts of love," a course of remedy Ali is happy to supply (20). Furthermore, as the love relationship between Ali and the Princess begins, their stichomythic dialogue is in the formal register of courtly discourse. For instance, when Ali protests her worthiness as a lover, the following exchange ensues:

> "Lady" … "there must be many in your kingdom better equipped than I am."
> "They have not your treasure …". (20)

Here the formal diction and inverted syntax echo the elevated discourse of the courtly love tradition. Then, however, Winterson undercuts that refinement and formality with bluntness, colloquialism, and even vulgarity. By the end of the last encounter, Ali reports, "All afternoon I fucked her" (22). In this "courtly" romance, as Ali retells it, the lovers' "refined" and distant conversation is counter-pointed by a raw, bawdy relationship; the romance becomes an earthy, fleshly, sexual tale, as much about concrete bodies as about ennobled spirits. This commingling of high and low, courtly and vulgar elements in her romance results in an ironization of romance that recalls Jean de Meun's bawdy extension of Guillaume de Lorris's courtly love material in the medieval *Romance of the Rose*.[42]

Yet, as much as this "Romance of the Tulip" seems to shift Winterson's courtly love game, turning it towards "real," physical bodies and away from the realm of pure imagination, this story also undercuts that movement. The story between the Princess and Ali traces the slow quest from conversation to kissing to consummation, yet that consummation is impeded by a seemingly insurmountable obstacle: Ali's gender. She is female rather than male (as the Princess initially assumes). At the crucial moment when the consummation of their love could be destroyed by the revelation of the tulip as tulip, the Princess regards the tulip metaphorically. She says to Ali, "but you are *like* a flower" and "[the bulbs] are *like* sweet chestnuts" [emphasis mine] (21), despite Ali's initial efforts to acknowledge the tulip itself. Ali then adopts the same game by responding allegorically, "This one is Key of Pleasure, and this one is Lover's Dream" (21); the center she calls her "Stem of Spring" (22). It is this figurative play that makes possible their sexual consummation. Ali notes, "I felt my disguise come to life. The tulip began to stand" (22). Because they are able to think metaphorically – that is, to "carry beyond" reality – they are able to do what seems impossible within the constraints of the ordinary world. In a fantastical consummation of their love, Ali explains, "Very gently the Princess lowered herself across my knees and I felt the firm red head and pale shaft plant itself in her body. A delicate green-tinted sap dribbled down her brown thighs. All afternoon I fucked her" (22). Paradoxically, then, this story about the very physical act of "fucking" is accomplished only through the characters' imaginative actions; figurative play quite literally makes their passionate intercourse possible.

As *The.Powerbook* progresses, Winterson presents other versions of courtly love that affirm the imaginative power of language and love in the face of "real world" constraints. Winterson's retelling of Dante's Paolo and Francesca tale emphasizes Francesca's unhappy fate as *malmariée* and the salvific power of courtly love. Whereas Dante never described the background of Francesca's marriage, instead having her speak of her love for Paolo as if it existed in a social and political vacuum, Winterson supplies background details that offer a rationale for Francesca's love.[43] According to Winterson's Francesca, her husband, Gianciotto, was as ugly as he was unkind, and she describes her waiting woman as a "gaoler" meant to keep her confined in an unhappy marriage (127). In Winterson's account, unlike in Dante's, Francesca's marriage is a political one, arranged by her father supposedly as a "condition of peace" (124). By contrast to this purely pragmatic marriage, the courtly relationship between Paolo and Francesca is one Winterson describes positively in Platonic as well as Christian imagery. It is the light against which the darkness of the father's castle is negatively defined; it is an annunciation as well as a resurrection in Francesca's once-dead life. As Francesca explains:

> The horrors of my nights with him [Gianciotto] might have been bearable if I had not been taught a different way. The grave of my childhood life and the grave of my married life might have crumbled into one another without distinction, if Paolo had not kissed me and raised me from the dead for those few wide-open days. (127)

Indeed, Winterson represents the passion of these courtly lovers as so powerful that it transcends God's own power. Turning the Dantean whirlwind into a fickle force of fortune rather than a perpetual punishment, Winterson has Francesca proclaim, "We are as light now as our happiness was, lighter than birds. The wind carries us where it will, but our love is secure. No one can separate us now. Not even God" (129).[44] Here Winterson ironically echoes the language of St. Paul, suggesting that the eternal devotion of Francesca to Paolo is more perdurable even than the bond of God's love.

Winterson uses these medieval lovers to illustrate once again the imprisoning constraints of marriage and the quest of characters like Francesca and Paolo to find passion that is pure and free of social, political, religious, and gender constraints. She echoes that quest in recapitulating the tale of Lancelot and Guinevere, the medieval courtly love story par excellence. In Winterson's metafictional allegorization of that tale, Winterson figures the author as Lancelot the rescuer ("My name is Lancelot"), and the reader as Guinevere

("'Lancelot du Lac,' you said, rowing your body over me") (68). Lancelot's body and the romance text are represented as synonymous. In the guise of Lancelot, the narrator says, "I was the place where you anchored. I was the deep water where you could be weightless. I was the surface where you saw your own reflection. You scooped me up in your hands" (68). Thus Lancelot – the author/narrator whose physical body is the romance text – becomes the place where Guinevere (the reader) can escape her "dead marriage" and find freedom as she reads the book (Lancelot) and hovers over it, reading (68).

This metafictional allegory is further amplified through the quest that the contemporary e-writer Ali pursues elsewhere in the novel. As the Lancelot–Guinevere allegory suggests, the e-writer of this novel is involved in her own love relationship – this one with the reader as beloved. The e-writer's problem, like the problem of many medieval lovers named in Winterson's novel, is how to woo her lover, win her favor, and seduce her to leave the world to which she is wedded. In this metafictional allegory, however, the reader's spouse is not necessarily a flesh-and-blood husband, but rather the ordinary, everyday world, which vies with the author's world for attention and affection. As Ali describes this "husband," he is "a man built like a dining car – solid, welcoming, always about to serve lunch" (38). And she laments that:

> Inside [the] marriage there were too many clocks and not enough time. Too much furniture and too little space. Outside her marriage, there would be nothing to hold her, nothing to shape her. The space she found would be outer space. Space without gravity or weight, where bit by bit the self disintegrates. (39)

Here Winterson describes the reader's fearful prospect, the self-annihilation she faces should she choose to enter the narrative, submit to passion, and lose herself in its world. Yet that world is described as a "foreign city" bringing "relief from identity" (45) as from the fixed body the beloved was asked to relinquish before entering the writer's costume shop.

Just as the reader fits the role of the beloved *malmariée*, the e-writer Ali herself could easily be characterized as a conventional courtly lover, longing to meet her love and lamenting the distance between her and her beloved, the reader. The story itself is variously figured as a castle, a forest, a labyrinth, and a body, through which she seeks her lover, much as Ariosto's Orlando once sought the fleet-footed Angelica, realizing that, in a very literal sense, she cannot be completed without her lover's gaze; Ali fears, "If I do not find her, I will never find myself. If I do not find her, I will die in this forest, water within water" (238). And, indeed, she imagines the story she is writing as a kind of "gallehaut," encouraging herself by saying, "Go home and write the story again. Keep writing it because one day she will read it" (243). Thus the book is the ultimate "go-between," ennabling her to bridge the seemingly insurmountable gap between herself and the one she seeks to woo – her reader.

And Ali seems to recognize the impossibility of a final consummation of love between her and her reader, asserting, "My search for you, your search for me, is a search after something that cannot be found" (78). For, there are obvious ways in which author and reader must always remain separate. As Celia Shiffer notes, "To put something into words is to be already at a distance from the thing to be spoken, but speaking is the only means by which we can hope to reach the Thing (and we are meant to trust in words to recover it)."[45] And so Ali continues, "Only the impossible is worth the effort" (78). With this conviction, she hazards yet one final plea to her disdainful lady, begging the reader's touch for her gift and imploring her to "Open it. Read it" (243). In this way, the courtly love paradigm structures the relationship between author and reader, drawing the reader into a relationship with her author that is distant and idealized but at the same time infused with potential passion, creating an erotic relationship that is fulfilled only through Winterson's language and the reader's imagination.

That Winterson would use such a transcendent ideal for love and art – one more familiar to medieval than to postmodern culture – is perhaps not surprising given the Christian background that shaped and inevitably still shapes her thinking; yet she seeks a transcendence that is not moored to a specifically Christian ideology. As Louise Horskjær Humphries notes:

Central to her writing seems to be ontological questions about the creation of identity and the nature of humanity, and, in relation to these, two very significant concerns are those of love and language. For Winterson, transcendence – going beyond oneself in search for an "other" – is absolutely essential for the creation of a person, and both art and love seem to carry with them a promise of transformation, of transcendence.[46]

Winterson's intensely lyrical, metaphorical prose pursues transcendence in just the way the medieval courtly poets once did. For she seeks to move beyond the boundaries of the ordinary, everyday world, with its political, social, religious, and gender constraints and instead to create an ideal aristocratic world – a "courtly" domain for contemporary inhabitants. In her view, that domain is the special province of true lovers and true artists who believe in the power of the imagination to create and ennoble reality.[47]

In *The Passion* and *The.Powerbook*, therefore, I submit that Winterson uses the medieval courtly love tradition in two primary ways to show how language moves beyond ordinary reality to create and transform. On the one hand, Winterson employs the courtly love tradition as a vehicle for exploring relationships deemed transgressive within conventional society – in the case of her earlier novel, for imagining the dynamics of same-sex relationships in a world dominated by domestic marriages and for preserving within heterosexual relationships a proper passion. On the other hand, she employs the courtly love paradigm as a metafictional allegory for exploring the relationship between author and reader. In her earlier novel she uses courtly love unironically, as a way of mapping an ideal ethical relationship between lover and beloved, but in her later work, she also allegorizes and ironizes her courtly love material, much as Jean de Meun once did with Guillaume de Lorris's courtly love material.

In both novels, Winterson illustrates how language – narrative and poetry – confers identity, creates relationships, and constitutes a veritable world, in which "atom and dream" (*The.Powerbook*, 241) are equally powerful. In this sense, Winterson implicitly levies a serious argument against those critics of literature and history who view courtly love as "merely" a literary fiction because of its distance from historical reality. For Winterson, the fiction of courtly love does not reflect reality; it is much more powerful than that. Rather, it shapes and creates reality. As one of the final pages in *The.Powerbook* proclaims, inverting the archetypal symbol of mimesis, "The world is a mirror of the mind's abundance" (223).

NOTES

1. For instance, Susana Onega's 1993 essay on *The Passion* describes that novel as one "clogged with literary allusions," yet the literary allusions she names range from "Homer and Euripides to Joyce, Pushkin and Borges," with no mention of anything medieval. See Susana Onega, "*The Passion*: Jeanette Winterson's Uncanny Mirror of Ink," *Miscelánea: A Journal of English and American Studies* 14 (1993): 113–29 (125). I address Winterson's use of medieval legendary material in my 1999 dissertation "Medieval Illuminations: Patterns of Medievalism in the Fiction of Jeanette Winterson, Iris Murdoch, and John Fowles." In that study, however, I examine Winterson's medievalism only in relation to her 1985 novel *Oranges Are Not the Only Fruit*.

2. Jean-Michel Ganteau, "Hearts Object: Jeanette Winterson and the Ethics of Absolutist Romance," in Susana Onega and Christian Gutleben, ed., *Refracting the Canon in Contemporary British Literature and Film* (Amsterdam: Rodopi, 2004), 165–85 (166).

3. Jeanette Winterson, *Lighthousekeeping* (Orlando, FL: Harcourt, 2004), 115, 143.

4. Carolyne Larrington, "Happily Ever After," rev. of *Weight*, by Jeanette Winterson, *Times Literary Supplement*, 18 November 2005, 23.

5. The six books included two Bibles, a concordance to the Old and New Testaments, *The House at Pooh Corner*, *The Chatterbox Annual 1923*, and Malory's *Morte d'Arthur*. See Jeanette Winterson, *Art [Objects]: Essays on Ecstasy and Effrontery* (New York: Alfred A. Knopf, 1996), 153. The fact that Winterson's early reading was divided largely between religious works and romance stories puts Winterson in a tradition of female readership dating back to the Middle Ages. As Roberta Krueger notes, "pious works and didactic works comprised the greatest portion of books associated with medieval women, even in the case of women not renowned for their piety [...]. But romances comprise the second largest genre owned and/or transmitted by women [...]. The widespread female readership of Arthurian romance in England can be seen in records of female ownership of romances variously about Tristan, Lancelot, Arthur, and Merlin in the fourteenth and fifteenth centuries." Roberta L. Krueger, "Questions of Gender in Old French Courtly Romance," in Roberta L. Krueger, ed., *The Cambridge Companion to Medieval Romance* (Cambridge: Cambridge University Press, 2000), 132–49 (135).

6. Jeanette Winterson, "Biography," <http://www.jeanettewinterson.com/pages/content/index.asp?PageID=207> [accessed 11 January 2008].

7. Helen Barr, "Face to Face," interview with Jeanette Winterson, *English Review* 2 (1991): 30–33 (31–32).

8. Barr, "Face to Face," 32.

9. Bill Hampl, an early reviewer of *The.Powerbook*, noticed parallels in the structure of the love relationships in these two novels, but he did not identify them as courtly love patterns. Bill Hampl, "High Seas of Cyberspace," review of *The.Powerbook*, by Jeanette Winterson, *Gay and Lesbian Review Worldwide* 8.1 (Jan./Feb. 2001): 44–45 (44).

10. Marian Eide, "Passionate Gods and Desiring Women: Jeanette Winterson, Faith, and Sexuality," *International Journal of Sexuality and Gender Studies* 6.4 (October 2001): 279–91 (285).

11. Gaston Paris, "Études Sur Les Romans De La Table Ronde. Lancelot du Lac. II. *Le Conte de La Charrette,*" *Romania* 12 (1883): 459–534 (518–19).

12. Bernard O'Donoghue, *The Courtly Love Tradition* (Manchester: Manchester University Press, 1982), 96.

13. E. Talbot Donaldson, "The Myth of Courtly Love," *Ventures* 5 (1965): 16–23 (17).

14. As Kelly explains: "[Paris] introduced [*amour courtois*] in 1883 as a critical term to describe the peculiar kind of love conventions first seen in Chrétien's *Lancelot*, but later came to apply it to earlier works, especially the lyrics of the troubadours, where it designated a different combination of conventions from that of *Lancelot*." Henry Ansgar Kelly, "The Varieties of Love in Medieval Literature According to Paris," *Romance Philology* 40.3 (February 1987): 301–27 (324).

15. James A. Schultz, *Courtly Love, the Love of Courtliness, and the History of Sexuality* (Chicago: University of Chicago Press, 2006), 159.

16. Joachim Bumke, *Courtly Culture: Literature and Society in the High Middle Ages*, trans. Thomas Dunlap (Woodstock, NY: The Overlook Press, 2000), 360. For further discussion of scholarly views on the courtly love tradition, Roger Boase offers a still-useful, comprehensive survey of theories about courtly love such as those Schultz and Bumke refer to here. See Roger Boase, *The Origin and Meaning of Courtly Love: A Critical Study of European Scholarship* (Manchester: Manchester University Press, 1977).

17. Joan M. Ferrante, "Cortes' Amor *in Medieval Texts,*" *Speculum* 55.4 (October 1980): 686–95 (686).

18. Ferrante, "Cortes' Amor," 695. Here it is interesting to note that Winterson read literature at Oxford University (St. Catherine's College) in the late 1970s, receiving her M.A. in 1981. See Daniel Jones and John D. Jorgensen, ed., "Winterson, Jeanette," *Contemporary Authors* 58 (Farmington Hills, MI: Gale, 1997): 443–46 (443). Her university education may have given her additional exposure to medieval literature and even to the scholarly

debate about courtly love, which was in full swing at the time Winterson received her university education. Indeed, the material presented in Ferrante's essay was initially gathered for a debate between Ferrante and Donaldson at the International Medieval Congress in May 1979 (Ferrante, "Cortes' Amor," 686).

19. Schultz, *Courtly Love*, 159.

20. Schultz, *Courtly Love*, 159.

21. Schultz, *Courtly Love*, xx, 160.

22. Schultz, *Courtly Love*, xx.

23. Sarah Kay, "Courts, Clerks, and Courtly Love," in Krueger, ed., *The Cambridge Companion*, 81–96 (81).

24. Kay, "Courts, Clerks," 92.

25. Kay, "Courts, Clerks," 81.

26. Schultz, *Courtly Love*, xxi.

27. Notwithstanding the nineteenth-century setting that dominates parts of *The Passion*, Judith Seaboyer still sees something medieval in Venice, the imaginary city Winterson contrasts to Napoleon's historical empire. Seaboyer writes that Winterson is a writer who has "discovered a means of articulating late-twentieth-century concerns not from the vantage point of the abstract metropolis of modernity, or the edge city of postmodernity, but from within the contained symbolic landscape of the medieval city–Renaissance *urbs* that is Venice." See Judith Seaboyer, "Second Death in Venice: Romanticism and the Compulsion to Repeat in Jeanette Winterson's *The Passion*," *Contemporary Literature* 38.3 (1997): 483–509 (483). Likewise, Helene Bengtson intuits echoes of medieval romance in *The Passion* by observing, "The custom-made geography of romance quests, with an adventure and a lady for each knight, has much in common with the fluid Venetian topography that meets Henri and Villanelle in *The Passion*: the Venetian cityscape is a testing-ground which, like the dangerous wilderness of chivalric romance, supplies the challenges which will bring out the errant knight's merit." See Helene Bengtson, "The Vast, Unmappable Cities of the Interior," in Helene Bengtson, Marianne Borch, and Cindie Maagaard, ed., *Sponsored by Demons: The Art of Jeanette Winterson* (Odense, Denmark: Scholar's Press, 1999): 17–26 (18).

28. Jeanette Winterson, *The.Powerbook* (London: Jonathan Cape, 2000), 95.

29. Jeanette Winterson, *The Passion* (New York: Vintage, 1989), 4.

30. Marie de France, "Laustic," in Robert Hanning and Joan Ferrante, ed., *The Lais of Marie de France* (Durham, NC: Labyrinth, 1982), 155–59 (lines 114–16).

31. Lisa Moore, "Teledildonics: Virtual Lesbians in the Fiction of Jeanette Winterson," in Elizabeth Grosz and Elspeth Probyn, ed., *Sexy*

Bodies: The Strange Carnalities of Feminism (London: Routledge, 1995), 104–27 (112).

32. A story element reminiscent of many medieval folktales and romances – just witness Boccaccio's tale of Roussillon and Cabestanh, the ninth story of the fourth day in *The Decameron*. In that tale, Roussillon forces his wife to eat her lover's heart, which he has brutally ripped from the lover's chest after murdering him. See Giovanni Boccaccio, *The Decameron*, trans. John Payne (Berkeley: University of California Press, 1982), 350–53.

33. Ganteau, "Hearts Object," 175. Or, as another recent critic, Jago Morrison, has observed (not without disapproval), Winterson's fictional career increasingly explores "Love in terms of the agapeic tradition" (169), a tradition that entails the "shedding of earthly ties, a transcendence of fleshly concerns, the recognition and acceptance of a freely given, freely taken gift of love" (179). See Jago Morrison, "'Who Cares About Gender at a Time Like This?' Love, Sex and the Problem of Jeanette Winterson," *Journal of Gender Studies* 15.2 (July 2006): 169–80.

34. Onega, "*The Passion*," 125.

35. O'Donoghue, *Courtly Love Tradition*, 117.

36. By contrast, other critics have seen in the ending a strictly tragic outcome; as Seaboyer puts it, "[H]e remains an exile unable to navigate the labyrinth and is swallowed up in madness and despair." Seaboyer, "Second Death," 485. But as Bengtson points out, such a reading depends on privileging Villanelle's view of Henri, not his own (21), and it further privileges her final view of "real life" over his imaginative construction of life, in a valuing of ordinary "reality" over imagination that is not supported elsewhere in Winterson's essays or fiction. Bengtson, "Vast, Unmappable Cities," 21.

37. Bengtson, "Vast, Unmappable Cities," 24.

38. O'Donoghue, *Courtly Love Tradition*, 125.

39. Ulf Cronquist, "Hypertext, Prosthetics, and the Netocracy: Posthumanism and Jeanette Wintersons [sic] *The.Powerbook*," in Carmen Rosa Caldas-Coultard and Michael Toolan, ed., *The Writer's Craft, The Culture's Technology* (Amsterdam: Rodopi, 2005), 47–56 (47).

40. Jeannine DeLombard, "Control Option Delete," rev. of *The. Powerbook*, by Jeanette Winterson, *Lambda Book Report* 9.5 (Dec. 2000): 24–25 (24).

41. Jan Rosemergy, "Navigating the Interior Journey: The Fiction of Jeanette Winterson," in Abby H. P. Werlock, ed., *British Women Writing Fiction* (Tuscaloosa: University of Alabama Press, 2000), 248–69 (248).

42. As one critic describes the contradictory currents within *Romance of the Rose*: "[I]f Guillaume is courtly and elegant, Jean is bourgeois and realistic; if the one is lyrical, pictorial, incisive, idealistic, the other is

philosophical, encyclopedic, digressive, satirical." See Maxwell Luria, *A Reader's Guide to the Roman de la Rose* (Hamden, CT: Archon, 1982), 10. Winterson captures both of those currents within the scope of *The.Powerbook*. And, indeed, at least one Winterson reviewer noticed her taking a similar strategy in the 1997 novel *Gut Symmetries*: Katy Emck described Winterson's "third voice" in that novel as the "voice of lyric love, which mixes dizzy troubadour longing with whispery religiosity and fruits-of-the-earthiness." Katy Emck, "On the High Seas of Romance," rev. of *Gut Symmetries*, by Jeanette Winterson, *Times Literary Supplement*, 3 January 1997, 21.

43. As much as Winterson draws upon the medieval past for the substance of her stories, she also resists it; the narrator Ali remarks, "Break the narrative. Refuse all the stories that have been told so far [...] and try to tell the story differently – in a different style, with different weights" (53).

44. Cf. St. Paul in Romans 8:38–39: "For I am sure that neither death, nor life, nor angels, nor principalities, nor things present, nor things to come, nor powers, nor height, nor depth, nor anything else in all creation, will be able to separate us from the love of God in Christ Jesus our Lord." Thus, Winterson appropriates St. Paul's rhetoric, but in order to exalt a secular, courtly love relationship. *The New Oxford Annotated Bible with the Apocrypha*, Revised Standard Version, ed. Herbert G. May and Bruce M. Metzger (New York: Oxford University Press, 1977).

45. Celia Shiffer, "'You see, I am no stranger to love': Jeanette Winterson and the Extasy of the Word," *Critique: Studies in Contemporary Fiction* 46.1 (Fall 2004): 31–52 (36).

46. Louise Horskjær Humphries, "Listening for the Author's Voice: 'Unsexing' the Wintersonian Oeuvre," in Bengtson et al., ed., *Sponsored by Demons*, 3–16 (16).

47. As Kasia Boddy puts it, "Love and art are religious experiences for Winterson's protagonists – acts of faith and creation – and the true artist, and true lover, must always have something of the mystic and the martyr about her." Kasia Boddy, "Love, again," rev. of *The.Powerbook*, by Jeanette Winterson, *Times Literary Supplement*, 1 September 2000, 9.

New Golden Legends:
Golden Saints of the Nineteenth Century

Clare A. Simmons

In the first half of the nineteenth century, the British printing and publishing industry underwent a transformation of such a scale that some observers seem to have found parallels with William Caxton's first introduction of the printing press into England.[1] Early printed books produced by Caxton, his successor Wynken de Worde, and others became sought-after collectibles. While the bibliomania of the early 1800s was limited to the wealthy, it helped foster an interest in the book both for its contents (generally, the older the better) and for its appearance. As the number of readers expanded, new forms of publication, and especially periodicals, brought not only words but also style to a broader reading public. The word "style" connotes both the imitation of earlier forms (homage, pastiche, parody, or a combination of all three) and the visual appearance of earlier forms made possible by new methods in printing. Many of the new periodicals of this time, including the most familiar example, *Punch*, which commenced publication in 1841, display not their newness but their indebtedness to tradition by imitating the kinds of lettering used by Caxton and other early printers and by incorporating illuminated letters and illustrations in the style of medieval texts. Some of them also adopt medieval genres. At the same time, these publications often show a discomfort with the kind of medieval recuperation on which their success depends.

One of the most popular of Caxton's productions was the *Golden Legend*, Jacques de Voragine's thirteenth-century compilation of devotional stories rendered into English. Caxton's apprentice Wynken de Worde continued to produce editions at least into the 1520s, and nineteenth-century writers often make reference to these later editions, which presumably were more accessible.[2] The concept of the legend, and to some extent this debt to the early history of printing, was reworked by authors in the early 1800s, perhaps the supreme example being Thomas Hood's bizarre poem "Miss Kilmansegg and her Precious Leg," subtitled "A Golden Leg-end." A poem about what might now be called a bionic leg might at first consideration seem far removed from medievalism. Yet medievalism here, as often in nineteenth-century British writing, becomes a means, probably an overdetermined means, to talk about changing circumstances of the contemporary world. For Hood, creator of such famous puns as "a cannon-ball took off his legs/ So he lay down his arms,"[3] the pun on Golden Legend and Golden Leg might be enough justification for his subtitle. I would suggest, though, that Hood was conscious of the structure of Golden Legends, and used the model of a saint's life as a form of social commentary, while not entirely endorsing the recuperation of the concept of the legend.

The word "legend" itself was undergoing a revival or even a recreation at the time that Hood wrote. *Legenda* as in *Aurea Legenda* has the meaning of something to be read,[4] as its Latin origin from the gerundive form of *legere* suggests. Peter G. Bietenholz makes a useful distinction between myth and legend by noting that myths have a universality while legends retain "at least some ties with documented historical events or specific geographical locations."[5] The stories of saints' lives, which reminded readers of names, dates, and places, ostensibly had the purpose of inspiring their audience to Christian faith and conduct, although very possibly the sexual implications, nudity, torture, and dismemberment in the stories of the martyrs may also have attracted a less devotional readership.

The change in the meaning of the word "legend" to a traditional story often with elements of the fantastic seems to have come after the English Reformation, at least partly as a direct repudiation of the Golden Legend. For Protestants, the stories of the marvelous doings of the saints detracted from the Christian's personal relationship with God. For example, John Foxe's *Actes and Monuments*, which creates a new Protestant hagiography proclaiming its basis in historical events rather than in legend, quotes a letter by Nicholas Sheterden, writing to his brother in 1555. Sheterden questions the authority of Roman Catholic theologians by reminding his brother that if the priests "had studied God's word, the author of truth, as they have done logick, and Duns [Scotus], with the legend of lies, they should have been so expert in the truth, as they be now in bald reasons."[6] Francis Bacon similarly invokes the *Golden Legend* as something beyond the power of rational belief in his essay "Of Atheisme" when he writes, "I had rather believe all the fables in the Legend, and the Alcoran, then that this universall frame is without a minde."[7] The *Oxford English Dictionary* records the first English use of the word "legend" in the sense of "an unauthentic or non-historical story" about the same time, in Thomas Purchas's *Pilgrimage*: "That yee may know the Indians want not their Metamorphoses and Legends [...]."[8] Even here, though, the term "legend" is paired with another specific book (Ovid's *Metamorphoses*), so it might still refer specifically to the *Golden Legend*.

Even in the eighteenth century, uses of the word "legend" tend to recall saints' lives. For example, the only use of the word in Francis Grose's *Provincial Glossary, with a Collection of Local Proverbs, and Popular Superstitions* (1787) is in connection with a story about the De Tracy family, who traced their origins to one of the murderers of Thomas Becket.[9] Similarly, the first volume of David Hume's *History of England* (1762) might be expected to use the word "legend" in describing the origins of the English people. Again, Hume only uses the word directly to reference saints' lives when he states that after Becket's murder, "Endless were the panegyrics on his virtues; and the miracle, operated by his relicts, were more numerous, more nonsensical, and more impudently attested, than those which ever filled the legend of any confessor or martyr."[10]

But the word "legend" underwent a revival in the early nineteenth century as a more general interest in national, local, and oral traditions emerged and tales of the marvelous could be appreciated not as miracles but as survivals of past beliefs. The *British Library Catalogue* lists one book title containing the word "legend" or "legends" from the period 1700 to 1800. From 1800 to 1850, it lists 80-odd, and from 1850 to 1900 it lists over 400. The trend in these titles is to use the word "legend" not in its original sense of something to read, but as something passed down through the oral tradition.

In the first half of the nineteenth century, we see the word "legend" bridging the written and the oral, as something that seems to be passed down by oral tradition, frequently in having elements of the fantastic or supernatural, but that reaches its audience in written form.

The most familiar example for many readers will be Washington Irving's "Legend of Sleepy Hollow," first published in *The Sketch-Book of Geoffrey Crayon* in 1818–19. R. H. Barham's contribution was the *Ingoldsby Legends*, again published piecemeal in *Bentley's Miscellany* in the 1830s. The role of *Bentley's* in creating the idea of the legend is significant. The very first number, published shortly before Queen Victoria's accession in 1837, contains a ballad titled "The Legend of Manor Hall," written by Thomas Love Peacock. The first of Barham's pieces followed in the second number. "The Legend of Hamilton Tighe," written in iambic couplets, tells the story of the headless ghost of a young officer that haunts the three people who conspired to murder him. Many of the succeeding tales draw on the oral traditions of the fictional Ingoldsby family and use "legends" in this new sense of traditional stories supposedly retold as fireside tales.

Yet beginning with "A Lay of St. Nicholas" in the third (1838) volume, Barham also drew upon the tradition of the "golden legend" by composing a number of "lays" about miraculous doings of medieval saints. Like the word "legend," the word "lay" was undergoing a recuperation at this time. B. G. Niebuhr, whose lecture-history of Rome was translated into English in 1837–38, had suggested that the early history of Rome would have been preserved by poets in the form of heroic lays, and that this would have been a source for Livy's history.[11] The future Lord Macaulay used this theory as the inspiration for his *Lays of Ancient Rome*, published in 1841. At the time Barham wrote, then, the word "lay" was closely associated with legends of supposedly historical people and places. Barham does not seem to have limited himself to the best-known stories associated with particular saints, but instead incorporates a variety of common folk-motifs. In "A Lay of St. Nicholas," for example, the story is not one of the best-known stories about Nicholas as in the *Golden* Legend, such as his miraculous childhood or his bestowal of gifts. Instead, following in the tradition of the "loathly lady," the saint reveals an aristocratic damsel in distress as a devil in disguise:

> O'er a pint and a quarter of holy water
>   He made a sacred sign;
> And he dash'd the whole on the *soi-disant* daughter
>   Of old Plantagenet's line!
> Oh! Then did she reek, and squeak, and shriek,

> With a wild unearthly scream;
> And fizzled, and hiss'd, and produced such a mist,
>   They were all half-choked by the steam.
> Her dove-like eyes turn'd to coals of fire,
>   Her beautiful nose to a horrible snout,
> Her hands to paws with great nasty claws,
>   And her bosom went in, and her tail came out.
> On her chin there appear'd a long Nanny-goat's beard,
>   And her tusks and her teeth no man mote tell;
> And her horns and her hoofs gave infallible proofs
>   'Twas a frightful Fiend from the nethermost Hell![12]

In this poem, Roman Catholic ritual such as the power of holy water actually works, yet the humorous tone makes it clear that Barham is not betraying his profession as an Anglican clergyman. The poem places the Golden Legend within the folklore tradition, so that stories of the saints are no longer devotional stories, but folktales of the marvelous and privileged for that reason rather than for their ability to inspire piety. Most of these verse-stories begin with the indefinite article ("A Lay of [...]"), which seems to stress the possibility of more and more such tales.

Barham directly references Caxton's *Golden Legend* in "A Lay of St. Dunstan," but again the story that follows is not one of the narratives of St. Dunstan included in the *Golden Legend*, such as how he pinched the devil's nose with his blacksmith's tongs, or even a story from Bede. The Lay of St. Dunstan is described as:

> A particular fact in the life of the Saint,
> Which, somehow, for want of due care, I presume,
> Has escaped the researches of Rapin and Hume,
> In recounting a miracle, both of them men, who a
> Great deal fall short of Jacques, Bishop of Genoa,
> An Historian who likes deeds like these to record:
> See his *Aurea Legenda*, by Wynkyn de Worde.

Rapin and Hume, representative of rationalist party historians of the eighteenth century, cannot match Jacques de Voragine, although, interestingly, the Ingoldsby narrator references Wynkyn de Worde's printing of the *Golden Legend* from 1521 rather than Caxton himself. That the narrator's tongue is firmly in his cheek is indicated when the miraculous story that follows is actually a retelling of "The Sorcerer's

Apprentice," probably most familiar at this time from Goethe's ballad "Der Zauberlehrling" (1797). In keeping with the theme of golden legends, Dunstan is in the story a goldsmith with a magic broomstick to do his household chores. Dunstan takes on a lay brother called Peter, Peter asks the broomstick to bring him beer, the broomstick cannot be stopped, and he breaks it in half. Then two broomsticks come, the narrator says:

> [...] loaded with Meux's entire;
> Combe's, Delafield's, Hanbury's, Truman's, no stopping –
> Goding's, Clarenton's, Whitbread's continued to drop in,
> With Hodson's pale ale, from the Sun Brewhouse, Wapping.

After this shameless use of brewery names, the bard adds:

> The firms differ'd then, but I can't put a tax on
> My memory to say what their names were in Saxon. (164)

St. Dunstan intervenes, but not in time; Peter is drowned in beer and petrified; his stone form is now in a "handsome glass-case" at Goldsmith's Hall. Barham thus preserves both the "golden" and the "legend" part, but even though he includes a moral, "Keep clear of Broomsticks, Old Nick, and three XXXs," the devotional aspect of the Legends is gone.

In contrast, Thomas Hood chose to recapture and restructure the devotional tone of the Golden Legend in his directly contemporary poem "Miss Kilmansegg and Her Precious Leg." Hood originally wrote this very long – over 2,000 lines – poem for publication in serial form in the *New Monthly Magazine* in 1840–41, and his correspondence reveals that he also composed it as a serial, the earlier parts having appeared in print before he wrote the conclusion; he wrote to a friend on 1 February 1841 that "[...] at last, I have killed her, instead of her killing me; not my wife, but Miss Kilmansegg, who died very hard, for I found it difficult to get into the tone and story again after two months' interruption."[13] The poem was reissued with illustrations by John Leech, best known for his work in *Punch*, in the *Comic Almanac* of 1842.[14] It is hard to determine exactly what level of understanding of the allusions to the *Golden Legend* Hood expected of his readership, but the pattern of the poem follows that of a typical saint's life. In the *Golden Legend*, the saint's holiness very often manifests itself at birth: for example, St. Nicholas:

> was born of rich and holy kin [...]. Then the first day that he was washed and bained, he addressed him right up in the bason, and he would not take the breast nor the pap but once on the Wednesday and once on the Friday, and in his young age he eschewed the plays and japes of other young children. He used and haunted gladly holy church; and all that he might understand of holy scripture he executed it in deed and work after his power.[15]

St. Dunstan prompted miracles before he was born:

> S. Dunstan was born in England, and our Lord showed miracles for him ere he was born. It was so that on a Candlemas day, as all the people were in the church with tapers in their hands, suddenly all the lights in the church were quenched at once, save only the taper which S. Dunstan's mother bare, for that burned still fair. Whereof all the people marvelled greatly; howbeit her taper was out, but by the power of our Lord it lighted again by itself, and burned full bright, so that all the others came and lighted their tapers at the taper of S. Dunstan's mother. (3:87)

Such stories of childhood are rarer of female saints, although St. Germaine identified St. Genevieve as saintly while she was a child, informing her parents that:

> God hath given to you so noble lineage, know ye for certain that the day of her nativity, the angels sang and hallowed great mystery in heaven with great joy and gladness; she shall be of so great merit against God. And of her good life and conversation many shall take ensample, that they shall leave their sin and shall convert them to God, and shall live religiously, by which they shall have pardon and joy perdurable. (3:131)

Similarly, St. Katherine was holy and learned from girlhood:

> when this holy virgin was born she was so fair of visage and so well formed Katherine in her members that all the people enjoyed in her beauty, and when she came to seven years of age, anon after she was set to school, where she profited much more than any other of her age, and was informed in the arts liberal, wherein she drank

plenteously of the well of wisdom, for she was chosen to be a
teacher and informer of everlasting wisdom. (7:5)

More typically, however, female saints' stories start when they reach
marriageable age. In her study of medieval virgin martyrs, Karen
Winstead notes that:

> Most of the standard ingredients of virgin martyr legends are
> found in the accounts of most early Christian martyrs, male or
> female: the saint refuses to participate in pagan sacrifices, debates
> her antagonist, affirms the fundamental tenets of Christianity,
> destroys idols, performs miracles, and endures excruciating
> torments. What distinguishes the legends of most female martyrs
> from those of their male counterparts is a preoccupation with
> gender and sexuality.[16]

When non-Christians want to marry them, they refuse and remain
steadfast to their devotion to Christ, often through horrible torments
that lead to their martyrdom. For example:

> S. Agatha the virgin was right fair, noble body and of heart, and
> was rich of goods. This glorious virgin served God in the city of
> Catania, leading a pure and holy life. Quintianus the provost of
> Sicily, being of a low lineage, was lecherous, avaricious, and a
> miscreant and paynim, and for to accomplish his evil desires
> fleshly, and to have riches, did do take S. Agatha to be presented
> and brought tofore him, and began to behold her with a lecherous
> sight; and for to have her himself, he would have induced her to
> make sacrifice unto the idols.

St. Agatha, of course, refuses and goes through horrible torments,
including imprisonment, mutilation, and burning, before going to her
heavenly reward.

As in the case of Agatha, and of course the archetypal virgin
martyr, St. Katherine, whose father is a king, the majority of these
saints are described in Caxton's translation as "nobly born," and
wealth, especially in the form of gold, comes into the stories in a
number of ways. St. Nicholas gives gold to protect people from
poverty or exploitation. St. Dunstan, who is sometimes described as a
blacksmith making shoes for horses and on one occasion for the Devil,
is a goldsmith in the Golden Legend. Similarly, St. Loye is a goldsmith

who miraculously makes the King of France two golden saddles out of the same gold and gives away all his wealth to the poor: "he loved well poor people, for all that he won and might win he distributed it to them, in so much that oft he was almost naked" (3:121). In the life of St. Loye and others in the *Golden Legend*, the primary function of gold is to help the poor, and the saints' disregard of gold shows their focus on real wealth, the Kingdom of Heaven.

In "Miss Kilmansegg and Her Precious Leg," Hood follows the pattern of the saints' lives in giving her pedigree, her birth, and her christening, each in sections headed by Caxton-style Gothic type.[17] He also emphasizes the role of gold in her life. In "Her Pedigree," the Kilmansegg family is said to have become wealthy:

> In the Golden Age of Farming;
> When golden eggs were laid by the geese,
> And Colchian sheep wore a golden fleece [...].[18]

In this opening section of the poem, Hood both uses the structure of the saints' legend and also sprinkles his poem with references to classical myths, seemingly not distinguishing between Christian and classical mythology. After listing golden apples, bulls, asses, bees, and so on, the narrator then suggests that this is itself legend:

> Such was the tale of the Kilmansegg Kin,
> In golden text on a vellum skin,
> Though certain people would wink and grin,
> And declare the whole story a parable –
> That the Ancestor rich was one Jacob Ghrimes,
> Who held a long lease, in prosperous times,
> Of acres, pasture and arable.

The wealth comes from investments and the high price of wheat due to the Corn Laws and the Napoleonic Wars, making the wealth new rather than old. Nevertheless, all the trappings of rank are presented to the "infant Kilmansegg," whose father is also Jacob. Perhaps Hood was thinking of Jacques de Voragine, since the father of the Golden Legend is also known by the Latin version of his name, Jacobus, but the name also recalls the great folklorist Jakob Grimm. Miss Kilmansegg has a golden rattle as soon as she is born, and her birth is celebrated by a huge party. Her baptism is celebrated in a vessel that recalls the legendary exploits of early Protestants:

> The Font was a bowl of American gold,
> Won by Raleigh in days of old,
> In spite of Spanish bravado [...] (lines 336–38)

In an ironic reversal of the *Golden Legend*, which painstakingly explains the meaning of saints' names, the poem informs us that Miss Kilmansegg was given six Christian names – and then does not state what they were!

The most important distinction, though, is that whereas in the Golden Legend saints are marked out by their holiness, Miss Kilmansegg is a special person only because of her wealth. In her childhood, her toys are gold, while her education increases her expectations:

> Long before her A B and C,
> They had taught her by heart her L.S.D.,[19]
> And as how she was born a great Heiress;
> And as sure as London is built of bricks,
> My Lord would ask her the day to fix,
> To ride in a fine gilt carriage and six,
> Like her Worship the Lady Mayoress. (lines 471–78)

Unlike the virgin saints of the *Golden Legend*, who seek to avoid marriage to devote their lives to Christ, Miss Kilmansegg is raised to believe that her life goal is being a wife.

It is then that disaster ensues, one that ought to remind Miss Kilmansegg of her common mortality. Her horse Banker bolts, and the heiress finds herself in a version of a more recent medievalist trope, the Wild Ride of Leonora. Burger's ballad about the young woman who is carried off by the ghost of her lover was known in various English versions, notably the translation by Sir Walter Scott. Yet at the same moment that she is elevated to a heroine of modern medievalist romance, she is reduced to the level of an everyday worker. Her, life, says the narrator, is "not worth a copper," so that she is just as vulnerable as a factory hand: "She shudders – she shrieks – she's doom'd, she feels/ To be torn by powers of horses and wheels,/ Like a spinner by steam machinery!" (lines 666–68). The result is the amputation of her leg, which Miss Kilmansegg bears "bravely," only then to insist that her replacement leg is not wood but gold.

The defining moment of many of the virgin martyrs of the *Golden Legend* is to go against the moral values of their fathers by proclaiming their Christianity. Miss Kilmansegg's defining moment is not when she rejects her father's idolatrous values but takes them further by insisting on:

> All sterling metal – not half and half.
> The Goldsmith's mark was stamped on the calf –
> 'Twas as pure as from Mexican barter!
> And to make it more costly, just over the knee –
> Where another ligature used to be,
> Was a circle of Jewels, worth shillings to see,
> A new-fangled Badge of the Garter! (810–18)

Whereas her accident threatened to make her ordinary, the excess of Miss Kilmansegg's leg makes her extraordinary, and also something of an exhibitionist: a young lady of the early Victorian period would not normally be showing others her upper leg, but Miss Kilmansegg's conspicuous expenditure is only effective if she exposes her (artificial) self.

Miss Kilmansegg's self-exposure continues when she is the star of her own fancy ball. She appears as the Goddess Diana (who in classical mythology was a virginal figure, but simultaneously a huntress), and takes a part in "Rich and rare were the gems she wore."[20] This appears to be some kind of charade based on the Thomas Moore poem about how in medieval Ireland, a young woman could wander at will in precious jewelry and not be in danger of attack, an ironic fore-shadowing of Miss Kilmansegg's future life. She then performs a minuet, which she finishes "off with a whirligig bout,/ And the Precious Leg stuck stiffly out, Like the leg of a *Figurante!*" (1255–56).[21] The night after the ball, she dreams she is transformed into gold:

> For, by magical transmutation,
> From her Leg through her body it seem'd to go,
> Till, gold above, and gold below,
> She was gold, all gold, from her little gold toe
> To her organ of Veneration!"[22] (1380–84)

In her dream she becomes "a Golden Idol," the very thing the saints of the Golden Legend such as St. Agatha will give their lives to avoid worshipping. She envisions herself, still in her Diana attire, all of gold, standing "On a Plinth of the selfsame metal [...]/ For the whole world's adoration" (1390–91). Leech's illustration shows her on a plinth, with the figure of a naked man with a small tail prostrate before her. He has many heads, representing the wealthy professions. Miss Kilmansegg is not just practicing idolatry, but converting others to it.

The result is that rather than pledging herself to a life of virtuous chastity like the saints of the Golden Legend, Miss Kilmansegg marries at the first opportunity she has to "A Foreign Count." To this point, Hood has characterized the lovers of gold as pagan, but the "Count" is hinted to be Jewish, with "a hooky nose, and his beard half-shorn,/ Like a half-converted Rabbin" (1469–70). Their relationship proves an unhappy one: although she has desired the distinctions of the landed gentry, the new Countess does not enjoy life at her country seat, while the Count ignores her and spends her wealth in dissipation with his cronies:

> In vain she sat with her Precious Leg,
> A little exposed, *à la* Kilmansegg,
> And roll'd her eyes in their sockets!
> He left her in spite of her tender regards,
> And those loving murmurs described by the bards,
> For the rattling of dice and the shuffling of cards,
> And the poking of balls into pockets! (1997–2003)

Hearing of "dangerous leagues" and "intrigues," she now dreams that she has "married the Devil!" (2034).

Once the Count has run through the Kilmansegg money, the idolatry ends, and "without any ossification at all,/ The limb became what people call/ A Perfect bone of contention" (2195–98). Now it is no longer a symbol of wealth but tying up capital, people now start to criticize the leg, so that the Countess hears:

> [...] in language low,
> That her Precious Leg was precious slow,
> A good 'un to look at but bad to go,[23]
> And kept quite a sum lying idle.

After she tears up her will, her husband, who is determined to be "the

Golden Leg's sole Legatee" (2231), uses it to beat her to death, then steals it:

> For gold she had lived, and she died for gold –
> By a golden weapon – not oaken;
> In the morning they found her all alone –
> Stiff, and bloody, and cold as stone –
> But her Leg, the Golden Leg, was gone,
> And the "Golden Bowl was broken!"[24]

Since her golden leg killed her, the coroner's jury – meeting, of course, at a public house called the Golden Lion – bring in a verdict of suicide, "Because her own Leg had killed her!" Hood tacks on a moral about the power of gold, but it is hardly necessary. The reader can see that whereas in the *Golden Legend*, death is a moment of triumph, Miss Kilmansegg's end is proof that the worship of money is self-destructive, a modestly trite conclusion to a poem that in every way has been about excess. Hood has sculpted a new Golden Legend, but it returns to a conventional moral standard, albeit one focusing on the material rather than the spiritual world.

If Hood has failed to escape the moral lessons of the *Golden Legend*, he, like Barham, has at least had fun with the structure. Is this straightforward parody with the simple goal of ridiculing the original? I would suggest instead that Barham and Hood each found a value in the concept of the legendary tale as a means of expressing the nineteenth century's recognition that post-Reformation England did not need to reject its medieval past. While the use of humor fulfills the authors' need to distance themselves from a whole-hearted embrace of the medieval, they still seem somewhat envious of how the saints of old rejected the material for the spiritual in a way no longer possible in modern capitalist society.

In fact, the legend's moment was about to arrive. Writers of the early nineteenth century were so successful in recouping the notion of the legend that when Henry Wadsworth Longfellow called his 1851 dramatic poem *The Golden Legend*, he was able to combine the medieval concept of the saintly narrative with a twelfth-century German tale without any humorous self-deprecation. Critics in both Britain and the United States praised the work for its authentic recapturing of the medieval[25] – which, if it were true rather than legendary, would be a miracle indeed.

NOTES

1. On the cultivation of English reading audiences, see Jon P. Klancher, *The Making of English Reading Audiences, 1790–1832* (Madison: University of Wisconsin Press, 1989). Caxton is an important figure in the bibliomania of this time.

2. See, for example, the instance of R. F. Barham, below. The British Library has copies of the *Golden Legende* [sic] printed in 1483, 1493, 1498, 1503, 1521, and 1527; only the first of these was printed by Caxton himself, and all but one of the others are attributed to Wyken de Worde.

3. "Faithless Nelly Gray," in *Selected Poems of Thomas Hood, Winthrop Mackworth Praed and Thomas Lovell Beddoes*, ed. Susan J. Wolfson and Peter J. Manning (Pittsburgh, PA: University of Pittsburgh Press, 2000), 23. Quotations from Hood's poetry follow this edition except in the use of type-face.

4. I am not here discussing the second meaning of "legend," an inscription to be read.

5. Peter G. Bietenholz, *Historia and Fabula: Myths and Legends in Historical Thought from Antiquity to the Modern Age* (Leiden: E. J. Brill, 1994), 3.

6. John Foxe, *Book of Martyrs* (London: John Fuller, 1760), 271.

7. Francis Bacon, "Of Atheisme," in his *Essays*.

8. Purchas, *Pilgrimage* (London: William Stansby for Henrie Fether-stone, 1614), 506.

9. Francis Grose, *A Provincial Glossary, with a Collection of Local Proverbs, and Popular Superstitions* (London: S. Hooper, 1787).

10. David Hume, *The History of England, From the Invasion of Julius Caesar to the Accession of Henry VII*, 6 vols. (London, A. Millar, 1762), 1:297.

11. B. G. Niebuhr, *The History of Rome*, trans. Julius Charles Hare and Connop Thirlwall, 3rd ed., 6 vols. (London: Taylor and Walton, 1837–38), 1:xx ff.

12. R. H. Barham, *The Ingoldsby Legends* (London: Routledge, n.d.), 191.

13. *The Letters of Thomas Hood*, ed. by Peter F. Morgan (Toronto: University of Toronto Press, 1973), 451–52.

14. Leech's illustrations take three main forms: illustrations of characters and events in the story; illustrations of points made by the narrator; and moral illustrations that seem to represent his own commentary. The last illustration, for example, is a child-sized miser sitting on the lap of Death dressed as a nursemaid.

15. "Life of St. Nicholas" (2:49). All references to Caxton's version of the *Golden Legend* follow the online full-text version, *Medieval Sources: The Golden Legend* <www.fordham.edu/halsall/basis/golden legend>.

16. Karen A. Winstead, *Virgin Martyrs: Legends of Sainthood in Late Medieval England* (Ithaca, NY: Cornell University Press, 1997), 5–6.

17. When the poem was reprinted in the *Comic Annual* for 1842, Gothic type appears nowhere else in the volume. "Miss Kilmansegg" is the first 100-odd pages in the 300-page pocket volume.

18. Lines 15–18. Subsequent references follow Wolfson and Manning's edition by line numbers.

19. "L.S.D." stands for pounds, shillings, and pence.

20. The Leech illustration shows her with a money-bag labeled "£100,000" in place of her left leg.

21. A Figurante is a ballet-dancer.

22. The "Organ of Veneration" is, in phrenological terms popular at the time, part of the head; since Hood was, though, such a great punster, we may suspect a smutty *double-entendre*.

23. The Countess is being described as though she were a horse, ironic since a horse was the cause of her need for a golden leg.

24. The reference is to Ecclesiastes (12:6), the book of the Bible best known for its condemnation of human vanity.

25. For example, the *New York Times* notes, "The manners, life, scenes, cities, customs of the time are illustrated with charming fidelity. The only other book we remember of equal excellence in the portraiture of the middle ages is the Heinrich Von Ofterdinger of Novalis" (17 January 1852, 2).

A Remarkable Woman?
Popular Historians and the
Image of Eleanor of Aquitaine

Michael Evans

The word "remarkable" is perhaps the most commonly used adjective in descriptions of Eleanor of Aquitaine. The entry devoted to her in one recent encyclopedia of the Middle Ages opens with the statement that she "was one of the most remarkable women of the twelfth century."[1] Pick up one of the many popular biographies of her, or even some of the more scholarly works, and you will be informed that Eleanor was an outstanding figure, whose remarkable career distinguishes her from any other woman in what is assumed to be a backward and misogynist age. Eleanor's political career is certainly remarkable enough: wife of two kings; mother of two more (or three, depending on how we count them) and (although this is less frequently remarked upon) of two queens; crusader; rebel; governor and regent. But she has also been viewed as patroness of the troubadours, defender of Occitan national identity, carrier of southern culture to the benighted north, Amazon warrior, and proto-feminist, not including the wilder legends that make her a lover of Saladin, murderess, and demonic mother.

The idea of Eleanor's exceptionalism runs through the popular image of her like letters through a stick of rock candy. Douglas Boyd, in his popular biography of 2004, calls Eleanor "[c]harismatic, beautiful, highly intelligent and literate, but also impulsive and proud." She "did not conform to preconceptions of medieval European womanhood,"[2] and was an "extraordinary woman" who "lived a remarkable life."[3] For Alison Weir (writing in 1999), Eleanor was "remarkable in a period when females were invariably relegated to a servile role [...] an incomparable woman."[4] The 1993 work *Queen Consorts of England* by Petronelle Cook states that "[i]f a prize were given for England's liveliest queen, Eleanor of Aquitaine would undoubtedly win."[5] Marion Meade, writing in 1977, asserts that "although Eleanor of Aquitaine [...] lived at a time when women as individuals had few significant rights, she was nevertheless *the* [my emphasis] key political figure of the twelfth century."[6] Amy Kelly, who in 1950 wrote the nearest there is to a scholarly English-language biography of Eleanor, is more sober, but still personalizes Eleanor rather than seeking to locate her in the context of twelfth-century queenship: "This account of Queen Eleanor and her century is offered as a study of individuals who set their stamp on events of their time, rather than as a study of developing systems of politics, economics, or jurisprudence."[7]

From the gushing prose of Boyd to the more sober reflections of Kelly, there is a consensus that Eleanor was a remarkable individual, who shone despite the limits placed on women of her time. As such, she has become for many "la première héroïne du combat feministe ou bien de l'indépendence occitane [...]" ("the first heroine of the feminist movement or even of Occitanian independence"), in the words of Georges Duby.[8] Yet a brief survey of royal or aristocratic women of Eleanor's world shows that powerful women were far from unusual. If we look at Eleanor's predecessors as Anglo-Norman queens of England, we find many examples of women wielding political power.[9] Eleanor's mother-in-law, the Empress Matilda, was engaged in a long and bitter struggle for the English crown. Less remembered is the fact that, for a substantial period in 1141, her principal antagonist was another woman, Matilda of Boulogne, who led the fight on behalf of her husband Stephen of Blois, who had been captured by the forces of the Empress. Among previous Anglo-Norman queens, Matilda of Flanders (wife of William the Conqueror) and the two wives of Henry I (Matilda of Scotland and Adeliza of Louvain) had all played some role in governing England during their husbands' absences.

It might be objected that these women were dutiful wives holding temporary power only on behalf of "their" men, who do not measure up to Eleanor's supposedly rebellious and independent character. But King Stephen's mother (and the Empress Matilda's aunt), Adela, countess of Blois, was another twelfth-century woman of independence and resolution. Ruler of the county of Blois in her husband's absence on crusade, she is said to have persuaded him to return to the East after he had rather ignominiously abandoned the crusade, and to have continued to rule the county after his death on the same expedition. And if we wish to seek a proto-feminist rebel woman, we need look no further than Juliana, illegitimate daughter of Henry I, who attempted to assassinate him with a crossbow.[10]

These women are just a few examples from one dynasty, the Anglo-Normans. But they illustrate in brief the fact that twelfth-century women from the ruling classes were able to wield considerable power. Eleanor was merely an outstanding example of a common type. She may have been "remarkable" in the extent to which she asserted her independence, but she had access to a remarkably rich inheritance, the Duchy of Aquitaine. Eleanor's power was derived not so much from a remarkable personality (of which, given the nature of twelfth-century sources, we can know little), but from her inheritance, in her own right as sole heiress, of a duchy that covered approximately one-third of the surface area of the kingdom of France.

Why, then, is there such apparent unanimity about the exception-alism of Eleanor? I will argue that this image of Eleanor is derived not from contemporary or near-contemporary sources, but from post-medieval historians, particularly popular historians of the nineteenth and twentieth centuries.

It is true that Eleanor was already a figure of legend in the thirteenth century, when the romance *Richard Coeur de Lion* portrayed her as a demonic figure, suggesting that she already possessed a reputation out of the ordinary. However, many of the modern historians who dismiss such legends as fairy tales have themselves created a mythology of Eleanor, and it is this mythology that has shaped our view of her.

RáGena DeAragon has posed the question "do we know what we think we know about Eleanor?"[11] We have remarkably little evidence of her life from twelfth-century historians. Georges Duby reckoned that we have only nine sources for her life.[12] Odo of Deuil, chronicler of and eyewitness to the Second Crusade, scarcely mentions Eleanor's presence in the French contingent.[13] W. L. Warren, biographer of Henry II, asserts that "to judge from the chroniclers, the most striking fact about Eleanor is her utter insignificance in Henry II's reign."[14] John Carmi Parsons and Bonnie Wheeler parody Churchill, arguing that "[r]arely in the course of historical endeavor has so much been written, over so many centuries, about one woman of whom we know so little."[15] These flimsy foundations seem insufficient to support 400-page popular biographies. To challenge Boyd's statement cited earlier, we simply cannot say with any certainty that Eleanor *was* "charismatic, beautiful, highly intelligent and literate." We do not know what she looked like: no portraits exist of her, and descriptions of her beauty are purely conventional,[16] as are depictions of her in seals, in a stained-glass window, on her effigy, and (possibly) in sculpture and painting; her intelligence and literacy might be inferred, but cannot be definitely ascertained, as her surviving letters were probably written on her behalf by her secretary, Peter of Blois; and her personality might be surmised from her actions, but again, with very little certainly, as medieval chronicles are poor guides to the motives and inner world of the actors. Their authors were less concerned with individual psychology than with describing the working of God's will through human history. In the words of John of Salisbury, one of our sources for Eleanor's life, chronicles were written "so that the invisible things of God may be clearly seen by the things that are done, and men may by examples of reward or punishment be made more zealous [...]."[17]

The development of the image of Eleanor can be traced in popular histories in English in the nineteenth and twentieth centuries. Three works have arguably done most to form and popularize that image for English-language readers; those of Agnes and Elizabeth Strickland, Amy Kelly, and Marion Meade. There have been many biographies of Eleanor; notable works not covered in this essay include Melrich Rosenberg's 1937 biography of Eleanor, the first published in English (if we exclude the Stricklands', which was part of a larger work), and a biography by Curtis Walker.[18] Yet neither of these had the same impact as those of the Stricklands, Kelly, or Meade. Amy Kelly's 1950 biography of Eleanor overshadowed both Rosenberg's and Walker's work, especially the latter, which was published in the same year. Kelly's and Meade's biographies have never gone out of print and are available in paperback to a mass readership. In contrast, that of Rosenberg is long out of print, and Walker's work, having appeared in a paperback edition in 1960,[19] appears not to have been reprinted since the 1970s. More recent popular biographies by Weir and Boyd, mentioned above, largely retread the ground covered by Kelly and Meade. It is also of note that the Stricklands, Kelly, and Meade were all women, and the influence (or otherwise) of the feminist movement on these authors will be considered in this essay. It will also assess the extent to which the myth-making about Eleanor in works of popular history has had an impact upon academic historians.

I will focus here on incidents from Eleanor's early career, including her time as queen of France. This period in her life, about which we know comparatively little, offers perhaps the most fertile ground for conjecture and myth-making. There is a tendency to assume that because Eleanor was "remarkable," her personality must have manifested itself in her early years. In the words of Marion Facinger:

> [B]ecause her later career was extraordinary, there has been a tendency to fabricate an early queen consonant with the later one. A dispassionate examination of the documentation for the first ten years of Eleanor's career as queen of France, however, reveals almost no information about either her activities or her influence. Her presence in the royal *curia* is unnoted, her name rarely appears on Louis's charters, and no sources support the historical view of Eleanor as bold, precocious, and responsible for Louis VII's behavior.[20]

Leaving aside the medieval and early modern myths about Eleanor, which were easily identified as such by historians, we can locate the beginning of myth-making in serious history to the work of Agnes Strickland and her sister Elizabeth in the nineteenth century. Their twelve-volume *Lives of the Queens of England*, published in the 1840s, was a Victorian best-seller.[21] The work was credited jointly to the two sisters; in fact Agnes, the more lionized of the two, worked principally on the early modern and modern queens, while Elizabeth wrote the biographies of medieval queens, including that of Eleanor. The sisters viewed themselves as serious historians. While excluded by their sex from academia, they approached their research in a spirit of serious scholarship, making use of available archives and expressing a belief in writing (in Agnes's words) "facts, not opinions."[22] Their biography of "Eleanora of Aquitaine" helped popularize the view of Eleanor as an outstanding figure: "As a sovereign, she ranks among the first of female rulers."[23]

Nevertheless, the Stricklands' portrait of Eleanor was highly opinionated and often misleading. They introduced the idea that Eleanor was a flighty young girl who grew into a mature ruler: she was "among the very few women who atoned for an ill-spent youth by a wise and benevolent old age."[24] They described, and went some way toward popularizing, an entirely fictitious incident in Eleanor's life. This was the claim that, when her husband Louis VII and his lords took the cross at Vézelay in 1147, the queen and her ladies put in a fancy-dress appearance as Penthesilea and her Amazons:

> When queen Eleanora received the cross [...] she directly put on the dress of the Amazons; and her ladies, all actuated by the same frenzy, mounted on horseback, and forming a light squadron, surrounded the queen when she appeared in public, calling them-selves queen Eleanora's bodyguard. They practised Amazonian exercises, and performed a thousand follies in public, to animate their zeal as practical crusaders. By the suggestion of their young queen, this band of mad-women sent their useless distaffs, as pres-ents, to all the knights and nobles who had the good sense to keep out of the crusading expedition.[25]

The Stricklands' moralizing is repeated throughout their account of Eleanor on crusade. They blamed the "freaks of Queen Eleanor and her female warriors"[26] for the failure of the crusade, another myth that has no basis in any contemporary source.[27] They also repeated the medieval myth that Eleanor had an affair with Saladin, who would have been about ten years old at the time.[28]

The Stricklands' view of Eleanor seems to be a product of their Victorian morality and conservatism. Agnes, the more celebrated of the sisters, was anti-Catholic, being a great supporter of the Anglican establishment (hence her disapproval of the Crusades), and anti-feminist, refusing to lend her support to a petition for women's prop-erty rights.[29] They enjoyed the support of Queen Victoria, who requested Agnes's autograph for her collection, and to whom they dedicated their work.[30] Thus their mildly feminist admiration for Eleanor as a female ruler was tempered by their horror at her "ill-spent youth." Eleanor the crusader, taking on a male role, was a "freak," compared to the older, wiser Eleanor, spending her "benevolent old age" looking after the interests of her sons. Their ambivalent attitude to Eleanor could be viewed as a reflection of their own experiences. Agnes may have been a conservative supporter of the establishment, but she and her sister also suffered from the restrictions set upon women. The State Paper Office, which housed many of the archives to which they needed access, was effectively barred to women. However, they were able to count upon friends in high places and gained access to the archives when Lord Melbourne, a friend and confidant of the queen, became Home Secretary.[31] The independent women writers might therefore view Eleanor as a role model; the conservatives who were fêted by the establishment might disapprove of her alleged high spirits and independence. The older, sober Eleanor matched more closely the character of their own royal benefactress.

We may also detect an element of Francophobia in the contrast drawn between the bad young queen of France and the good old queen of England. Popular biographers of Eleanor – British ones especially – frequently contrast Eleanor's first husband, Louis VII of France, with her second, the Plantagenet king of England Henry II. Louis is portrayed as weak, monkish, and unmanly, no fit match for the strong and independent Eleanor, who was easily able to manipulate him but lacked the maturity to do so for good ends. In contrast, Henry is represented as young and vigorous, and able to tame the unruly queen. Thus, for the Stricklands, Eleanor "swayed the king of France according to her will and pleasure."[32] This view of Louis as a weak king is not an invention of the Stricklands and can be seen in contemporary sources. John of Salisbury characterized Louis as "puerile" in his love for Eleanor, while William of Newburgh records Eleanor's famous alleged comment that she had "married a monk."[33] But, as John Parsons points out, William's comment was made nearly half a century after the event it purports to describe.[34] It is easy to see how such comments (which, significantly, derive from English chroniclers) may have been reinforced by a prevailing Francophobia in nineteenth-century England. The image of the weak Louis versus the vigorous, manly Henry continues to this day, with an added element of sexuality. To cite one modern author, Louis was "not particularly virile" whereas Henry "was made from the same strong mettle as his great-grandfather, William the Conqueror, and was as virile and as much of a ladies' man as his grandfather, Henry I [...]."[35] Alison Weir describes Eleanor as "sensual," Louis as "sexually withholding" and Henry as "aggressively virile."[36] Even Elizabeth A. R. Brown, a dispassionate and skeptical historian of Eleanor, echoes such language in her comment that, after dispatching his wife to govern Poitou in 1168, Henry "could indulge his appetites [...] as he wished."[37]

The anti-feminism in earlier accounts of Eleanor's life came under challenge in the twentieth century. Amy Kelly's *Eleanor of Aquitaine and the Four Kings*, written in 1950, is still perhaps the best biography of Eleanor available in English to a general audience. Kelly had spent a lifetime in female education when she wrote this work, having been head of Bryn Mawr School (a girls' school in Maryland, not to be confused with the women's liberal arts college of that name in Pennsylvania) and professor of English at Wellesley College. She authored a report on liberal arts education for women in 1927, and this gives us some insight into her philosophy. For her, history was seen in materialist terms as "but the record of what men, with their pressing biological needs, have done to get on as practically as possible in an environment that limits them [...]."[38] She believed that a history and social science curriculum "should give intelligent students a very shrewd understanding of the causes of wars, the debasement of politics and statesmanship and the reasons for many social maladjustments, and should make them curious, critical and tolerant with respect to current social movements."[39] Yet against this radical analysis, Kelly also advocated an education for women that reconciled their aspirations with the reality of their social condition "so that conflicts do not arise to impair the quality of women's work or disturb social order."[40] Kelly's materialist view of history is at odds with her desire, cited previously, to approach Eleanor's life "as a study of individuals." However, Eleanor does seem an ideal subject of study for a type of limited feminism that wishes to promote women without disturbing the social order. As a strong female figure, she offered a role model for women in a history dominated by men. Yet as a member of the ruling elite, she was still a figure from the Great Men (and, very occasionally, Great Women) school of history.

Kelly's biography was well-received in academic circles on its publication. "At long last – a scholarly biography of Eleanor of Aquitaine" enthused A. C. Krey in a review in *The American Historical Review*.[41] Loren C. McKinney, reviewing the book in *Speculum*, praised it as an "impressive achievement."[42] Yet although more sober and scholarly than the Stricklands, and lacking their judgmental tone, Kelly nevertheless repeats some of their errors. For example, the claim that Eleanor and her ladies dressed as Amazons on the Second Crusade reappears several times in the course of her book, as we are told that "she appears to have kept en route her role as Penthesilea, which, as it is said, had been such a success and inspiration at Vézelay," despite the absence of any medieval source referring to this incident.[43] Some of her assumptions seem to have become the model for later, uncritical biographers. For example, she cites a diatribe of Bernard of Clairvaux against the attire of ladies, adding "to whom if not the queen and her suite does the abbé allude?"[44] This attribution is taken as fact, without qualification, by the subsequent biographers Meade and Weir. Meade presents Bernard's comments in his letter to the virgin Sophia as "the only physical portrait of Eleanor."[45] Yet the letter nowhere refers to Eleanor, and the sole reference to a queen or queens is a general and rhetorical one: "The ornaments of a queen have no beauty like the blushes of natural modesty which color the cheeks of a virgin."[46] Read in context, this is part of Bernard's general aim to encourage his reader to turn from the beauty of worldly things to the contemplation of heaven, not a specific criticism of Eleanor, or any other particular queen. And yet Meade makes it the basis for an imagined portrait, and Weir has Bernard meeting Eleanor at the Council of Sens in 1140, and claims that his letter to Sophia is a shocked description of the finery of the queen and her ladies whom he encountered there.[47]

But perhaps Kelly's greatest contribution to muddying the waters about Eleanor is her promotion of the myth of the queen as the leading patron of troubadours and, specifically, as hostess of the Courts of Love alongside her daughter Marie, countess of Champagne. Kelly was a literary scholar by background, rather than a historian, and seems to have been drawn to Eleanor as a subject via her interest in the literature of the twelfth century.[48] There is insufficient space here to rehearse the arguments about the historicity of these courts, which were described vividly in the *Tractatus de Amore et de Amoris Remedio* of Andreas Capellanus. The notion that the courts were actual assemblies, rather than a literary device created by Andreas, has been repeatedly challenged by historians and literary scholars, most recently in Jean Flori's biography of Eleanor.[49] Elizabeth A. R. Brown states simply that the existence of the Courts "has no basis in fact."[50] One of the key critics of this notion, John F. Benton, wrote in 1961 that "[t]here is no evidence to show that Marie ever saw her mother or communicated with her after Eleanor left the court of France when Marie was seven [...]."[51] Yet the legend continues to reassert itself, particularly in association with Eleanor, as if the combination of a romantic notion and a romantic queen is too much to resist. Given the stubborn longevity of this myth, it is not surprising that we detect a somewhat frustrated tone in the works of scholars who have to repeatedly refute it, as seen, for example, in the somewhat tautological title of Benton's later article "The Evidence for Andreas Capellanus Re-Examined Again."[52]

Kelly's promotion of the myth of Eleanor as a hostess of the Courts of Love begins not in her 1950 biography, but in an article that appeared in *Speculum* in 1937.[53] This article displays many of the poorly grounded assumptions and much of the romanticization that would characterize Kelly's later Eleanor biography, and those of her successors. Two extracts serve to illustrate the heightened romantic tone in which even her scholarly work was written. Describing Eleanor's return to Paris after the Second Crusade, Kelly asks:

> Was it not intolerable that the foremost queen in Christendom [...] should lodge in the indifferent quarters of the king's routiers, while the empress of Byzantium dwelt apart from all vulgar contacts in purple pavilions, in harems rich with tapestries and silken hangings, among tiled fountains and chirruping golden birds [...]?[54]

Kelly's conclusion sees Eleanor as a heroine of feminism and modernity, being dragged away to captivity by Henry II, the representative of the ruling patriarchal order:

> For the moment the feudal system triumphed. Sedition looked out from barred windows upon a world of havoc. But ideas had gone forth from the high place in Poitiers which survived to shed a brightness in the world when rods had fallen from the hands of feudal kings and bolts had rusted in the Tower of Salisbury.[55]

There is little critical analysis of Andreas' work in Kelly's *Speculum* article, which consists largely of a potted biography of Eleanor and an imaginative reconstruction of the process of one of the Courts of Love.[56] The author's reasoning that Eleanor and Marie de Champagne presided together at such courts in Poitiers is based on assumptions, not evidence. She begins by arguing that "[p]resumably, although Andreas does not so state, the place of assembly is Poitiers," and that Marie *could* have been present at Eleanor's court while the latter was governing Aquitaine from 1170 to 1174: "Nothing we know of Marie's life precludes the assumption that she was in Poitiers in the period in question."[57] By the middle of the article, Marie's supposed presence has become fact, "*when* [my emphasis] she journeyed down from Paris or Troyes to assume her place at the court of Poitiers [...]."[58]

Despite the efforts of scholars such as Benton, the myth of Eleanor and Marie's Courts of Love refuses to die. Meade repeated it,[59] and one recent book about Eleanor aimed at high-school students bears the title *Eleanor of Aquitaine, Courtly Love, and the Troubadours.*[60] Weir, unusually among popular historians, accepts the scholarly consensus on the Courts of Love, but goes on to assert that it is "probably true, *although there is little evidence to support it,* [my emphasis] that Eleanor encouraged troubadours and poets to come to her court and receive the benefits of her patronage."[61]

It must be concluded that Amy Kelly is largely responsible for the longevity of the myth. Well before Benton's work, scholars were skeptical about Andreas' Courts of Love. As early as 1842, the German philologist Friedrich Diez cast doubt upon their historicity.[62] In the same year that Kelly's *Speculum* essay appeared, Sidney Painter was damning Rosenberg's biography, subtitled *Queen of the Troubadours and the Courts of Love*, with the following faint praise: "The quality of popular historical literature would be vastly improved if enthusiastic and talented amateurs could be persuaded to confine themselves to the historical novel. Had Mr. Rosenberg chosen this type of literary expression, I believe that this book would have been an unqualified success."[63] It is possible that the myth of the Courts of Love would have died around this time, had not Kelly given it new life. In the words of John C. Moore, reviewing a collection of papers on Eleanor's patronage published in 1976, "[t]he refulgent light that seems in these papers to be shining from Eleanor's court comes rather from the splendid prose of Amy Kelly [...]."[64] June Hall McCash writes that "Marie's function at the court of Poitiers was in large measure a product of the fertile imagination of Amy Kelly."[65]

American author Marion Meade's biography of Eleanor was published in 1977. This has been described as a feminist interpretation of her life,[66] and Meade seems to have been drawn to Eleanor on this basis, viewing the twelfth century as a period that saw "the burgeoning of a feminist movement."[67] The choice of subjects of Meade's other works certainly reflect a feminist interest. They include *Stealing Heaven*, a novel about Héloïse and Abelard (the subtitle, significantly, gives their names in that order) that sympathizes predominantly with the former; a novel about a female troubadour at the time of the Albigensian Crusades; a biography of Dorothy Parker; and *Bitching*, a collection of interviews with women described by its current publisher as "[o]ne of the classic books from the Second Wave of Feminism."[68] Her Eleanor biography, however, reads in places more like romantic fiction than feminist history, reflecting perhaps Meade's background in journalism, rather than academia. In addition, her claim to bring a new female perspective to the subject ignored the fact that two women – Elizabeth Strickland and Kelly – had already written biographies of Eleanor.[69]

Her prose style makes Meade's one of the more readable Eleanor biographies, and she plays less fast and loose with history than some popular biographers. For example, Eleanor's Amazonian exploits do not make it into her account. However, despite her claim that "I did not find it necessary to fictionalise Eleanor's life. Her history, what little is known of it, is novel enough,"[70] Meade does precisely that, inventing details that we cannot possibly know. Her journalistic desire to tell a good story often clashes with the historian's admission that we have a paucity of sources on Eleanor. For example, we are told that Eleanor "a highly literate woman, left no intimate record of herself, no letters, diaries, or poetry [...]," leaving us to speculate as to how therefore Meade knows that she is highly literate.[71] After vividly describing Eleanor's early childhood, Meade tells us that "[h]er name first appeared in the records in 1129 [...]" when she would have been, by Meade's account, at least seven years old.[72] Meade admits in a note that her description of Eleanor's education is "entirely inferential," and later informs us that Eleanor was "exceptionally beautiful" before admitting that "there is not a single word about what she looked like."[73]

Meade's feminism, set out in the introduction to the book, does not appear to inform the text itself beyond a restatement that Eleanor was a remarkable woman, "one of the most politically astute women of the medieval era,"[74] a contestable verdict given that Eleanor's misjudgment in supporting her sons' rebellion in 1173 led to a decade and a half of imprisonment and powerlessness. For a feminist author, she is remarkably quick to fall back upon clichéd ideas about gender roles, as seen in her treatment of Louis, whom she stereotypes as unmanly.[75] Her picture of Eleanor can occasionally be patronizing, as in her claim that she went on crusade out of boredom and a desire for adventure.[76] We see asserted again the Stricklands' image of the young Eleanor as a silly, flighty girl: "her natural exuberance had reasserted itself, and she was [...] enjoying herself to the utmost [...]" and "she planned to enjoy herself once she reached the pleasure palaces of Constantinople."[77] Too often Meade, like so many popular biographers, falls back on references to Eleanor's character and personality to back her judgments, even though we can only make inferences about these traits. For example, we are offered this character sketch of the fifteen-year-old Eleanor, who at that age had barely appeared in the written record: "Her restless temperament, her vanities and self-centeredness, her bold flirtatious manner, [were] combined with a certain tomboyishness [...]." Later we are told that she "had matured into a saucy, hot-blooded damsel [...]."[78]

The image of Eleanor in Kelly and Meade's works has set the template for the popular view of Eleanor today, demonstrated in such contemporary popular biographies as those of Weir and Boyd, mentioned at the beginning of this essay. Dubious assertions are made about Eleanor, which are backed by appeals to what we "know" about her character. Thus Alison Weir, repeating the myth about Eleanor's Amazonian exploits on crusade, admits that "[m]ost historians dismiss the tale as pure legend, because there are no contemporary accounts of it, but it is in keeping with what we know of Eleanor's character [...]."[79] Meade uses the same reasoning to describe the same incident: "From what most people knew of their flamboyant queen, the tale sounded completely in character."[80] Yet what we "know" of Eleanor's character is limited and largely based on inference. At its worst, this process becomes circular. How do we know Eleanor dressed as an Amazon? Because it was consistent with her character. How do we know it was consistent with her character? Because she performed outrageous actions such as dressing as an Amazon.

Does any of this matter to the academic historian, beyond merely being an irritant? Scholars have gone a long way in the last half-century toward creating what one has called "a realistic image" of

Eleanor.[81] Does popular history have any impact on the more sober world of academe? I would argue that it does, because scholars are themselves not immune to the appeal of the Eleanor myth. Georges Duby writes of her legend that "je connais même des historiens très sérieux dont elle continue d'enflammer l'imagination et de la dévoyer" ("there are even serious historians whose imagination it continues to inflame and lead to error").[82]

Virginia Berry, who edited and translated Odo of Deuil's chronicle of the Second Crusade, expressed surprise at the small part played by Eleanor in the narrative and suggested that references to her were erased in a rewriting after her divorce from Louis VII.[83] It would be unsurprising if Odo, Louis's chaplain, had chosen not to refer to the king's former wife, and it may be significant that his account ends with the French army's arrival in Antioch, before Eleanor's supposed infidelity with Raymond of Antioch, one scandal of which she was accused in her own lifetime. Yet in the lack of any compelling evidence for any active rewriting (only a single manuscript of Odo's work is extant), this theory must be viewed as another example of supposition based on what we think we know of Eleanor: we think we know she behaved scandalously; therefore we assume that descriptions of her scandalous behavior were excised. In a review of Berry's edition published in *Church History* in 1949, Quirinus Breen of the University of Oregon admits that "a desire to know precisely how Eleanor carried on bears the reader forward, but he [sic] will be disappointed,"[84] illustrating again how academic historians are far from immune to the allure of the scandalous image of Eleanor.

Roy Owen, a former professor of French at St. Andrews University, analyzed the life and legendary afterlife of Eleanor in his work of 1993. As a literary scholar, Owen is at his strongest in analyzing the legends that surrounded Eleanor, but a little too prone to speculation when approaching her life. He gives some credence to the story of Eleanor's Amazonian performance; while acknowledging it as a legend, he asserts that the Byzantine historian Niketas Choniates "surely had Eleanor herself in mind when he described the arrival of [armed women among] the crusaders at Constantinople."[85] Yet Niketas never mentions Eleanor by name, referring to a woman named "Goldfoot" [Chrysopous] among the *German* forces.[86] Likewise, Owen was unwilling to entirely discount the idea of the Courts of Love.[87] In the first section of his work, a brief biography of Eleanor,

Owen too often uses speculative constructions. To cite just two examples, in describing Eleanor's girlhood in an Aquitaine steeped in the troubadour culture Owen claims that "we can imagine [...] with what special awe she came to learn of the rumbustious doings of her talented but reprobate grandfather [William IX],"[88] and that "we can imagine her captivated by the exciting new vogues in poetry and story-telling that were being enthusiastically exploited at her father's court [...]."[89] By my count, the construction "we can imagine," or variations thereon, occurs fourteen times in Owen's book. Overcooked descriptions like those cited above seem to betray the influence of Amy Kelly and other romanticizing historians of Eleanor.

Martin Aurell has criticized the "psychological approach" so often taken to the study of Eleanor.[90] In his recent book on the Angevin Empire, he mentions two such recent examples of professional historians. David Crouch, referring to the young William Marshall, claims that "Queen Eleanor of England was rather taken by his youthful charm."[91] Jacques Le Goff, in an interview given to *L'Express* magazine about courtly love in 2002, went so far as to call Eleanor "une vraie garce, uniquement préocupée par le pouvoir et le sexe" ("a real tart, uniquely preoccupied by power and sex").[92]

To conclude, the popular historians of Eleanor have created an image of her, and of medieval women as a whole, that is misleading. The misogynist medieval and late-modern legends of Eleanor found their way into the Stricklands' disapproving Victorian accounts of the foolish and rebellious young Eleanor. Twentieth-century historians promoted a more feminist view of Eleanor, stressing her strengths and her power. But these accounts have themselves built on earlier legends and too often rely on speculation and inference. Moreover, by stressing the exceptionalism of Eleanor, they obscure the wider picture of twelfth-century women. Ironically, in promoting a stereotypical view of medieval women as downtrodden by a patriarchal society and religion, they could be seen as doing women's history a disservice. The attempt to make an exception of Eleanor is part of the modern desire to make ourselves feel more comfortable about our own age by exaggerating the ignorance and poverty of others. This view of the Middle Ages is expressed in the words put into Eleanor's mouth by James Goldman in *The Lion in Winter*: "It's 1183 and we're barbarians!"

NOTES

1. Norman F. Cantor, ed., *The Pimlico Encyclopedia of the Middle Ages* (London: Pimlico, 1999), 154.

2. Douglas Boyd, *Eleanor, April Queen of Aquitaine* (Stroud: Sutton, 2004), 1.

3. Boyd, *Eleanor, April Queen*, 2.

4. Alison Weir, *Eleanor of Aquitaine, by the Wrath of God, Queen of England* (London: Jonathan Cape, 1999), 355.

5. Petronelle Cook, *Queen Consorts of England: The Power Behind the Throne* (New York: Facts on File, 1993), 29.

6. Marion Meade, *Eleanor of Aquitaine: A Biography* (New York: Hawthorn, 1977; rpt. London: Phoenix, 2001).

7. Amy Kelly, *Eleanor of Aquitaine and the Four Kings* (Cambridge, MA: Harvard University Press, 1950). For a more scholarly and up-to-date biography in English, see Ralph V. Turner, *Eleanor of Aquitaine: Queen of France, Queen of England* (New Haven, CT: Yale University Press, 2009).

8. Georges Duby, *Dames du XIIe Siècle, 1: Héloïse, Aliénor, Iseut et quelques autres* (Paris: Gallimard, 1995), 30. (English translation, Georges Duby, *Women of the Twelfth Century, Volume 1: Eleanor of Aquitaine and Six Others*, trans. Jean Birrell [Chicago: University of Chicago Press, 1997], 15.)

9. For a good discussion of Eleanor in context, see RáGena C. DeAragon, "Wife, Widow, and Mother: Some Comparisons between Eleanor of Aquitaine and Noblewomen of the Anglo-Norman World," in Bonnie Wheeler and John Carmi Parsons, ed., *Eleanor of Aquitaine: Lord and Lady* (New York and Basingstoke: Palgrave, 2002), 97–114; and Lois L. Honeycutt, "*Alianora Regina Anglorum*: Eleanor of Aquitaine and her Anglo-Norman Predecessors as Queens of England," in Wheeler and Parsons, ed., *Eleanor of Aquitaine*, 115–32.

10. Orderic Vitalis, *The Ecclesiastical History*, ed. and trans. Marjorie Chibnall, 6 vols. (Oxford: Oxford University Press, 1969–80), 6:212–15.

11. RáGena DeAragon, "Do We Know What Think We Know?: Making Assumptions about Eleanor of Aquitaine," *Medieval Feminist Forum* 34 (2004): 14–20.

12. Duby, *Dames du XIIe Siècle*, 15–17.

13. Odo of Deuil, *De profectone Ludovici VII in orientem*, ed. and trans. Virginia Gingerick Berry (New York: Columbia University Press, 1948).

14. Quoted in D. D. R. Owen, *Eleanor of Aquitaine: Queen and Legend* (Oxford: Blackwell, 1993), 49.

15. Bonnie Wheeler and John Carmi Parsons, "Prologue. Lady and

Lord: Eleanor of Aquitaine," in Wheeler and Parsons, ed., *Eleanor of Aquitaine*, xiii–xxix (xxix).

16. Duby, *Dames du XIIe Siècle*, 14–15.

17. John of Salisbury, *Historia Pontificalis*, ed. and trans. Marjorie Chibnall (Oxford: Clarendon Press, 1986), 3.

18. Melrich V. Rosenberg, *Eleanor of Aquitaine: Queen of the Troubadours and the Courts of Love* (Boston: Houghton Mifflin, 1937); Curtis H. Walker, *Eleanor of Aquitaine* (Chapel Hill: University of North Carolina Press, 1950). Although published by a university press, Walker's book seems to have been aimed at a mass readership and includes illustrations by M. S. Nowicki. It shares with other popular treatments of Eleanor's life a tendency towards speculation and romanticization, as when the author describes Eleanor and Marie de Champagne discussing interior decorations (161–62), cited in Elizabeth A. R. Brown, "Eleanor of Aquitaine Reconsidered: The Woman and Her Seasons," in Wheeler and Parsons, ed., *Eleanor of Aquitaine*, 1–54 (3).

19. Curtis H. Walker, *Eleanor of Aquitaine*, 2nd ed. (New York: Lancer Books, 1960). This edition was clearly aimed at a popular audience. Lancer published mass-market paperbacks including the *Conan the Barbarian* series.

20. Marion F. Facinger, "A Study of Medieval Queenship: Capetian France (987–1237)," in William M. Bowsky, ed., *Studies in Medieval and Renaissance History* 5 (Lincoln: University of Nebraska Press, 1968), 1–47 (7–8). It should be noted that Marion Facinger is *not* the same person as Marion Meade, although they are identified as such by Wheeler and Parsons in the bibliography of their *Eleanor of Aquitaine, Lord and Lady*, 478, 493.

21. Agnes and Elizabeth Strickland, *Lives of the Queens of England*, 12 vols. (London: Henry Colburn, 1840–47).

22. Mary Delorme, " 'Facts not Opinions' – Agnes Strickland," *History Today* 38:2 (1988): 45–50.

23. Strickland, *Lives of the Queens*, 1:378.

24. Strickland, *Lives of the Queens*, 1:378.

25. Strickland, *Lives of the Queens*, 1:313. For myths about Eleanor on crusade, see Frank McMinn Chambers, "Some Legends of Eleanor of Aquitaine," *Speculum* 16 (1941): 459–68.

26. Strickland, *Lives of the Queens*, 1:314.

27. Curtis H. Walker, "Eleanor of Aquitaine and the Disaster at Cadmos Mountain on the Second Crusade," *American Historical Review* 55 (1949–50): 857–61.

28. Strickland, *Lives of the Queens*, 1:316–17.

29. Delorme, "Facts not Opinions," 49.

30. Delorme, "Facts not Opinions," 45.

31. Delorme, "Facts not Opinions," 46.

32. Strickland, *Lives of the Queens*, 1: 312.

33. John of Salisbury, 61–62; William of Newburgh, *A History of English Affairs*, ed. and trans. Patrick Gerald Walsh and M. J. Kennedy (Oxford: Aris and Phillips, 1988), 128–29.

34. John Carmi Parsons, "Damned If She Didn't and Damned When She Did: Bodies, Babies, and Bastards in the Lives of Two Queens of France," in *Eleanor of Aquitaine: Lord and Lady*, 247–99 (268).

35. Cook, *Queen Consorts*, 30–31.

36. Cited in Brown, "Eleanor of Aquitaine Reconsidered," 35, n. 20.

37. Brown, "Eleanor of Aquitaine Reconsidered," 12.

38. Amy Kelly, *A Curriculum to Build a Mental World: A Proposal for a College of Liberal Arts for Women* (Baltimore, MD: Bryn Mawr School, 1927), 32.

39. Kelly, *A Curriculum*, 33.

40. Kelly, *A Curriculum*, 3–4.

41. A. C. Krey, review of *Eleanor of Aquitaine*, by Amy Kelly, and *Eleanor of Aquitaine*, by Curtis H. Walker, *American Historical Review* 56:1 (1950): 84–87 (84).

42. Loren C. McKinney, review of *Eleanor of Aquitaine*, by Amy Kelly, and *Eleanor of Aquitaine*, by Curtis H. Walker, *Speculum* 26:1 (1950): 166–70 (167).

43. Kelly, *Eleanor of Aquitaine*, 38.

44. Kelly, *Eleanor of Aquitaine*, 20.

45. Meade, *Eleanor of Aquitaine*, 78.

46. *The Letters of St Bernard of Clairvaux* (Chicago: Henry Regnery, 1953), ed. and trans. Bruno Scott James, 175; cited in Meade, *Eleanor of Aquitaine*, 79.

47. Weir, *Eleanor of Aquitaine*, 35–36.

48. Parsons and Wheeler, "Prologue," xvi.

49. Jean Flori, *Aliénor d'Aquitaine: la reine insoumise* (Paris: Payot, 2004), 337–83. In a review of this book, Elizabeth A. R. Brown expresses the hope that it may dispose of the myth "once and for all," but this may be too optimistic. *English Historical Review* 120 (2005): 503–4 (503).

50. Brown, "Eleanor of Aquitaine Reconsidered," 2.

51. John F. Benton, "The Court of Champagne as a Literary Centre," *Speculum* 36 (1961): 551–91 (589). June Hall McCash, "Marie de Champagne and Eleanor of Aquitaine: A Relationship Reexamined," *Speculum* 54 (1979): 698–711, offers a more moderate position, arguing that we cannot discount the possibility of a literary connection between Eleanor and Marie, but accepts that there is no firm evidence linking them in Marie's adult lifetime.

52. John F. Benton, "The Evidence for Andreas Capellanus Re-examined Again," *Studies in Philology* 59 (1962): 471–78.

53. Amy Kelly, "Eleanor of Aquitaine and her Courts of Love," *Speculum* 12 (1937): 3–19. The theme was clearly a popular one, as in the same year, and independently of Kelly, Melrich V. Rosenberg wrote the book *Eleanor of Aquitaine: Queen of the Troubadours and the Courts of Love*.

54. Kelly, "Eleanor of Aquitaine and her Courts of Love," 8.

55. Kelly, "Eleanor of Aquitaine and her Courts of Love," 18–19.

56. Kelly, "Eleanor of Aquitaine and her Courts of Love," 5–10, 15–17. A similar reconstruction can be found in Kelly's *Eleanor of Aquitaine and the Four Kings*, 165–67.

57. Kelly, "Eleanor of Aquitaine and her Courts of Love," 4–5. In fact, Kelly gives the wrong dates for Eleanor's period of rule in Aquitaine, which occurred in 1168–73.

58. Kelly, "Eleanor of Aquitaine and her Courts of Love," 12.

59. Meade, *Eleanor of Aquitaine*, 252.

60. ffiona [sic] Swabey, *Eleanor of Aquitaine, Courtly Love, and the Troubadours* (Westport, CT: Greenwood, 2004). Swabey acknowledges that "no evidence exists to support" the idea that the Courts of Love were real (71), but the title of her book illustrates the extent to which courtly love and the troubadour culture are inextricably linked with Eleanor in the popular imagination.

61. Weir, *Eleanor of Aquitaine*, 181–82.

62. Frédéric [Friedrich C.] Diez, *Essai sur les Cours d'Amour*, trans. Ferdinand de Roisin (Paris: Labitte, 1842).

63. Sidney Painter, review of *Eleanor of Aquitaine: Queen of the Troubadours and the Courts of Love*, by Melrich V. Rosenberg, *Speculum* 12 (1937): 411–12 (411).

64. John C. Moore, review of *Eleanor of Aquitaine: Patron and Politician*, ed. William W. Kibler, *Speculum* 53:1 (1978): 148–49 (148).

65. McCash, "Marie de Champagne and Eleanor of Aquitaine," 698 n. 2.

66. See, for example, M. Markowski, "Medieval Sourcebook," <http://www.fordham.edu/halsall/source/eleanor.html> [accessed 9 October 2007].

67. Meade, *Eleanor of Aquitaine*, x.

68. Marion Meade, *Stealing Heaven: The Love Story of Heloise and Abelard* (New York: W. Morrow, 1979) (a film based on the novel was produced in 1988); *Sybilie* (New York: W. Morrow, 1983); *Dorothy Parker, What Fresh Hell Is This?* (New York: Penguin, 1989); *Bitching* (London: Garnstone Press, 1973; rpt. New York: Authors Guild, 2001).

69. Parsons and Wheeler, "Prologue," xvii.

70. Meade, *Eleanor of Aquitaine*, xi.

71. Meade, *Eleanor of Aquitaine*, ix.

72. Meade, *Eleanor of Aquitaine*, 26. Or five years old, if we accept the dating of Eleanor's birth to 1124. See Flori, *Aliénor d'Aquitaine*, 31.

73. Meade, *Eleanor of Aquitaine*, 437 n. 24, 34, 35.

74. Meade, *Eleanor of Aquitaine*, 62.

75. Meade, *Eleanor of Aquitaine*, 44–46.

76. Meade, *Eleanor of Aquitaine*, 88–89.

77. Meade, *Eleanor of Aquitaine*, 99–100, 105.

78. Meade, *Eleanor of Aquitaine*, 27, 34–35.

79. Weir, *Eleanor of Aquitaine*, 51.

80. Meade, *Eleanor of Aquitaine*, 87.

81. Edmond-René Labande, "Pour une image véridique d'Aliénor d'Aquitaine," *Bulletin de la Société des antiquaires de l'Ouest*, 2nd series 2 (1951): 175–234. See also Martin Aurell, "Aliénor d'Aquitaine (1124–1204) et ses historiens: la destruction d'un mythe?" in J. Paviot and J. Verger ed., *Guerre, pouvoir et noblesse au Moyen Âge. Mélanges en l'honneur de Philippe Contamine* (Paris: Presses de l'Université de Paris-Sorbonne, 2000), 43–49; Elizabeth A. R. Brown, "Eleanor of Aquitaine, Parent, Queen and Duchess," in William W. Kibler, ed., *Eleanor of Aquitaine: Patron and Politician* (Austin and London: University of Texas Press, 1976), 9–34; and Brown, "Eleanor of Aquitaine Reconsidered," 1–54; Flori, *Aliénor d'Aquitaine*; Jane Martindale, "Eleanor of Aquitaine," in Janet L. Nelson ed., *Richard Coeur de Lion in History and Myth* (London: Kings College London Centre for Late Antique and Medieval Studies, 1992), 17–50.

82. Duby, *Dames du XIIe Siècle*, 15 (*Women of the Twelfth Century*, 6).

83. Odo of Deuil, *De profectione*, xxiii n. 67.

84. Quirinus Breen, review of *Odo of Deuil: De profectione Ludovici VII in orientem*, by Virginia Gingerick Berry, ed. and trans., *Church History* 18 (1949): 57.

85. Owen, *Eleanor of Aquitaine*, 149.

86. Niketas Choniates, *'O City of Byzantium': Annals of Niketas Choniates*, ed. and trans. H. J. Magoulis (Detroit, MI: Wayne State University Press, 1984), 35; Niketas Choniates, *Historia*, ed. I. A. Van Dieten, 2 vols. (Berlin and New York: Walter de Gruyter, 1975), 2:60.

87. Owen, *Eleanor of Aquitaine*, 65. Brown, "Eleanor of Aquitaine Reconsidered," 2.

88. Owen, *Eleanor of Aquitaine*, 7.

89. Owen, *Eleanor of Aquitaine*, 11.

90. Aurell, "Aliénor d'Aquitaine et ses historiens," 45–46.

91. David Crouch, *The Image of Aristocracy in Britain, 1000–1300*

(London: Routledge, 1992), 131, cited in Martin Aurell, *The Plantagenet Empire*, trans. David Crouch (Harlow: Pearson, 2007), 286 n. 72.

    92. *L'Expresse*, 11 July 2002, 78, cited in Aurell, *The Plantagenet Empire*, 286 n. 72.

The New Seven Deadly Sins

Carol Jamison

The Seven Deadly Sins website, a site devoted to all modern aspects of the Seven Deadly Sins, features this telling statement about the current status of the Seven Deadly Sins in modern culture:

> We at the Seven Deadly Sins Homepage pride ourselves on our commitment to keeping alive the vital historical tradition of the Seven Deadly Sins. But sometimes, like the Second Amendment to the U.S. Constitution, you wonder if the people who framed the original concepts would have felt differently if they could have peered into the future and seen all the crazed goings-on in our age. In a time as rich with sin and evil as ours, it seems that the Seven Deadly Sins might need a little bit of updating.[1]

The very existence of The Seven Deadly Sins website is itself evidence that the concept of the Sins has, in fact, been updated in some surprising and curious ways. This essay will explore how the Seven Deadly Sins have been both adopted and adapted by today's secular culture and will also reveal some commonalities between medieval and modern portrayals of the Sins.

The rich tradition of the Seven Deadly Sins began in the Middle Ages. As laid down by Pope Gregory the Great in the sixth century, the Seven Deadly Sins thoroughly infiltrated medieval society. In 1215 the Fourth Lateran Council encouraged the education of clergy in counseling penitents during confessions. The Council advised priests to instruct penitents about the Seven Deadly Sins in order that the penitents might better understand the nature of their transgressions. Subsequently, the Seven Deadly Sins began to appear not only in numerous pastoral treatises meant to educate the clergy and in sermons themselves, but also in secular literature.

Sin scholars Morton Bloomfield and, more recently, Richard Newhauser both recognize the extent to which the Sins infiltrated medieval culture beyond their pastoral function. In his definitive work on the Sins, Bloomfield writes that "medieval man was fascinated, as we are, by the Sins, but more than that, he believed in them. For most men in the Middle Ages, the Sins were as real as the parish church itself and readily entered into everyday life."[2] Identifying literary works that feature the Sins as a generic classification, Newhauser writes that "[the pastoral treatise] fulfilled varied functions in the course of its long history; certainly some of these functions came to include private meditation and public reading in surroundings not under the immediate control of church authorities."[3]

Robert of Brunne's early fourteenth-century *Handlyng Sinne* offers a vivid demonstration of how, even in the Middle Ages, the concept of the Seven Deadly Sins had entertainment value that transcended their religious purpose. *Handlyng Sinne*, an adaptation of the *Manuel des péchés*, contains a collection of exempla that illustrates the Sins. Although intended as didactic, this lively narrative had popular appeal that mainstreamed into secular culture and encouraged a number of imitators and continuations.

But the extent to which the Sins infiltrated secular medieval culture is perhaps best evidenced by the fact that two of England's most famous fourteenth-century writers, John Gower and Geoffrey Chaucer, both wrote secular works that draw upon the penitential tradition to incorporate the Seven Deadly Sins. Larry Scanlon credits Chaucer with moving the exempla from the clerical to the lay. Scanlon explains that "Chaucer's frequent recourse to the exemplum enabled him to translate cultural authority from the Latin discourse of the church to the vernacular."[4] Chaucer directly presents the Sins in the final tale of *The Canterbury Tales*, "The Parson's Tale." The Parson presents a pastoral treatise on the Sins that itself shows a clear distinction between the secular and clerical traditions. By distinguishing between the "draf" of many of the previous tales and the "whete" of his pastoral treatise, Chaucer's Parson invites readers to reconsider the previous tales (including romance and fabliaux) in the context of the treatise on Sins and thus bridges the gap between the clerical and secular traditions.

The Sins appear in each of Gower's three works, most prominently in the *Confessio Amantis*, in which, according to Gerald

Kinneavy, "the confession device is a massive working principle in the poem."[5] Scanlon describes the structure of Gower's work as "[disposing] its exempla according to the penitential framework of the Seven Deadly Sins and their subcategories, specifically recalling *Handlyng Synne*, a text where the penitential and sermon exemplum traditions converge."[6] The *Confessio Amantis* is organized around a mock confession in which Venus' priest, Genius, presents a series of narratives, many secular in origin, intended as commentary on the Seven Deadly Sins. This confessional framing narrative melds religious with courtly material as the unhappy lover Amans is counseled by Genius, who relates the Sins to Amans' status as lover. As Ardis Butterfield explains, Gower "makes the language of confession and the language of love less incompatible than they may seem."[7]

In addition to John Gower and Geoffrey Chaucer, other secular writers and artists in the Middle Ages and Renaissance employed the Sins, using them as allegorical tools and as social and political commentary, weaving them not only into framed narratives, but also into dream visions, poems, and plays. As Bloomfield notes, the Seven Deadly Sins as they appeared in the Middle Ages "passed into art and literature, associating themselves with and linking themselves to various strands in Western thought and life [...]," forming a long-standing tradition that still thrives today.[8]

Secular portrayals of the Sins in medieval works were never completely severed from their religious origins, as illustrated by Gower's *Confessio Amantis*, ostensibly about courtly love, though taking the form of a confession that ends with penance. Modern portrayals of the Sins, however, are often devoid of religious association. The number seven, it seems, has become merely a convenient number to employ when making lists of things one is better off avoiding, and the term "deadly" is almost always used tongue-in-cheek. The utter secularization of the Seven Deadly Sins in much of today's pop culture accounts for the most radical change of the concept from the Middle Ages to today.

To name just a few of the modern manifestations of the Sins one can find on the Internet and in the media, consider the following sampling of the 216,000 titles revealed in a Google search: "The Seven Deadly Safety Sins," "The Seven Deadly Culinary Sins," "The Seven Deadly Sins in the Workplace," "The Seven Deadly Sins of Home Remodeling," "The Seven Deadly Sins of Corporate Management," "The Seven Deadly Sins of Kid Culture," "The Seven Deadly Sins of Chess," "The Seven Deadly Sins of Powerpoint Presentation," "The Seven Deadly Sins of Dating," "The Seven Deadly Sins of Geekdom," "The Seven Deadly Sins of Outsourcing," "The Seven Deadly Sins of Science Fiction," and "The Seven Deadly Sins of Email." The "Seven Deadly Sins of Email" offers a particularly vivid illustration of how far removed these lists are from the original Sins by citing such infractions as using company email for personal messages, failing to heed copyright laws, and failing to double-check addresses, hardly Sins that could result in the eternal damnation of the soul, the medieval penalty for Deadly Sin.

Among the most recent lists of Sins is an article from 17 September 2008, a reaction to the current financial market crisis, "The Seven Deadly Sins of Deregulation." The author, Robert Kuttner, attributes the financial crisis to "corruption, mingled with incompetence," an idea that medieval church officials would likely agree to be a reason for the creation of the original Seven Sins.[9] Like most medieval authors, including Chaucer, Kuttner includes remedies for his Sins in the form of "The Three Necessary Financial Reforms." Whereas Chaucer recommends such remedies as fasting for gluttony and meekness for wrath, Kuttner's remedies include providing leverage limits for banks, regulating financial institutions regardless of size, and policing conflicts of interest in financial institutions. Like the plethora of Sin topics previously mention, Kuttner's use of the term "Deadly Sins" is a clear indication of how dramatically the notion of the Sins has changed and how creatively modern culture makes use of the Sins schema.

The list of titles drawing upon the Sins schema is seemingly interminable, with new lists created to comment upon almost every current event. Most often, though, current lists of Sins provide entertaining advice for today's culture. In addition to Robert Mannyng of Brunne's lively portrayal of sin exempla, other works evidence that, even in the Middle Ages, the Sins were perceived as entertaining and even somewhat attractive. Referencing a fourteenth-century poem in which the devil defends each of the Sins with persuasive rhetoric, Bloomfield provides further evidence for the attractiveness of the Sins in the Middle Ages. Continuing in the Renaissance, Christopher Marlowe's *The Tragical History of Dr. Faustus* similarly shows the attractiveness of the Sins, which appear as a successful diversion to distract Faustus who has momentarily reconsidered his bargain with the devil – twenty-four years of worldly pleasure in exchange for his soul. In the fourteenth-century poem, the devil ultimately loses his argument about the attractiveness of the Sins, and Faustus, although too late, attempts to repent by offering to burn his books.

However, the Sins as they appear in today's popular culture seem vaguely, if at all, connected to the notion of repentance. In her article on the Seven Deadly Sins in *The Simpsons*, popular-culture scholar Lisa Frank concludes with this apt remark about the changes in the traditional notion of the Sins: "The only difference [in modern portrayals of the Sins] is that now we work with our vices instead of against them."[10] Playing on the cliché that good chocolate is "sinful," The House of Dorchestor candy manufacturer offers a line of chocolates called "the Seven Deadly Sins." The advertisement asks, "Which sin box contains your chocolate? Will you open the 'LUST' box, or are 'PRIDE' or 'ENVY' more appropriate [...]?! One can follow this theme with Individual gift 'Sin' bars and 'Mini Sins Pack' now available as part of the Seven Deadly Sins brand."[11] One can consult several websites that offer detailed instructions on how to throw a dinner party based on the theme of the Seven Deadly Sins. One can choose Seven Deadly Sins backgrounds and graphics for MySpace and YouTube sites. Self-proclaimed sinners might play a board game or video game that encourages players to find entertaining ways to commit the Sins. One can flaunt his or her Sin of choice by purchasing Seven Deadly Sins wrist bands, posters, skateboarding shoes, screensavers, mouse pads, grinders from the Cape Herb and Spice Company, baseball caps, Halloween costumes, coffee mugs, and, from 7DeadlyClothing.com, hooded zipper jackets and tee shirts.

One can purchase Seven Deadly Sins motivational posters from The Parody Place. Drawing on the medieval practice of linking the Sins to various animals, the pride poster predictably displays a peacock and has the following text: "It's not easy being the smartest person in this office. You're brilliant, funny, and darned attractive, too [...]. Do what anybody in your shoes would do. Go rub everybody's noses in it."[12] One can also take numerous online quizzes with such titles as "Which of the Seven Deadly Sins are you?"[13] and "What's Your Sin?"[14] After answering a series of questions about, for example, what kind of vehicle one drives and how much one gives to charity, the online quizzes give results that measure or graph an individual's level of sin.

Far from serious, the sin quizzes are clearly meant to be entertaining, one of them acknowledging that it was created "to show off the drawings" the creator had made of the Sins.[15] Despite their lack of seriousness, these popular depictions of the Sins are revealing evidence of society's current tendency to treat the Sins as comic material.

Perhaps our politically correct culture is responsible for this desire not simply to laugh at our Sins, but even to flaunt them. The Seven Deadly Sins website reinterprets the Sins in an inoffensive manner for today's easily offended population. The old sin of pride is now self-esteem; anger is assertiveness; envy, appreciation; greed, enterprise; lust, libido; gluttony, appetite; and sloth, stress-management.[16] Putting it in slightly different terms, P. J. O'Rourke in *The Weekly Standard* finds that "modern society has turned [the Sins] into virtues: building self-esteem, dreaming your dream, exercising gourmet tastes, having satisfying sex for life, speaking truth to power, being relaxed and centered. And Gordon Gekko said it all about greed."[17]

In *Skipping towards Gomorrah: The Seven Deadly Sins and the Pursuit of Happiness in America*, syndicated sex columnist Dan Savage regards a sinful lifestyle as a basic human right. He opens his work with this provocative comment: "The very pursuits that make some Americans happy [...] are considered downright sinful by social conservatives. By itself, this attitude wouldn't be a problem if these other Americans were content to avoid those activities they regard as sinful and recognize the rights of others to do the same."[18] Using the form of a travelogue, Savage tours America in a humorous yet revealing celebration of the Sins in America. By equating sinfulness with happiness, Savage recasts the Sins in terms of desirable behaviors to which all Americans have a basic right.

When not transformed into positive attributes by secular culture, the Sins today might be reinterpreted as illnesses or genetic flaws. Frank Furedi, Professor of Sociology at the University of Kent, explains that:

> Western culture can only make sense of the act of sinning as a symptom of some regrettable psychological disease. Behaviour that was once denounced as sinful [might be] today discussed through the language of therapy rather than the language of morality. The old deadly Sins tend to be looked upon as personality disorders that require treatment, rather than transgressions that deserve punishment.[19]

For Furedi, lust has become "sex addiction"; gluttony, "food addiction"; wrath, "road rage," "air rage," and other such rages; avarice and envy, "the inevitable outcomes of consumerism"; sloth, "chronic fatigue," and pride, no longer a sin at all but "one of the prime virtues of our time."[20]

Molecular biologist John Medina uses science to contextualize the Sins for today's society. His work, entitled *The Genetic Inferno: Inside the Seven Deadly Sins,* employs Dante's presentation of the Sins as a framework for a study on the genetic roots of human behavior. He explains his view of the primary difference between the Sins in the Middle Ages and the Sins today: "the medieval mind thought about creation in terms of a soul within a body, not a collection of neurons creating a brain."[21] Medina gives biological explanations for each of the Seven Sins. Thus, his chapter on gluttony provides a scientific explanation of appetite and includes a two-page diagram revealing a study on rat brains that attempts to isolate the hunger gene, and his chapter on envy contains a discussion of the biological effects of depression and its link to envy. Despite his reliance upon the Sins as framework, Medina's purpose is actually to study the workings of the human brain, a decided departure from the medieval purpose of using the Sins to understand the state of the human soul.

Despite our tendency to celebrate or analyze them, one *can* detect some medievalism in current depictions of the Seven Deadly Sins. Journalist Suzanne Fields writes that "The conditions of life have changed radically since [the conception of the Seven Deadly Sins], but the normal perils of the soul have not."[22] Her point is well illustrated by recent articles in *The Chronicle of Higher Education* delineating the Seven Deadly Sins of both students and professors. Using the traditional Seven Sins, these articles demonstrate that, although the Sins have changed in some ways to suit our society, they remain essentially constant. Anger, for example, is now exemplified by disgruntled students who rage about their professors on RateMyProfessors.com or by faculty members who have shouting matches over differences in ideology.[23] Regardless of their modern secular contexts, these actions fit the typical medieval description of wrath as described in medieval pastoral treatises: "the Wrathful man wants vengeance"; he may be "angry over minutia" and "easily moved to attack others verbally or bodily."[24] Depictions of the Sins in the pastoral treatises of the Middle Ages were intended to lead to confession although most modern depictions of them seem unaware of this fact. However, the author of the *Chronicle* articles concludes, although mock-seriously, that his own account of the Sins of professors is "a confession [...] which may, perhaps, become as helpful to others as it has to me."[25]

Even the ways in which we incorporate the Sins into modern popular culture are not all new. In the Middle Ages, both Gower and Chaucer placed the Sins in framed narratives. Although Chaucer's work is framed around a pilgrimage, for Gower in *The Confessio Amantis*, the Sins function as the primary framing device. The 1995 movie *Se7en* borrows upon this medieval practice of employing the Sins as a framing device, in the film to link a series of murders, each committed to illustrate one of the Sins. Similarly, author Lawrence Block is editing collections of short stories linked by the Sins; Oxford University Press has published a philosophical series organized around the Sins; and author Robin Wasserman writes a series of teen romances connected by the Sins. The popularity of Wasserman's series is evidenced by a website created by the publisher of the series, Simon & Schuster.[26] One must note, however, that though the Sins function as framing devices in these modern examples, their purpose is not to expound on the theme for moral purposes, as is clearly the case for both Gower throughout the *Confessio Amantis* and Chaucer in "The Parson's Tale."

Early writers including Gower, Chaucer, William Langland, and, in the Renaissance, Edmund Spenser all incorporated the Sins into works that had political connotations or served as social commentary. Langland's *Pier's Plowman* molds the Sins into social satire by portraying them as representations of characters from various social estates. Serving as a commentary on ecclesiastical corruption, wrath, for example, is depicted as a friar and gardener at a convent whose wrathful actions include spreading false rumors: "I was sum tyme a frere,/ And þe couentes Gardyner for to graffe ympes" (I was some-time a friar and the convent's gardener to graft shoots).[27] Likewise, medieval portrayals of gluttony are frequently situated in the social setting of the alehouse, hinting at a general corruption that extends beyond the individual. Envy, too, can be contextualized in social settings as vividly demonstrated in John Gower's version of the Constance narrative. Constance's mother-in-law is so envious of Constance's estate that she incites a massive slaughter in her kingdom that includes the death of her own son, who is Sultan.

The Sins today are still used as social and political commentary. Various journalists and bloggers have accused Bill Clinton, George W. Bush, and Dick Cheney of committing the Seven Deadly Sins of politics, which in various accounts include the traditional Sins of lust, greed, and wrath, with a few new Sins especially for today's politician: political incorrectness, bullying the press, and warmongering, to name a few. John Pitney, Jr., for example, dedicates an entire article to the Sins of Bill Clinton.[28] A blog list on The Information Paradox website, on the other hand, delineates the Sins of Bush and Cheney.[29]

Certainly, the 2008 presidential election provided new opportunities for political uses of the Sins. Katherine Mieszkowski cites Bush's Seven Deadly Environmental Sins, each followed by a remedy extracted from Obama's environmental agenda.[30] John Ortberg lists the Sins of politics and evangelicals in response to the 2008 election. Orberg's list is directed to voters who are guilty of such Sins as "Messianism," or the sin of believing that "a merely human person or system can usher in the eschaton" and "Easy Believism," "the sin of believing the worst about a candidate you disagree with."[31] In a press release publicizing his recently released *American Drama Series*, author Jack Eadon shamelessly connects his novels about the Sins to President Obama's campaign and election.[32] The seven novels in Eadon's series depict contemporary Americans struggling against the Sins. "Similar to President Obama's recent message," Eadon claims, "the *American Drama Series* really captures what the individual can do to bring about the rebirth of America."[33] Whereas medieval authors often used the Sins as political commentary, Eadon uses politics to endorse his depiction of the Sins.

As in the Middle Ages, the Sins still lend themselves to allegorical interpretation, offering rich fodder for scholars in the field of popular culture. *Gilligan's Island* seems an especially rich, if low-brow, source for sin allegory, inspiring a slew of articles that attribute the Sins to the cast of characters. In one version, the Sins emerge allegorically as Marianne represents lust; Ginger, envy; the Captain, wrath and gluttony; the Professor, pride; and the Howells, greed and sloth. Gilligan, whose antics "keep the others trapped," is Satan himself.[34] Lisa Frank's previously mentioned article in *The Journal of Popular Culture* traces episodes of *The Simpsons* that are, in her reading, allegorical representations of the Sins. For example, she cites an episode entitled "The Simpsons and Delilah," in which Homer, who

purchases a ridiculously expensive bottle of hair tonic to cure his bald-
ness, serves as an allegorical representation of pride, and another,
"Lisa's Rival," in which Lisa is challenged by an equally intelligent
new student.[35]

The longstanding visual appeal of the Sins is evidenced both in
medieval art and literature. Medieval wall paintings of the Seven
Deadly Sins can be found in a number of churches including some
in Dorset and Warwickshire. The Sins are also incorporated into
manuscript illuminations and religious-themed murals. Medieval
artists depicted the Sins as branches from trees, in the form of
wheels, arranged around the body of Christ, riding on animals, and
surrounding the figures of both men and women.[36] Contemporary
artists are equally creative, yet more likely to display their works in
art galleries and even on the Internet rather than on church walls.
The winner of a 2005 online art contest on the Seven Deadly Sins
depicts a procession of the Sins in ballpoint and ink;[37] South
African artist Kendall Greers displayed a series of neon depictions of
the Sins at the Stephen Friedman Gallery in London in 2006;[38] and
art professor Sheehan Saldana of City University of New York has
created a website to display one student's digital imaging of the
Sins.[39] Featured on the Seven Deadly Sins website are British artist
Nick Hunter, who has created a series of woodcarvings of the Sins
and digital illustrator Tim Dry, who has produced a series of
computer-generated Sin art.

In October 2008, Atlanta Photography hosted an art show
featuring photographs based on the theme of the Seven Deadly Sins.
The guidelines for the show reveal contemporary artists' continued
interest in the Sins:

> The Seven Deadly Sins. Since the 6th century, they have pervaded
> our popular culture. We find them everywhere, from the pulpit to
> the silver screen. Whether you find them repugnant or delightful,
> there is no denying the strength of the imagery that these seven
> words conjure up. And October is the perfect month for us to
> explore the darker side of humanity.[40]

Less seriously but equally dependent upon art, CartoonStock features
a series of ten cartoons that are largely dependent upon visual effect.
Among the more memorable of the cartoons is a drawing of a sloth
lazily hanging from a tree branch. The sloth comments, "at least I'm

not accused of being envious, lustful, greedy, prideful, gluttonous, or wrathful."[41]

The phenomenon of YouTube gives new meaning to visually appealing processions of the Sins as sometimes amateur video producers depict the Sins accompanied by music. Among the amateurs are bands with such disturbing names as Rage, Destruction, Fairyfromhell, and technozeus, all with videos entitled "The Seven Deadly Sins." The successful Los Angeles-based, post-grunge band Flogging Molly has a popular song entitled "We're seven drunken pirates, we're the Seven Deadly Sins" for which various YouTube artists pair the rollicking lyrics (Envy and its evil twin/ Its crept in bed with slander/ Idiots they gave advice/ But sloth it gave no answer) with visuals to present a procession of the pirates demonstrating each of the Sins.[42] Also on YouTube, one can view the "punk cabaret band" The Tiger Lillies in a performance at Soho Theatre in March 2008.[43] Their version of the Seven Deadly Sins, entitled "7 Deadly Sins: A Sinful Punk Caberet," is a theatrical song featuring Punch and Judy. The puppets display signs with the names of each Sin followed by a brief enactment of the Sin while the Tiger Lillies perform in the background.

One of the more artistic of the many YouTube videos on the Sins is created by swirls of sand on a black background. The sand is maneuvered to form, in procession, the names of each sin followed by a symbolic depiction. For gluttony, the swirls of smoke form a gaping mouth; for wrath, a knife surrounded by fire, and for greed, a groping claw.[44] A number of videos have also been created to show scenes from Bertolt Brecht's drama on the Seven Deadly Sins, performed by the Royal Ballet in 2007. In all of these modern examples, the artistic displays of the Sins are a major departure from medieval renderings on church walls. Clearly, today's visual displays are for artistic purposes alone and not to incite viewers to reflect upon and repent of their own sinfulness. However, the visual appeal of the Seven Deadly Sins in these modern art forms in many ways recalls visually appealing depictions of the Sins in the Middle Ages and Renaissance.

Particularly colorful literary depictions of the Sins feature in the works of Renaissance authors Edmund Spenser's *The Faerie Queene* and Christopher Marlowe's *The Tragical History of Dr. Faustus*. In each of these works, the Sins are vividly described in dazzling processions that distract both Spenser's Red Cross Knight and Marlowe's Dr.

Faustus. The Red Cross Knight is amazed by the visual splendor of the House of Pride, "whose glorious view/ Their frayle amazed senses did confound."[45] In Scene Five of *The Tragical History of Dr. Faustus*, Beelzebub promises to show the Sins in "their own proper shape and likeness," and, following the procession, Faustus responds that "this sight doth delight my soul."[46] In both works, however, the splendor of the Sins is undermined, in Spenser by the sandy foundation of the House of Pride, and in Faustus by Satan's intent to ensnare Faustus' soul. More than vivid descriptions, the colorful processions of Sins are thematically significant to both writers. They provide temporary distractions for the Red Cross Knight and Faustus, demonstrating that both have gone astray from virtuous paths. Most modern portrayals of the Sins rarely have deeper moral implications.

However, even today some portrayals of the Seven Deadly Sins retain their original function as ordained by the Fourth Lateran Council, to teach lay people. In *The Seven Deadly Sins Today*, Henry Fairlie uses the model of the Seven Deadly Sins to explain modern society's frailties and weaknesses. Fairlie's concluding chapter, "The Paths of Love," offers advice as to how sinners today might redeem themselves.[47] Psychologist Solomon Schimmel and theologian Graham Tomlin each also write self-help books that describe current manifestations of the Sins and offer ways that we might overcome them.[48]

Mary Eberton, a research fellow at the Hoover Institution, has recently written a series of educational articles entitled "The Seven Deadlies Revisited" for the online journal *The Catholic Thing*. In each of the articles, Eberton brings new relevance to the Sins, promising to connect them to current events or "pulses of the Zeitgeist." Considering the previous examples of the Sins in today's secular society, it is perhaps not surprising that Eberton opens her series on the Sins with a comment about their entertainment value: "Why don't we hear about something interesting from the pulpit once in a while – like, say, the Seven Deadly Sins?"[49] Despite this comment, Eberton's articles are intended to be read seriously and are not merely entertainment.

Through Amazon.com, one can purchase a number of Biblical study guides on the topic of the Sins, including a DVD Bible study based on *Gilligan's Island* and the *Workbook on the Seven Deadly Sins*, an eight-week Bible study program. Although they are a far cry from the pastoral treatises of the Middle Ages, the proliferation of these

resources providesfurther evidence that the Sins are still used as theo-
logical tools and are occasionally topics for sermons.

Certainly, the concept of the Sins remains part of the Catechism
of the Catholic Church and is there clearly defined: "Vices can be clas-
sified according to the virtues they oppose, or also be linked to the
capital Sins which Christian experience has distinguished, following
St. John Cassian and St. Gregory the Great. They are called 'capital'
because they engender other Sins, other vices."[50] However, the Sins are
never listed explicitly in the Bible, and they are not detailed in the
Catechism. Perhaps the fact that they are not officially Biblical
doctrine, coupled with their prominence in today's popular culture,
accounts for the reasons that, in religious circles, emphasis on the
Seven Deadly Sins has waned. *White Stone Journal* accounts for the
Church's lack of focus on the Sins: "Some people feel it is better to
take a more positive approach and not dwell on sin. Others believe
that all sin is equally repugnant to God, so any classification is wrong.
Still others just want to forget the whole thing since they are saved
[…]."[51] Furedi blames this shifting emphasis on controversy within
the Catholic Church: "A powerful sense of moral defensiveness,
combined with an awareness that its teaching seems out of touch with
the modern world, means the Church finds it difficult to assert its
authority with any conviction. As a result, many churches feel increasingly uneasy about preaching the Seven Deadly Sins to their flocks."[52]

Recently, however, in a brief but significant moment, the Catholic Church made an apparent attempt to reclaim the Seven Deadly
Sins, indicating concern over contemporary portrayals of the Sins.
The Church's actions could be seen as an attempt to rescue the Seven
Deadly Sins from the throes of popular culture and to revitalize their
function within the Church. On 8 March 2008, newscasts reported
that the Vatican had listed new Seven Deadly Sins. Interestingly, this
new list of Sins arose from a similar concern to that of The Fourth
Lateran Council in 1215. The 2008 week-long training seminar in
Rome was, much like the Fourth Lateran Council, intended to
educate priests and encourage a revival of the practice of confession.
Journalist David Willey explains that a survey conducted by the Catholic University ten years ago revealed that "60% of Italians have
stopped going to confession altogether" and that "the situation has
certainly not improved in the last decade."[53] The decline in confession
is further evidenced by a 2008 survey revealing that 75 percent of

Catholics in the United States rarely, if ever, attend confession.[54] The training seminar evidences the Church's concern with these numbers. The so-called new list of the Sins was gleaned from an interview by Bishop Gianfranco Girotti shortly after the training seminar. This interview was published in *L'Osservatore Romano*, the Vatican newspaper, and came as the Pope noted not only the the falling numbers of Roman Catholics going to confession, but also the "decreasing sense of sin" in today's "secularized world."[55]

Following the week-long Lenten seminar, Bishop Girotti, head of the Apostolic Penitentiary, urged priests to take account of "new Sins which have appeared on the horizon of humanity as a corollary of the unstoppable process of globalisation."[56] Although the Bishop did not specifically make a list, the idea of seven new Sins emerged from his response to the question "what are the 'new Sins'?" The Bishop noted "various areas today in which we adopt sinful behavior," and from his comments, the media constructed what came to be known as the new Seven Deadly Sins. As delineated by the *Times* of London, they are: 1) drug abuse, 2) morally debatable experimentation, 3) environmental pollution, 4) causing poverty, 5) social inequality and injustice, 6) genetic manipulation, and 7) accumulating excessive wealth.[57] The creation of this list, at least momentarily, turned the minds of the public to the subject of the Seven Deadly Sins as a serious issue.

But it also aroused controversy, particularly on Internet blogs. Some bloggers saw the list as an attempt of the Catholic Church to recover from recent controversy. Furedi rationalized that "In [today's] climate, is it any surprise that moral entrepreneurs in the Catholic Church want to re-brand sin, and have decided to cobble together a shopping-list of new no-nos for the twenty-first century consumer?"[58] "Recycle or go to Hell" became the motto of some of those ridiculing the Bishop's statement. O'Rourke argued that the new Sins "have no gravitas. Imagine the reaction in the confessional when you say, '[forgive me] Father, I have littered.'" O'Rourke further explained that the items on the new list do not involve willpower and thus are not Sins at all: "Pollution is not a passion we resist with an agony of will for the sake of our immortal souls"[59]

The Catholic weekly journal in its editorial blog criticized the mass media's interpretation of the interview, arguing that the Bishop's intent was to point out the social aspects of sin and to provide relevant examples: "The Vatican's intent seemed to be less about adding to the traditional 'deadly' Sins [...] than reminding the world that sin has a social dimension, and that participation in institutions that themselves sin is an important point upon which believers need to reflect."[60] The Bishop himself explained that his comments stemmed from this desire: "If yesterday sin had a rather individualistic dimension, today it has a value, a resonance, beyond the individual, above all social, because of the great phenomenon of globalization. [...] its consequences are wider and more destructive."[61] Father Gerald O'Vollins, former professor of theology at the Papal University in Rome, explains the increased emphasis on the social aspects of sin: "I think the major point is that priests who are hearing confessions are not sufficiently attuned to some of the real evils in our world [...]. They need to be more aware today of the social face of sin – the inequalities at the social level. They think of sin too much on an individual level."[62]

As verified by the Vatican website, the social aspect of sinning is not new: "The catechetical tradition recalls ancient social Sins 'that cry to heaven': the blood of Abel, the sin of the Sodomites, the cry of the people oppressed in Egypt [...]".[63] Even in the Middle Ages, the Sins, though individual in nature, had social consequence. Wrath, for example, is often associated with war, and envy might lead one to burn his neighbor's house. While Bishop Girotti's comments emphasize the prominence of the social aspects of sin today, they do not to replace the traditional medieval list of Seven Deadly Sins. As one blogger wrote, "Just to clear up any confusion, the original Sins, Pride, Envy, Gluttony, Lust, Anger, Greed and Sloth are still in effect," and another commented that "the [new] list of social Sins is basically an updated version of venial Sins with an enhanced global perspective."[64]

Perhaps Bishop Girotti's statements were misconstrued by the press because, as James Martin explains, the press possesses a "general unfamiliarity with the contemporary Catholic tradition of social sin" and sought a sexier headline than "Vatican Official Deepens Church's Reflection on Longstanding Tradition of Social Sin."[65] Obviously, the Bishop's intent was to delineate the prominence of social Sins today in order to emphasize the continued need for Catholics to go to Confession. He did not intend to replace the traditional list of Seven Deadly Sins. Although the Church made no official comment on the Bishop's commentary, the events of March 2008 show that the Church has a continued interest in sin, and perhaps the Bishop's comments create a way that the Seven Deadly Sins might again be appropriated as a serious matter that is relevant to today's society.

Bishop Girotti's comments indicate his concern with one of the major aspects of the traditional Sins: the notion of Charity as remedy. In most of the popular culture examples previously mentioned, the Sins are not portrayed seriously and are rarely attached to any notion of confession, so remedies and repentance are not an option. However, the Catechism of the Catholic Church explains that Charity and repentance are mandatory: "The root of sin is in the heart of man [...]. But in the heart also resides charity, the source of the good and pure works, which sin wounds."[66] Depictions of the Sins in the Middle Ages were almost always connected with repentance. Gower establishes Charity as the remedy for sin in the conclusion of the *Confessio Amantis*: the main character Amans, ultimately revealed to be Gower himself, acknowledges his old age, repents of his foolishness in pursuing a love affair, and renounces love except "thilke love which that is/ Withinne a mannes herte affermed,/ And stant of charite confermed."[67] Chaucer concludes each of the Parson's presentations of the Sins with a remedy, and Langland cites as his remedy for the Sins the Seven Christian Virtues: Abstinence, Humility, Charity, Chastity, Patience, Peace, and Generosity.

The connection between virtues such as Charity and social responsibility are evident in Newhauser's account of Charity in medieval pastoral treatises on the Sins, which defines Charity as "joy among true brethren."[68] Agreeing that Charity remains a crucial aspect of Sins old and new, Bishop Girotti claims that repentance today "takes on a (special) social dimension," and that to receive absolution, "it is required that one also demonstrate outstanding purity and show evidence of fervent charity."[69] Considered from this perspective, the Bishop's comments indicate renewed interest in Charity as it reflects social responsibility and a reconnection of the Sins to the notion of repentance.

Despite Bishop Girotti's misconstrued interview, there is officially no new list of Seven Deadly Sins. Rather, the old Sins have taken some curious new forms that reflect our increasingly secular world and the prevalence of technology. Whereas the Sins originally moved from the pulpit to popular literature and art, they are now displayed on YouTube videos and paraded on tee shirts. Their prevalence is obvious not only in our tendency to concoct lists of imaginary new Sins to label our current vices, but also in our tendency to celebrate, rather than repent of, the traditional ones. It is not surprising that the Catholic Church should be alarmed by some of these modern depictions? In a world where Sins are often flaunted and may be completely disconnected from the notion of repentance, one must wonder: where is redemption?

Although the Catholic Church had no immediate response to the media's construction of a new list of Seven Deadly Sins, several recent events indicate a continued concern with the secularization of the Sins, and some may even be delayed reactions to the media attention surrounding Bishop Girotti and his comments. In June 2008, several months after the Bishop's comments, the Catholic journal *La Civiltà Cattolica*, which is reviewed by a Vatican official, published an article on the role of the Sins in today's culture.[70] The author, Jesuit Father Giovanni Cucci, reacts to a 2005 survey indicating that most people believe the medieval notion of Seven Deadly Sins is no longer applicable in today's society. Using seven headlines from *The New York Times* that illustrate modern manifestations of the Seven Deadly Sins, Father Cucci argues that the traditional Seven Deadly Sins are still relevant and that the Church's role in helping individuals to overcome Sin has not been replaced by psychotherapy or science.[71]

On 13 and 14 January 2009, the Vatican offered a two-day conference to reveal the function of the Apostolic Penitentiary, the institution that handles the absolution of Sins so severe that the Pope alone can handle them. Writing for the *Catholic News Service*, Cindy Wooden explains that the Penitentiary is "probably the most secret of any Vatican office."[72] About the role of the Apostolic Penitentiary, Bishop Girotti commented that "Even though it's the oldest department of the Holy See, it's very little known – specifically because by its nature it deals with secret things." Girotti added an explanation for the Church's decision to reveal the inner workings: "We want to relaunch the sacrament of penance."[73] Journalist Wooden notes that "the media flocked" to the symposium, indicating that perhaps the Church is beginning to use the media, rather than ignoring or struggling against it, in an attempt to reappropriate the Sins.[74]

Most recently, on 9 February 2009, the *New York Times* reported that Catholic churches worldwide have begun to reinstate the granting of indulgences, "reminding [Catholics] of the church's clout in mitigating the wages of sin."[75] The renewed emphasis on indulgences, which actually began in 2000, is gaining popularity as churches continue to search for ways to attract Catholics to confession. Whereas the Fourth Lateran Council was designed to help penitents better understand the nature of their confessions, the Church's current actions are primarily to encourage Catholics to treat sin as a serious matter and to attend confession in the first place. The *Times* quotes Reverend Gilbert Martinez commenting on his parishioners' reactions to the indulgences: "I had a number of people come in and say, 'Father, I haven't been to confession in 20 years, but this' – the availability of an indulgence – 'made me think maybe it wasn't too late.'"[76] The return of indulgences appears to be yet another indication that the Church is alarmed by contemporary society's casual approach to the Sins.

The recent media attention initiated by Bishop Girotti's so-called new Seven Deadly Sins may have reminded the public, perhaps even informed some for the first time, that the Sins are socially relevant today and still important to the Church. Certainly, the idea of the new Seven Deadly Sins has provided new opportunities for the Church to remind the public of the continued relevance of the Sins, evidenced by the Church's recent decisions to reinstate indulgences and to reveal the inner workings of the Apostolic Penitentiary. Regardless of the Church's reaction, the Sins continue to permeate our culture, serving primarily to delight and entertain. However, they also reveal much about our current culture, and, at least occasionally, they still serve as religious instruction and guidance.

NOTES

1. *7 Deadly Sins*, <http://www.deadlySins.com/>.

2. Martin Bloomfield, *The Seven Deadly Sins: An Introduction to the History of a Religious Concept, with Special Reference to Medieval English Literature* (Lansing: Michigan State College Press, 1967 [c. 1952]), xiv.

3. Richard Newhauser, "The Pardoner's Tale and Its Generic Affiliations," in David Raybin and Linda Taite Holley, ed., *Closure in the Canterbury Tales: The Role of the Parson's Tale* (Kalamazoo: Western Michigan University, 2000), 45–76 (52).

4. Larry Scanlon, *Narrative Authority and Power* (New York: Cambridge University Press, 1994), 248.

5. Gerald Kinneavy, "Gower's *Confessio Amantis* and the Penitentials," *The Chaucer Review* 19.2 (1984): 144–61 (156).

6. Scanlon, *Narrative Authority*, 248.

7. Ardis Butterfield, "*Confessio Amantis* and the French Tradition," in Siân Echard, ed., *Companion to Gower* (Cambridge: D. S. Brewer, 2004), 169.

8. Bloomfield, *The Seven Deadly Sins*, xiv.

9. Robert Kuttner, "Seven Deadly Sins of Deregulation – and Three Necessary Reforms," *The American Prospect* (17 September 2008): <http://www.prospect.org/cs/articles?article=seven_deadly_Sins_of_deregulation_and_three_necessary_reforms>.

10. Lisa Frank, "The Evolution of the Seven Deadly Sins: From God to the Simpsons," *The Journal of Popular Culture*, 35.1 (2001): 95–105 (104).

11. The House of Dorchester Chocolates, <http://www.chocolates-uk.co.uk/bestselling.htm>.

12. Seven Deadly Motivational Posters, <www.dumbentia.com/gallery_Sins.htm>l.

13. "Which One of the Seven Deadly Sins Are You?": <http://www.youthink.com/quiz.cfm?action=go_detail&sub_action=take&obj_id=1364>.

14. "The Seven Deadly Sins Quiz": <http://www.4degreez.com/misc/seven_deadly_Sins.htm>l.

15. "Which One of the Seven Deadly Sins Are You?"

16. *7 Deadly Sins*, <http://www.deadlySins.com/>.

17. P. J. O'Rourke, "Seven New Deadly Sins," *The Weekly Standard* 13.29 (14 June 2008): <http://www.theweeklystandard.com>.

18. Dan Savage, *Skipping towards Gomorrah: The Seven Deadly Sins and the Pursuit of Happiness in America* (New York: Dutton Adult, 2002), 1.

19. Frank Furedi, "The Seven Deadly Personality Disorders," *Spiked* (12 March 2008):
<http://www.spiked-online.com/index.php?/site/article/4862/>.

20. Furedi, "The Seven Deadly Personality Disorders."

21. John Medina, *The Genetic Inferno: Inside the Seven Deadly Sins* (Cambridge: Cambridge University Press, 2000), 99.

22. Suzanne Fields, "Pope Benedict Comes with an Ancient Rebuke," *Clear Politic* (14 April 2008):
<http:www.realpolitics.com/articles/2008/04/pope_benedict.html>.

23. Thomas H. Benton (pseudonym), "The 7 Deadly Sins of Professors," *The Chronicle of Higher Education* (12 May 2006), and "The 7 Deadly Sins of Students," *The Chronicle of Higher Education* (14 April 2006):
<http://chronicle.com/jobs/news/2006/05/2006051201c.htm>.

24. Richard Newhauser, *The Treatise on the Vices and the Virtues in Latin and the Vernacular* (Turnhout: Brepols, 1993), 63 and 61.

25. Benton, "The 7 Deadly Sins of Professors."

26. The Website of Simon & Schuster, <www.SimonSays.com>.

27. William Langland, "The Vision of William Concerning Piers the Plowman," in Thomas J. Garbaty, ed., *Medieval English Literature* (Lexington, MA: D. C. Heath and Company, 1984), 138–39.

28. John Pitney, Jr., "The Seven Deadly Sins of Politics: What's Wrong with Clinton? Let Us Count the Faults," *Reasonline* (April 1998):
<http://www.reason.com/news/show/30588.htm>.

29. "George W. Bush, Dick Cheney, and The Seven Deadly Sins" (20 March 2008):
<http://www.theinformationparadox.com/2008/03/george-w-bush-dick-cheney-and-7-deadly.html>.

30. Katherine Mieszkowski, "Bush's Seven Deadly Environmental Sins," *Salon* (22 January 2009):
<http://www.salon.com/env/feature/2008/11/08/bush_environmental_Sins/index.html>.

31. John Ortberg, "John Ortberg's Lessons from the Election: The Seven Deadly Sins of Evangelicals in Politics," *Christian Today* (11 November 2008):
<http://blog.christianitytoday.com/outofur/archives/2008/11/john_ortbergs_l.html>.

32. Jack Eadon, *American Drama Series* (Tustin, CA: Eloquence Press, 2009).

33. "American Drama Series Links Individual Conquest of the Seven Deadly Sins to Obama's Call for National Rebirth" (4 February 2009):
<http://www.prweb.com/releases/2009/02/prweb1950994.htm>.

34. Josef Rosenburg, "The Seven Deadly Sins of Gilligan's Island,"

Gilligan's Island Web Ring (1999):
<http://www.members.tripod.com/TTLF/gilligan.html>.

35. Frank, "The Evolution of the Seven Deadly Sins: From God to the Simpsons," 98, 101.

36. Phillip Lindley, "Seven Deadly Sins and Seven Corporal Works of Mercy," University of Leicester (20 December 2001):
<http://www.le.ac.uk/arthistory/seedcorn/contents.html>.

37. EBSQ Self Representing Artists, "Seven Deadly Sins" (9 February 2005): <http://www.ebsqart.com/ArtShows/sh_45.htm>.

38. Stephen Friedman Gallery, <http://www.stephenfriedman.com/>.

39. Sheehan Saldana, Art 3041 Special Topics: Digital Imaging (Fall 2008): <http://blsciblogs.baruch.cuny.edu/zsheehan/>.

40. Atlanta Photography, "Seven Deadly Sins Exhibit Submission" (October 2008):
<http://www.atlantaphotography.org/content/seven-deadly-Sins-exhibit-submission>.

41. CSL CartoonStock, "Seven Deadly Sins Cartoons":
<http://www.cartoonstock.com/directory/s/seven_deadly_Sins.asp>.

42. Flogging Molly, "The Seven Deadly Sins," <www.youtube>.

43. The Tiger Lillies, "7 Deadly Sins: A Sinful Punk Cabaret," <www.youtube>.

44. McCrawfishMAC, "7":
<http://ie.youtube.com/watch?v=RUnll0QgnuE&feature=channel_page>.

45. Edmund Spenser, "The Faerie Queene," *The Complete Works in Verse and Prose of Edmund Spenser*, ed. Risa S. Bear (Portland: University of Oregon, 1995):
<http://darkwing.uoregon.edu/%7Erbear/queene1.html#Cant.%20IIII>.

46. Christopher Marlowe, *The Tragical History of Dr. Faustus*, ed. David Scott Kastan (New York: W. W. Norton and Company, 2004).

47. Henry Fairlie, *The Seven Deadly Sins Today* (Washington, DC: New Republic Books, 1978; rpt. Notre Dame, IN: University of Notre Dame Press, 1995).

48. Solomon Schimmel, *The Seven Deadly Sins: Jewish, Christian, and Classical Reflections on Psychology* (Oxford: Oxford University Press, 1997); and Graham Tomlin, *The Seven Deadly Sins: And How to Overcome Them* (Oxford: Lionhudson, 2008).

49. Mary Eberton, "The Seven Deadlies Revisited," *The Catholic Thing* (18 September 2008 – 8 December 2008):
<http://www.thecatholicthing.org/index.php?option=com_content&task=view&id=94>.

50. Catechism of the Catholic Church, Article 8: "Sin":
<http://www.vatican.va/archive/ccc_css/archive/catechism/p3s1c1a8.htm>.

51. WhitestoneJournal.com (4 January 2009):
<http://www.whitestonejournal.com/seven_deadly_Sins/>.

52. Furedi, "The Seven Deadly Personality Disorders."

53. David Willey, "Fewer Confessions and New Sins," *BBC News Channel* (10 March 2008):
<http://news.bbc.co.uk/1/hi/world/europe/7287071.htm>.

54. Mark M. Gray and Paul M. Pearl, *Sacraments Today: Belief and Practice among U.S. Catholics*, Center for Applied Research in the Apostale (CARA), Georgetown University (2008):
<http://cara/georgetown.edu/sacramentsreport.pdf>.

55. Bishop Gianfranco Girotti, "The New Forms of Social Sin," interview by Nicola Gori, translated into English by Istuto Acton, *L'Osservatore Romano* (9 March 2008):
<www.vatican.va/newsservices/or/oreng/index.htm>.

56. Girotti, "The New Forms of Social Sin."

57. Richard Owen, "Seven New Deadly Sins: Are You Guilty?" *TimesOnline* (8 March 2008):
<http://www.timesonline.co.uk/tol/comment/faith/article3517050.ece>.

58. Furedi, "The Seven Deadly Personality Disorders."

59. O'Rourke, "Seven New Deadly Sins."

60. James Martin, S.J., "In All Things," *America: The National Catholic Weekly* (10 March 2008):
<http://www.americamagazine.org/blog/entry.cfm>.

61. Girotti, "The New Forms of Social Sin."

62. Willey, "Fewer Confessions and New Sins."

63. Catechism of the Catholic Church, Article 8: "Sin."

64. Our group blog, *America: The NationalCatholic Weekly* (10 March 2008): <http://www.americamagazine.org/blog/entry.cfm>.

65. James Martin, S.J., "In All Things."

66. Catechism of the Catholic Church, Article 8: "Sin."

67. John Gower, *The English Works of John Gower*, ed. G. C. Macaulay (New York: Oxford University Press, 1969), VIII, 3162–64.

68. Newhauser, *The Treatise on Vices and Virtues*, 63.

69. Girotti, "The New Forms of Social Sin."

70. Father Giovanni Cucci, "Are the Capital Vices Still Relevant Today?" *La Civiltà Cattolica* (7 June 2008):
<http://www.laciviltacattolica.it/>.

71. Carol Glatz, "Seven Deadly Sins Alive and Well Today, Says Jesuit Journal," *Catholic News Service* (June 2008):
<http://www.catholicnews.com/data/stories/cns/0803010.htm>.

72. Cindy Wooden, "For 830 years, Apostolic Penitentiary has Focused on Forgiveness," *Catholic News Service* (January 2009):

<http://www.catholicnews.com/data/stories/cns/0900179.htm>.

73. Nicole Winfield, "Vatican Secret Confession Tribunal Opens Up," *YahooNews* (14 January 2009):
<http://news.yahoo.com/s/ap/20090114/ap_on_re_eu/eu_vatican_confession_crisis;_ylt=AibQPa4GlwVQ4CtzwbD5d.h0bBAF>.

74. Wooden, "For 830 years."

75. Paul Vitello, "For Catholics, A Door to Absolution is Reopened," *New York Times* (9 February 2009):
<http://www.nytimes.com/2009/02/10/nyregion/10indulgence.html?_r=2&em=&pagewanted=all>.

76. Vitello, "For Catholics."

Contributors

CARLA A. ARNELL is Associate Professor of English at Lake Forest College, where she teaches courses in medieval literature and the British novel. Her scholarly work has focused on medievalism and postmodern religious fiction, and she has contributed articles on that topic to journals such as *Studia Mystica*, *Christianity and Literature*, and *The Modern Language Review*.

AIDA AUDEH is Associate Professor of Art History at Hamline University in St. Paul, Minnesota. She has published widely on French artists' interest in Dante in the eighteenth and nineteenth centuries, with articles appearing in such publications as *Annali d'Italianistica*, *Dante Studies*, and the *Journal of the Iris and B. Gerald Cantor Center for the Visual Arts at Stanford University*. She is a contributing author to *Dante in the Nineteenth Century: Reception, Portrayal, Popularization* (Peter Lang Publishing Group, forthcoming), and is co-editor of and contributing author to *Dante in the Long Nineteenth Century: Nationality, Identity, and Appropriation* (Oxford University Press, forthcoming).

JANE CHANCE, Andrew W. Mellon Distinguished Chair in English at Rice University, has taught medieval literature and the study of women and gender since 1973. A specialist in myth reception and medievalism, she has published twenty-two books and nearly a hundred articles and reviews and delivered invited lectures all over the world. Among her Tolkien books are *Tolkien's Art: A Mythology for England* (1979; 2001) and *The Lord of the Rings: The Mythology of Power* (1992; 2001); she has also edited *Tolkien the Medievalist* (2003); *Tolkien and the Invention of Myth* (2004); *Tolkien's Modern Middle Ages*, with Alfred Siewers (2006); and two issues of *Studies in Medievalism*, on the *Twentieth Century* (1982) and *The Inklings* (1991). Her most recent book, *The Literary Subversions of Medieval Women* (2007), received the SCMLA Prize, as did *Medieval Mythography: From Roman North Africa to the School of Chartres* (2004).

PAM CLEMENTS is a Professor of English at Siena College in Albany, New York. Her scholarly work, which reflects her teaching and research interests, includes articles on Anglo-Saxon poetry, pedagogy of medieval studies, science fiction and fantasy, and nineteenth-century women's diaries. For seven years, she was Director of Convivium: Siena Center for Medieval and

Early Modern Studies. In recent years, she has published many poems and essays in literary journals such as *Kalliope*, *Earth's Daughters*, *The Pacific Review*, *The Palo Alto Review*, and *The Baltimore Review*. She is currently compiling a book of poetry titled *Natural Science*. Siena College, with Pam as organizer, hosted the 2009 Studies in Medievalism conference.

ALAIN CORBELLARI, born in 1967, is Professor of Medieval French Literature at the University of Lausanne. He completed his doctoral dissertation – "Joseph Bédier écrivain et philologue" – at the Sorbonne in 1996, and it was published by Droz in 1997. He is the author of *La voix des clercs* (Droz, 2005), as well as the editor and translator of Henri d'Andeli's *Dits* (Champion, 2003). He also edited several volumes about the reception of the Middle Ages, the Middle Ages and Comics, and Ernest Renan and Charles Albert Cingria. His numerous publications cover various topics, such as medieval literature, modernity and its reception of medieval literature, and the history of medieval studies. He is a member of the History of the Romance Philology Research Group, directed by Michel Zink at the Collège de France.

ROBERTA DAVIDSON received her Ph.D. in medieval literature from Princeton University. She is a Professor of English at Whitman College, and, in 2005, she co-authored *Macbeth for Murderers*, an account of her experience teaching Shakespeare to maximum security inmates at the Washington State Penitentiary. Her other published work includes articles on Sir Thomas Malory, gender in the Middle Ages, and Arthurian popular culture.

MICHAEL EVANS is an adjunct professor in the Department of History at Central Michigan University. He received his Ph.D. from the University of Nottingham. He is the author of *The Death of Kings: Royal Death in Medieval England* (Hambledon and London, 2003) and is currently working on a book about the image of Eleanor of Aquitaine. His other research interests include the Crusades, gender in the Middle Ages, and the Robin Hood legend. He is a member of the Society for the Study of the Crusades and Latin East, and was formerly the associate editor of the society's journal *Crusades*.

NICKOLAS HAYDOCK is a professor of English at the University of Puerto Rico, Mayaguez, where he teaches courses on medieval English literature, film, the classical tradition, medievalism, and literary theory. His *Movie Medievalism: The Imaginary Middle Ages* (McFarland, 2008) introduces and attempts to theorize this phenomenon. More recently he edited with E. L. Risden a collection of essays on orientalist medievalism in film entitled

Hollywood in the Holy Land (McFarland, 2009). His latest book is *Recursive Readings: The Place of Robert Henryson's Testament of Cresseid* (Cambria. He lives contentedly on the enchanted isle with his enchanting wife Socorro.

CAROL JAMISON is Professor of Medieval Literature and Linguistics at Armstrong Atlantic State University in Savannah, Georgia. She teaches a variety of courses including Chaucer, Early English Literature, Arthurian Literature, History of the English Language, and Advanced Grammar. Her research interests include Arthurian legend, fabliaux, and Old English litera-ture. She has published articles in *Studies in Philology, Studies in Medieval and Renaissance Teaching,* and *Women in German Yearbook.* Her current project is entitled "Harry Potter and the Grail Quest."

STEPHEN MEYER is an Associate Professor in the Department of Fine Arts at Syracuse University. His research specialty is early nineteenth-century opera, and he has published articles on Beethoven, Mozart, Marschner, and others in numerous scholarly journals, including the *Journal of the American Musicological Society* and the *Cambridge Opera Journal.* His book *Carl Maria von Weber and the Search for a German Opera* was published in 2003 by Indiana University Press, and he has recently published an opera libretto on the subject of Sir Gawain and the Green Knight. He has been the recipient of numerous awards, including a Fulbright scholarship and awards from the National Endowment for the Humanities and the DAAD (Deutsche Akademischer Austauschdienst). Forthcoming articles concern the history of the sound recording of Wagner's Grail operas; the role of technology in the early music movement; and medievalist iconography of romantic music.

E. L. RISDEN, Professor of English at St. Norbert College, teaches medieval and Renaissance literature and Classical myth. He has published thirteen books, including most recently *Heroes, Gods, and the Role of Epiphany in English Epic Poetry* (McFarland, 2008), *A Living Light* (Wipf and Stock, 2009), and *Hollywood in the Holy Land* (co-edited with Nick Haydock) (McFarland, 2009). He is currently working on projects on medieval narratology, the transition from medieval to Renaissance mind, and Tolkien's ideas.

CAROL L. ROBINSON is Assistant Professor of English at Kent State University Trumbull. She is co-editor of a collection of essays on cyberpunk science-fiction writer William Gibson, and editor of a forthcoming anthology of essays on neomedievalism in film, television, and electronic games. She has works published or forthcoming on *Sir Gawain and the Green Knight*, Everyman, Monty Python, Charles Chaplin, William Gibson,

Willy Conley, Peter S. Cook, The Flying Words Project, medievalist video games and films, digital and analog communication, and communication chaos. Her areas of interest include Arthurian literature, Chaucer, video games, semiotics, American Deaf culture, and visual-kinetic communication. She is also a founding member of the Medieval Electronic Multimedia Organization (<http://medievalelectronicmultimedia.org/>).

CLARE A. SIMMONS is Professor of English at The Ohio State University. She is the author of *Reversing the Conquest: History and Myth in Nineteenth-Century British Literature*; *Eyes across the Channel: French Revolutions, Party History, and British Writing 1830–1882*, and papers and articles on nineteenth-century British literature and medievalism. The co-editor of *Prose Studies*, she also edited the essay collection *Medievalism and the Quest for the "Real" Middle Ages* and Charlotte Mary Yonge's *The Clever Woman of the Family*. Her current project is titled *Popular Medievalism in Britain 1789–1851*.

RICHARD UTZ is Professor and Chair in the English Department at Western Michigan University. He is the author and/or editor of more than a dozen book-length publications, including: *Culture and the Medieval King* (2008), *Falling into Medievalism* (2006), *Speculum Sermonis* (2005), *Postmodern Medievalisms* (2005), *Chaucer and the Discourse of German Philology* (2002), *Medievalism in the Modern World* (1998), and *Literarischer Nominalismus im Spätmittelalter* (1990). His work in the area of medievalism focuses on the roles of nationalism, memory, and academic discourse in the reception of medieval culture.

VERONICA ORTENBERG WEST-HARLING is a graduate of the Sorbonne and Oxford universities, who has taught at the universities of Durham, Lampeter, and Oxford as a medieval historian. She has published three books and numerous articles and is a Fellow of the Royal Historical Society and a lecturer at Oxford University. Her research has been in the societies and cultures of the early medieval West, in particular in their transformation from the Late Roman world into the Romano-Germanic world in Italy, Spain, France, and Anglo-Saxon England, with a particular interest in historical anthropology, notably in perceptions of the sacred in medieval society and the association of female political power and virginity. In the last few years she has published and lectured on medievalism from the sixteenth century onwards, especially in the areas of popular culture and new media in the last hundred years.

Previously published volumes

Volume I

1. Medievalism in England
Edited by Leslie J. Workman. Spring 1979

2 Medievalism in America
Edited by Leslie J. Workman. Spring 1982

Volume II

1. Twentieth-Century Medievalism
Edited by Jane Chance. Fall 1982

2. Medievalism in France
Edited by Heather Arden. Spring 1983

3. Dante in the Modern World
Edited by Kathleen Verduin. Summer 1983

4. Modern Arthurian Literature
Edited by Veronica M. S. Kennedy and Kathleen Verduin. Fall 1983

Volume III

1. Medievalism in France 1500–1750
Edited by Heather Arden. Fall 1987

2. Architecture and Design
Edited by John R. Zukowsky. Fall 1990

3. Inklings and Others
Edited by Jane Chance. Winter 1991

4. German Medievalism
Edited by Francis G. Gentry. Spring 1991
Note: Volume III, Numbers 3 and 4, are bound together

IV. Medievalism in England
Edited by Leslie Workman. 1992

V. Medievalism in Europe
Edited by Leslie Workman. 1993

VI. Medievalism in North America
Edited by Kathleen Verduin. 1994